Lisbon

WORLD BIBLIOGRAPHICAL SERIES

General Editors:
Robert G. Neville (Executive Editor)
John J. Horton

Robert A. Myers   Hans H. Wellisch
Ian Wallace   Ralph Lee Woodward, Jr.

John J. Horton is Deputy Librarian of the University of Bradford and was formerly Chairman of its Academic Board of Studies in Social Sciences. He has maintained a longstanding interest in the discipline of area studies and its associated bibliographical problems, with special reference to European Studies. In particular he has published in the field of Icelandic and of Yugoslav studies, including the two relevant volumes in the World Bibliographical Series.

Robert A. Myers is Associate Professor of Anthropology in the Division of Social Sciences and Director of Study Abroad Programs at Alfred University, Alfred, New York. He has studied post-colonial island nations of the Caribbean and has spent two years in Nigeria on a Fulbright Lectureship. His interests include international public health, historical anthropology and developing societies. In addition to *Amerindians of the Lesser Antilles: a bibliography* (1981), *A Resource Guide to Dominica, 1493-1986* (1987) and numerous articles, he has compiled the World Bibliographical Series volumes on *Dominica* (1987), *Nigeria* (1989) and *Ghana* (1991).

Ian Wallace is Professor of German at the University of Bath. A graduate of Oxford in French and German, he also studied in Tübingen, Heidelberg and Lausanne before taking teaching posts at universities in the USA, Scotland and England. He specializes in contemporary German affairs, especially literature and culture, on which he has published numerous articles and books. In 1979 he founded the journal *GDR Monitor*, which he continues to edit under its new title *German Monitor*.

Hans H. Wellisch is Professor emeritus at the College of Library and Information Services, University of Maryland. He was President of the American Society of Indexers and was a member of the International Federation for Documentation. He is the author of numerous articles and several books on indexing and abstracting, and has published *The Conversion of Scripts and Indexing and Abstracting: an International Bibliography*, and *Indexing from A to Z*. He also contributes frequently to *Journal of the American Society for Information Science*, *The Indexer* and other professional journals.

Ralph Lee Woodward, Jr. is Professor of History at Tulane University, New Orleans. He is the author of *Central America, a Nation Divided*, 2nd ed. (1985), as well as several monographs and more than seventy scholarly articles on modern Latin America. He has also compiled volumes in the World Bibliographical Series on *Belize* (1980), *El Salvador* (1988), *Guatemala* (Rev. Ed.) (1992) and *Nicaragua* (Rev. Ed.) (1994). Dr. Woodward edited the Central American section of the *Research Guide to Central America and the Caribbean* (1985) and is currently associate editor of Scribner's *Encyclopedia of Latin American History*.

VOLUME 199

Lisbon

John Laidlar

Compiler

CLIO PRESS
OXFORD, ENGLAND · SANTA BARBARA, CALIFORNIA
DENVER, COLORADO

British Library Cataloguing in Publication Data

Laidlar, John
Lisbon. – (World bibliographical series; v. 199)
1. Lisbon (Portugal) – Bibliography
I. Title
016.9'469425

ISBN 1–85109–268–4

ABC-CLIO Ltd.,
Old Clarendon Ironworks,
35A Great Clarendon Street,
Oxford OX2 6AT, England.

———————

ABC-CLIO Inc.,
130 Cremona Drive,
Santa Barbara,
CA 93117, USA.

Designed by Bernard Crossland.
Typeset by Columns Design Ltd., Reading, England.
Printed and bound in Great Britain by Bookcraft (Bath) Ltd., Midsomer Norton.

THE WORLD BIBLIOGRAPHICAL SERIES

This series, which is principally designed for the English speaker, will eventually cover every country (and some of the world's principal regions and cities), each in a separate volume comprising annotated entries on works dealing with its history, geography, economy and politics; and with its people, their culture, customs, religion and social organization. Attention will also be paid to current living conditions – housing, education, newspapers, clothing, etc. – that are all too often ignored in standard bibliographies; and to those particular aspects relevant to individual countries. Each volume seeks to achieve, by use of careful selectivity and critical assessment of the literature, an expression of the country and an appreciation of its nature and national aspirations, to guide the reader towards an understanding of its importance. The keynote of the series is to provide, in a uniform format, an interpretation of each country that will express its culture, its place in the world, and the qualities and background that make it unique. The views expressed in individual volumes, however, are not necessarily those of the publisher.

VOLUMES IN THE SERIES

To my wife,
daughter and father

Contents

Contents

Contents

Contents

Preface

Compilation

Prior to the current publication, no recent general bibliography dedicated to Lisbon has been available in either English or Portuguese, apart from the brief *Bibliografia sobre Lisboa* of Vanda de Freitas (1992). Significant Portuguese library exhibition catalogues published by the Biblioteca Nacional (National Library) and the Instituto Britânico (British Institute) have, to some degree, filled the void, as has the list of some 180 modern Portuguese publications on Lisbon mounted on the Internet by Hugo de Carvalho as part of his *Lisbon Pages*. Although this bibliography has drawn on all of the above sources, the bulk of the present entries has, however, derived initially from library and booktrade catalogues, in card, book and electronic form, as well as from visits to bookshops in Manchester, London and Lisbon itself. A short overview of the English-language entries included in this work now follows, by way of a preface to the bibliography itself.

Brief Review of the English Literature of Lisbon

For the English reader, the longstanding British religious communities in Lisbon, particularly the English College seminary and the Bridgettine nuns of Sion Abbey, provided the earliest significant corpus of English material on Lisbon, including Thomas Robinson's *Anatomie of the English nunnery* (1622). These are supplemented by accounts of those who crossed the Lisbon Inquisition, such as George Buchanan in 1550, Hugo Gurgeny in 1606 and John Coustos in 1743, whilst several modern works by the Reverends Croft, Michael Williams and Sharratt cover the full history of the English College. In the 18th century the curative Lisbon diet drink was imbibed by James Boswell and others and generated a medical literature of its own. The terrible Lisbon earthquake of 1755 prompted numerous eyewitness accounts from the city's appreciable English-speaking community, as well as geological, philosophical and religious explanations of the event, the latter most notably from John Wesley and George Whitefield. The Marquês de Pombal's subsequent rebuilding of Lisbon has been widely described in English, especially by Boxer, Maxwell and França. The rise and fall of the powerful commercial body, the English Factory in Lisbon, is also amply treated by 20th-century historians such as Fisher, Lodge and Walford.

From the mid-18th to early 19th century a number of British literary and other figures recorded visits to Lisbon, including Udal ap Rhys (c.1749), Henry Fielding (in 1754), Richard Twiss (in 1772), Arthur Costigan (in 1778-79), William Beckford (in 1787, 1793-95, 1795-96, 1798-99), James Murphy (in 1789-90), Robert Southey (in 1796 and 1800-01) and Lord Byron (in 1809). The Peninsular War halted such visits but prompted many British military men to publish memoirs of Lisbon, including Semple (1809) and Walter Henry (1811) before upper-class tourists, including Charles Beaufoy (in 1820), Earl Carnarvon (in 1827), Dora (Wordsworth) Quillinan (in 1846) and Lord Tennyson (in 1859), discovered the city. Enobled British visitors such as Lady Jackson continued to frequent Lisbon (1873) but, by the mid-19th-century they were joined by the upper-middle classes as exemplified by T. M. Hughes (in 1846), W. E. Baxter (in 1850-51) and a clutch of adventurous clerics such as Neale (1855), Oldknow (1855) and Smith (in 1870). Invalids, including Henry Matthews (1817) sought out Lisbon's mild climate, a trend which generated aids such as *The invalid's guide* by Cooper (1840). In the latter part of the 19th century medical climatologists, notably Madden, Scoresby-Jackson and Dalgado encouraged visits by other ailing British visitors. The mid- and late 19th century also saw the emergence of the tourist guide from the embryonic *Lisbon guides* (1800 and 1853) and *Strangers' guide* (1848) through Neale (1855) and Macedo (1874) to Baedeker (1898).

Early 20th-century travellers to Lisbon included Inchbold (1907), Baker (1912) and the American, Wood (1913). Other well-heeled visitors recorded their visits to Lisbon both before and after the Second World War, including John Gibbons (1931), Sacheverell Sitwell (1926-53), Lady Gordon (1932), Clive Holland (1934) and Oswell Blakeston (1955). The Catholic priests, Martindale (1949) and Tole (c.1959) continued the tradition of clerical visitors to Lisbon. Some excellent, colour tourist guides have appeared in Britain in the 1990s including *The rough guide* and the three complementary titles in the *Insight* series, whilst several excellent colour maps of Lisbon have also emerged, particularly from Germany.

A significant number of 20th-century English literary works have been set in Lisbon by authors who include Kingsley Amis, Arthur

Quiller-Couch and Ann Bridge. The city has also been used as an exotic backdrop to popular romances by Barbara Cartland, Iris Danbury and Tom Hopkinson, whilst its neutrality during the Second World War engendered novels of intrigue by Eberhart and Lambert as well as English translations of Frederic Prokosch and Erich Remarque's wartime accounts of the city. In the last two decades many English translations of Portuguese literary works set in Lisbon have become available, notably novels by Eça de Queiroz and José Saramago, together with the poetry of Pessoa. On the historical and academic front, several studies of the 1147 reconquest from the Moors, the earthquake and rebuilding of Lisbon, and of the capital's flourishing modern architecture have appeared. Less demanding are the many 1980s and 1990s editions of colour, illustrated books emanating from Portugal, particularly concerning Lisbon's historical buildings, gardens, ceramic art and museums. Such works increasingly appear either wholly in English or with an English summary but, sadly, many of them are avoidably blemished by imperfect translation. The emergence since the 1970s of the British Historical Society of Portugal has generated an excellent journal and more than twenty books on Lisbon in English. Lisbon's exceptional diversity of public transport has also generated a sizeable number of English-language books describing its trams, buses, funiculars, street-lifts and trains.

In central Lisbon amongst the best bookshops for modern material on Lisbon are: Livraria Portugal, Rua do Carmo 70-74, 1200 Lisboa; Livraria Bertrand, Rua Garrett 73, 1200 Lisboa; and Livraria Municipal, Avenida da República 21, 1050 Lisboa. The last is run by the Câmara Municipal de Lisboa (Lisbon City Council) and its stocks include its copious publications on the city.

Specialist organizations include: Amigos de Lisboa (Friends of Lisbon), Palácio da Mitra, Rua do Açúcar, 1900 Lisboa; British Historical Society of Portugal, Rua da Arriaga 13, 1200 Lisboa; and Gabinete de Estudos Olisiponenses (Office for Lisbon Studies), Palácio do Beau Séjour, Estrada de Benfica 368, 1500 Lisboa.

Scope of this Work

The goal of this bibliography is to provide the English-speaking reader with details of accessible printed sources of information on as wide a range of aspects of Lisbon as possible. Consequently, the large majority of the entries are works published in English or which contain an English summary. However, English material is not available in some subject areas, such as descriptions of the various districts of the city of Lisbon. Some works in Portuguese and a handful in French have therefore been included but publications have had to contain a significant amount of illustrative or graphical matter to justify their inclusion. In only a handful of cases, where a Portuguese work is a recognized classic, or in the case of Lisbon's newspapers, has this criterion not been applied.

Few past or present travellers to Lisbon fail also to visit those western coastal suburbs of Lisbon which lie along the Tagus estuary, as far as Cascais, or the historic royal towns of Queluz and Sintra, inland to the north-west of the capital. These places are therefore included within the geographical scope of this bibliography. It is my hope that this work will be of use not only to those researching aspects of Lisbon's history or to prospective visitors to the Portuguese capital, but also to the general reader. I have attempted, therefore, to provide entries which, if read *in toto*, may convey some idea of the city's appearance, its glories, disasters and way of life. This compilation may also be of some value to readers in Portugal as it brings together for the first time references to a large corpus of material about their capital city.

Arrangement of the Bibliography

The overall subject arrangement is essentially that prescribed for all volumes in the World Bibliographical Series. Entries within each subject are arranged by author's surname or corporate name, or in the case of anonymous works and periodicals, by the work's title. For Portuguese names, the last part of compound surnames is the filing element. For foreign titles of publications, an English translation is given in brackets. Where a work has its own translated title, this is given without brackets, in bold typeface, after the original title. Titles are reproduced as in the publication and thus do not always conform to modern orthography. The pagination given is that of the last numbered page; prefatory sequences in roman numerals are excluded. An index is appended of authors, titles and subjects, together with a brief note of major Portuguese works which fall outside the scope of the bibliography itself.

Acknowledgements

Written help has been gratefully received from Mr Clive Gilbert (British Historical Society of Portugal), Ms Ana Novo (Instituto Britânico, Lisbon), S^{ra}. Vanda de Freitas (Biblioteca Municipal de Lisboa), Mr Colin Clarkson (Cambridge University Library), Dr Robert Howes (University of Sussex Library), Mr A. G. Johnson (The P.S.V. Circle) and Professors Clive Willis (University of Manchester) and

Allan Williams (University of Exeter). The helpfulness and efficiency of staff at the British Library in London and at the Biblioteca Nacional in Lisbon have been greatly appreciated. Sincere thanks are also due to Ms Claire Diamond, formerly Librarian of Canning House Library, London. I am, of course, especially indebted to my colleagues in the John Rylands University Library of Manchester and, in particular, the Inter-Library Loans, Acquisitions and Special Collections departments. My colleague, Mrs Jacquie Sen, assisted me in the medical aspects of this bibliography and without the technical aid of my colleague Mr Charlie Hulme in acquiring and installing my computer equipment, this bibliography would have been far less complete and the work of compilation much more laborious. I am also most grateful to the editor of this volume, Julia Goddard, whose helpfulness and patience during its production were invaluable. Above all, however, I must thank my wife, Dana, and daughter, Katherine, for their willingness over the last year to entertain themselves during the many hours of compilation at home and whilst I trawled through bookshops and libraries on what, ostensibly, were family holidays in Lisbon and London. My wife's assistance with the proofreading of the text and indexing of entries has also been invaluable; any remaining errors are my responsibility.

I should be delighted to receive any notification of corrections, omissions or details of subsequently published material on Lisbon which might be included in any re-edition of this work. Such information may be sent to the address below.

July 1997

John Laidlar
John Rylands University Library of Manchester
Oxford Road
Manchester M13 9PP
England
(E-mail address: john.laidlar@man.ac.uk)

Introduction

Site of the City

Lisbon is mainland Europe's most westerly capital city and, with the only marginal exception of Athens, it is also its most southerly. It is situated at 38° 43' north and 9° 09' west, on the northern bank of the estuary of the *Rio Tejo* (River Tagus). This is the longest river in Iberia, flowing for 1,000km from its origins in the Sierra de Albarracín, near Cuenca in Spain, to its outlet into the Atlantic Ocean by the Torre de S. Julião, some 15km west of Lisbon. At Lisbon, the Tagus is nearly 2km wide, but 40km upstream of the city it opens out into the so-called *mar de palha* (sea of straw), a 13km-wide bay. Lisbon's position is thus on the fringe of a huge natural harbour, adjacent to Atlantic sea lanes through which an estimated 75 per cent of the world's tanker traffic passes. In addition to trade to and from the Americas, Lisbon has for centuries also been an important port of call for vessels travelling from northern Europe to ports in the Mediterranean and Africa. This favourable nautical location, combined with its correspondingly adverse position for overland communication at the edge of the European land mass, were significant factors in Lisbon's development as a major maritime city. Indeed, with its docks extending for 15km along the Tagus, Lisbon has recently been marketing itself, quite aptly, as 'Europe's Atlantic Capital City'.

The city, like Rome, is traditionally said to be built on seven hills. Although the authoritative *Guia de Portugal* will identify these as the hills of the Castelo, Santa Catarina, S. Vicente, S. André, Santana, S. Roque and Chagas, the visitor will feel with some justification that many other elevated parts of the city could equally be added to the list. The undulating panorama of Lisbon visible from the Tagus has beguiled countless writers over the last two hundred years. Today, the Baixa (or Lower City), the central commercial heart of Lisbon which starts at the imposing riverfront square (the Praça do Comércio, or Terreiro do Paço), is flanked to the west by the Bairro Alto (the High

District) and to the east by the elevated area of Alfama. Alfama is surmounted by the Castelo de São Jorge (St George's Castle), which reaches a height of 112m above sea level. The Baixa itself rises relatively gently, through the main square of central Lisbon, the Rossio (otherwise known as the Praça D. Pedro IV), northwards up the wide Avenida da Liberdade to the Parque Eduardo VII (Edward VII Park), about 3km from the riverfront. One of the highest man-made points on the western city skyline remains the imposing 18th-century Estrela Basilica, 3km to the west of the city centre, which rises to over 137m. Further west still, slightly inland, lies the extensive Monsanto forest park with its fort which stands at 230m above sea-level. Some 4km to the west of Lisbon, beyond the docks of Alcântara, is the historic riverside suburb of Belém, which forms the western boundary of the modern city on the way to the coastal resorts of Estoril and Cascais, the latter being 27km from Lisbon. Nowadays the northern horizon is dominated by modern buildings, notably the tower of the Amoreiras shopping centre. Along the Tagus, to the east of the city lie more docks and the industrial suburbs of Xabregas, Beato and Poço do Bispo.

The Baixa lies on blue clay and other chiefly alluvial deposits, where in ancient times there was an inlet of the River Tagus. However, the higher areas which flank both sides of the Baixa are primarily of limestone. Looming across the river from Lisbon are the cliffs of Almada which extend down-river from Cacilhas to the small port of Trafaria, both of which towns are linked by ferry to Lisbon. Behind Lisbon rise the formerly volcanic hills of the Serra de Sintra, an impermeable granite range which rises to 529m at the Cruz Alta and which on the Atlantic coast forms the so-called Rock of Lisbon (Cabo da Roca), a landmark to British sailors over the centuries and mainland Europe's most westerly point. Fault lines both out at sea and on land are still active and have resulted in a number of serious earthquakes in the Lisbon area.

Today, Lisbon lies within the administrative area of the Concelho de Lisboa (Council of Lisbon) which occupies some 87.44 sq.km, a relatively large area in respect of its size of population, when compared with other European capitals. The Concelho de Lisboa is one of the fifteen councils which make up the Distrito de Lisboa, whose population of 2,052,910 (1992) resides in a total area of 2,757 sq.km on both sides of the River Tagus, at a population density of 745 inhabitants per sq.km. Some twenty per cent of Portugal's entire population resides within the Distrito de Lisboa, a proportion which has grown markedly in the 20th century. The city's most westerly *freguesia* (parish or administrative ward), is Belém, which borders on the Concelho de Oeiras whilst the city's other western and northern borders are with

Amadora and Sintra. Its north-eastern neighbour is Loures, whose jurisdiction actually begins approximately half way along the main runway of Lisbon's international airport at Portela de Sacavém. The Concelho de Lisboa administers a population of 610,880 (1992) at a density of 7,272 per sq.km and consists of fifty-three *freguesias*, each with its own *junta*, or local council (see p. xlix-l).

Climate

Lisbon's position gives it an Atlantic climate influenced by the Gulfstream, but with Mediterranean influences which combine to make it exceptionally mild in winter, with frost and snow being exceptional. The summer temperatures rise sharply to the east, away from the Atlantic and inland from Lisbon. The average temperature in summer is 21°C, in autumn 16.7°C, in spring 14.5°C, and in winter 10°C, while the annual median is 15.75°C. On average, there are 136 days of rain per year producing 61.5cm in Lisbon, forty fewer such days than in Paris but as many more as occur in Rome. This benign climate has led to Lisbon and the Estoril coast, to the west, being a popular destination for north Europeans. From the 18th to the early 20th century invalids, particularly British consumptives, came to Lisbon seeking climatic and thermal-water cures for their ailments. Amongst the many infirm visitors to Lisbon were Henry Fielding and Lord Tennyson. In the mid-18th century the fashionable Lisbon diet drink also attracted British sufferers from venereal diseases to the Portuguese capital, whilst in the early 20th century the area around Monte Estoril, with the further attraction of its naturally therapeutic waters, became a celebrated health resort. Such natural advantages, as well as Portuguese political neutrality, were also instrumental in the settlement in the Estoril area of many of Europe's displaced monarchs in the first half of the present century. Today, the coastline between Estoril and Cascais continues to enjoy a substantial tourist trade, although it has been spared the worst excesses of package tourism.

Historical Origins

According to a tradition perpetuated by sources such as Luís Vaz de Camões's 16th-century national epic, *Os Lusíadas* (The Lusiads), Lisbon is said to have been founded by the Greek hero Ulysses, during his odyssey after the Trojan Wars. This myth probably stems from the similarity between the hero's name and *Alis Ubbo*, the name by which the Phoenicians knew the local settlement which they occupied from about 1200 BC, and which translates into Portuguese as *enseada amena* or 'pleasant inlet'. This is an accurate geographical description of its site, particularly as at that time the Tagus encroached into the area now known as the Baixa. In fact, there is archaeological evidence of a settlement on the present site of Lisbon as early as the mesolithic period (c.7000 BC) and substantial heaps of sea-shell waste found in the lower Tagus area testify to a significant period of static human habitation in the area, dating from c.5000 BC. Certainly, by 3000 BC there was an established settlement on the present site of Lisbon and evidence of other neolithic townships in the nearby lower Tagus valley has been found. The Phoenicians were in Spain from about 1200 BC and they also established a trading settlement known as Olisipo on the site of Lisbon about that time. They occupied the hill on which the castle now stands, spreading southwards down towards the Tagus river. The Phoenicians were succeeded in Lisbon by the Greeks and Carthaginians.

Around 205 BC, during the 2nd Punic War, the Romans occupied Lisbon and by around 200 BC the indigenous inhabitants of Iberia had been largely absorbed into the Roman Empire, although local resistance continued. The consul, Decimus Julius Brutus, took Olisipo in around 137 BC, before marching north to confront Viriato, the Celtic leader of the peoples known to the Romans as the Lusitanians. The Romans divided what is modern-day Portugal into a northern and southern province respectively named Gallaecia (Galicia) and Lusitania, the latter embracing parts of both modern Portugal and Spain, with its capital at Emerita Augusta (Mérida). Around 60 BC Julius Caesar, the *propraetor* in the west of the Roman Empire, attempted to pacify the Lusitanians from his base in Lisbon. Caesar was also responsible for raising the settlement to the status of a *colonia romana* which was named after him as *Felicitas Julia*. As such it was the only town in the area whose residents enjoyed the benefits of Roman citizenship. Three road connections were built in Roman times between Lisbon and Mérida, of which two ran south of the Tagus, whilst a further road ran to Braga in northern Portugal. Significant evidence of the Roman period in Lisbon has been found under modern Lisbon, including remains of *thermae* (baths) under the Rua da Prata in the Baixa area, of a temple near the present cathedral, and of a theatre dedicated to Nero discovered in 1798 near the Rua de S. Mamede in the Alfama district near the castle. Evidence of a Roman garum manufactury has also been found near the Casa dos Bicos (House of the Facets), just to the south-east of the Baixa. Although the Emperor Constantine legalized Christianity in the early 4th century, a schism remained between the Catholics and the Arians. By the end of that century, Potamius (*fl.*360), the first recorded Bishop of Lisbon, had allegedly embraced the Arian heresy.

Portugal remained a Roman province until 407 AD when the Alans, Suevi (Swabians) and Vandals moved in to Lusitania from Germany, taking advantage of the Romans' own difficulties with the barbarians in Italy. By 410, the Alans had taken Lisbon. As they and the Swabians and Vandals began to trouble the Roman Empire, Rome contracted its former enemies, the Visigoths, to impose order on them. By around 419 AD the Christian Visigoths had driven out the Alans and were in possession of Lisbon, which they named Olisipona, and by 585 they had incorporated much of Portugal into their empire. It was they who built the forerunner of today's Lisbon cathedral and also the early city walls, erroneously styled the *cerca moura* (Moorish wall), since any structure of extreme antiquity was loosely deemed to be Moorish. This wall was some 1,250 metres long and enclosed about 15 hectares.

In 711 Muslims invaded the Iberian peninsula and within two years Lusitania, including Lisbon, had fallen into their hands. The city thereafter went under the Arabic name of Ilixibuna. This was the start of a period of occupation lasting more than four centuries, although it was punctuated by brief Christian occupations. As early as 796 the city was attacked by Christians in the shape of the raiding forces of Alfonso II of Asturias but was back in Moorish hands by 811. In 844 a force of Normans encircled the town and sacked the surrounding area. They returned but were fought off at a battle just outside Lisbon in 966. In between these two attempts, in 851, the town was sacked by the King of Asturias. whilst in 955, Ordoño III of León, raided Lisbon but the Muslims once again soon regained their control. Fernando I of Castile also attacked Lisbon in 1060 whilst in 1093, his successor, Alfonso VI actually captured it briefly from the Muslims. Three years later Alfonso assigned the County of Portugal, effectively the northerly portion of the modern country, to Henry of Burgundy, his son-in-law. However, before the Christians could assert themselves in Lisbon, the Almoravides, puritanical Berbers emanating from Africa via Morocco, moved through Spain to take Lisbon in 1111. The Almoravides, in turn, were soon succeeded by the even more zealous Almohads.

In 1140 Afonso Henriques, the son of Henry of Burgundy, attempted but failed to capture Lisbon with the aid of Crusaders *en route* to the Holy Land. These overseas forces included English warriors, such as the Veal brothers from Dartmouth, and mark one of the first instances of Anglo-Portuguese cooperation. However, Afonso's second attempt to capture Lisbon from the Moors, in 1147, was successful, following a four and a half-month siege conducted with the assistance of German, Flemish, English and French Crusaders. These forces were intercepted in Oporto whilst on their way to the Holy Land as part of the Second Crusade and following a stirring sermon from the Bishop of Oporto, they travelled on to Lisbon with him. One of the English Crusaders, Gilbert of Hastings, became the Bishop of Lisbon soon after the city's liberation, replacing the Mozarabic bishop who was killed after the siege for collaborating with the ruling Moors. Gilbert established the Sarum (Salisbury) rite in Lisbon, which remained in force in Portugal until the 16th century.

After the 1147 reconquest, half of the Lisbon populace was Mozarabic, that is to say local Christians who had accepted Moorish rule. They were tolerated in their ghettoes, the *mourarias,* but were considered to be second-class citizens. In the century following the reconquest, Christianity was physically asserted by the construction of a number of churches and convents. Indeed, the church of Santa Maria dos Mártires was built on the alleged burial site of the Crusaders who died during the siege. Other early churches included those of Madalena (1164) and Santa Justa (1173). Also in 1173, the remains of St Vincent, Lisbon's patron saint, were brought by King Afonso to Lisbon from Cape St. Vincent in southern Portugal. According to legend, ravens accompanied the vessel bearing his remains and to this day this bird remains a symbol of Lisbon. As at the Tower of London, live ravens were kept over a long period at Lisbon Cathedral but although St Vincent is the city's patron saint, St Anthony of Padua is equally revered there. He was born in Lisbon in 1195 and a church and museum in his name today stand in front of Lisbon Cathedral.

Throughout the 13th century Christianity was further bolstered by the construction of numerous convents, including those of saints Francisco (1217) and Domingos (1241), as well as of the Espírito Santo (Holy Spirit, 1279) and Trindade (Trinity, 1283). The predominant religious orders in Lisbon at this time were the Dominicans and Franciscans. On the secular front, although the first *foral da cidade* (city charter) was granted to Lisbon in 1179, giving it privileges from the Crown, it was not until 1255 that Afonso III made Lisbon the capital of Portugal in preference to Coimbra. Regular *Cortes* were held in Lisbon thereafter. Particularly after the Christian recapture of Seville from the Moors in 1288, maritime trade and shipbuilding increased in Lisbon. The city's relative stability during the reign of Dinis (1279-1325) was reflected in 1290 in the foundation of the *Estudos Gerais* (College of General Studies), the forerunner of the University of Lisbon and in 1294 by the first reference to commercial establishments in the Rua Nova dos Mercadores (Merchants' New Road). However, in 1537 the University was to move to Coimbra and was not re-established in Lisbon until 1911. Despite the stability implicit in Lisbon's educational and commercial activities, Dinis still felt it necessary to construct a new riverside defensive city wall in 1294 to defend the city's population of about 15,000.

The Later Middle Ages

Despite the setbacks of a large earthquake on Christmas night in 1337 and of plague from 1348, Lisbon was an established international seaport by the 1350s. Indeed, Fernão Lopes, the royal chronicler, estimated that at that time 400-500 ships regularly anchored in the Tagus, of which only half were Portuguese vessels. Under Fernando I (1367-83) commerce was further stimulated by steps taken to protect Portugal from overseas trade competition. Notwithstanding this, by the end of the 14th century, a considerable colony of Genoese, English, Flemish, Lombard and Breton merchants and traders was established in Lisbon. In fact, by 1353, the merchants of Lisbon and Oporto were sufficiently organized and powerful to negotiate a commercial treaty with Edward III of England.

However, the latter part of the 14th century was a period of strife. By 1373 King Fernando I (1367-83) was allied to England's John of Gaunt against Enrique II of Castile, a kingdom to which the Englishman laid claim through his Castilian wife. However, Fernando's attempt to invade Castile ended in failure in 1371 and two years later Enrique retaliated by sacking the central Rua Nova and Jewish quarter (*judiaria*) of Lisbon. In the ensuing brief period of peace, Fernando erected further substantial walls around Lisbon, now known as the *cerca fernandina* (1373-5), which encompassed 103 hectares, an area more than six times larger than the Moorish walls.

In Lisbon in 1381 Edmund, Earl of Cambridge, John of Gaunt's brother, betrothed his six-year-old son Edward to ten-year-old Beatriz, King Fernando of Portugal's heir. However, after an abortive Anglo-Portuguese assault on Castile, Fernando made peace with its king, Juan I, in 1383 and reneged on Beatriz's betrothal, promising her instead to Juan himself. When Fernando died, later in the same year, Beatriz's Spanish mother, Leonor Teles, became regent and established a pro-Spanish régime in conjunction with her Galician lover, the Count de Ourém. To forestall Juan's annexation of Portugal, a popular revolt was orchestrated by several cities of the realm, notably Lisbon, where the rising was led by Álvaro Pais, a city burgher. Pais supported the claim to the throne of the so-called Mestre de Avis (Master of the Order of Avis), an illegitimate son of Pedro I of Portugal (1357-67), who was proclaimed King João I of Portugal in the Lisbon churchyard of S. Domingos Regedor. In the conflict João murdered Queen Leonor's lover and his supporters threw her ally, the Bishop Martinho Annes, off the tower of the city's Cathedral, an event later chronicled in *The Lusiads*. The Castilians, with the help of members of the Portuguese nobility, responded by besieging Lisbon (1384) but an outbreak of pestilence forced their withdrawal.

At this time the city walls confronting the assailants were 6.5km long with seventy-seven towers and thirty-eight gates, protecting a city with a population of about 60,000. Castilian claims were decisively rebuffed in June 1385 by Nun'Álvares Pereira, with the assistance of English archers, at the battle of Aljubarrota some 110km north of Lisbon.

In 1385 João I was confirmed as King by the Cortes of Coimbra in preference to his half-brother, Pedro I's illegitimate son by Inês de Castro, and he assigned to the hero of Aljubarrota, Nun'Álvares, the title of Constable of Portugal. The King also renewed the civil privileges of Lisbon and cemented ties with England through the Treaty of Windsor (1386) and his marriage, the following year, to Philippa of Lancaster, daughter of John of Gaunt. Around 1393 work started in Lisbon on the Convento do Carmo, to be the city's largest church, overlooking the city centre. This was built over the following thirty years as a celebration of the national independence of Portugal, earned at Aljubarrota. By a curious twist, the battle's hero Nun'Álvares Pereira later became a monk at the Carmo convent where he died in religious poverty. In 1996 excavations were carried out in the Carmo ruins which allegedly uncovered his remains.

The reign of King João (1385-1433) was particularly important for Lisbon as it signalled the new importance of the lower aristocracy, the city's bourgeoisie and, in some cases, its artisans in contrast to the declining influence of the nobility. This process is also reflected in João's acceptance of the so-called Casa dos 24 (House of the 24) which consisted of two representatives of the twelve major craft guilds of Lisbon in which, in their early days, both Jews and Christians participated. Led by the *juiz do povo* (people's judge, or lord mayor), the delegates and four deputies of the Casa dos 24 had important rights to attend the Council of Lisbon and make representations to the Crown, privileges which lasted until the 19th century. During the early 15th century the Royal Court became firmly established in Lisbon where a state bureaucracy developed, including the creation of offices of the *contador-mor* (chief accountant or treasurer), who looked after the royal finances, and of other *contadores* who administered local affairs. The embryonic Portuguese diplomatic service was also established, with the king's ambassadors being despatched from headquarters in Lisbon. The administrative importance of the city was further underlined by the founding of the national archives, the Torre do Tombo (Tower of the Archives). As early as 1418 Fernão Lopes, the royal chronicler, was keeper of the Tombo and used its records for his celebrated histories of Portugal.

The Age of Discoveries

As well as João's diplomatic links with England, his reign also witnessed the birth of Portugal's own overseas expansionism, particularly after peace had been made with Castile in 1411. In 1415, the Portuguese with English help took Ceuta, on the north African coast, and by 1419 they had reached Madeira, and the Azores by 1427. Maritime expansion continued off west Africa, with the Portuguese arriving at Cabo Verde (Cape Verde Islands) in 1445 and Senegal in 1446. Lisbon's role as a maritime capital, orchestrating the burgeoning empire, had begun and by 1417 its population stood at an estimated 63,750, organized into twenty-three *freguesias*, with a growing bourgeoisie. The capital's role in these explorations was typified by the Lisbon merchant Fernão Gomes's attainment of rights to explore the Guinea coast in 1469. North European involvement in Lisbon's trade also grew as is shown by the establishment in 1472 of a Flemish merchants' brotherhood. Under King João II (1481-95), overseas exploration and trading continued apace. Diogo Cão reached the Congo river and Angola (1482) and five years later Bartolomeu Dias sailed from Lisbon to round the Cape of Good Hope in 1488.

It was under King Manuel I (1495-1521), however, that Lisbon derived its greatest benefit from what is now known as the Age of Discoveries. On 8 July 1497, Vasco da Gama set sail from Lisbon (Belém) to find the sea route around the Cape to the East Indies. After reaching Calicut in India, his fleet returned to Lisbon with spices in 1499, the same year that Pedro Álvares Cabral set out from the Tagus for the Indies but, *en route*, encountered Brazil. News of Cabral's discovery of Brazil reached Lisbon in 1501 and by 1503 Venetian and German merchants and financiers, such as the famous Fuggers, had bases in the Portuguese capital, as the city outstripped Genoa, Venice and other Mediterranean ports in importance. Exotic goods traded in Lisbon included African gold and ivory, Eastern spices and silks and Persian carpets, and the city also became a centre of navigational and maritime excellence. The new art of printing belatedly reached Lisbon from northern Europe in 1489, although books had been printed in Coimbra from at least 1487. The first eleven Portuguese incunabula were actually works in Hebrew but from 1495 Lisbon established itself as the centre for printing in the vernacular.

However, despite its momentous maritime achievements, Lisbon was subject to domestic strife during Manuel's reign. In 1496, the influence of his Spanish wife led the King to follow the example of the Spanish monarchs, Fernando and Isabella, by ordering the dissolution of the *judiarias* and *mourarias*, the Jewish and Moorish ghettoes. Indeed, many of Portugal's Jews had only recently come to Portugal, after expulsion from Spain in 1492. Those who now refused to convert were brought, by Manuel's orders, to Lisbon where more of them were coerced to adopt Catholicism or exiled. Worse was to follow, however, in 1506. After a Jew had cast doubt on an allegedly miraculous light shining on a crucifix in the Lisbon church of S. Domingos, the Dominicans orchestrated a large-scale slaughter of the local Jews. As many as 2,000 Jews may have been killed before Manuel put an end to the disorder. In response, he executed fifty of the culprits and shut down the convent of S. Domingos. He also briefly suppressed the Casa dos 24, but this body was re-established by 1508.

The overseas discoveries brought wealth which financed the construction of fine new buildings in Lisbon. One of the most notable was the Jerónimos (Hieronymite) monastery at Belém, conceived in 1499 and built, initially, by Boytac from early 1501. The monastery and church are arguably the finest surviving examples of what became known as the Manueline style of architecture, a form of late Gothic, using contemporary maritime motifs such as ropes, anchors, armillary spheres and other navigational instruments. Another Manueline masterpiece, Madre de Deus (Mother of God) church, at Xabregas to the east of the city centre, was erected in 1509. Its fine ceramic tilework has recently been given a new lease of life as the nucleus of a Museu do Azulejo (Museum of Ceramic Tilework). One notable Lisbon building of this time which no longer survives was the magnificent Paço da Ribeira (Royal Riverside Palace), which was started in 1500 to replace the *Paço da Alcáçova*, the old Moorish castle, as the royal residence. During its existence the Riverside Palace witnessed a flourishing court life with many of the plays of Gil Vicente being produced there in the period to 1536. Manueline architecture also graced fortifications such as the small Torre de Belém (Tower of Belém) built in the Tagus by 1521, probably by Arruda, as part of the river defences of Lisbon. Today, following the alteration of the course of the river, it stands only marginally off-shore. Another survivor of this period is the curious pointed-stone Casa dos Bicos, which was built in central Lisbon in 1523 by the Albuquerque family. It was controversially restored, by the re-erection of a top floor, during the 1980s. At this time of expansion in the early 16th century, part of modern Lisbon's central square, the Rossio, was still in use for the grazing of cattle, with commercial activity being centred nearer the river on the Rua Nova d'el-Rei.

As well as architecture, King Manuel also patronized a thriving Lisbon School of painting, which developed around Jorge Afonso. The 1530s, however, witnessed a number of less pleasant events in the capital. In 1531 a very substantial earthquake necessitated a programme of rebuilding whilst, in 1537, the anti-semitic King João III set up the

awesome Catholic Inquisition in Lisbon. That same year he closed
Lisbon University and moved it to Coimbra, in central Portugal. By
1540 Lisbon had witnessed its first *auto-da-fé* (trial of faith) and seven
years later the Inquisition produced its first index of prohibited books.
In 1551 yet another earthquake struck, causing much destruction. A
more insidious development was Lisbon's deep involvement in the
trade in slaves between Africa, Portugal and Brazil. Indeed, about ten
per cent of Lisbon's population of 113,706 (1557) were estimated to be
black slaves or mulattos. Large numbers of Lisbon's citizens were
killed in both 1569 and 1575 by pestilential epidemics.

The Occupation by Spain

A self-inflicted wound of more lasting proportions was the disastrous
crusade to Africa of the young King Sebastião in 1578. When he set off
from Lisbon with 500 ships, 17,000 men and 9,000 camp-followers on
a crusade to vanquish the Moors of North Africa, he set in train a
sequence of events which ended with Portugal's loss of independence.
Routed at the Battle of Alcácer-Quibir in Morocco, Sebastião and some
8,000 men were killed and 15,000 captured. This left the aged Cardinal
of Lisbon, Henrique, to assume the throne for two years before his
death in 1580. Although António, Prior de Crato, a cousin of the dead
king, was welcomed in Lisbon as his successor, the army of a rival
claimant, Philip II of Spain, bombarded and captured the waterside
citadel at Cascais, to the west of Lisbon. The Spaniards, under the
Duque de Alba, pushed on towards Lisbon and triumphed at the battle
of Alcântara, leaving Philip and his Spanish successors in possession of
Portugal from 1580 till 1640. Philip did have a legitimate claim to the
throne; like the Prior, he was a cousin of Sebastião, and his mother and
first wife were both Portuguese. Philip actually spent from December
1580 to February 1583 in Portugal and the state carriage in which he
allegedly travelled is the prize possession today of Lisbon's Museu dos
Coches (Museum of Coaches), at Belém. The Spanish occupation
weakened Portugal partly through the indirect effect of Spain's wars in
Holland, but also as a result of the Spaniards' barring the Dutch from
Lisbon. This was a factor in the creation of the Dutch East India
Company and the Dutch seizure of Portuguese possessions in
Indonesia, Ceylon, Angola, Brazil and São Tomé.
    The Spanish occupation was also a period of much intrigue in
Lisbon. Catholic and Protestant conflict in northern Europe brought to
Lisbon both the Bridgettine nuns in 1594, originally from London, and
the Catholic seminarists of the English College in 1628 from Douai,
France, communities which both survived in Lisbon for over 250 years.

Alleged English 'spies' such as Richard Butler were also to be found in Lisbon. During the occupation, Lisbon's harbour was used as the launching point for the ill-fated Spanish Armada of 1588. Following its defeat, Francis Drake, Sir John Norris and the Earl of Essex sailed to Lisbon in 1589 to mop up the remains of the Spanish fleet. Norris and Essex's forces landed at Peniche, some 70km north west of Lisbon, expecting to be embraced by supporters of the Prior de Crato. When these did not materialize, Norris's forces straggled on to Lisbon, where Drake failed to rendezvous with them. Following this débâcle, the remaining forces retreated to Cascais and out of Portugal.

Another large earthquake hit Lisbon during the Spanish occupation (1597), its effects being most serious in the hilly area of Santa Catarina to the west of the city centre. Philip II's successors largely neglected Portugal other than as a source of income and, indeed, it was following the Spanish Conde de Olivares's excessive demands for taxes and for the country to enlist in fighting the Catalans, that there was a rising in Lisbon on 1 December 1640. The conspirators gathered in the Terreiro do Paço and their successful revolt resulted in the establishment of João IV (1640-56) as founder of the Royal House of Braganza. Fittingly, João's ducal origins traced back to the family of another national hero, Nun'Álvares, the victor at Aljubarrota (1385) where Portugal had previously asserted its independence from Spain. However, fighting against the Spaniards continued intermittently and in 1661 the Spaniards even seized the towns of Borba and Évora to the south-east of Lisbon. Not until their defeat at the Battle of Ameixial in 1663 was their threat removed and Évora recaptured.

Lisbon was also the scene of difficult diplomatic episodes with both the English and the Dutch. In 1650 Prince Rupert of the Rhine, nephew of the recently executed Charles I of England, and Prince Maurice arrived in the Tagus at the head of a Royalist fleet. They were shortly followed by Admiral Blake and a Commonwealth flotilla. King João was faced with trying to balance his sympathies for a Catholic monarchy against the need to deal with the *de facto* Protestant rulers of a historic ally. Much wrangling and a tense confrontation in the Tagus took place before Blake was induced to withdraw. Fighting against the Dutch also continued in the 1640s and 1650s, and although the Portuguese permanently lost some possessions, especially in the East, they regained territory in Brazil in 1654. The Dutch even blockaded Lisbon in 1657, when Portugal was ruled by the crippled and mentally defective Afonso VI (1656-67), and peace was only made with them in 1661. The year before the Dutch blockade, the British fleet also entered the Tagus with the aim of enforcing the 1654 Treaty with Britain, which had effectively been imposed on the Catholic Portuguese by the Puritan

Commonwealth. However, a more amicable pact was made with England in 1662 when Catherine of Braganza married Charles II of England, after leaving Lisbon amidst great ceremony.

The discovery of significant deposits of gold in Brazil in the mid-1690s brought a second era of splendour to Lisbon from around 1697. This, and other overseas sources of wealth led to a period of baroque extravagance and artistic endeavour in the city, albeit to the detriment of the Portuguese economy. In 1703 the first Methuen treaty between England and Portugal, named after the English minister in Lisbon, John Methuen, granted import duty privileges to Portuguese wine arriving in England, but also permitted English cloth to be imported into Portugal, further weakening her economy. The English Factory, a group of English merchants, became an increasingly powerful force in Lisbon's commercial life over the ensuing hundred years. However, gold continued to pour into the capital to mask such problems, with, for example, 16,000 pounds weight recorded as arriving in Lisbon in 1705. This wealth also gave King João V (1706-50) the leverage to induce the Pope, in 1708, to allow Lisbon to have two ecclesiastical jurisdictions with an archbishop overseeing each of two cathedrals in the city. The newer, the Sé Patriarcal in the Bairro Alto area, burnt down in 1756. In 1716, the King also persuaded the Pope to agree to the creation of a cardinal-patriarchate in Lisbon, a *coup* achieved by assisting the papacy in a naval crusade against the Turks, and by lining the Vatican's coffers. In effect, a form of state-controlled Church existed in Portugal, run from Lisbon.

João V also spent large sums on patronizing the arts. The Italian musician, Domenico Scarlatti was brought to the Lisbon Court and José da Silva's operas were also lavishly staged. From 1717, the German-born architect J. F. Ludovice (Ludwig) built the enormous Mafra palace, 45km north of Lisbon, which was intended as the Versailles of Portugal. Nevertheless, some significant public works were also effected in Lisbon at this time, most notably the construction between 1731 and 1748 of the main portion of the Aqueduto das Águas Livres (Free Waters Aqueduct) by Manuel da Maia and Custódio José Vieira. This links Caneças, to the north-west of Lisbon, with the Mãe d'Água reservoir at Amoreiras in northern Lisbon. As it crosses the Alcântara valley the aqueduct is supported by thirty-five arches, the tallest being 66m high. It supplied water to Lisbon until the mid-20th century but public access to it was withdrawn in the mid-19th century after a series of suicides and gruesome murders on its parapets. Including its various tributaries, the aqueduct system extends for 58km.

Between 1721 and 1745 about £250,000 of gold was imported into Portugal annually from Brazil. However, such wealth was powerless to prevent an epidemic of yellow fever in 1723 and also stimulated an increased demand for imports, especially from England, whilst local industry stagnated. Money was nevertheless still lavished on new palaces, both at Belém in 1725 and at Queluz, 30km to the north-west of Lisbon, where work started on a new building in 1747.

The Great Earthquake of 1755

In 1750 King João died and was succeeded by José I (1750-77). On the morning of 1 November 1755, All Saints' Day, most of Lisbon's inhabitants were attending mass in the city's churches. At around 9.30am an earthquake, centred in the Atlantic off Lisbon, shook the city and was accompanied by a massive tidal wave. The earthquake has since been estimated at a strength of around 7.9 on the Richter Scale and its effects on land and sea were allegedly felt in England and beyond. The initial shock lasted for an estimated five to seven minutes and was followed by many lesser ones over succeeding days. However, the damage caused by the earth movement was exceeded by the many fires which broke out in its wake. Some witnesses attributed the flames to the myriad candles burning in the churches at the time of the disaster, whilst others blamed arsonists seeking to take advantage of the chaos to plunder the ruins. Indeed, a number of British sailors were amongst those who were executed for looting in the ruins. The destruction was worst along the waterfront area of the Baixa, where the alluvial deposits under the buildings could not withstand the shocks as effectively as the limestone outcrops of the castle and Bairro Alto areas which, like the Águas Livres aqueduct and the Belém area, survived largely intact. In central Lisbon, the sumptuous royal palace on the waterfront was destroyed with all its splendours, including its library. Many other architectural and artistic treasures were lost, as well as important historical manuscripts and printed works. Amongst the debris was the recently completed Italianate showpiece Teatro da Ópera do Tejo (Tagus Opera House, 1755), along with many churches and public buildings such as the Casa da India (India House), which controlled Portugal's overseas trade to the East, the Custom House, the Inquisition Palace, and the convents of S. Domingos and Carmo. The imposing shell of the Carmo church has been left in ruins to this day as a memorial to the disaster. Estimates of the death toll vary wildly with 30,000 being about the median. The royal family was at Belém at the time, so was spared, but over seventy Britons died in the disaster, prompting the British government to donate £100,000 to the recovery of Lisbon. The cataclysm led to literary, religious and philosophical outpourings across Europe from authors who included Voltaire, Kant and John Wesley.

Sebastião de Carvalho e Melo, the Minister of Foreign Affairs and War (1750-56), took charge of the situation whilst his King's reaction was typified by his subsequent insistence on never sleeping in a masonry-built building for fear of another earthquake. In contrast, his Minister remained calm and gave his famous orders to bury the dead and feed the living before setting about the task of rebuilding the city. Four options were considered, including abandoning Lisbon and building a new city at Belém. Ultimately Carvalho e Melo oversaw the clearing of both the ruins and also of many surviving buildings in the area from the river-front to the Rossio square and their replacement by an impressive grid-iron of tall, neo-Classical buildings, the Baixa, which today forms the heart of Lisbon. The new buildings even incorporated strengthened walls designed to minimize damage in any future earthquake. By 1775 reconstruction had included a massive bronze equestrian statue of José I by Machado de Castro, complete with medallion of Pombal, sited in the new Praça do Comércio (measuring 192m by 177m), which replaced the Terreiro do Paço, in front of the Baixa. To generations of British sailors this was therefore known as Black Horse Square.

After the earthquake Carvalho e Melo became the all-powerful Minister of State (1756-77) and successively Conde de Oeiras (1759) and Marquês de Pombal (1770), the name by which he is generally known today. The less appealing side of Pombal can be seen in his reaction to the 1758 assassination attempt against King José I near Belém. The ringleaders of the conspiracy, including the Marquis and Marchioness of Távora, their two sons and the Duke of Aveiro, were tried and subjected to gruesome and fiery executions near Belém Palace in 1759, where a small monument still marks the spot. That same year, Pombal dissolved the Jesuits in Portugal and had Malagrida, one of the Order's leaders, burned at the stake. Malagrida had been a favourite of João V and made his name as preacher to the native indians of Brazil before he fatally criticized Pombal. Another source of tribulation to Pombal in the 1750s was the serious decline in gold and sugar income coming to the city. Despite this, however, in 1764 a start was made on the construction of the Passeio Público, a route out of Lisbon to the north and in 1774 Pombal also built a new Paço do Concelho (Town Hall) for the city. For himself, he constructed an impressive palace at Oeiras, 18km to the west of the capital. Although the Marquis made attempts to reorganize Portuguese trade and industry, his failure to do so successfully and to reform the Portuguese transport infrastructure had as serious a negative impact as his positive success in rebuilding Lisbon.

In 1777 José I died and Pombal was promptly dismissed from office and his medallion removed from the King's statue in the Praça do

Comércio, although his son remained as president of the Lisbon municipality. The new monarch, Maria I (1777-1816), moved her Court to the recently constructed rococo palace of Queluz, outside Lisbon. However, she was mentally unstable and in 1792 her son, João VI, became regent. Nevertheless, during her reign there were some significant developments in the field of learning. Not least, in 1779, the Academia das Ciências de Lisboa (Lisbon Academy of Sciences) was established, although it was somewhat derided by supercilious late 18th-century English visitors. Then, in 1796 the Real Biblioteca Pública de Lisboa (Royal Public Library of Lisbon), forerunner of today's Biblioteca Nacional (National Library), was founded. On the ecclesiastical front, in 1779, work commenced on the imposing Estrela Basilica (1790) by Mateus Vicente and Reinaldo Manuel, in the west of Lisbon.

In spite of the initiatives of the new Royal Library, the Academy of Sciences and, in 1793, the opening of the new Teatro de S. Carlos opera house in Lisbon, the nation's agriculture remained backward and its industry was likewise well behind northern European developments. Before these problems could be addressed, they were to worsen when, in 1801, Spain and France declared war on Portugal and forced her to close her ports to the Royal Navy. Nevertheless, Anglo-Portuguese commercial trade did continue with, for example, Brazilian cotton being shipped to England through Lisbon. Despite the French threat, the Regent, João went ahead with the construction, from 1802, of a huge new royal palace at Ajuda, 5km west of Lisbon, although the building is still incomplete today.

Also in 1802, General Jean Lannes was sent to Lisbon as French Minister. He demanded from Portugal the expulsion of Spanish royalists who had fled there after his country had invaded Spain and he also extorted money from Portugal to allow her to remain neutral in a western Europe otherwise overrun by France's armies. The respite was short, for in April 1805 General Junot was sent to Lisbon, to replace Lannes and to demand that the Portuguese declare war on their old ally, England, as well as deny access to its ports to English vessels. The French also sought the arrest of all Britons in Portugal and expropriation of their assets. Consequently, in September 1806 the Prince Regent felt obliged to bar the British Fleet from Portugal. Even so, Napoléon was not satisfied and in 1807 sent an ultimatum to Portugal to declare itself against England or be invaded. After much diplomatic effort by Strangford, the Portuguese Court and an estimated 15,000 supporters fled Lisbon in November 1807. The Royal entourage headed for Rio de Janeiro under the protection of Sir Sidney Smith and the Royal Navy. In all, fifteen Portuguese warships and twenty merchantmen left Lisbon on 29 November and the following day, the French forces entered the Portuguese capital.

Peninsular and Civil Wars, 1807-34

Although Junot's 15,000 men were bedraggled after their campaign, they met no resistance in Lisbon except from brief popular riots when the Portuguese flag was removed from the castle. Important figures such as the Archbishop of Lisbon acquiesced in the occupation. However, after the Royal Navy had blockaded Lisbon and troops under Arthur Wellesley (Lord Wellington) had triumphed at the battles of Roliça and Vimeiro in 1808, Junot's possession of the city became untenable. The controversial Convention of Sintra (1808) generously allowed Junot to withdraw by sea with his army largely intact and without making reparations to Portugal. The following year William Carr Beresford was put in charge of reorganizing the army of Portugal but, undeterred, French forces again headed for Lisbon. Once more they were defeated by Wellington at Buçaco (Bussaco, 1810) some 230km north of Lisbon. They were then forced by a lack of provisions, exacerbated by Wellington's scorched-earth policy, to withdraw before his masterly defensive Lines of Torres Vedras, created about 60km north of the capital.

Although by 1811 British and Portuguese troops had driven the French from Portugal, the country's economy and trade were by then in a parlous state. Much of Lisbon's Brazilian trade had been lost to Britain and some 75 per cent of state revenues were dissipated in supporting Beresford's armies. Local dissent grew and was fuelled by Beresford's execution of the Grand Master of Masons, and Liberal general, Gomes Freire (1817).

Although the exiled royal family of João VI was invited back from Brazil to Portugal in 1813 and George Canning was even sent to Lisbon to receive him, the king failed to return. Soon a Liberal revolution, fomented in Oporto in 1820, spread to Lisbon where its forces were welcomed and supported by the *juiz do povo* who subscribed to the cause of an elected parliament along the Spanish constitutional model of 1812. Marshal Beresford, who had sailed to Brazil to consult the absent monarch, was then refused permission to re-land in Portugal and the regency of the absent João VI was replaced by Liberals, a move much welcomed in Lisbon. In this anti-clerical atmosphere, the infamous Lisbon Inquisition was abolished and the city's Patriarch refused to take an oath to the new draft constitution. Belatedly, in 1821, the Portuguese court of João VI returned to Lisbon, leaving Crown Prince Pedro in Rio. Although João accepted the new constitution, his Spanish queen, Carlota Joaquina and second son, Dom Miguel, refused to do so. She was therefore stripped of her Portuguese citizenship and exiled to the Ramalhão palace, near Sintra, where she became a focus of dissent. Outside the country, too, many European countries refused to recognize the new Liberal régime in Lisbon.

Although the Banco de Lisboa had been set up in 1821, its creation could not disguise the fact that the Portuguese economy was in a parlous state, all the more so after 1822 when Pedro declared Brazil's independence from Portugal and thereby cut off gold revenues and other trading income to Portugal. Conflict between supporters of an authoritarian monarchy, epitomized by Dom Miguel, and the more liberal constitutional monarchists ensued. In 1823, much of the Lisbon garrison defected to Miguel, who was the rallying-point for protest against the Constitution of 1822. The radical liberal government resigned in May 1823 and on 30 May, King João VI joined the revolt against the radicals. The following year D. Miguel tried once again to take over the Lisbon garrison and was briefly hailed as King but his revolt was again defeated. Although pardoned by João, Miguel was despatched to Vienna to calm the situation at home.

However, in 1826, João VI died leaving his son, the Brazilian Emperor Pedro, as heir to the Portuguese throne. Pedro proposed a new constitution, the *Carta Constitucional*, which Sir Charles Stuart conveyed to Lisbon on 7 July. This document proposed two chambers of parliament and also, in an attempt to reunite the warring factions, the betrothal of Pedro's young daughter, Dona Maria Glória, to the errant D. Miguel, her uncle. This centrist *Carta Constitucional* was espoused in Portugal by General Saldanha, the Marquis of Pombal's great-grandson. However, in 1828, Miguel returned to Lisbon and finally seized the throne, dismantling the constitutional régime, many of whose supporters fled, including Saldanha. A Liberal revolt in Lisbon in 1831 failed but, the following year, D. Pedro returned from Brazil with English and French support to confront King Miguel. In 1833 Miguel's fleet was destroyed by Admiral Charles Napier and the Duque de Terceira's Liberal army entered Lisbon. By 1834 Miguel had been finally defeated and banished from Lisbon for good. Although the young Maria Glória was the titular monarch (as Maria II), her father Pedro IV, who had abdicated in her favour in 1826, was the effective ruler. Even though Miguel was now out of the way, domestic strife continued and, in 1836, the Liberal *Setembristas* faction revolted in Lisbon and took over from their Conservative rivals. They abolished the 1826 *Carta Constitucional*, reinstating instead a version of the more radical 1822 constitution.

The Modern Era (1834-1997)

In the early part of the 19th century, visitors to Lisbon frequently remarked on the packs of wild dogs and the cries of 'Água vai!' ('Water on its way!') which presaged the ejection of slops from upper windows onto unsuspecting passers-by. In the mid-19th century many improvements were made to the city's infrastructure, including the opening of public cemeteries at Alto do S. João and Prazeres (by 1835), the introduction of gas light (1836) and the erection of a fine new town-hall, the neo-Classical Paços do Concelho (1865-80) to serve its population of 197,000 (1864). Nevertheless, Lisbon was still a relatively insanitary metropolis, regularly afflicted by epidemics. In 1855 and 1857 cholera, then yellow fever, ravaged Lisbon and in 1861 even King Pedro V died of typhus, as did Albert, the Prince Consort of Britain. On a more positive note, Lisbon's international connections were improved by new telegraph lines (1854), the Carregado to Lisbon railway link (1856) and the opening of the Santa Apolónia international railway terminus to the east of the city centre (1865). Five years later, the Eastern Telegraph Company laid a submarine cable, complete with telegraph station at Carcavelos, which connected Lisbon to London as part of the British colonial link to India.

Lisbon's population continued to expand rapidly in the last quarter of the 19th century, rising from 227,000 in 1878 to 243,000 by 1885, and to 300,964 in 1890. By the turn of the century, the city had more than 350,000 inhabitants. To accommodate this rapid influx of population from rural areas new workers' districts at Alcântara and Xabregas were created between 1870-90, whilst better housing was erected in the D. Estefânia and Campo de Ourique areas. Lisbon's citizens also benefitted from the introduction of *americanos,* or horse-drawn trams, which were introduced to the city on the coastal Cais do Sodré to Santa Apolónia route in 1873. That year also witnessed the final element of the post-earthquake reconstruction of the Baixa: the triumphal arch across the riverside end of the Rua Augusta was completed, to a design by Veríssimo José da Costa and A. Calmels. Lisbon city planners also initiated the construction of the imposing 90m-wide Avenida da Liberdade (1879-86) which was to stretch for 1.5km as the main artery northwards out of the city, replacing the Passeio Público. The perennial problem of Lisbon's water-supply was alleviated by the opening of the Barbadinhos pumping station in 1880 which continued to supply the city till 1967 and survives today as the Museu da Água (Water Museum). The railway finally arrived in the very heart of Lisbon with the construction between 1887 and 1892 of the ornate, Moorish-style Rossio station and the adjacent Avenida-Palace Hotel. Rossio is probably the only rail terminus in the world in which the platforms are sited on the sixth floor of the station building.

On the international front, the British Ultimatum of 1890, which required Portugal to renounce territorial claims in Africa, provoked anti-British demonstrations in Lisbon and a political crisis. The extent of British influence at that time is reflected in the estimated 30,000 British sailors who visited Lisbon that year, in addition to those of the Channel fleet and the 2,000 British residents of the capital. Furthermore, many of Lisbon's advances in communications and commerce were implemented by British-controlled enterprises. The city's progress was, however, sadly punctuated by the regular litany of natural and man-made misfortunes which have struck throughout its history. There were major fires at the Arsenal da Marinha (Naval Arsenal) in the city centre in 1883 and in the Deputies' Chamber in the parliament building at S. Bento in 1895; between these a cholera epidemic swept through the city in 1891.

Nevertheless, recreational and commercial advances were also made in the mid and latter parts of the 19th century. The impressive Teatro D. Maria II was erected in the Rossio between 1842 and 1846, while in 1860 Thomas Price established a longstanding circus in the Salitre area. Also in the 1860s the Lisbon Cricket Club was founded and this, despite its name, also helped to introduce football to the city. Lisbon Zoological Gardens were inaugurated in 1884, whilst an imposing Moorish-style bullring was built near the cricket field site at Campo Pequeno in 1892, to replace an arena at Campo de Santana. Major market buildings were constructed at Campo de Santa Clara (1877), Avenida 24 de Julho (1881), S. Bento (1881) and Praça Figueira (1885), whilst the Alcântara market followed in 1905.

In order to transport the vastly increased population of the city, modern American-built electric tramcars were introduced on the riverside route to Belém from 1901, albeit on a narrow 90cm gauge which had been chosen largely to frustrate illegal use of tramlines by rival horse-drawn trams. The following year saw the inauguration of the Santa Justa *elevador* (street-lift) to connect the Baixa to the elevated Chiado area. A similar street-lift between the Praça do Município and Public Library had been constructed in 1897 but soon fell out of use. By 1906 electric trams were also running from the city centre north to Campo Grande and some of those same vehicles remained at work, albeit in reserve service, in 1996. However, by 1907 the motor-car had also begun to make its mark, when Lisbon's first taxis were introduced. The scale of city development prompted the creation of the Prémio Valmor (Valmor Prize) which has been awarded to architects and owners of worthy new Lisbon buildings from 1903 to date. Amidst this social and physical change, came reminders of tradition with British royal visits to Lisbon from King Edward VII (1903) and by Queen Alexandra (1905). Amongst the King's duties in the city were the inauguration of the new Royal British Club and of the park which now bears his name, the Parque Eduardo VII.

However, the Portuguese monarchy itself was far from popular. In 1906 King Carlos I dissolved the Portuguese Cortes and the Lisbon municipality and, in the following year, he bestowed dictatorial prime-ministerial powers on João Franco. On 31 January 1908, the King signed a decree allowing his prime minister to deport political enemies to Timor. However the next day King Carlos and Crown Prince Luís Filipe were shot dead by assassins in the Praça do Comércio in Lisbon as they passed in their carriage whilst returning from Vila Viçosa palace. There followed a period of political turmoil with six governments before October 1910 and Lisbon a hotbed of Republicanism. On 5 October, after fighting in the streets of Lisbon, a Republic was declared from the balcony of the Town Hall. Carlos's son, King Manuel II, fled into exile in Twickenham, England but political chaos continued. Indeed, the United States envoy in Lisbon in the 1920s, Norval Richardson, claimed that there were 150 prime ministers in a twelve-year period after the 1910 Revolution, one of whom, Sidónio Pais, was even assassinated at the Rossio railway station in 1918.

Despite Portugal's entry into the First World War in 1916, following her seizure of German merchant ships in Lisbon harbour, the country remained riven by internal conflict to the extent that, in 1919, Monarchist forces shelled the city from the heights of the Monsanto fort. Such political instability and the weakness of the economy prompted the establishment of a military dictatorship in May 1926, headed by General Gomes da Costa. But in 1927, as well as a significant earthquake in the city, there were risings in Lisbon and Oporto. The ousted Republicans fought armed battles in the streets of the capital, especially in the northern district of Rato, before General Carmona asserted martial law and assumed the President's mantle. He appointed António de Oliveira Salazar as his Minister of Finance and this little-known academic succeeded in balancing the national budget soon after.

The interwar years saw further large increases in population, from 484,664 in 1920 to 591,939 by 1930, as more rural dwellers were drawn to the city. To meet the strain, several major transport initiatives were taken in Lisbon. In 1928, at Cais do Sodré, a new Lisbon terminus building was erected for the busy commuter and recreational railway line to Cascais. The parallel Marginal road to Cascais was upgraded and along the route of this road and railway the suburbs of Estoril,

Cascais and Caxias developed. At nearby Cruz Quebrada a new national sports stadium was erected in the 1940s, with a dedicated link from both the Cascais railway and the Lisbon tram systems. In the city itself, a modern ferry-boat terminal, the Estação do Sul e Sueste (South and Southeast Station) was opened near the Praça do Comércio in 1931 as the necessary staging post for rail travellers wishing to reach the Alentejo and Algarve. To avoid this tortuous journey, an ambitious plan was hatched in 1934 to build a bridge across the Tagus which would have linked the northern district of Beato with Montijo on the southern bank, had the project not been aborted. A number of monumental, to some monolithic, buildings were erected in Lisbon in the 1920s and 1930s including the Instituto Superior Técnico (Higher Technical Institute, 1927) and the Casa da Moeda (National Mint, 1934-36). Lisbon also acquired an ambitious peripheral network of new motorway-type roads which were built between 1938 and 1948 through the vision of Duarte Pacheco, President of Lisbon City Council and Minister of Public Works.

During the Second World War, Portugal remained neutral. This stance and its relative proximity to the USA helped to swell Lisbon's population to 694,389 (1940). Political refugees *en route* to North America arrived in significant numbers and the city became a centre for the intrigue of both Allied and Axis spies. Lisbon Airport, then at Granja do Marquês near Sintra, was one of the few places in western Europe from which commercial flights continued after the outbreak of war and British, German and Italian airlines operated side by side there. To commemorate the tercentenary in 1940 of Portugal's restoration of its independence from Spain a large international exhibition was installed at Belém but, because of the war, visitors from overseas were very limited in number. A legacy of the exhibition can be seen in the striking Padrão dos Descobrimentos (Monument to the Discoveries) at Belém which, although only erected in 1960 on the 500th anniversary of the death of Henry the Navigator, was actually a recreation of a design for the 1940 celebrations.

Under the fiscally rigid régime of Salazar, who had become Prime Minister in 1932, civil liberties were circumscribed but attempts were made to modernize Lisbon during and after the War. Residential districts at Restelo and Alvalade were developed between 1940 and 1945, whilst in 1948 the impressive Rocha Conde de Óbidos maritime terminal was opened at Alcântara docks. A massive Fonte Monumental (monumental fountain) decorated the modern concrete public buildings of the Alameda from 1948 and broad new avenues were driven north out of the city over the next two decades, such as the Avenida dos Estados Unidos and the Avenida do Brasil. The city's population reached 783,226 by 1950, and extensive estates rose up to the northeast of the city centre at Olivais Sul and Norte (1955-60) to house the increasing numbers. In 1954 the large Santa Maria hospital opened, although this was perversely sited beneath the noisy final approach to Lisbon airport as, equally unfortunately, was the new National Library of Lisbon, opened in 1969. Nearby, a new campus was built for the University of Lisbon at Campo Grande in northern Lisbon, designed by Pardal Monteiro (1957-61). Growth prompted an administrative reorganization of the city which resulted in 1959 in the current delineation of fifty-three *freguesias*. The capital also installed a small underground railway system, the Metropolitano de Lisboa, which opened in 1959 using two-car trains which soon proved inadequate for their traffic.

The benevolence of the Armenian oil magnate Calouste Gulbenkian, who had lived in Lisbon for more than a decade before his death in 1955, gave the city an international attraction in the form of the Gulbenkian Museum, which also boasted theatre, concert and library facilities built in a landscaped park at Palhavã between 1960 and 1969. The complex was completed by a Centro de Arte Moderna (Modern Art Centre) in 1983. A striking near-replica of the Cristo Rei (Christ the King) statue at Rio de Janeiro was erected in 1959, at Almada, by the Mothers of Portugal in thanks for Portugal's survival of the Second World War. This stands 85m high and fine views of Lisbon can be had across the Tagus from the summit of its concrete pedestal on the riverside cliffs opposite Alcântara. However, the most dramatic transformation to the face of Lisbon was the nearby construction of the Ponte Salazar (Salazar Bridge, 1962-66), now known as the Ponte 25 de Abril (25 April Bridge), spanning the Tagus between Alcântara and Almada. At 2.278km long, with a centre span of 1,013m it had the longest central span of any steel suspension bridge in Europe but is now ranked behind those which cross the Bosphorus and England's River Humber. The Lisbon bridge crosses the Tagus at a height of 70m and its foundations reach down 79m to basalt rock, which was a world record depth for a bridge at the time of construction.

The 1960s also saw Lisbon's emergence in the international sporting world with triumphs in European competitions by the Lisbon football teams Benfica (1961 and 1962) and Sporting (1964). In the 1970s and 80s Lisbon's athletes brought world sporting honours to the city, whilst the nearby Estoril circuit has become firmly established as a Grand Prix motor racing venue. Lisbon's sporting fanaticism is reflected in its supporting weekly newspapers produced by its own major football teams, as well as three national sports newspapers. Despite the material advances and the success on the sports field, there was a darker side to life in Lisbon in the 1960s. Apart from the limitations imposed by the State and the ever-watchful eyes of the PIDE secret police, the country had become embroiled in overseas colonial wars. Although in 1951 Portugal had made its colonies into provinces which were theoretically equal in status to continental Portugal, this did not forestall the Indian seizure of the Portuguese possessions of Goa, Diu and Damão in 1961 nor protracted wars of independence in Angola, Guiné-Bissau and Mozambique from the early 1960s. By 1968 there were over 100,000 Portuguese troops attempting to maintain colonial power in these African territories. The sight of troop ships at the Lisbon quayside and the return of soldiers' bodies became a grim routine, only partly masked by nationalistic medal-award ceremonies in the city. Even after Salazar had been incapacitated by a cerebral haemorrhage in 1968 the colonial wars continued under his successor as prime minister, the academic lawyer Marcelo Caetano. Opposition was suppressed and such modern developments as Lisbon's skyscraper Sheraton Hotel (1972) masked the country's true economic plight. All was to change on 25 April 1974 when, in the early hours, factions within the Army seized key points in Lisbon and elsewhere. They surrounded the Carmo barracks in upper central Lisbon where Caetano had taken refuge and by the end of the day, power was theirs. Apart from four deaths in Lisbon, caused by the PIDE secret police, the revolution was bloodless.

However, as the country came to grips with its new freedoms, myriad political parties sprang up. The city's streets were daubed with political slogans and fly-posters, and its squares were filled by left-wing rallies and marches. A counter-coup by the first post-revolution President, General Spínola, failed but in late 1975 the army re-imposed a degree of order on the political and economic chaos. As the country extricated itself from its colonial territories with indecent haste, it unleashed a major social problem at home, particularly in Lisbon. Huge numbers of colonists and citizens, fearful for their futures in the newly independent African territories, came back to Portugal. Lisbon's airport and docks witnessed chaotic scenes and hotels bulged at the seams. The possessions of these *retornados*, packed into crates and containers, piled up in the docks and other open spaces. The housing infrastructure of Lisbon could not cope and shanty towns sprang up around the periphery of the city. Even legal housing suffered as regulations introduced under Salazar fixed domestic rent at such low levels that owners could not afford repairs. This in turn led many to sell to developers who subsequently erected new multi-storey blocks to capitalize on the rent laws. Inflation was rampant.

The presidency of Ramalho Eanes (1976-86) brought a degree of stability accompanied by the right-wing and centrist governments of

Francisco Sá-Carneiro and, later, Aníbal Cavaco e Silva's Social Democrats. In 1986 Portugal joined the European Community and has since benefitted from EC-funded projects. Large shopping centres have grown up in Lisbon notably at Amoreiras (1980-86), where Tomás Taveira produced a controversial multi-coloured tower complex. In 1994 Lisbon received international recognition as the European Capital of Culture, an honour which also helped to reawaken local pride in the city. The arts enjoyed a renaissance as new museums such as the Museu da Cidade (City Museum), Museu do Chiado (Chiado Museum), the Centro de Arte Moderna (Modern Art Centre) and the museums of tiles, costume, water and electricity were set up in Lisbon in the 1980s and 1990s. In the suburbs, too, an international modern art museum was opened in Sintra in 1996. The Lisbon buildings of Portuguese architects such as Taveira and Álvaro Siza enhanced their growing international reputations. The fort-like Centro Cultural de Belém, Lisbon's equivalent of the Centre Pompidou in Paris, was opened in time for Portugal's presidency of the Council of Europe in 1992. As many of the older underground railway platforms were extended and new stations built, bringing the total to twenty-five (1996), they were decorated by innovatively designed ceramic tilework, a revival of an historic craft of Lisbon. Quality of life was simultaneously improved by pedestrianization of major city-centre streets in the Baixa and the closure of the Praça do Comércio as a car park. A marked decline in Lisbon's population in the 1980s and 1990s, as peripheral suburbs grew, has also helped to relieve pressure on the urban infrastructure. Today the city's population is over 100,000 lower than in the 1970s.

Regrettably, the great advances made in Lisbon in the postwar period have been punctuated by a regular sequence of major fires in historic buildings. In addition to the gutting, in 1959, of the historic S. Domingos church near the Rossio, where many royal funerals and baptisms had taken place, and of the nearby Teatro D. Maria II five years later, a major fire which started with an electrical fault in the Grandella department store destroyed eighteen buildings in the Chiado shopping and commercial district in 1988. Some 2,000 jobs were lost and although the area is now back in use, some parts of it currently (1996) remain in ruins. However, a positive effect of the Chiado disaster was to induce Lisbon to think carefully about its urban planning, the architect Álvaro Siza being charged with the reconstruction project. Lamentably, another fire destroyed the upper part of the magnificent 19th-century Lisbon Town Hall on 7 November 1996 and this has now given the city another major rebuilding project.

Following the fillip given by its nomination as European Capital of Culture in 1994, Lisbon's development received another boost in 1993 with its successful candidature to host the prestigious Expo 98 event. Work is now (1996) well advanced to regenerate the chosen site in the Olivais dockland area of north-east Lisbon. Lisbon is keen not to follow the mistakes of other World Expo cities and is aiming to build structures which will have a useful function after the event and its planners have therefore been keen to incorporate housing into the scheme. The project also incorporates a new international railway station, Lisboa Oriente (Lisbon East, 1996) and the city's internal transport infrastructure is also being upgraded, with a Metro link to the Expo area. The Metropolitano system is also being extended south-westwards to Cais do Sodré, to link with the Cascais railway line which is being upgraded at the Lisbon end (1996). In addition, Carris, the city's transport operator introduced ten new high-capacity articulated trams in 1995 and these have increased journey speeds by 50 per cent to 13km/hour on the route to Belém. Work, approved in 1993, has now started on adapting the Ponte 25 de Abril both to take more lanes of road traffic and to incorporate a railway crossing of the Tagus which had been part of the bridge's original plans in the 1960s. This rail link, using new double-decker trains, will remove the present need to take a ferry across the Tagus to Barreiro to catch trains to the Algarve and Alentejo. A new and controversial 11km second road bridge across the Tagus, the Ponte Vasco da Gama, is also taking shape near the Expo site, despite conservationists' protests that the bridge threatens an area of nature conservation.

Lisbon Today

Although the internationalization of Lisbon, especially since the 1980s, is readily apparent and is epitomized by the arrival in Lisbon of such names as McDonalds, Marks and Spencer and Coca-Cola, city centre side-streets such as the Rua dos Correeiros still boast significant numbers of largely unspoilt traditional restaurants and small businesses. Family-run bars, grocers and hardware shops can also still be found in significant numbers within yards of the Praça do Comérico on such streets as the Rua do Arsenal. However, tangible signs of modernity are increasingly evident in the modern shopping centres (*centros comerciais*) of Lisbon, the arrival of international hotel chains and of English-language satellite television. The cost of living, ridiculously cheap twenty years ago, in the mid-1990s largely matches that of Britain and other material indexes, such as car ownership, continue to rise, although taxis and public transport are still very heavily used. Modern urban problems of drug-taking, homelessness and crime exist but are arguably less visible in the streets than in British or North

American cities. The popular press of Lisbon also bears favourable comparison with that of Britain in its avoidance of titillation and prurient scandalmongering. Likewise, the size of the crowds to be seen at the annual *Feira do Livro* (Book Fair) in Lisbon, when dozens of open-air kiosks are opened for three weeks to market books, is remarkable. *Fado*, the doleful traditional vocal and instrumental music of Lisbon, still survives in the Bairro Alto and Alfama districts, albeit often these days in a commercialized form aimed at overseas tourists, whilst vibrant African nightclubs have sprung up to cater for the sizeable immigrant population.

For much of the 20th century, under the Salazar régime, Lisbon was regarded as a somewhat backward capital of an anachronistic imperial nation. In the last twenty years it has largely divested itself of this image and embraced Europe and modernity. In this process it has managed largely to retain its historical character, traditions and wealth of old buildings, whilst making material and cultural advances to the benefit of most of its citizens, which have included programmes to rehabilitate the most run-down, old quarters of the city. National recognition of the city's progress can be seen in the election of Lisbon's former mayor, Jorge Sampaio, as President of Portugal in January 1996. Internationally, although many tourists are attracted both to the city and to the nearby Estoril coast, it has not been swamped by visitors to the degree endured by other European capitals such as London, Paris, Rome and Amsterdam. Its role as European Cultural Capital in 1994 and its forthcoming hosting of the Expo 98 event have epitomized the transformation of Lisbon into an increasingly prosperous and efficient city of growing international status.

The Administration of Lisbon

Following the Reconquest of Lisbon from the Moors in 1147, there were just three *freguesias* (parishes) in the city, a number which had grown to ten (S. Vicente, Mártires, Sta Justa, Sta Maria da Sé, Madalena, Sta Cruz do Castelo, S. Bartolomeu, S. Martinho, S. Jorge and S. Pedro de Alfama), by the end of the 12th century. By 1375 the number of parishes had grown to twenty-three and, in the 16th century, to thirty-five. The addition of S. Sebastião da Pedreira, Mercês and Sta Isabel during the 18th century brought the total to thirty-eight. In 1886 four over-arching *bairros administrativos* (administrative districts) were created and in the 20th century new parishes have been carved out of the older ones bringing the total by 1959 to the current total of fifty-three, divided into the four *bairros administrativos*.

These fifty-three parishes, each led by a President, constitute one of fifteen *concelhos* (councils) comprising the *Distrito de Lisboa*, which straddles both banks of the lower Tagus and reaches north to Torres Vedras. The *Concelho de Lisboa* is administered by the *Assembleia de Lisboa (AL)* and the *Câmara Municipal de Lisboa (CML)*. It is one of Portugal's 305 *municípios* which collectively comprise 4,182 *freguesias*.

The CML is the executive arm of the city administration whilst the AL is its deliberative body. The AL is elected by universal suffrage with a four-year mandate and its members comprise the Presidents of the *Juntas de Freguesia* and elected members in equal numbers, plus one. The AL approves the CML's plans of action and sets local taxes as well as arranging loans proposed by the CML. The CML comprises up to sixteen elected *vereadores* (town councillors), with the person who heads the voting list becoming the President of the CML, a post analogous to that of Chief Executive of a British metropolitan borough or an American city mayor. The CML is effectively the city council and it executes the decisions of the AL through its dozen *Direcções Municipais* (Municipal Directorates). The CML headquarters are the

Paços do Concelho (Town Hall) situated in the Praça do Município, between the Praça do Comércio and Cais do Sodré.

Freguesias (Parishes)

The fifty-three current *freguesias* of Lisbon are:

Ajuda
Alcântara
Alto Pina
Alvalade
Ameixoeira
Anjos
Beato
Benfica
Campo Grande
Campolide
Carnide
Castelo
Charneca
Coração de Jesus
Encarnação
Graça
Lapa
Lumiar
Madalena
Mártires
Marvila
Mercês
Nossa Senhora de Fátima
Pena
Penha de França
Prazeres
Sacramento

Santa Catarina
Santa Engrácia
Santa Isabel
Santa Justa
Santa Maria de Belém
Santa Maria do Olivais
Santiago
Santo Condestável
Santo Estêvão
Santos-o-Velho
S. Cristóvão e S. Lourenço
S. Domingos de Benfica
S. Francisco Xavier
S. João
S. João de Brito
S. João de Deus
S. Jorge de Arroios
S. José
S. Mamede
S. Miguel
S. Nicolau
S. Paulo
S. Sebastião da Pedreira
S. Vicente de Fora
Sé
Socorro

Lisbon and Its People

General

1 **Lisbon in the years 1821, 1822 and 1823.**
Marianne Baillie. London: John Murray, 1824. 2 vols.
One of the most extensive contemporary accounts, in English, of life in Lisbon and Sintra in the volatile period of Portuguese liberal unrest following the Peninsular War (1808-14), by the poetess and writer, Mrs Marianne Baillie. At the start of the two and a half years spent there with her husband, her avowed intention was 'to enter [. . .] into the society of the natives', but she found the Portuguese 'by no means social, or encouraging towards foreigners' and she judged the famed views of Lisbon 'greatly over-rated'. As well as recounting the social activities of her circle, Mrs Baillie also experienced two minor earthquakes in Lisbon. The volumes are illustrated by some rather naive illustrations of local types, including nuns, friars and a 'fisherman's family of Pedroiços', near Belém.

2 **Cities of Europe: Oporto and Lisbon. Reprodução facsimilada do original bilingüe inglês-francês, com tradução em português.**
(Facsimile reproduction of the original bilingual French-English edition, with a Portuguese translation.)
Robert Batty. Lisbon: Instituto da Biblioteca Nacional e do Livro; Imprensa Nacional-Casa da Moeda, 1996. 119p.
An attractive facsimile reproduction from Lieut. Col. Batty's *Select views of some of the principal cities of Europe from original paintings*, first published in London in 1832. The twelve original colour plates of Lisbon and Oporto are reproduced complete with protective crepe overlays. The six pictures of Lisbon show 'Belem Castle' (i.e. the Torre), 'Convent of St Geronymo, Belem', the Largo do Pelourinho and views of Lisbon from the 'Rua de San Miguel', Nossa Senhora da Monte and Almada. Interestingly, opposite most of the plates is the same view in outline with a key by Batty to identify the main features shown. A brief text in English and French describes each picture.

1

3   **In Portugal.**
    Aubrey F. G. Bell.   London; New York: John Lane, The Bodley Head,
    1912. 227p.
In twenty-nine chapters, Aubrey Bell seeks primarily to differentiate Portugal from
Spain in the perception of the English reader. After general information on Portuguese
customs and travel arrangements, chapters X to XII (p. 71-98) specifically portray
Lisbon, Belém and Sintra. Descriptions of Lisbon street life and visits to sights, such
as Henry Fielding's grave, are included. As might be expected from the scholarly
author, the text is more liberally scattered with Portuguese terminology than other
books written for an English audience.

4   **Letters from Portugal, on the late and present state of that Kingdom.**
    John Blankett.   London: J. Almon, *c.*1777. 66p.
An anonymous work, attributed to Lieutenant John Biankett, which comprises
seventeen letters written from Lisbon in the first half of 1777, coinciding with the
death of King José I and the resultant fall from grace of his chief minister, Pombal.
The latter's achievements are chronicled, as are developments in trade and politics.
The book is a useful source of detailed information about Lisbon, including statistical
details of shipping movements in its port, which show that in 1774 and 1775 English
vessels outnumbered the combined totals of all other nations' ships which docked
there, including Portuguese vessels.

5   **Sketches of the country, character and costume, in Portugal and
    Spain, made during the campaign, and on the route of the British
    Army in 1808 and 1809. Engraved and coloured from the drawings
    by the Rev. William Bradford, with incidental illustrations &
    appropriate descriptions of each subject, etc.**
    Rev. William Bradford.   London: John Booth, 1809. 24p.
Bradford was chaplain to the British Army expedition to Spain and Portugal during
the Peninsular War (1808-14). His artistic skills as revealed in these *Sketches* are
somewhat limited. Nevertheless, this folio volume of his many engravings, which
follow a twenty-four page textual introduction and index, does vividly convey the
contemporary appearance both of topographical landmarks, such as the Lisbon
aqueduct and Sintra, and, more interestingly, of local people such as a Lisbon lady in
her walking dress, a local police guard and the regiment of Alcântara.

6   **Breve história da olisipografia.** (Brief history of writings on Lisbon.)
    Fernando Castelo Branco.   Lisbon: Instituto de Cultura
    Portuguesa, 1980. 112p. (Biblioteca Breve, vol. 47, Série Pensamento e
    Ciência).
A survey of the work of twelve Portuguese 'Olisipographers', or writers on Lisbon,
with a short section on overseas writers on the city. The writers covered include Júlio
de Castilho, Gomes de Brito, Pastor de Macedo, Robert Southey, William Beckford
and William Dalrymple. The volume is completed by a short anthology of extracts
from some of the cited works.

7 **Ruas de Lisboa: notas para a história das vias públicas lisbonenses.**
  Obra póstuma. (Streets of Lisbon: notes for the history of the public
  thoroughfares of Lisbon. Posthumous work.)
  J. J. Gomes de Brito.   Lisbon: Sá da Costa, 1935. 3 vols.
  One of the fundamental works of Lisbon historiography. It provides an alphabetical
  directory of street names with each entry comprising information on the source of the
  name and on historical events which have taken place there.

8 **Portugal.**
  Roy Campbell.   London: Max Reinhardt, 1957. 206p.
  In this idiosyncratic book, completed just before his death, the poet Roy Campbell
  addresses aspects of Lisbon in his final two chapters. The penultimate chapter (nine)
  covers 'Fado: the music of Lisbon and the gipsies', whilst the last chapter, 'A word
  about Lisbon', is, curiously, a translation of the Comenadador's speech on Lisbon
  from the 17th-century play *El burlador de Sevilla* (The trickster of Seville) by the
  Spanish dramatist, Tirso de Molina. Other chapters on the history of Portugal also
  touch on Lisbon.

9 **Tableau de Lisbonne en 1796. Suivi de Lettres écrites de**
  Portugal sur l'état ancien et actuel de ce royaume, traduites de
  l'anglois. (Picture of Lisbon in 1796. Followed by Letters written from
  Portugal on the former and present state of that kingdom, translated from
  the English.)
  J. B. F. Carrère.   Paris: H.-J. Jansen, 1797. 442p.
  An account, arranged thematically, of the author's impressions of Lisbon. Topics
  include streets, buildings, climate, crime, the theatre, waste-disposal and seats of
  learning. The author is dismissive of many aspects of Lisbon life and, for example,
  mocks the monumental efforts of the Academia das Ciências to produce a dictionary
  of the Portuguese language. He is also critical of the degree of literary and scientific
  prowess in the city. This is, nevertheless, a wide-ranging review of Lisbon in the late
  18th century, accompanied in this edition by letters attributed to John Blankett (see
  item no. 4).

10 **La vie quotidienne au Portugal après le tremblement de terre de**
   Lisbonne de 1755. (Daily life in Portugal after the Lisbon earthquake of
   1755.)
   Suzanne Chantal.   Paris: Hachette, 1962. 281p. (La Vie Quotidienne).
   The first of the three sections of this book is principally concerned with the 1755
   Lisbon earthquake and its aftermath. The text is heavily derivative and, at times,
   sententious, being based on the writings of contemporary travellers and observers. A
   further consequence of using these sources is that the book focuses mainly on the
   major cities of Lisbon, Oporto and Coimbra rather than on the whole country, as its
   title implies. Thus the second section of the work concentrates on the Royal Court,
   Church and nobility, whilst the final part addresses food, drink, entertainment and
   other aspects of Lisbon life.

11   **Lisboa desaparecida.** (Disappeared Lisbon.)
     Marina Tavares Dias.   Lisbon: Quimera, 1988-96. 5 vols.
The authoress had a regular column in the 1980s in the Lisbon newspaper *Diário Popular* in which she wrote about the city, its history and customs. Disturbed by the despoliation of Lisbon by planners, particularly in the 1940s and 1950s, Dias here seeks both to animate her readers to respect their urban heritage and to remind them of bygone scenes. Although written in Portuguese, these folio volumes each have nearly 200 pages packed with photographs and drawings supplemented by reproductions of old maps, contemporary shop catalogues and similar ephemera. These vividly illustrate Lisbon life during the late 19th and 20th centuries.

12   **Tipos e factos da Lisboa do meu tempo.** (Characters and facts from
     the Lisbon of my lifetime.)
     Calderon Dinis.   Lisbon: Editorial Notícias, 1993. 326p.
Calderon Dinis provides a fascinating visual review of Lisbon life as he illustrates in his own drawings the diverse characters encountered and events experienced during a lifetime spent in the city from the early years of the 20th century. Approximately half of this folio volume comprises fine colour reproductions of his caricatures of Lisbon 'types' together with numerous black-and-white photographs and drawings of Lisbon scenes and characters. All manner of Lisbon folk are shown in colour, from fishwives to priests, dustmen to policemen. The text describes city locations, events and notable citizens such as the poet, Fernando Pessoa and the medical pioneer, Egas Moniz.

13   **A picture of Lisbon, taken on the spot, being a description, moral,
     civil, political, physical and religious of that capital, with sketches of
     the government, character and manners of the Portuguese in
     general.**
     A Gentleman, many years resident at Lisbon.   London: Henry Colburn,
     1809. 242p.
A rather inchoate, yet wide-ranging collection of fifty-nine chapters on Lisbon. Whilst the author believes that the 'new-erected part of the city is beautiful', he finds the old part of the city 'confined, stagnant and pestilential', a view reinforced by his being drenched by slops thrown out of an upstairs window, a common practice in Lisbon's old and undrained quarters. The writer provides an intriguing snapshot of Pombal's building of the Baixa area after the 1755 earthquake, at a time when only a number of its streets had been constructed. He comments, too, on the backwardness of Lisbon social customs, and particularly on the lot of women who are not allowed outdoors without escort. It appears to have been written earlier than Semple's account (see item no. 269), published in the same year, of military activities in the city as it faced the threat of renewed French occupation.

14   **O trabalho e as tradições religiosas no Distrito de Lisboa. Exposição
     de etnografia.** (Work and religious traditions in the District of Lisbon.
     Ethnographic exhibition.)
     Governo Civil de Lisboa.   Lisbon: Governo Civil de Lisboa, 1991.
     469p. bibliog.
This folio volume includes 568 illustrations, predominantly photographs, of the life, work and traditions of the *saloios*, the rural inhabitants of the so-called Lisbon

peninsula, which embraces Oeiras, Loures, Amadora, Cascais, Sintra and Mafra. The illustrations, many in colour, include old prints, postcards and sketches which depict artefacts as varied as farm tools, ceramics, articles of clothing and animals, as well as local people. The book also depicts those elements of rural life which impinged on the city of Lisbon, such as the sale of fish and natural produce, and the popular tradition of religious processions.

15 The real Lisbon: the complete guide to life in Lisbon.
A Guia.   Lisbon: A Guia, 1995. 156p. maps.

A pocket guide to Lisbon crammed with practical information, addresses and lists, together with colour maps. It aims to suggest to visitors and residents how to get the most out of their leisure time in the city. As such, it lists restaurants, bars, sports arenas and information on cultural establishments in Lisbon.

16 Coast of the sun.
Henry C. James.   London: Jarrolds, 1956. 176p.

Illustrated with black-and-white photographs, this book includes Estoril and Lisbon in its uncontroversial portrayal of life in Portugal in the decade after the Second World War, as witnessed at first hand by the author.

17 The Portuguese: the land and its people.
Marion Kaplan.   Harmondsworth, England: Penguin Books, 1991. 396p. 5 maps. bibliog.

Apart from many passing references to Lisbon, there is a section specifically on the city and its buildings, both ancient and ultra-modern. A 'travel advisory' section gives practical information and an excellent bibliography provides pointers for further reading.

18 Portugal illustrated in a series of letters. Embellished with a map, plates of coins, vignettes and various engravings of costumes, landscape scenery etc.
Rev. W. M. Kinsey.   London: Treuttel, Würtz & Richter, 1828. 500p. map.

William Morgan Kinsey's letters, addressed to a Mr Bayley and friends, were written during a visit to Portugal in 1827 which was devised to gather information on the country for the edification of his fellow-countrymen. Although adorned with fine engravings and a substantial section of coloured watertint drawings of Portuguese costume, the book is unindexed, rendering it difficult to locate specific references. However, Lisbon and Sintra are covered in the early part. As well as providing factual information as to which trades were practised in which Lisbon streets, and advice to avoid eating local meat, Kinsey also warns the reader of the principal bodily disorders prevalent in Lisbon. These allegedly included apoplexy, paralysis, liver complaints and inflammation of the bowels. As a Protestant clergyman, he lays much of the blame for the country's backwardness on the Catholic Church's representatives.

19   **Portugal: its land and people.**
     W. H. Koebel, illustrated by S. Roope Dockery.   London: Archibald
     Constable, 1909. 405p.

The first five chapters cover Lisbon, with subsequent sections also covering 'Round
about Lisbon' (p. 3-136). A further chapter describes a journey to Lisbon from
Oporto. Although the text itself gives a positive and comprehensive account of the
history, attractions and experiences of Lisbon, it is the excellent illustrations which
particularly mark out this quality publication. It contains reproductions of more than
twenty watercolours, whilst over fifty early photographs capture the reality of
Lisbon's streets in the late 19th and early 20th centuries, making it one of the few
works to illustrate this period for an English audience.

20   **Lisboa.** (Lisbon.)
     Alfredo Mesquita.   Lisbon: Perspectivas & Realidades, 1987. 631p.
     bibliog.

A folio-sized re-edition of Mesquita's monumental study of Lisbon life, first published
in 1903. With 402 fine engravings of Lisbon scenes and types, the work has
substantial value for the reader with no Portuguese. This photographic reprint of the
original edition has been enhanced by a so-called bibliographical table which provides
a much-needed index to many of the persons cited in the original text. Whilst the
engravings are themselves indexed, it is difficult to find specific references to
buildings and locations within the book.

21   **A general view of the State of Portugal, containing a topographical
     description thereof in which are included, an account of the physical
     and moral state of the Kingdom, together with observations on the
     animal, vegetable and mineral productions of its colonies. The
     whole compiled from the best Portuguese writers and from notices
     obtained in the country.**
     James Murphy.   London: T. Cadell Jun. & W. Davies, 1798. 272p.
     map.

A wide-ranging handbook of the country arranged into thirty chapters, which cover
the physical geography of the country, as well as its history, trade, language, culture
and customs. Information relating to Lisbon is plentiful but is scattered throughout the
text. Fifteen fine engravings, mostly based on the architect-author's sketches, include
depictions of the bay of Lisbon, showing the Torre de Belém, the equestrian statue in
the Praça do Comércio and 'A courrier from Lisbon to Oporto'.

22   **O povo de Lisboa: tipos, ambiente, modos de vida, mercados e
     feiras, divertimentos, mentalidade. Exposição iconográfica, Junho/
     Julho, 1978-1979.** (The working class of Lisbon: social types,
     environment, ways of life, markets and fairs, entertainments, mentality.
     Iconographic exhibition, June/ July, 1978-79.)
     Museu de Artes Plásticas dos Coruchéus.   Alvalade, Lisbon: Museu de
     Artes Plásticas dos Coruchéus, [1979]. 298p. bibliog.

A catalogue of some 660 items from an exhibition held in the Coruchéus Museum of
Plastic Arts to show the life of the lower classes of Lisbon from the mid-17th century.

The work is divided into eight sections, each with a brief introductory essay. The copious illustrations form a vivid portrayal of Lisbon street life through the ages.

23   **Portugal.**
     Henry Myhill.   London: Faber & Faber, 1972. 248p. map. bibliog.
When commissioned to write a book about Portugal, a country not known to him, the author enterprisingly joined a language course at Lisbon University. His assimilation of the country's history and his enjoyment of his assignment are reflected in this country-wide survey, of which the first two chapters (to p. 70) cover Lisbon and its environs. The opening chapter, 'The city of Ulysses', has four numbered sections: 'Under Pombal'; 'Beneath the Castle'; 'Around Estrela'; and 'Museums: Belém'. The first three of these cover, respectively, the central city area, the Alfama district and the Estrela, Chiado, Lapa and other districts of Lisbon. The second chapter, 'Within the lines of Torres Vedras', includes the western Lisbon suburbs of Oeiras, Carcavelos, Estoril, Cascais and Sintra. Thirty-two black-and-white photographs are included as are several useful appendices, one of which is an especially concise history of Portugal.

24   **Traits and traditions of Portugal collected during a residence in that country.**
     Julia Pardoe.   London: Saunders & Otley, 1833. 2 vols.
A generally rather romantic account of 'pleasant Portugal' and of Julia Pardoe's 'unceasing enjoyment' there during a period of accompaniment to her father who was one of Sir William Clinton's army entourage. The factual chapters are interspersed with Portuguese 'legends'. Educated in a European convent and conversant with the Portuguese language, Julia Pardoe was able to gain admittance to convents and converse with nuns, as well as with the Infanta Regent, whom she encountered on her first day in Lisbon. There is an account of the arrival of D. Miguel, the royal pretender, in Lisbon. She records, too, the seamy side of Lisbon life: animal corpses, packs of dogs and black pigs in the streets as well as the burials, without coffins, of poor children. In the locality of Lisbon, she also visited Sintra and Sacavém.

25   **Lisboa.** (Lisbon.)
     Jörg Schubert.   Lisbon: Distri Cultural, 1982. 216p. bibliog.
Replete with colour plates and monochrome illustrations of Lisbon, this large-format general introduction is a translation of the Austrian original, *Lissabon*. Despite its title, the work ranges as far afield as Évora, Coimbra, Cacilhas, Arrábida and Queluz. The sections on Lisbon are arranged by urban areas. There is an extensive bibliography, which includes works in English, and a chronological table of Portugal's history.

26   **Portugal and Madeira.**
     Sacheverell Sitwell.   London: Batsford, 1954. 242p. map.
Based on information gleaned during five visits to Portugal between 1926 and 1953, this informed introduction to the country is divided into eight geographical sections. Chapters two and three cover Lisbon (p. 68-89) and Belém, Sintra and Queluz (p. 90-108), whilst ten of the book's seventy-one black-and-white photographs are of the Lisbon area. Sitwell captures the bustle of Lisbon street life, with its knifegrinders and fishwives, as well as giving lengthy accounts of the Museu dos Coches, the cathedral and other major historical buildings.

27 **Things seen in Portugal, the garden of the West, a land of mountains and rivers, of the vine, the olive & the cork tree & of ancient buildings richly carved, picturesque peasantry & hardy fishermen.**
    M. F. Smithes. London: Seeley, Service & Co., 1931. 156p. map.

This book's title reveals the somewhat lyrical perspective of its author towards Portugal. The two chapters specifically on Lisbon and Sintra (p. 28-55) are certainly no exceptions so far as this uncritical attitude is concerned. Black-and-white photographs record the city as it was around 1930.

28 **Lisbon.**
    Carol Wright. London: J. M. Dent, 1971. 88p. 2 maps.

The authoress, a travel and cookery writer, has divided this book into sections headed 'Morning', 'Noon', 'Night' and 'Out of bounds' and attempts to give 'a changing picture of the day in Lisbon'. As such, she has produced an impressionistic rather than an exhaustively factual guidebook. Eleven black-and-white photographs accompany the text, which is complemented by an index.

29 **Cities of the world: a compilation of current information on cultural, geographical and political conditions in the countries and cities of six continents, based on the Department of State 'Post Reports'. Volume 3, Europe and the Mediterranean Middle East.**
    Edited by Margaret Walsh Young, Susan L. Stetler. Detroit, Michigan: Gale Research Company, 1985. 788p. maps.

The section on Lisbon includes a basic map which includes the US Embassy as one of only a handful of identified sites. Indeed, this volume is clearly intended for the United States citizen intent on a protracted residence in Lisbon, for details of schools in the city for English-speaking children are prominent, as is information on organizations such as the Lions and Rotary clubs of Lisbon. Details are also provided of sports and health clubs, entertainment, restaurants and sea-bathing conditions in the Lisbon area.

Books of photographs

30 **Lisboa.** (Lisbon.)
    Afonso Manuel Alves, António Sacchetti, Moura Machado, The Image Bank, Paula Neves. Lisbon: Comissão de Promoção da Exposição Internacional de Lisboa 1998, 1991. unpaginated.

A collection of 139 colour photographs of Lisbon by different hands, designed to attract visitors to the city of Lisbon in advance of the international exhibition, Expo 98. The foreword, by António Mega Ferreira, is printed in English as well as Portuguese. Twenty-six of the architectural projects which are integral parts of the Expo 98 initiative are also richly illustrated, with accompanying parallel Portuguese and English descriptive texts, in *Lisbon Expo 98: projectos*. *Lisbon Expo 98 projects*, edited by Luiz Trigueiros and Cláudio Sat, with Cristina Oliveira, translation by Mark Cain (Lisbon: Blau, 1996. 216p. [Blau Monographs]).

31 **Lisboa do nosso olhar: a look on Lisbon.**
José Antunes. Lisbon: Câmara Municipal de Lisboa, 1991. 61p.
A bilingual, Portuguese and English, coffee-table book of pleasant colour photographs of Lisbon sights. It is accompanied by a short essay on the city by the contemporary writer, Baptista Bastos.

32 **Lisboa ribeirinha.** (Riverside Lisbon.)
Arquivo Municipal, Câmara Municipal de Lisboa, text by Miguel
Gomes Martins. Lisbon: Livros Horizonte, 1994. unpaginated. bibliog.
A volume of 201 black-and-white photographs from the 19th and 20th centuries illustrating life on the Lisbon riverside. The oldest photographs included here date back to the 1860s and the collection depicts social extremes, ranging from visiting dignitaries to ambulatory street vendors. A bibliography of more than fifty references completes the work. The publication marked the end of a series of exhibitions jointly arranged by the Lisbon City Council and the Sociedade Lisboa 94 to commemorate the city's role as European Capital of Culture in 1994.

33 **7 olhares.** (Seven viewpoints.)
Arquivo Municipal, Câmara Municipal de Lisboa. Lisbon: Livros
Horizonte, 1994. 109p. bibliog.
One of a number of publications produced under the umbrella of the Lisbon 1994 European Capital of Culture initiative. This volume, in landscape format, presents dozens of photographs of Lisbon from the City Council's archives. The compilation differs from other modern collections both in that it is limited to the work of seven named photographers or studios and that it spans a wide period of time, from the latter years of the 19th century up to, and including, the 1950s. Also many of the photographs were not originally produced for the postcard or tourist market and so convey an unvarnished picture of everyday life in Lisbon.

34 **A short account of the view of Lisbon now exhibiting in Henry Aston Barker's Panorama, Leicester Square.**
Henry Aston Barker. London: Published by the Author, 1812. 12p.
The major part of this publication is a fascinating folding diagram showing, in monochrome, the circular panorama of Lisbon painted by Barker on 10,000 sq.ft. of canvas as one of the series of one-shilling shows mounted at the Leicester Square Panorama in London, founded in 1793. The diagram shows the skyline and coast from the mouth of the River Tagus to the east of Lisbon itself, with a numbered key showing forty-one buildings or features of interest on both sides of the river. It is based on a view made from a ship in the Tagus estuary by John Burford. The text describes the chief features and provides historical details associated with the buildings in question.

35 **Lisboa, Queluz, Sintra, Estoril, Cascais.**
Carlos Vitoriano da Silva Barros, Renée Foulomeau Pesquiet.   Lisbon:
R. N. Tours, 1988. 30p. bibliog.
A volume produced for tourists of which the main feature is 119 unpaginated colour photographs of the city of Lisbon and of its nearby resorts and attractions. These are preceded by a short introductory essay, in English, of a necessarily superficial nature, given its primary audience.

36 **Lisboa 1942, Cecil Beaton, Lisbon 1942.**
Cecil Beaton.   Lisbon: British Historical Society of Portugal, Fundação Calouste Gulbenkian, British Council, 1995. 101p.
A large-format, illustrated catalogue of the evocative professional photographs taken by Cecil Beaton (1904-80) in Lisbon during the Second World War. The pictures were rediscovered in the Imperial War Museum, London and exhibited in Lisbon's Ajuda Palace in October and November 1995. Beaton came to Lisbon in 1942 primarily to photograph Portuguese government ministers whose images, with those of other local dignitaries such as Archbishop Cerejeira, feature amongst the thirty-five here reproduced from the 203 surviving in London. Photographs of Queluz and the Marquês de Fronteira's palaces are also included here. Captions are in both English and Portuguese as is a brief essay by Beaton recounting his Lisbon experiences. This account is a slightly abridged version of chapter seven of his book, *Near East* (London: B. T. Batsford, 1943, p. 139-49), in which a number of his Lisbon photographs are also reproduced.

37 **Portugal.**
Yves Bottineau, photographs by Yun.   London: Thames & Hudson, 1957. 280p. map.
The fourth of the six chapters (p. 162-220), in this regionally arranged collection of 168 photographs, covers Lisbon and the Tagus river area. Twenty-seven monochrome photographs of Lisbon and Sintra are included, these being a mixture of pictures of buildings, works of art and street scenes. The text, written in the form of a guided tour, includes a history of Lisbon. It also provides details of museum layouts, such as that of the Museu de Arte Antiga.

38 **Lisboa: imagens d'*A Capital.*** (Lisbon: images from *A Capital.*)
A Capital.   Lisbon: Editorial Notícias, 1984. unpaginated.
This folio volume comprises 213 black-and-white photographs of Lisbon, published as a permanent record of a readers' photographic competition organized by the Lisbon evening newspaper, *A Capital*. Unlike most other photographic compilations which have Lisbon as their subject and which are almost invariably in colour, this monochrome collection portrays the city as seen by its citizens during their day-to-day routines.

39 **Os melhores postais antigos de Lisboa.** (The best old postcards of Lisbon.)
Marina Tavares Dias.   Lisbon: Químera, 1995. 134p.
A collection of fine reproductions, on art paper, of fifty colour and monochrome postcards of Lisbon, mostly from the first decade of this century. The selection

concentrates on street scenes rather than tourist sights and consequently includes pictures of street vendors, trams and cafés. Intended as a homage to the postcard producers of 1900, the volume includes brief details of their company histories. There is also a chronology which assists in placing the cards in their historical context. The selection reflects the choices of six major postcard collectors whose personal 'top twenties' are listed.

40 **Photographias de Lisboa, 1900.** (Photographs of Lisbon, 1900.)
   Marina Tavares Dias. Lisbon: Quimera, 1991. 2nd ed. 205p.

Through its use of commercial postcards as well as the work of street photographers, this album captures both the touristic and everyday aspects of Lisbon life as it was at the turn of the century.

41 **Portugal.**
   Photographs by Graham Finlayson, introduction and notes on the plates by Frank Tuohy. London: Thames & Hudson, 1970. 203p. map.

Part two of this A4-size book of 11 colour and 106 black-and-white photographs is entitled 'Lisbon and its surroundings' (p. 101-61). This section includes pictures of the suburbs of Belém, Queluz and Sintra as well as of Lisbon city centre, with an accompanying textual description. A preliminary essay outlines the history of Portugal.

42 **Lisboa: inclinações e desvios.** (Lisbon: inclinations and diversions.)
   Henrique Dinis da Gama. Oporto, Portugal: Editorial Afrontamento, 1993. unpaginated.

An evocative, colour, photographic essay on contemporary Lisbon. It concentrates on the artistic portrayal of urban details, such as tramlines, tree trunks and window casements, rather than coldly objective reproductions of buildings or scenes in their entirety.

43 **Lisboa, qualquer lugar, Lisboa, qual Lisboa!** (Lisbon, any place, Lisbon, some place!)
   Grupo Iris, texts by Alberto Pimenta, photographs by Agostinho Gonçalves, Américo Silva and others. Lisbon: Diferença Comunicação Visual, 1994. unpaginated.

Comprises eight sections, each one by a different photographer, of ten photographs of Lisbon scenes, people and buildings. Most are contemporary, except those of Jean Dienzaide from 1954. Each section is accompanied by a fictional narrative which has an English and French translation.

44 **Lisbon: photos and text.**
   Manfred Hamm, Werner Radasewsky. Berlin: Nicolai, 1994. 236p.

An impressive photographic journey, in colour, around Lisbon which is characterized by shots taken from unusual angles. Thus, tall monuments, like that to Pombal at the Rotunda, are curiously depicted in close-up from above.

45 **Souvenir album, Lisbon.**
    Photographs by Claude Huber, text by Ken Bernstein.   New York:
    Berlitz, [1995]. 128p.

The English-language edition of a work aimed at the tourist market and also published in German, French and Spanish. It comprises striking colour photographs of mostly well-known sights in Lisbon with a short textual description of the city.

46 **Lisbon from the sky.**
    Photographs by Filipe Jorge, text by Clara Mendes, Maria Calado.
    Lisbon: Argumentum, 1995. 2nd English ed. 112p. map.

Made up almost entirely of colour aerial photographs of Lisbon, this large-format publication has been published in several European languages, including a Portuguese version entitled *Vista do céu*. As the well-produced photographs are accompanied by only brief captions, the book's practical value is primarily to those who know Lisbon well. The first-time visitor to Lisbon, or transitory tourist, will find it difficult to identify the locations easily without use of the book's map and may therefore view it primarily as a coffee-table book.

47 **Vistas aéreas de Lisboa. Aerial views of Lisbon.**
    Photographs by Gustavo Leitão, text by João Constantino, English
    translation by Jonathan Weightman.   Lisbon: Meribérica/ Liber, 1996.
    151p.

A large-format collection of colour aerial pictures of contemporary Lisbon which includes a descriptive text in English.

48 **Lisbon and the surrounding country.**
    Frederic P. Marjay.   Lisbon: Livraria Bertrand, under the patronage of
    the Study Group Amigos de Lisboa, 1956. 26p. (Colecção Romântica).

The somewhat uncritical text of this large-format book meanders over a number of themes, including Lisbon's role as a sea port, the districts of Belém and Alfama, St Anthony of Lisbon, the Conquest of Lisbon in 1147, 'Wandering around Lisbon', 'The New Lisbon' and 'Places of interest around Lisbon'. However, it is the eighty-four unnumbered pages of monochrome photographs of the Lisbon area which are the book's chief allure. These include historical monuments in Lisbon and Belém and modern roadways and buildings, such as the Sporting Lisbon football stadium. There are also a number of photographs of Cascais, Estoril, Sintra, Queluz, Vila Franca de Xira and the Ribatejo.

49 **Portugal.**
    Text by F. P. Marjay.   Neuchâtel, Switzerland; Paris: Édns Ides et
    Calendares, 1953. 80p. (Collection des Ides Photographiques, no. 6).

Eighty impressive black-and-white photographs and a brief linking text make up this large-format volume. Nineteen of the pictures are of locations in Lisbon or Sintra, including the Praça de Londres, Alfama, the castle, the cathedral and Belém.

50 **Portugal.**
Frederic P. Marjay. Lisbon: Livraria Bertrand, 1967. 40p. map.
(Romantic Portugal Collection).
Although it only contains a small amount of paginated text, over 200 further pages of
photographs, some of which are in colour, are appended to this volume. Many of these
illustrations are of Lisbon and the surrounding area. The introductory text of this
coffee-table book is in both Portuguese and English and ranges over Portuguese
history, culture, industry, tourism and the major conurbations.

51 **Bilhetes postais antigos do Largo do Rato à Praça D. Luís:**
    persistências e inovações no decorrer de quatro décadas. Old
    postcards of the Seventh Hill.
José Manuel de Silva Passos. Lisbon: Livros Horizonte, 1994. 109p.
bibliog.
The city of Lisbon is traditionally said to be built on seven hills, of which the seventh
is that between Largo do Rato in north-west Lisbon and D. Luís square near the
waterfront, at Cais do Sodré. This reproduction of mostly coloured postcards records a
district which has remained largely free of major redevelopment in the present
century. The text is in both Portuguese and English. The same author has also
produced *O bilhete postal ilustrado e a história urbana de Lisboa. The illustrated
postcard and the urban history of Lisbon* (Lisbon: Caminho, [1994]), which contains a
multitude of reproductions of views of Lisbon.

52 **Fotografias de Lisboa à noite.** (Photographs of Lisbon at night.)
Luís Pavão. Lisbon: Assírio e Alvim, 1983. 155p.
Well over 100 black-and-white photographs, and two in colour, portray both the work
routines and seamy sides of Lisbon night life. Thus there are pictures of transport
depots and railway stations being cleaned, of cat-catchers and of newspaper printers at
work alongside portraits of vagrants, drunks, bar-girls, transvestites and *fado* houses.
Descriptions of each photograph are given in a preliminary section of the book whose
images derive from the 5,000 pictures taken by Pavão over a four-month period
shortly before publication. His selection concentrates on the Baixa, Cais do Sodré,
Bairro Alto and Avenida districts of the city. Of related interest is *The photographers
of Lisbon, Portugal, from 1886 to 1914* (Rochester, New York: University Educational
Services, International Museum of Photography at George Eastman House, 1990.
156p. bibliog.), which is Pavão's illustrated academic thesis.

53 **Tempos idos: Lisboa, ruas.** (Bygone times: Lisbon, streets.)
Edited by Camacho Pereira. Lisbon: Rotep, 1973.
A collection of thirty-six engravings from such sources as the magazines *Revista do
Ocidente* and *A Ilustração Portuguesa*, accompanied by eight pages of textual
introduction. Amongst the scenes reproduced are views of Campo de Santa Clara,
Rossio and Xabregas.

54 **Antigos lugares de vender, Anciens lieux de vente, Old selling places: Feira da Ladra, Mercado da Ribeira.**
Photographs by Mariano Piçarra, text by Carlos Medeiros, translated by Paula Mendes Coelho, Sheilah Cardno.   Lisbon: Fundação Luso-Americana para o Desenvolvimento, 1994. unpaginated.
A collection of thirty-three black-and-white photographs illustrating commercial activity in Lisbon's open-air Thieves' Market (*Feira da Ladra*) in the Alfama district and the Ribeira (Riverside) indoor fish, vegetable, flower and fruit market, near Cais do Sodré. The original Ribeira market building was erected by Pombal in 1771 but was demolished in 1882 and replaced by the more modern structure in use today. The photographs range from general views of stallholders and customers to more artistic compositions of man-made artefacts or natural produce on market stalls.

55 **Lisbon. English edition.**
Werner Radasewsky, photographs by Joachim Holz.   Lisbon: Distri, 1993. 64p.
The English edition of a work first published in Munich (Verlag C. J. Bucher, 1993). Clearly aimed at the tourist market, the main section of this book includes many colour photographs of the sights of Lisbon, with accompanying descriptions, whilst its final section collects together practical information about the city and is enhanced by black-and-white photographs.

56 **Lisbon: the city and the river.**
Isabel Salema, photographs by Afonso Manuel Alves, Luís Leiria de Lima, English version by Joan Ennes.   Lisbon: Publicações Dom Quixote, 1989. 127p.
A collection of high-grade colour photographs of Lisbon, arranged into eight sections. These cover buildings, monuments and street scenes, with modern constructions such as those at Picoas being included as well as Manueline and earlier architectural gems. There is brief textual accompaniment to the photographs and a short history of Lisbon.

57 **Portugal no. 1º quartel do séc. XX documentado pelo bilhete postal ilustrado. Da 1ª Exposição Nacional de Postais Antigos, Bragança, 1984.** (Portugal in the first quarter of the twentieth century as documented by the picture postcard. From the 1st National Exhibition of Old Postcards, Braganza, 1984.)
Vicente de Sousa, Neto Jacob.   Braganza, Portugal: Câmara Municipal de Bragança, 1985. 509p. bibliog.
In this large, folio volume, over 5,000 postcards are reproduced, albeit in small monochrome format. Over 500 of these are illustrations of Lisbon buildings or scenes. A further twenty-eight cards are shown both in full-size and in colour and these include three of Lisbon. In addition, there is an introductory essay and details of the major postcard producers and artists whose works are featured on postcards. A very brief summary is given in French, German and stilted English.

58   **É fácil amar Lisboa. It is easy to love Lisbon.**
Luís Forjaz Trigueiros.   Lisboa: Verbo, 1989. 86p.

A guide to the sights of Lisbon, copiously illustrated by colour photographs of the city, including Belém. Modern buildings, such as the Amoreiras complex, are represented as well as more traditional tourist sights. The work has parallel Portuguese and English texts.

59   **Esta Lisboa.** (This Lisbon.)
Alice Vieira, photographs by António Pedro Ferreira.   Lisbon: Caminho, 1994. 199p.

A collection of colour photographs of Lisbon, which, unlike most such compilations, is aimed at the local population rather than the tourist market. Many of the pictures are consequently of everyday Lisbon streets and scenes rather than the historic monuments.

60   **Portugal.**
Text by Hellmut Wohl, Alice Wohl, introduction by Alexandre O'Neill, photographs by Nicolas Sapieha, design by Gianfranco Cavaliere.
London: Frederick Muller in association with Summerfield Press, 1983. 205p. map.

Although this coffee-table book consists of text on Portugal's history and traditions interwoven with three 'photographic essays', it is the latter which are its chief attraction to those readers with an interest in Lisbon. One of the 'photographic essays', entitled 'Lisbon and surroundings' (p. 21-59), comprises some sixty colour photographs both of the city and as far afield to the north and west as Sintra, Colares and Mafra. Subjects depicted vary from innovative angles on tourist sights to everyday scenes in Lisbon's streets.

Geography

General

61 **Les périphéries de Lisbonne.** (The outskirts of Lisbon.)
P. Limouzin. *Annales de Géographie*, no. 541, vol. 97 (May-June 1988), p. 359-65. maps. bibliog.

Limouzin studies the rapid growth in the metropolitan area of Lisbon's proportion of the national population, from 12.9% (1920) to 26.1% (1981), which has been mostly on the periphery of Lisbon. Limouzin contrasts the northern growth area, particularly around Sintra, with the pattern of housing and industrial development in the Barreiro area, opposite Lisbon across the Tagus. The influences on Lisbon's suburban development of factors such as the Tagus bridge, completed in 1967, clandestine housebuilding, shanty towns and industrial competition from the Third World, are all assessed.

62 **Spain & Portugal. Volume II: Portugal.**
K..Mason. London: Naval Intelligence Division, 1942. 450p. 89 maps. bibliog. (BR502A Geographical Handbook Series).

One of a series of illustrated naval handbooks which, in fact, constitute a physical, economic and social geography of the country, combined with a wealth of historical and practical travel information. In this last category a detailed itinerary is given of rail and road routes from Lisbon. The work is divided into sixteen chapters, plus appendixes which include one on 'The Lisbon Earthquake 1755'. In all, the volume has more than fifty index entries for Lisbon.

63 **Atlas de Lisboa: a cidade no espaço e no tempo.** (Atlas of Lisbon:
the city in space and time.)
Pelouro da Cultura da Câmara Municipal de Lisboa and Gabinete de
Estudos Olisiponenses. Lisbon: Contexto, 1993. 142p. maps. bibliog.
Despite its title, this is not an atlas in the conventional sense, rather a highly visual
historical geography of Lisbon, preceded by a short textual introduction and a useful
chronological table. Although it reproduces many historical maps, aerial photographs
and recent city plans, most are too small and unlettered to be used as maps and they
form, rather, a colourful decoration to a study of the evolution of the geographical site
of Lisbon. Indeed, the maps are accompanied by a large number of historical
engravings, photographs of buildings and even reproductions of postcards, which
would not generally be found in a true atlas.

Bibliografia geográfica de Portugal. (Geographical bibliography of
Portugal.)
See item no. 682.

Districts

64 **Lisboa: freguesia da Lapa.** (Lisbon: parish of Lapa.)
Maria Paula Alves, Sérgio Infante. Lisbon: Contexto, 1992. 61p.
3 maps. bibliog. (Guias Contexto).
One of a series of visually attractive colour guides to Lisbon districts which includes
maps and a suggested walking route around the locale. Lapa is an area well known to
British visitors as the home of the British Embassy, in the Rua de S. Domingos.
Amongst the illustrations are past and present views of S. Bento, the Portuguese
parliament building, and of the imposing Estrela basilica. Also portrayed are modern
tilework, residential streets and the Estrela gardens.

65 **Lisboa: freguesia de Santos-o-Velho.** (Lisbon: parish of
Santos-o-Velho.)
Maria Paula Alves, Sérgio Infante. Lisbon: Contexto, 1992. 55p.
3 maps. bibliog. (Guias Contexto).
Santos-o-Velho lies on the riverfront, to the west of the Lisbon city centre. Its roots
are in a hermitage built after the reconquest of Lisbon from the Moors in 1147 to
honour three children allegedly killed by order of the Roman Emperor, Diocletian, in
307 BC. It was also the site of the Paço Real de Santos (Royal Palace of Santos, 1501)
but as this book shows, it is better known today for the maritime passenger terminal of
Rocha Conde de Óbidos (1945), its dockland bars, the Museu de Arte Antiga
(Museum of Ancient Art) and the first railway station out of Lisbon on the busy
coastal line to Cascais. The book's many colour pictures concentrate on present-day
buildings but also include some historical engravings and a photograph of a model of
the Santos area before the ravages of the 1755 earthquake affected it.

66 **Lisboa: freguesia de Carnide.** (Lisbon: parish of Carnide).
Maria Calado, Vítor Matias Ferreira. Lisbon: Contexto, 1991. 60p.
3 maps. bibliog. (Guias Contexto).

Carnide lies on the north-west fringes of Lisbon and comprises two nuclei, Carnide itself and Luz. Carnide's origins trace back to the 13th century, but it was in the 15th century that the pilgrimages to Nossa Senhora da Luz (Our Lady of the Light) began in the area. By the 17th century the area was a summer retreat for wealthy Lisbon dwellers, a role boosted by the havoc wrought on the central area of Lisbon by the 1755 earthquake. A further boom occurred between 1960 and 1981 when the population grew threefold to 13,370. Today Carnide boasts multi-storey dwellings for city workers as well as palatial old residences, 18th-century churches and the 19th-century Colégio Militar (Military College), with a nearby underground station linking it to the city centre. Here many colour photographs and illustrations reflect this diverse district.

67 **Lisboa: freguesia da Encarnação, Bairro Alto.** (Lisbon: parish of Encarnação, Bairro Alto.)
Maria Calado, Vítor Matias Ferreira. Lisbon: Contexto, 1992. 77p.
3 maps. bibliog. (Guias Contexto).

This guide to the parish of the church of Encarnação (the Incarnation), in Lisbon's elevated western quarter, includes the Praça Camões, the gardens and belvedere of S. Pedro de Alcântara, the churches of S. Roque and Loreto, as well as the steep Rua do Alecrim, which connects the Chiado area to Cais do Sodré on the riverfront. In addition to a number of colour photographs of the ecclesiastical buildings in the area, there are pictures of a number of eating establishments, for which the area is celebrated.

68 **Lisboa: freguesia da Graça.** (Lisbon: parish of Graça.)
Maria Calado, Vítor Matias Ferreira. Lisbon: Contexto, 1993. 61p.
3 maps. bibliog. (Guias Contexto).

Devotion to Nossa Senhora da Graça (Our Lady of Grace) can be traced back to the early 14th century in this area, which occupies high ground below the castle. The district of Graça accommodates several 17th-century palaces as well as the imposing convent of Nossa Senhora da Graça, which was rebuilt after the 1755 earthquake had badly damaged the original edifice. Colour illustrations in this guide include pre- and post-earthquake views, interior and exterior pictures of the convent and other ecclesiatical premises, as well as of the gardens, tilework and patios.

69 **Lisboa: freguesia dos Mártires.** (Lisbon: parish of Mártires.)
Maria Calado, Vítor Matias Ferreira. Lisbon: Contexto, 1991. 60p.
3 maps. bibliog. (Guias Contexto).

The Mártires (Martyrs) parish covers much of the area better known as the Chiado, in the western centre of the city, a district famed for its fashionable literary and artistic associations. The parish dates back to the reconquest of the city from the Moors in 1147 and this book provides a detailed chronology up to present times. Numerous colour photographs depict the area today and monochrome illustrations show bygone scenes. The text concludes with an assessment of the impact of the 1988 fire in the Chiado and the rebuilding plans for the area.

70 **Lisboa: freguesia de Santa Catarina, Bairro Alto.** (Lisbon: parish of
Santa Catarina, Bairro Alto.)
Maria Calado, Vítor Matias Ferreira.   Lisbon: Contexto, 1992. 69p.
3 maps. bibliog. (Guias Contexto).
A colourful guide to the Santa Catarina area of the Bairro Alto, Lisbon's westerly
upper quarter, where a hermitage was established in the 13th century. In 1597 an
earthquake caused serious damage in the area and in 1835 a major fire occurred in the
parish church, which led to its demolition in 1861. The parish also includes the church
of the Paulistas and was the location of the first offices of the *Diário de Notícias*
newspaper. In the 17th century a number of palaces were built in the Rua do Século
area, where Pombal was born in 1699. The English College seminary was also located
in this area. In the 19th century the area was popular with writers and the poet and
playwright, Garrett, established the national conservatory here. The area now has a
declining and ageing population.

71 **Lisboa: freguesia de Santo Estêvão, Alfama.** (Lisbon: parish of
S. Estêvão, Alfama.)
Maria Calado, Vítor Matias Ferreira.   Lisbon: Contexto, 1992. 76p.
3 maps. bibliog. (Guias Contexto).
The parish of Santo Estêvão (St Stephen) occupies a site on the slopes of the historic
Alfama district of eastern central Lisbon in which Christian worship has been
documented back to the latter part of the 12th century. Lisbon's impressive Museu
Militar (Military Museum) is to be found here on the site of a former military arsenal,
as is the former Celeiro Público (public granary) built during the era of Pombal in the
18th century. The book's plentiful colour photographs capture the street life of this
ancient quarter as well as depicting a number of its major buildings.

72 **Lisboa: freguesia de S. Miguel, Alfama.** (Lisbon: parish of S. Miguel,
Alfama.)
Maria Calado, Vítor Matias Ferreira.   Lisbon: Contexto, 1992. 76p.
3 maps. bibliog. (Guias Contexto).
This old parish in the southern portion of the elevated Alfama district houses the
famous Santa Luzia belvedere and the former Limoeiro gaol, as well as the parish
church of S. Miguel from which it takes its name. This church's origins go back to the
late 12th century and parts of the city's mediaeval walls are also located nearby. One
of Lisbon's most famous natural water sources, the Chafariz d'el Rei (The king's
fountain), also lies within the parish. The volume contains many colour photographs
of the area and a map on which the major locations are clearly marked.

73 **Lisboa: freguesia de S. Sebastião da Pedreira.** (Lisbon parish of
S. Sebastião da Pedreira.)
Maria Calado, Vítor Matias Ferreira.   Lisbon: Contexto, 1993. 60p.
3 maps. bibliog. (Guias Contexto).
Although a hermitage to St Sebastian was established there in the 16th century, the
parish is better known today for its modern avenues, which include those named to
honour the statesman Fontes Pereira de Melo and the Cinco de Outubro (5 October
1910 Revolution). Indeed, this district has won the prestigious Prémio Valmor (q.v.)
for contemporary Lisbon architecture more often than any other area of the city. The

Geography. Districts

Parque Eduardo VII, so named after the British king, Edward VII, who visited the city in 1903, is also in this district. Colour photographs depict many of the notable buildings, including the parish church, the Hotel Avis and the Rotunda with its landmark statue of Pombal.

74 **Pelas freguesias de Lisboa, 1: o termo de Lisboa, Benfica, Carnide, Lumiar, Ameixoeira, Charneca.** (Through the parishes of Lisbon: the limits of Lisbon, Benfica, Carnide, Lumiar, Ameixoeira, Charneca.) Carlos Consiglieri, Filomena Ribeiro, José Manuel Vargas, Marília Abel.   Lisbon: Câmara Municipal de Lisboa, Pelouro da Educação, 1993. 142p. map. bibliog. (Pelas Freguesias de Lisboa, vol. 1).

The first in a well-illustrated series of colour guides to Lisbon's fifty-three parishes. For each parish there are details of its territory, population, urban structure, institutions, public spaces and information about its history, socio-economic profile and historical heritage. An index of the streets in each parish is given but there is no accompanying map on which they may be found. Statistics of population and a chronological calendar are supplied, but an index would have been a useful adjunct.

75 **Pelas freguesias de Lisboa, 2: Lisboa oriental, São João, Beato, Marvila, Santa Maria dos Olivais.** (Through the parishes of Lisbon: eastern Lisbon, São João, Beato, Marvila and Santa Maria dos Olivais.) Carlos Consiglieri, Filomena Ribeiro, José Manuel Vargas, Marília Abel.   Lisbon: Câmara Municipal de Lisboa, Pelouro da Educação, 1993. 166p. map. bibliog. (Pelas Freguesias de Lisboa, vol. 2).

Ostensibly aimed at school and college teachers, to provide a focus for their local history studies, the attractive series of guides in which this volume appears, in fact, is useful to a much wider audience. They abound in colour photographs of high quality which show the major buildings and also many street and commonplace locations in each of the parishes covered. The text addresses each parish in turn, following a consistent format which covers history, socio-economic aspects and the physical heritage of each area. This volume covers the north-eastern area of the city, soon to be regenerated by the Expo 98 event at Olivais.

76 **Pelas freguesias de Lisboa, 3: de Campo de Ourique à Avenida. Santo Condestável, Santa Isabel, S. Mamede, Coração de Jesus.** (Through the parishes of Lisbon: from Campo de Ourique to the Avenue. Santo Condestável, Santa Isabel, S. Mamede, Coração de Jesus.) Carlos Consiglieri, Filomena Ribeiro, José Manuel Vargas, Marília Abel.   Lisbon: Câmara Municipal de Lisboa, Pelouro da Educação, 1995. 178p. map. bibliog. (Pelas Freguesias de Lisboa, vol. 3).

The third of Lisbon City Council's projected series of twelve volumes covering the parishes of the city. As usual the volume contains many fine colour photographs of modern and historic sights. The four parishes covered here form a band running across the north-west of the city centre. Details are provided of each area's spatial and population structure, its local institutions, open spaces, historical and socio-economic features as well as its cultural heritage as manifested by its historic buildings. The

20

streets in each parish are listed and population statistics and a chronological calendar are also supplied.

77   **Lisboa: freguesia de S. Paulo.** (Lisbon: parish of S. Paulo.)
Graça Índia Cordeiro, Joaquim Garcia.   Lisbon: Contexto, 1993. 65p.
3 maps. bibliog. (Guias Contexto).
The parish of S. Paulo includes the churches of Corpo Santo, Chagas and S. Paulo itself, as well as the lively Ribeira and 24 de Julho markets and the dockland bar area. In addition, the terminal stations of both the railway to Cascais and of the Tagus passenger and car ferries to Cacilhas are sited at Cais do Sodré, whilst another transport facility, the Bica street funicular, is also located nearby. The parish dates back at least to the early 15th century, although the current parish church had to be extensively rebuilt after the 1755 earthquake. The natural water sources in the area led, from 1850, to the operation of the Banhos de S. Paulo (St Paul's Baths), which were used both for washing and health purposes. Colour photographs and maps amply illustrate the district's attractions.

78   **Lisboa: freguesia de Sta Maria dos Olivais.** (Lisbon: parish of Sta Maria dos Olivais.)
Francisco da Silva Dias, Tiago da Silva Dias.   Lisbon: Contexto, 1993. 71p. 5 maps. bibliog. (Guias Contexto).
Olivais is the largest of Lisbon's parishes and occupies the north-eastern border of the city, adjoining Loures. It embraces most of Lisbon Airport and the modern residential districts of Olivais-Sul, Olivais-Norte and Encarnação. In this book, a brief chronology and history trace the parish back to its roots in 1397, the destruction of its church in the 1755 earthquake and its rapid growth as a residential area between 1960 and 1970, when its population rose from 11,896 to 55,065. Major developments planned for the area include a new civic centre and the enormous Expo 98 international exhibition to be held on the Olivais dockside, which will include a major new international railway station as well as housing developments.

79   **O Rossio.** (The Rossio.)
Marina Tavares Dias.   Lisbon: Ibis Editores, 1990. 96p. 2 maps. bibliog. (Guias de Lisboa pelos Olisipógrafos, no. 1).
This guide to the history of the main square of Lisbon, the Rossio, is packed with monochrome photographs of the area through the ages. The text comprises extracts from the writings of celebrated Olisipographers (writers on Lisbon) and also includes a list of all the buildings in the Rossio, with their past and present functions.

80   **São Domingos de Benfica: roteiro.** (St. Domingos de Benfica: guide.)
Jorge M. Rodrigues Ferreira, with assistance from Carlos Biscaya.
Lisbon: Junta de Freguesia de São Domingos de Benfica, 1991. 136p. map.
A lavish colour guide to the parish of S. Domingos de Benfica, which became one of Lisbon's fifty-three parishes (*freguesias*) in 1959. The parish contains the famous Estádio da Luz, the home of the Sport Lisboa e Benfica club. It also embraces the Lisbon zoo at Sete Rios, the celebrated Palácio do Marquês da Fronteira and part of the 18th-century Lisbon aqueduct. Photographs, mostly in colour, show the major locations within the area.

81 **A sétima colina: roteiro histórico-artístico. The seventh hill: historical and artistical [sic] guide.**
José Augusto França. Lisbon: Livros Horizonte/ Departamento de Intervenção Urbana da Sociedade Lisboa 94, 1994. 158p. map. bibliog.
Describes the route from Cais do Sodré, by the River Tagus, to the Largo do Rato in Lisbon, containing some thirty-five sites which are described and illustrated, almost exclusively in colour. At the end of the book is a section on twelve statues and sculptures to be found on the route. There is an abridged, and rather stilted, English translation of each section of the book.

82 **Lisboa: freguesia de Belém.** (Lisbon: parish of Belém.)
Eduardo de Freitas, Maria Calado, Vítor Matias Ferreira. Lisbon: Contexto, 1993. 81p. 3 maps. bibliog. (Guias Contexto).
Santa Maria de Belém, to give it its full name, is the most westerly parish of Lisbon and probably the best known abroad, since it was not only the starting point for Vasco da Gama (1597) and other voyages of discovery, but is also the site of the magnificent 16th-century Manueline monuments of the Torre de Belém and the Jerónimos monastery, which survived the ravages of the 1755 earthquake. Belém is also home to the controversial Centro Cultural, an enormous fort-like building, opened to coincide with Portugal's presidency of the European Community in 1992. Six major museums and the striking Padrão dos Descobrimentos, a monument to the Discoveries, are also located at Belém, as is the presidential residence, the Museu dos Coches and the Restelo stadium, home of Belenenses football club. Colour photographs illustrate these major sights, as well as the riverside dock and houses.

83 **Lisboa: freguesia do Castelo.** (Lisbon: parish of the Castle.)
Helena Pinto Janeiro. Lisbon: Contexto, 1993. 77p. 3 maps. bibliog. (Guias Contexto).
The parish boundaries of Santa Cruz do Castelo have remained largely unaltered since the 1147 reconquest of the castle from the Moors. The parish's history, including its damage by the 1755 earthquake is chronicled here. The many photographs, mostly in colour, show more recent developments, not least the striking clearance between 1938 and 1940 of the barracks and other buildings which had abutted the castle walls and concealed the impressive crenellated castle walls visible today.

84 **Lisboa: freguesia da Sé.** (Lisbon: parish of the Cathedral.)
Ana Cristina Lourenço, Helena Pinto Janeiro. Lisbon: Contexto, 1992. 65p. 3 maps. bibliog. (Guias Contexto).
A colourful, illustrated guide to the area around Lisbon's cathedral, whose origins are Visigothic. The cathedral's history, along with that of the nearby church of St Anthony, who was born in Lisbon, the Limoeiro gaol and the Casa dos Bicos, are all covered. Illustrations also include some of the Moorish and Roman remains discovered in the area, as well as more modern local ceramic tilework adornments to buildings.

85   **Lisboa: freguesia de Santiago.** (Lisbon: parish of Santiago.)
     Ana Cristina Lourenço.   Lisbon: Contexto, 1993. 77p. 4 maps. bibliog.
     (Guias Contexto).
A pocket history of the historic Santiago parish, on the southern flank of the castle
hill. Amongst the local buildings dealt with in detail are the palaces of Belmonte and
Azurara, the Limoeiro gaol and the Roman theatre remains of the Rua S. Mamede, the
only such site in Portugal, which was excavated in the 1960s. Many colour
photographs depict the area which, despite losing almost a third of its population since
1960, still has a population density twice that of Lisbon's average.

86   **Chiado: o incêndio.** (Chiado: the fire.)
     A. Sacchetti.   Venda Nova, Portugal: Bertrand Editora, 1989. 129p.
An A4-format book of vivid colour photographs of the disastrous fire in the Chiado
area of central Lisbon in 1988, accompanied by a short textual introduction. The
captions to the photographs are all to be found at the back of the volume which makes
identification of the location of individual photographs difficult.

Jerónimos. (The Jerónimos Church and Monastery.)
See item no. 409.

Torre de Belém: English guide. (Tower of Belém: English guide.)
See item no. 500.

Mosteiro dos Jerónimos: English guide. (Jerónimos Monastery: English guide.)
See item no. 502.

Belém Palace its guests, its secrets and its daily life.
See item no. 504.

**The Palace and gardens of Fronteira: seventeenth- and eighteenth-
century Portuguese style.**
See item no. 505.

Gravuras de aguarelas de Belém. (Watercolour prints of Belém.)
See item no. 585.

A fronteira. (The frontier.)
See item no. 596.

Suburbs

87   **Palace of Queluz: the gardens.**
     Simonetta Luz Afonso, Angela Delaforce, photographic essay by
     Nicolas Sapieha.   Lisbon: Quetzal, [1995]. 136p.
Despite the book's title, the introductory text actually outlines the history of the Royal
Palace at Queluz rather than just its gardens. Nevertheless, the many black-and-white

photographs which follow do concentrate on the grounds and exterior of the building, which is located some fifteen kilometres west of Lisbon, and was built in a lightweight Rococo style by King José I, from 1747. Queen Maria I moved the Royal Court to Queluz during her reign (1777-1816).

88 **Landscapes of Portugal: Sintra, Cascais, Estoril: a countryside guide.**
Brian Anderson, Eileen Anderson.   London: Sunflower Books, 1995.
Updated printing. 65p. maps.

A pocket-sized book written for the independent traveller, originally published as *Landscapes of Portugal: Estoril coast and Costa Verde* (London: Sunflower Books, 1991. 64p + 64p. maps). The text comprises details of car tours through the Serra de Sintra and Estremadura as well as nine walks. Mileages and timings are given for the tours and walks. Plans of Sintra, Estoril and Cascais are provided along with local bus times and topographical maps at a scale of 1:50,000. The same authors' *Lisbon and Central Portugal* was published in 1997 (London: Black. 248p. maps. [Regions of Portugal]). This work contains sections on subjects including food and drink, history, and suggestions for tours. These precede accounts of Lisbon and its environs which are illustrated by colour photographs and make up more than a half of the book. Excellent maps show clearly the locations of individual sights in Lisbon and its vicinity.

89 **Pena: palácio nacional.** (Pena: national palace.)
José Manuel Martins Carneiro.   Lisbon: ELO for Instituto Português
do Património Cultural, 1991. unpaginated. map.

A guide to the 19th-century Pena royal palace, perched on the hills high above Sintra. Built by Fernando de Saxe Coburg-Gotha, husband of Queen Maria II, it displays an eclectic variety of architectural and decorative styles. This guide is well-illustrated with colour photographs of the exterior and interior and of specific pieces of furniture, silverware and ceramic ware.

90 **Sintra na literatura romântica inglesa.** (Sintra in English Romantic
literature.)
J. Almeida Flor.   Sintra, Portugal: Câmara Municipal de Sintra, 1978.
31p. (Publicações da Câmara Municipal de Sintra).

Although the text of this essay is in Portuguese, it gives full references to a number of English-language accounts of Sintra from the 18th and 19th centuries, as well as including three full-page engravings of Sintra by W. H. Burnett. Amongst the sources covered are works by William Beckford, James Murphy, Robert Southey, J. Sherer, Dora Wordsworth (Mrs Quillinan), Lord Tennyson and Lord Byron.

91 **O Palácio Nacional de Sintra: residência querida de D. João I e D.**
Filipa de Lencastre. The Royal Palace of Sintra, favourite residence
of John I and Philippa of Lancaster.
Matilde Sousa Franco.   Sintra, Portugal: Palácio Nacional de Sintra;
The British Historical Society of Portugal, 1987. 48p. bibliog.

A book published in commemoration of the sixth centenary of the marriage in 1387 of King João I of Portugal to John of Gaunt's daughter, Philippa of Lancaster, and to coincide with the unveiling of a memorial plaque of Philippa at the Royal Palace of Sintra by the Prince and Princess of Wales. The authoress was, at the time, Director of the Palace and she provides a detailed, illustrated account of its origins and of those existing features most clearly linked to the period of João and Philippa's residence there. The text is in parallel Portuguese and English versions.

92   Goldenbook of Estoril coast.
Lisbon: H. Cerqueira; Interpropo, 1993- .

A companion volume to the *Goldenbook of Lisbon* (q.v.), which comprises a large-format, colour, hardback book aimed at tourists and visiting businessmen. It is full of attractive colour photographs and articles on the Estoril and Cascais area, with advertisements by local businesses. A new edition is produced every September.

93   Castles, caliphs and Christians, a landscape with figures: Monserrate.
Ida Kingsbury.   Lisbon: The British Historical Society of Portugal; Associação Amigos de Monserrate, 1994. 68p.

A posthumous edition of Ida Kingsbury's illustrated study of Monserrate, the magnificent country estate at Sintra, owned, during the 19th century, by the wealthy English writer, William Beckford. Kingsbury outlines the history of the area from Moorish times before giving a detailed account of the ownership of Monserrate by Gerald de Visme, a late 18th-century Englishman, resident for over forty years in Portugal. She also describes the period of Beckford's tenancy and that of the wealthy English businessman, Sir Francis Cook, who owned the property in the mid-19th century. Sintra and Monserrate's role as a centre of pilgrimage for North European writers, including Byron, Tennyson and Hans Christian Andersen, is also covered.

94   Towards the history of the municipality of Cascais in the Middle Ages.
A. H. de Oliveira Marques.   Lisbon: The British Historical Society of Portugal, 1993. 30p. map.

Oliveira Marques, a leading Portuguese historian, traces here the origins of the coastal town of Cascais from Palaeolithic times, through the four and a half centuries of Moorish rule, to the 15th century. He outlines the growth of the town as a fishing port and its early period as a satellite of nearby Sintra. In the Middle Ages its trade axis moved to the east, to Lisbon, as its maritime importance increased and by 1527 Cascais had a population approaching 2,000.

95   An historical journey along the Marginal.
Paulo Lowndes Marques.   Lisbon: The British Historical Society of Portugal, 1991. 46p. bibliog.

An informative exposition of the architectural and historical landmarks to be encountered when travelling westwards along the Marginal, the busy coast-road from Algés, on the outskirts of Lisbon, to the resort and fishing town of Cascais. Drawings illustrate a number of the notable houses, forts, monuments and other buildings along the route.

96   **Cascais: a terra e as gentes.** (Cascais: the land and the people.)
Niza Paiva.   Cascais, Portugal: NP-OMBS, 1995. 100p.
A collection of colour photographs of the landmarks in the fishing port and resort of
Cascais, which lies 27km (17 miles) to the west of Lisbon. Also included are pictures
of local celebrities and characters.

97   **Sintra: a borough in the wild.**
António Pena, Luís Gomes, José Cabral, Maria do Rosário Pinto, Sheila
Stapleton Garcia, Carlos Eduardo Stapleton Garcia.   Sintra, Portugal:
Câmara Municipal, 1993. 78p.
An illustrated introduction to the Sintra area, which lies some 30km (19 miles) north-
west of Lisbon, in a fine natural setting of rugged hills and luxuriant foliage which
justifies the book's title.

98   **Cintra: an English landscape garden in Portugal. Extracted from
'The Times' newspaper, Dec. 28, 1886.**
J. C. Robinson.   Chiswick, England: Privately printed, 1887. 18p.
Robinson gives a fulsome description of Sintra's natural environment together with
accounts of its buildings, including the so-called 'cork convent' (Convento dos
Capuchos) and various *quintas* (rural estates). Two engravings of Sintra are included
and an appendix comprising stanzas XIV-XVI and XVIII-XXIII of Canto I of Byron's
Childe Harold (see item no. 538), completes this large folio volume.

99   **Sintra: Palácio Nacional.** (Sintra: National Palace.)
Ana Maria de Arez Romão, Brito Correia, photographs by Luzes da
Ribalta, Francisco d'Almeida Dias.   Lisbon: ELO for IPPAR Instituto
Português do Património Arquitectónico e Arqueológico, 1995. 16p.
A high quality guidebook to the royal palace in the centre of Sintra, to the west of
Lisbon, whose most striking feature is two enormous conical chimneys over the
extensive kitchens. As well as the many excellent photographs, the text outlines the
history of the palace, built by King João I (1385-1433) and remodelled by King
Manuel (1495-1521), as well as providing a description of the interior of the building.

100   **Sintra.**
Vítor Serrão.   Lisbon: Editorial Presença, 1989. 107p. bibliog.
(Cidades e Vilas de Portugal, no. 6).
A guide to the history, architecture and natural splendours of the Sintra area by the
town's librarian. It is replete with colour photographs of the palaces, gardens and
scenery of the district. A number of black-and-white reproductions of historical
portrayals of Sintra are also included.

101   **Sintra: a landscape with villas.**
José Cornélio da Silva, Gerald Luckhurst, photographs by António
Homem Cardoso.   Lisbon: Inapa, [1995]. 2nd ed. 134p.
A large-format volume on the natural and man-made splendours of the Sintra area.
The English text, translated from the Portuguese edition, *Sintra: a paisagem e suas*

quintas (Lisbon: Inapa, 1989), covers themes such as Sintra's role in the Romantic movement, the architecture of the Royal palaces and the neighbouring chalets, and the relationship between Sintra and overseas artists and visitors. The mostly colour photographs show much more than the usual tourist sights of Sintra especially in their depiction of the many fashionable residences (*quintas*) built in the surrounding hillsides. Much of the same ground is covered in the multilingual *Sintra and its farm manors, Sintra et ses manoirs, Sintra und seine Landhäuser, Sintra e suas quintas* by Arturo D. Pereira, Felipa Espírito Santo Cardoso and Fernando Caladão Correia (Lisbon: Qualigrafe, 1983. 69p.) which is also illustrated by colour photographs.

102 **Cascais.**
Raquel Henriques da Silva.   Lisbon: Editorial Presença, 1988. 89p. bibliog. (Cidades e Vilas de Portugal, no. 1).
A companion volume to item no. 100. Cascais is situated on the Atlantic coast to the west of Lisbon and despite tourist developments, it has remained a thriving fishing port. The Portuguese text covers the history, architecture and 19th- and 20th-century development of the town but it is profusely illustrated with mostly colour photographs which give the English reader a good impression of its attractions.

103 **Sintra and its surroundings.**
Nuno Severiano Teixeira, Paulo Roberto.   Lisbon: Sage, 1994. 161p. (Tourist Guide).
A comprehensive and profusely illustrated guide for the English-speaking visitor to the historic town of Sintra and its rugged natural surroundings, which so impressed Byron and other British travellers. It is a translation of the authors' *Sintra e arredores: guia turístico* (1994).

Lisboa, Oeiras, Estoril, Cascais, Sintra. Touristic maps, Mapas turísticos.
See item no. 104.

Mapa dos arredores de Lisboa e guia turístico. (Map of the suburbs of Lisbon and tourist guide.)
See item no. 120.

O clima da região de Lisboa. (The climate of the Lisbon region.)
See item no. 122.

The climate of Lisbon and of the two health resorts in its immediate neighbourhood, Mont' Estoril on the Riveira of Portugal and Cintra.
See item no. 124.

The climate of Portugal and notes on its health resorts.
See item no. 125.

Elementos para o conhecimento do clima do Estoril. (Contributions towards a knowledge of the climate of Estoril.)
See item no. 130.

'Except the Lord build the house, their labour is lost that build it', Psalm 127. A guide to and brief record of the building of St Paul's Church, Estoril, Portugal together with an account of the origin of the Dicoese to which it belonged and what became of it.
See item no. 405.

Torre de Belém: English guide. (Tower of Belém: English guide.)
See item no. 500.

Mosteiro dos Jerónimos: English guide. (Jerónimos Monastery: English guide.)
See item no. 502.

Belém Palace.
See item no. 504.

Crescimento e diferenciação das áreas suburbanas de Lisboa e do Porto.
(Growth and differentiation of the suburban areas of Lisbon and Oporto.)
See item no. 522.

One day to Sintra & back.
See item no. 548.

'Cintra's glorious Eden'.
See item no. 569.

The Berardo Collection.
See item no. 649.

Maps

104 **Lisboa, Oeiras, Estoril, Cascais, Sintra. Touristic maps, Mapas turísticos.**
Vítor M. Batista.   Lisbon: Ciparte, 1996. 122p. 10 maps.
Despite its title, the excellent colour maps in this volume only occupy seventeen of its pages. The rest is taken up, for each location, with a short essay, street indexes and details of services, events, places to visit, culture, accommodation, gastronomy, entertainment and shopping opportunities. Liberally illustrated with colour photographs, this volume is particularly useful for its cartographic coverage of such Lisbon suburbs as Oeiras and Monte Estoril, which do not normally warrant maps in travel and tourist guides.

105 **Lisboa, Lisbon, Lissabon 1:14,000 city centre map.**
Berndtson & Berndtson. Fürstenfeldbruck, Germany: Berndtson,
1996. (B & B City Streets).

A highly original map whose geographical coverage is actually far greater than its title
implies. Its innovations include its being printed in colour on wipe-clean paper and
with the horizontal fold-line being free of print, thereby avoiding illegibility through
heavy use. It actually consists of seven separate maps showing the city as a whole
(1:14,000), the central area (1:8,500), Cascais and Estoril (1:10,000), the Lisbon
region (1:300,000), Portugal and southern Spain (scale unstated), the Castelo de São
Jorge (1:2,700) and a diagrammatic map of the Metro and tram system. Also included
are vivid colour barcharts of monthly temperature, rainfall, humidity and hours of
sunshine, as well as conversion charts for weights and measures. Another card map of
Lisbon which seeks to avoid damage by folding is the *Rand McNally City Flash:
Lisboa* map (Bern: Hallwag, 1996), with a scale of 1:16,000.

106 **Planta da rede dos transportes públicos da Carris.** (Map of the
public transport network of Carris.)
Companhia Carris de Ferro de Lisboa. Lisbon: Companhia Carris de
Ferro de Lisboa, 1996.

A folding colour map (approximately 41cm x 58cm) of the bus and tram system
operated by the Carris company, Lisbon's public transport enterprise. Its usefulness is
limited by the absence from the map of any street names; only the names of termini
and of districts are given. The reverse of the map includes lists of all services and a
black-and-white map of night services. In addition, there are lists of public facilities,
such as hospitals, museums, libraries, parks and sports stadia, and of the bus and tram
routes which serve them, together with a reference to their approximate location on
the map.

107 **Lisboa: mapa turístico, tourist map. 1:20,500.**
Dinternal. Lisbon: Dinternal, 1995.

An exceptionally clear, colour map of Lisbon which also includes inset maps of
Cascais, Estoril and Sintra. A street index is provided, as is information on hotels and
on tourist sights, such as *fado* houses.

108 **Lisboa, Lisbonne, Lissabon, Lisbon: roteiro de cidade, plan de
ville, Stadtplan, city map. 1:13,500.**
Falk Verlag. Hamburg, Germany: Falk Verlag, 1992. 15th ed.
(Falkplan Extra).

One of Falk's excellent series of clear colour maps of European cities. A notable
feature is that it is intricately folded so that the streets of central Lisbon are
immediately visible once the cover has been opened. An attached booklet provides a
detailed alphabetical index of street names and this, unusually, also includes separate
sections for the streets of Cascais and Estoril.

109 **Guia urbano de Lisboa.** (Urban guide to Lisbon.)
Forum Ibérica. Lisbon: Forum Ibérica, 1993. 93p. 116 maps.

Surprisingly, this claims to be the first detailed A to Z map book of Lisbon. It has been
created from aerial photographs and has employed modern cartographical techniques.

The result is a superbly detailed (1:5,000) and visually clear colour book of maps on which even selected house numbers are shown. The maps are preceded by an alphabetical index of streets and of public buildings such as churches, post offices and hospitals. It has an introduction and other explanatory information in English, French and Spanish, as well as in Portuguese. Although there is a grid-map of the city at the back of the volume, this lacks any place or street names. Consequently, the publication also comes with a separate and impractically large folding map which serves the same purpose of allowing the user to home in on a particular page of the atlas. On the reverse of the folding map is a 1:1,500 map of the Alfama district.

110   **Lisboa. City map. 1:13,400.**
Foto Vista.   [Lisbon?]: Foto Vista, [1995].
A more detailed than average tourist map of the city of Lisbon in which the careful use of colour further facilitates location-finding. As well as a street index, the map also gives details of accommodation, churches, museums and other tourist sights in the city.

111   **Portugal: touristic map, carta turística, carte touristique, Touristenkarte.**
Guia Turística do Norte.   Odivelas, Portugal: Guia Turística do Norte, [1990].
A 1:600,000 scale map (110cm x 51cm) of Portugal showing major roads, inter-town distances and notable buildings. The reverse has a striking three-dimensional map of the entire Lisbon city area, from Algés in the west to Moscavide in the east, and includes Almada, south of the Tagus. An inset map on the reverse shows the city centre area, also in three dimensions, and a further small map shows the roads around Lisbon. The three-dimensional maps show all the major buildings and monuments of Lisbon, whilst a smaller but similar map depicts Oporto.

112   **Lisboa: plantas e perspectivas. Lisboa, Estoril, Cascais.** (Lisbon: maps and perspectives. Lisbon, Estoril, Cascais.)
Hipergráfica.   Odivelas, Portugal: Hipergráfica, 1995.
This publication consists of two large, but rather luridly coloured maps on thick glossy paper which present a three-dimensional view of Lisbon and the surrounding coast. Their visual clarity is unfortunately partly offset by their lack of detail of those roads which are not main thoroughfares. The work also includes a list of hotels in the area.

113   **Lissabon. City map. Lisbonne, Lisbon, Lisboa. 1:15000.**
Kümmerly + Frey.   Bern: Kümmerly + Frey, [1995].
A very clear colour map of the city of Lisbon at a scale of 1:15,000 which has many features not found on most such maps. Thus, the routes of all bus, tram and Metro services are superimposed on the streets and there are also three smaller inset maps, in colour, at respective scales of 1:60,000, 1:150,000 and 1:1,000,000 showing progressively larger areas around the city. A fourth inset map shows the Lisbon Metro system. The reverse of the map includes a street index, six suggested city itineraries with maps, drawings and details of twenty-five buildings or monuments in Lisbon and a brief history of the city. The text throughout is given in German, French, Portuguese and English.

114   Atlas de cidades medievais portuguesas, séculos XII-XV, vol. I.
(Atlas of mediaeval Portuguese towns, XIIth-XVth centuries, vol. I.)
A. H. de Oliveira Marques, Iria Gonçalves, Amélia Aguiar Andrade.
Lisbon: Centro de Estudos Históricos da Universidade Nova de Lisboa,
1990. 96p. 19 maps. bibliog.
A collection, arranged into regions, of maps of widely-varying quality and detail of
major Portuguese towns and cities. The textual accompaniment comprises a mass of
facts about each city covered. In the case of Lisbon, (p. 55-60), details are given in
note form of population, produce, parish and street names, places of worship and
education, and sources of water together with much historical detail. A separate entry
covers the town of Sintra (p. 69-71). Lisbon's history from Roman to present times is
covered in the impressive *Atlas histórico de ciudades europeas: Península Ibérica*
(Historical atlas of European cities: Iberian Peninsula), edited by Manuel Guàrida,
Francisco Javier Monclús and José Luis Oyón (Barcelona, Spain: Salvat for the Centro
de Cultura Contemporànea de Barcelona, 1994. 334p. maps. bibliog.). This folio-sized
publication is the first in a series covering Europe's leading 100 cities. Lisbon's
geography and history are described by Maria Calado, Margarida de Souza Lobo and
Vítor Matias Ferreira in a section (p. 94-125, maps. bibliog.) replete with colour maps,
photographs and engravings which clearly illustrate the city's evolution.

**115   Euro-City Map 1:15,000, Lisbon. With tourist information, places
of interest, hotel accommodation and street index.**
R. V. Reise.   Berlin: R. V. Reise, [1995]. (Geo Center).
A full-colour map of the Lisbon city area which also shows the main public transport
routes. On the reverse is a street index and practical information about Lisbon, such as
emergency services and hotel lists.

116   Euro Holiday Map 1:250,000, Lisbon and its coastal region.
R. V. Reise.   Berlin: R. V. Reise, [1995]. (Geo Center).
A more wide-ranging but less detailed colour road map than its companion publication
in the Geo Center Series (see item no. 115). This map is intended for the motorist
whereas its companion is equally useful to the pedestrian visitor to Lisbon. On the
reverse of this map are twenty-eight suggested excursions, each with a small colour
photograph of the destination in question.

**117   Guia de ruas da cidade de Lisboa, com a lista do código postal de
todas as localidades do país. Roteiro actualizado.** (Guide to the
streets of the city of Lisbon, with the list of postcodes for all localities
in the country. Up-to-date street index.)
Roteiro.   Lisbon: Roteiro, 1995. 320p. map.
A handy pocket index, in alphabetical order, to the streets of Lisbon. Its usefulness
would be enhanced by a map with larger, and therefore more legible, lettering. It is
also a useful source of Lisbon and other Portuguese postcodes.

118   **Roteiro das ruas de Lisboa.** (Directory of the streets of Lisbon.)
       Lisbon: Editorial Notícias, 1994. 255p. map.
A small, pocket-sized alphabetical guide to the streets of Lisbon, with an accompanying folding map. Also provided are lists of addresses of public buildings, such as hospitals.

119   **Lisboa: planta e roteiro. Estoril e Cascais, 1994/95. 1:20,000.**
       (Lisbon: map and guide. Estoril and Cascais, 1994/95. 1:20,000.)
       J. R. Silva.   Lisbon: J. R. Silva, 1994.
A colour map of Lisbon and its western suburbs from one of Portugal's long-established cartography firms, published in English and French versions of the same title as the Portuguese original.

120   **Mapa dos arredores de Lisboa e guia turístico.** (Map of the suburbs of Lisbon and tourist guide.)
       J. R. Silva.   Lisbon: Agência Portuguesa de Revistas, [1985].
This large folding road map (1:100,000) covers the area from Torres Vedras in the north to Sesimbra in the south and from the Atlantic coast to Setúbal in the east. On the reverse are an index of places on the map, plus small monochrome maps of the centres of Lisbon, Estoril and Cascais, a mileage chart and lists of addresses of public services and tourist sights. There is also brief factual information on a number of the towns shown on the map.

121   **Cultural atlas of Spain and Portugal.**
       Mary Vincent, R. A. Stradling.   Oxford: Andromeda; New York:
       Facts on File, 1994. 240p. 34 maps. bibliog.
An attractive history of Iberia presented largely through good quality maps and illustrations, all in colour. The text is divided into sections on 'The physical background', 'A history of the Peninsula' and 'Geographical regions'. One of the essays covers 'Pombal and the rebuilding of Lisbon' and others of relevance to Lisbon address Portuguese tiles, Jews in Iberia and the 1974 Revolution. However, it is the maps which are the unique aspect of this publication for they graphically portray Lisbon's position in such historical contexts as the Roman Empire, the Visigothic expansion, the Moorish period and the Peninsular War. The geographical maps show agricultural land use, industries and historical monuments in the Lisbon area.

Atlas de Lisboa: a cidade no espaço e no tempo. (Atlas of Lisbon: the city in space and time.)
See item no. 63.

Climate

122 **O clima da região de Lisboa.** (The climate of the Lisbon region.)
Maria João Alcoforado. Lisbon: Centro de Estudos Geográficos,
Universidade de Lisboa, 1993. 347p. bibliog. (Memórias do Centro de
Estudos Geográficos, [15]).
This volume has an English summary (p. 315-20) but also has many charts and
diagrams which transcend any language barrier. The authoress variously uses data
from between twenty-eight and thirty-two weather stations in the Lisbon region, the
longest sequence of which is the 126 years of readings from the Lisbon Botanic
Gardens. She studies wind, rain, temperature and sunshine patterns, focusing on the
urban area of Lisbon.

123 **The climate of Portugal.**
J. C. de Brito Capello. *Scottish Geographical Magazine*, vol. XII
(1896), p. 150-51. 3 maps.
A brief summation of the climate of Lisbon and thirteen other towns in Portugal, the
Azores and Madeira, which is accompanied by useful isothermic maps of Portugal in
summer, winter and over the full year. The Lisbon readings are averages over the
period from 1856-85 and show temperature maxima and minima, humidity and
rainfall.

124 **The climate of Lisbon and of the two health resorts in its
immediate neighbourhood, Mont' Estoril on the Riviera of
Portugal and Cintra.**
D. G. Dalgado. London: H. K. Lewis, 1906. 50p.
Dr Dalgado was largely instrumental in reawakening interest in Lisbon and the nearby
Estoril area as therapeutic destinations for ailing visitors from northern Europe. Here
he describes the microclimates of Lisbon, Monte Estoril, which lies between Estoril
and Cascais, and Sintra, which lies inland. He makes favourable comparisons of the
Portuguese towns with the more fashionable French health resorts of Biarritz and
Nice. Climatic data from the end of the 19th century is used to support his case.

125 **The climate of Portugal and notes on its health resorts.**
D. G. Dalgado. Lisbon: Academia das Ciências; London: H. K.
Lewis, 1914. 479p. 6 maps. bibliog.
A section on 'Lisbon and its environs' (p. 354-60) is supplemented by separate entries
for Monte Estoril and the Portuguese Riviera, Sintra, Estoril and Poças, as well as the
São Paulo district of the city. There are general chapters on climate, flora and fauna,
each supplemented by a bibliography and an overall index. Whilst the meteorological
detail is of interest primarily to experts, the information on health resorts is more
accessible to the general reader who will be fascinated to learn, for example, that the
Lumiar district of Lisbon is deemed especially conducive to the treatment of
consumptives, whilst Benfica is recommended for sufferers from nervous complaints.
Charts of climatic data for 1904, a typical year, are provided.

126 **Influence de la continentalité sur le rhythme thermique au Portugal.** (Influence of continentality on the temperature in Portugal.)
Suzanne Daveau. *Finisterra: Revista Portuguesa de Geografia,*
vol. X, no. 19 (1975), p. 5-52.

An English summary is included in this study of temperature variations at and between three Portuguese locations which lie at or about 38° 45' in the northern latitudes; Cabo da Roca on the Atlantic coast, Lisbon and Elvas. Daveau's use of data for the period 1931-60 and her thorough assessment of winter and summer weather in 1967-69 demonstrate how average annual and daily temperature variations increase with progression eastwards. The Lisbon data is from the weather station in the *Jardim Botânico* (Botanic Gardens), to the west of the city centre.

127 **O clima de Portugal. Fascículo IV. Valores mensais e anuais dos elementos climáticos no período 1901-1930.** (The climate of Portugal. Fascicule IV. Monthly and annual values of the climatic elements in the periods 1901-30.)
H. Amorim Ferreira. Lisbon: Observatório do Infante D. Luíz, 1945.
179p.

Includes tables and charts showing readings of the atmospheric pressure, median, minimum and maximum temperatures, wind, humidity, rainfall totals and rain days for every month between 1901 and 1930, as recorded in Lisbon and a number of other sites in Portugal.

128 **O clima de Portugal. Fascículo VI. Estremadura, Ribatejo a Alto Alentejo.** (The climate of Portugal. Fascicule VI. Estremadura, Ribatejo and Alto Alentejo.)
H. Amorim Ferreira. Lisbon: Serviço Meteorológico Nacional, 1950.
48p.

In addition to a description of the climate in the Lisbon area, a section of charts records monthly rainfall, sunshine and temperature readings taken in Lisbon, at both the Ajuda and Belém weather stations, and in the suburbs at Monte Estoril and Queluz. The years covered vary from location to location but all include substantial sequences of years between the 1920s and 1940s.

129 **O clima de Portugal. Fascículo XVI. Região de Lisboa-Santarém.** (The climate of Portugal. Fascicule XVI. Region of Lisbon-Santarém.)
H. Amorim Ferreira. Lisbon: Serviço Meteorológico Nacional, 1965.
116p.

A description of the climate along the northern side of the Tagus estuary between Lisbon and Santarém. Thirty-two tables of data and nineteen charts are provided.

130 **Elementos para o conhecimento do clima do Estoril.** (Contributions towards a knowledge of the climate of Estoril.)
H. Amorim Ferreira. Lisbon: Academia das Ciências de Lisboa, 1940. 13p. (Academia das Ciências de Lisboa, Separata das Memórias, Classe de Ciências, III).
This brief essay on the climate of the seaside resort of Estoril also includes many tables and charts for both Monte Estoril and Lisbon for the period 1931-40. These record, month by month, statistics of rainfall, sunshine and temperature which amply demonstrate the area's exceptionally equable climate.

131 **The world weather guide.**
E. A. Pearce, C. G. Smith. Oxford: Helicon, 1994. 483p.
The section on Portugal in this book (p. 404-06) includes charts of climate data for Lisbon. These show the city's highest, lowest and average temperatures as well as precipitation measures for each month of the year. In addition, morning and evening relative humidity readings are provided.

The thermal springs and the climate of Estoril in chronic rheumatism and gout during winter.
See item no. 435.

Change of climate considered as a remedy in dyspeptic, pulmonary and other chronic affections.
See item no. 436.

On change of climate: a guide for travellers in pursuit of health.
See item no. 439.

Medical climatology.
See item no. 442.

River Tagus

132 **Os portos fluviais do Tejo.** (The river ports of the Tagus.)
Jorge Gaspar. *Finisterra: Revista Portuguesa de Geografia*, vol. V, no. 10 (1970), p. 153-204. 11 maps.
This study of the history of Tagus river transport has an English summary, as well as ten black-and-white photographic illustrations. Gaspar recounts how early trade consisted of foodstuffs being transported upriver from Lisbon, whilst livestock and timber came down to the capital. He also shows how the river trade accounted for the siting of various local industries, such as sawmilling and cork processing. In the period of union between Spain and Portugal (1580-1640), Philip II of Spain attempted to make the Tagus navigable for commerce from Lisbon as far as Aranjuez in central Spain but despite surviving the competition of railways, transport on the Tagus declined inexorably with the advent of bulk road transport.

133 **Roteiro das barras de Lisboa e do Rio Tejo até Valada.** (Guide to the river-bars of Lisbon and to the River Tagus as far as Valada.) Joaquim António Martins. Linda-a-Velha, Portugal: Published by the Author, 1995. 2nd ed. 379p.

The revised version of a work first published in 1972 which provides a comprehensive guide to the river Tagus between its mouth at the Atlantic Ocean, some nine miles below Lisbon, and Valada on the Tagus estuary, above the city, in the Ribatejo area. Its author is a former merchant navy captain and ex-head of the Lisbon river pilots' corporation. Although written in Portuguese, it is packed with illustrations, charts, diagrams and photographs, with virtually no aspect of the river omitted. Topics as diverse as navigational signal codes and radio frequencies, locations of sunken hazards and submarine cables are treated. Whilst it is of greatest practical value to professional and amateur users of the river, its profusion of illustrative material makes it accessible to the general reader.

134 **O Tejo.** (The Tagus.) Mário Pires. Lisbon: Câmara Municipal de Lisboa, [1965]. 41p.

An introduction, with text in English, French and German, as well as Portuguese, to the River Tagus at Lisbon. The text is supplemented by twenty pages of photographs, some of which are in colour. A more recent survey of the Lisbon riverside is provided by the Portuguese and English texts of *Lisboa do Tejo: a ribeirinha/ Lisbon: the riverside* by Pedro Brandão and Filipe Jorge (Lisbon: Argumentum, 1996. 60p. maps). This large-format book has abundant colour photographs arranged into ten riverside zones, as well as suggested itineraries and reviews of local bars, discothèques and cultural sights. It also provides details of port activity and of future planning developments.

Backwards out of the big world: a voyage into Portugal.
See item no. 290.

Mist in the Tagus.
See item no. 549.

Bibliografia do rio Tejo: margens e núcleos urbanos ribeirinhos. (Bibliography of the River Tagus: river banks and riverside towns.)
See item no. 684.

Geology

General

135 **On the geology of the neighbourhood of Lisbon.**
Daniel Sharpe. *Geological Society Transactions*, 2nd series, vol. VI
(1842), p. 107-33. map.

An expanded version of the author's paper on the geology of Lisbon published in the same journal in 1832. Here, he provides a detailed description of the geology of the Lisbon area, largely derived from personal explorations. The text is accompanied by thirteen coloured cross-sections of the countryside in and around Lisbon, clearly showing the rock formations in each case. Particularly fascinating is his description of the gold workings in the Tagus sands at Adiça and the parallel drawn between the sulphurous beds of Estoril and those of Caldas da Rainha, to which he attributes both towns' status as health resorts. An appendix addresses the 1755 Lisbon earthquake in which the author's own observations in Lisbon, including his inspection under drain covers, lead him to conclude that virtually all of the structural damage occurred in those lower streets of the city which were built on blue clay.

Earthquakes

136 **Le tremblement de terre de la vallée du Tage du 23 avril 1909.**
Note préliminaire. (The Tagus valley earthquake of 23rd April, 1909.
Preliminary note.)
Alfredo Bensaude. Lisbon: Librairie Ferin, 1909. 129p. 2 maps.

Although the 1755 earthquake was the worst to hit Lisbon, as recently as 1909, twenty-seven people were killed in the Tagus valley by a substantial earth movement.

The effects were felt in Lisbon, but the worst damage was in Benavente, some 25km to the north-west. This offprint (from the *Bulletin de la Société Portugaise des Sciences Naturelles*, volume IV) includes photographs of collapsed and damaged buildings as well as mathematical calculations of the earthquake's force and origins.

137 **Voltaire et le désastre de Lisbonne; ou, La mort de l'optimisme.**
(Voltaire and the Lisbon disaster; or, The death of optimism.)
Théodore Besterman. *Studies in Voltaire and the Eighteenth Century*,
vol. II (1956), p. 7-24.

The text comprises a lecture given in 1955 at the University of Geneva to mark the bicentenary of the Lisbon earthquake. Given the relative frequency of earthquakes in the 18th century, Besterman seeks to explain why the Lisbon disaster was so important. In response to the earthquake, Voltaire penned his *Poème sur le désastre de Lisbonne* (Poem on the Lisbon disaster), which went through twenty printings in 1756, its year of first publication. Besterman sees in this the end of its author's more optimistic phase.

138 **The history and philosophy of earthquakes from the remotest to the present times collected by the best writers on the subject, with a particular account of the phaenomena of the great one of November the 1st 1755 in various parts of the globe. By a Member of the Royal Academy of Berlin.**
John Bevis. London: J. Nourse, 1757. 351p.

The closing chapter of this treatise, 'Phaenomena of the great earthquake of November 1, 1755, in various parts of the globe' (p. 280-334), is a directory, arranged by country and then alphabetically by place, of the recorded effects of the Lisbon earthquake. As such it helps to explain why the Lisbon earthquake had such an impact on science, philosophy and literature across Europe.

139 **Some contemporary reactions to the Lisbon earthquake of 1755.**
C. R. Boxer. *Revista da Faculdade de Letras (Universidade de Lisboa)*, 2nd series, vol. XXII, no. 2 (1956), p. 113-29.

One of two articles by Boxer to commemorate the bicentenary of the Lisbon earthquake. This is the text of a lecture given at King's College, London, in 1955 and relies heavily on the contemporary account of the English Consul, Edward Hay of a disaster which Boxer likens in impact on the world to the Hiroshima atomic bomb of 1945. Boxer corrects a number of exaggerations surrounding the disaster such as the fact that there was no damage to British ships in the Tagus and also points out that a good harvest before the earthquake and fine weather afterwards lessened its potential effect. Boxer's other bicentennial contribution, 'Pombal's dictatorship and the Great Lisbon Earthquake' (*History Today*, vol. V, no. 11 [November 1955], p. 729-36), furnishes biographical details of the Marquis of Pombal, including his period as Portuguese envoy in London before his supervision of the recovery efforts following the earthquake made his name famous abroad. Boxer also notes that in response to the loss of seventy-eight of its own citizens in the earthquake, Britain gave the enormous sum of £100,000 to the Portuguese programme of recovery.

140   **Disaster at Lisbon: the great earthquake of 1755.**
      Charles B. Brooks.   Long Beach, California: Shangton Longley Press,
      1994. 263p. maps. bibliog.

A thorough, modern reassessment of the Lisbon earthquake which destroyed the
centre of the city in 1755. An extensive bibliography makes this a particularly useful
source.

141   **The 'demonic' earthquake: Goethe's myth of the Lisbon
      earthquake and fear of modern change.**
      Robert H. Brown.   *German Studies Review*, vol. XV, no. 3 (1992),
      p. 475-91.

The author sees the Lisbon earthquake in 1755 as Goethe's first experience of the
demonic. He questions Goethe's claim that the event caused him to experience
prolonged doubt of God's providence, not least because Goethe was only six at the
time of the disaster. The writer's claims for the effect of the cataclysm upon him were
thus somewhat exaggerated. A surviving account by Goethe's mother supports
Brown's hypothesis that it was the adult Goethe's fear of disorder and instability
which led him to magnify the true effect on him of the earthquake.

142   **The earthquake at Lisbon: a letter from a survivor, 1755.**
      Mr Chace, edited by Rev. P. H. Ditchfield.   *Cornhill Magazine*,
      series III, vol. XXVIII (1910), p. 705-15.

An abridged edition of a manuscript account of the Lisbon earthquake, written in June
1756, by an Englishman who was injured in the disaster. The building he was in was
damaged and he took refuge with a German resident of the city. After recounting his
own experiences, Chace gives a general description of the disaster pieced together
from his own observations and those of others.

143   **Great earthquakes, with 122 illustrations.**
      Charles Davison.   London: Thomas Murby, 1936. 286p. 14 maps.
      bibliog.

The opening chapter (p. 1-28) of this book covers the 1755 earthquake in Lisbon in
considerable detail, as a prelude to the description of fifteen other major earth
movements up to 1931. Davison illustrates how the Lisbon event was momentous
because of its duration (its first shock lasted five to seven minutes), its estimated toll
of up to 60,000 lives and the fact it was 'the first such event to be investigated on
modern scientific lines', thanks to Pombal's survey of the effects on Lisbon parishes
carried out soon after the disaster. Many instances of the actual and alleged effects of
the Lisbon earthquake on other parts of Europe and beyond are recorded. Sixteen
earthquakes in Lisbon between the years 1009 and 1915 are also chronicled here.

144   **Gentleman's Magazine and Historical Chronicle for the Year
      MDCCLV. Edited by Sylvanus Urban.**
      London: D. Henry & R. Cave, 1755. Vol. XXV ⌐5p.; vol. XXVI, 626p.

News of the Lisbon earthquake of 1 November is given in an entry dated 29
November 1755 (p. 521). This report claims that 100,000 were buried by the disaster
and that fires were caused by 'flames which issued from the bowels of the earth'. In

the December issue of the magazine, there are several substantial accounts (p. 554-62) from eyewitnesses, together with a general description of the city before the disaster. The witnesses quoted include Abraham Castres, the British envoy extraordinary in Lisbon, who recorded the actions taken to reorganize the English Factory, as well as describing the disaster. Four other accounts are given by eyewitnesses. In a Supplement to the *Magazine*, there are updates on the aftermath of the earthquake and further eyewitness accounts of the original and subsequent, lesser, earthquakes. The 1756 volume contains further accounts (p. 7-8, 67-72, 99-100).

145 Voltaire, Rousseau and the Lisbon earthquake.

Rita Goldberg. *Eighteenth Century Life*, vol. 13, new series 2 (1989), p. 1-20.

Following the Lisbon earthquake of 1 November 1755, Voltaire rapidly wrote his *Poème sur le désastre de Lisbonne* (Poem on the Lisbon disaster) at the end of the same month. Goldberg shows how the disaster caused Voltaire to question the optimistic view of the world as a benevolently organized unity. She argues that Voltaire here depicted the physical suffering of the victims of the earthquake rather than concentrating on the compassionate response of witnesses to such disasters, as was the case with Rousseau and other contemporary writers.

146 The Lisbon earthquake.

T. D. Kendrick. London: Methuen & Co., 1956. 170p. 2 maps. bibliog.

Written in the bicentennial year of the 1755 earthquake, this book concentrates on the 'earthquake theology and the end of optimism' engendered by the disaster, rather than on a minute investigation of the event itself. Nevertheless, much detail does emerge, not least that the damage by the subsequent fire caused more damage than the earthquake itself. Kendrick's references to minor earthquakes in London (1750) and Manchester (1777) underline how the Lisbon disaster had a striking relevance to the god-fearing population of Great Britain.

147 Letter from Mr J. Latham dated at Zsusqueira Dec. 11, 1755.

J. Latham. *Philosophical Transactions of the Royal Society*, vol. XLIX (1755), p. 411-13.

Latham had an unusual perspective on the earthquake as he was on board a ship on the Tagus at the time and saw the effect of the disaster simultaneously over a wide area of Lisbon. After landing near Lisbon, he also witnessed the tidal wave. He estimated the death toll at 60,000 and noted that 'the greatest factory, belonging to Great Britain was ruined in 24 hours'.

148 Principles of geology.

Charles Lyell. London: John Murray, 1834. 2 vols.

Volume II of this textbook contains a section on major earthquakes, including that at Lisbon in 1755. Lyell repeats a number of the more dramatic and fanciful accounts of the disaster. In most of these cases he attempts to adopt a rational explanation for such alleged phenomena as electric flames emanating from nearby mountains and volcano-like smoke being emitted from the hilltops around Lisbon. He also relays reports of the effect of the Lisbon disaster in other parts of Europe.

149 **Conjectures concerning the cause, and observations upon the phaenomena of earthquakes; particularly of that great earthquake of the first of November, 1755, which proved so fatal to the city of Lisbon, and whose effects were felt as far as Africa, and more or less throughout all Europe.**
Rev. John Michell. *Philosophical Transactions of the Royal Society,* vol. LI (1760), p. 566-634.

Michell attempts to address the earthquake in Lisbon from the scientific viewpoint of examining the evidence. He refutes the traditional view that the causes of earthquakes could be found in the preceding weather conditions and instead asserts that their origins are subterranean. However, he believed the cause to be underground fires which, when in contact with water, emitted a vapour which produced the 'elastic force' of an earthquake.

150 **O terramoto de 1755: testemunhos britânicos. The Lisbon earthquake of 1755. British accounts.**
Judite Nozes, Maria Leonor Machado de Sousa. Lisbon: Lisóptima Edições for the British Historical Society of Portugal, 1990. 277p.

A landscape-format anthology of parallel texts, in Portuguese and English, of contemporary accounts of the Lisbon earthquake of 1755. Eleven accounts are given from such contemporary sources as *The Gentleman's Magazine* (q.v.), and each is accompanied by appropriate prints from other sources. All of the texts originate in items to be found in the British Library, Public Record Office or the Henley family archives.

151 **The great earthquake at Lisbon.**
E. J. Pereira. *Transactions of the Seismological Society of Japan,* vol. XII (1888), p. 5-19.

The bulk of this paper, delivered in 1887, is an English translation of a rare pamphlet published in 1756 in Lisbon and here entitled *A new and faithful account of the earthquake experienced in Lisbon and over Portugal on the 1st of November, 1755.* The text is followed by discussions by members of the Society. The 1756 pamphlet is more scientific in its approach than most other contemporary accounts. It suggests that late tides presage such disasters and asserts that there is a temporal rhythm in their occurrence, based on the fact that major disasters occurred in 1309, 1531 and 1755. The author therefore predicts a major earthquake between 1977 and 1985. A list of Lisbon earthquakes between 1309 and 1755 is also provided.

152 **The Lisbon earthquake of November 1, 1755.**
Harry Fielding Reid. *The Bulletin of the Seismological Society of America,* vol. IV, no. 2 (June 1914), p. 53-80. map.

The author sees the Lisbon disaster as 'the most notable earthquake in history'. He seeks 'to correct some very exaggerated traditions and to apply our present knowledge of earthquakes to some phenomena not heretofore explained'. Reid surveys worldwide reports of geological, maritime and freshwater effects attributed to the Lisbon earth movement. The latter part of this thorough assessment includes some technical calculations but otherwise the article is eminently suitable for the general reader.

153 **Kant's theory of earthquakes and volcanic action.**
O. Reinhardt, D. R. Oldroyd. *Annals of Science*, vol. 40, no. 3 (1983), p. 247-72.

The authors present partial translations of several articles by Immanuel Kant on seismology, which derived from his interest in the Lisbon earthquake of 1755. Kant rejected the contemporary theory that earthquakes might originate in the gravitational pull of heavenly bodies and asserted, instead, his belief that volcanic eruptions arising from the interaction of sulphur and iron beneath the earth's surface were their cause.

154 **A copy of part of two letters written to Dr De Castro, dated from the Fields of Lisbon on the 7th of November and the 1st of December, 1755.**
John Mendes Saccheti. *Philosophical Transactions of the Royal Society*, vol. XLIX (1755), p. 409-11.

Saccheti set out to provide an authoritative account of the earthquake for members of the Portuguese nobility. Typically for the era he drew a connection between the weather conditions before the disaster and the earth movement itself. His studied approach contrasts with an accompanying report, *Observations made at Colares on the earthquake at Lisbon, of the 1st of November, 1755,* by 'Mr' Stoqueler, the consul of Hamburg at Lisbon (p. 413-18). Stoqueler gives a fanciful account of his observations of the Lisbon earthquake from his vantage point at Colares, where he allegedly saw flames issuing from the side of mountains and black smoke being emitted from the hillsides for several days after the event.

155 **The Scots Magazine.**
Vol. XVII (1755). Edinburgh: Sands, Donaldson, Murray and Cochran, 1755.

The November 1755 issue has extensive coverage of the Lisbon earthquake (p. 552-63 in double columns), and its record of British responses is particularly informative. This includes the reaction of both the House of Commons and of King George II, as well as a report of the account sent back to Britain by Sir Benjamin Keene from the British Embassy in Madrid. As well as granting the huge sum of £100,000 for emergency relief, the Royal Navy's man-of-war *Hampton Court* was promptly despatched with £50,000 worth of 'specie' and provisions. The 1756 issues of the magazine (especially those of January and February) include eyewitness accounts and updates of the destruction and rebuilding plans in Lisbon. They also provide a full description of the trial and execution of a number of English sailors for plundering silver plate from the earthquake ruins.

156 **Poem upon the Lisbon disaster, Poème sur le désastre de Lisbonne; ou, l'examen de cet axiome 'tout est bien'.** (Poem upon the Lisbon disaster; or, The study of that axiom 'all is well'.)
François Marie Arouet de Voltaire, translated into English by Anthony Hecht. Lincoln, Massachusetts: Penmaen Press, 1977. 33p.

A high-quality edition of Voltaire's famous poem on the Lisbon earthquake. This English version is illustrated by six wood engravings by Lynd Ward.

157 **Serious thoughts occasioned by the earthquake at Lisbon to which is subjoin'd An account of all the late earthquakes there and in other places.**
John Wesley. London, 1756. 6th ed. 36p.

As well as seeing the 1755 earthquake as a form of divine retribution for man's follies, Wesley cites a series of supposed related earthquakes in England and of alleged effects of the Lisbon earthquake around Europe. A postscript includes three eyewitness accounts of the disaster.

158 **A letter from a clergyman at London to the remaining disconsolate inhabitants of Lisbon, occasioned by the late dreadful earthquake and conflagration by which the great and populous city, with many other parts of that late flourishing kingdom, have been laid in ruins, to which is added A faithful account of Mr Archibald B-w-r's motives for quitting his office of secretary to the Court of Inquisition.**
George Whitefield. London: R. Griffiths, 1756. 4th. ed. 32p.

The first eighteen pages of this tract, dated 1 December 1755, concern the Lisbon earthquake. Whitefield, a Calvinistic Methodist, baldly tells the residents of Lisbon that the schism in the Church was 'your fault' and goes on to suggest to them that the divine retribution of the earthquake was prompted by the actions of the Inquisition and by other offences towards God. The second part of the publication discusses the iniquities of the Inquisition at Macerata.

159 **An account of the earthquake at Lisbon, Nov. 1, 1755, in two letters.**
Richard Wolfall. *Philosophical Transactions of the Royal Society*, vol. XLIX (1755), p. 402-07.

Wolfall makes a frequently made connection between the prevailing weather and the Lisbon earthquake, before describing its effects on land and as felt at sea by a ship's captain. Wolfall himself was in the Terreiro do Paço at the time of the disaster and survived uninjured. He estimated the major shock at five to seven minutes duration and counted some twenty-two shocks in all. He describes looting in the wake of the disaster and reports the resulting execution of one hundred offenders, including some English sailors.

Dictator of Portugal: a life of the Marquis of Pombal, 1699-1782.
See item no. 378.

Pombal: paradox of the Enlightenment.
See item no. 383.

Rebuilding the city, Pombal's Lisbon.
See item no. 521.

Pombaline Lisbon and art in the days of the Marquis of Pombal.
See item no. 524.

The reconstruction of Lisbon following the earthquake of 1755: a study in despotic planning.
See item no. 529.

The stone cutter of Lisbon.
See item no. 553.

Lady Good for Nothing.
See item no. 555.

Candide & Zadig.
See item no. 558.

Tourist and Travel Guidebooks

19th century

160   **Spain and Portugal: handbook for travellers.**
Karl Baedeker.   Leipzig, Germany: Karl Baedeker, 1898. 618p. maps.
Sections of this volume cover Lisbon (p. 514-39) and the 'Environs of Lisbon' (p. 539-46). The latter include Cascais, Estoril, Cacilhas and Sintra. Whilst the practical details of sights, accommodation, food, prices and transport around Lisbon were invaluable to the 19th-century visitor, today this guide provides a fascinating illustration of Lisbon in the 1890s. A thorough index makes reference easy and excellent maps show the city as it was at the turn of the century.

161   **The Lisbon guide, containing directions to invalids who visit Lisbon, with a description of the city and tables of the coin, weights and measures of Portugal.**
London: for J. Johnson by J. Crowder, 1800. 68p.
An idiosyncratic guide to Lisbon which includes the curious advice that visitors should take with them soap, butter, potatoes and fish sauce to Lisbon, as these commodities were in short supply there. Much detail of English lodging houses in Lisbon and local prices for hiring servants is provided, as is information on the bureaucratic process of obtaining a passport in Lisbon to allow travel outside the city. Although in its streets 'misery and filth meet the eye in every disgusting shape', Lisbon's opera is judged superior to London's. The sights of Belém and Cascais are included, as well as those of Lisbon itself. Despite its subtitle, there is little specific guidance for invalids other than brief information on curative baths.

162 **The Lisbon guide; or, An historical and descriptive view of the city of Lisbon and its environs, with notices of the chief places of interest in Portuguese Estremadura.**
Lisbon: Printed by António Joaquim de Paula, 1853. 348p.
One of the earliest extensive guides for the visitor to Lisbon which is not an opinionated travelogue. Following a long historical introduction (p. 1-61), a thorough and objective description of virtually every conceivable aspect of Lisbon is given. Inhabitants, from royalty and nobility downwards, are described, as are manners, customs, notable buildings and the city's institutions. Typical of the work's thoroughness is the detailed account of the activities of the Lisbon Medical Board. The author concedes that work is still required to improve the city's hygiene and he also expresses reservations at the 'fearful elevation' of the buildings in the Baixa, given that they are in an earthquake zone. Amongst the neighbouring towns also described here are Sintra, Arrábida and Tróia.

163 **A guide to Lisbon and its environs, including Cintra and Mafra, with a large plan of Lisbon.**
Joaquim António de Macedo. London: Simpkin, Marshall & Co.; Lisbon: Matthew Lewtas, 1874. 324p. map.
Macedo's work is an enormous advance in organization, comprehensiveness and detail over Lisbon guides of the first half of the 19th century. The text is split into three sections of preliminary, descriptive and supplementary information, completed by a good index and an enormous, gridded and folding map of the entire Lisbon city area. The preliminary section covers practical matters of arrival formalities, accommodation, finance and eating places. The descriptive chapter is sub-arranged into categories including squares, churches and convents, palaces, public amusements, libraries and even prisons. It covers Sintra and Mafra, as well as Lisbon, and includes a wealth of historical detail. The final supplementary section addresses topics such as royalty, nobility, communications, money, weights and measures.

164 **Handbook for travellers in Portugal, with a travelling map.**
John M. Neale. London: John Murray, 1855. 190p. map. bibliog.
Reverend Neale's book set a new standard in English-language travel guides to Portugal in its detail, organization and authoritativeness. The depth of Neale's researches is exemplified by his inclusion of even Scandinavian texts in his bibliography and in his prodigious English-Portuguese vocabulary of horse ailments and other useful phrases for visitors. He is equally thorough in his detail of how to obtain a residential or short-stay permit from the combined bureaucratic processes of the Lisbon Customs, the Civil Government and the British consul. As well as purveying information on Lisbon and its neighbourhood in the opening section of the book (p. 1-34), he also describes forty-seven itineraries for travellers in Portugal, including seventeen which start from Lisbon.

165   **The stranger's guide in Lisbon; or, An historical and descriptive**
view of the city of Lisbon and its environs, with notices of the chief
places of interest in Estremadura.
Lisbon: printed by A. J. P., 1848. 364p.

A pocket guide written for British visitors to Lisbon which, in addition, covers not only the well-trodden tourist paths to Sintra, Queluz and Benfica, but also less common suburban destinations such as Caxias, Paço de Arcos, Carcavelos, Odivelas and, across the Tagus, Trafaria. Historical information on Lisbon includes the assertion that the post-earthquake fires in 1755 were started by looters and that the cost of the disaster to Britain alone was £6.4 million. Statistics of shipping movements and other factual details are included alongside information on Lisbon customs and street life. An index would have been a useful adjunct to this fascinating pot-pourri of information.

20th century

166   **Lisboa.** (Lisbon.)
José Víctor Adragão, Natália Pinto, Rui Rasquilho.   Lisboa: Presença,
1985. 2nd ed. 208p. bibliog. (Novos Guias de Portugal).

A thorough guide to Lisbon, packed with colour plates which make it a useful introduction to modern-day Lisbon, even to the non-Portuguese reader. An index of buildings and areas of the city is included.

167   **Your guide, Lisboa.**
Aeroportos e Navegação Aérea.   Lisbon: Aeroportos e Navegação
Aérea, 1996. 105p. 4 maps.

A useful bilingual (English and Portuguese) pocket guide to Lisbon created by A. N. A., the Portuguese airports' authority. Its coverage includes the Cascais area and Sintra, and even places as far afield as Coimbra and Évora. Suggested tourist itineraries and extensive lists of museums, galleries and eating places are given. The entries include addresses and, for public buildings, their opening times and admission charges. Colour photographs of major sights are also included.

168   **All Lisbon and its surroundings.**
Barcelona, Spain: Editorial Escudo de Oro, 1995. 15th ed. 90p.
(Collection All Europe).

The English-language version of a guide produced in a number of European languages. It is aimed clearly at the short-stay tourist market and, with its excellent colour photographs of Lisbon and its environs, provides a more than adequate introduction to the city.

169   **A.A. Baedeker Lisbon.**
Automobile Association, original text by Eva Missler, English edition
by Alec Court.   Basingstoke, England: Automobile Association, 1996.
2nd English ed. 218p. maps.

Colour photographs and even floorplans of such sights as the Jerónimos monastery
and the Museu da Arte Antiga make this an attractive guide to the city which is useful
to car-driving and pedestrian visitors alike. It is easy to use as headings for the
individual sights and public transport details are given in the margins of each page,
making places easy to locate. The first of the three parts of the book covers nature,
culture and history, and the other two comprise alphabetical sections on city sights and
practical information. A large and clear, colour map (scale 1:16,000) is included in a
pocket attached to the book. This is a companion to the *A.A. Baedeker Portugal*
(Basingstoke, England: Automobile Association, 1993. 3rd English ed. 414p. maps.),
a volume which itself has a useful section on Lisbon (p. 209-31). In late 1997 the
same publisher expects to produce the *A.A. City Pack: Lisbon* (Basingstoke, England:
Automobile Association, 1997. 96p. maps).

170   **Pousadas of Portugal: unique lodgings in state-owned castles,
palaces, mansions and hotels.**
Sam Ballard, Jane Ballard.   Ashbourne, England: Moorland
Publishing, 1986. 173p. 53 maps.

Published in pocket-size format, originally for a wealthy North American readership,
this guide provides details of forty-two private and state-run hotels (*pousadas*),
including three in the Lisbon area. However, it is the latter part of the book, which
details thirteen suggested motoring itineraries, all of which either start, finish or pass
through Lisbon, which will be of at least equal interest to the visitor to the capital.
Maps are provided for each journey and for the location of the *pousadas* and the
hotels. There are also black-and-white photographs of most of the *pousadas*.

171   **Um passeio por Lisboa. A walk in Lisbon.**
António Alçada Baptista, Luís Filipe Cândido de Oliveira, Susan
Lowndes Marques, Rui Viana Pereira.   Lisbon: Direcção de Relações
Internacionais e Filatelia; Correios e Telecomunicações de Portugal,
1989. 48p.

A richly illustrated celebration of Lisbon, presented in the form of a city walk, which
is described in both English and Portuguese.

172   **The selective traveller in Portugal.**
Ann Bridge [pseudonym for Mary Dolling, Lady O'Malley], Susan
Lowndes.   London: Chatto & Windus, 1967. new, revised ed. 292p.
2 maps. bibliog.

First published in 1949, this new edition is an exceptionally well-informed and factual
description of the country. The book describes sights in the suburbs and outskirts of
Lisbon, such as Cruz Quebrada, Caxias and Oeiras, which are not normally covered in
English-language guides. In all, three chapters cover the Lisbon area (p. 40-89).
Black-and-white photographs, an appendix of practical information about life in
Portugal and a useful bibliography add to the volume's value.

173 **Portugal.**
Martha de la Cal. London: Collins, 1988. 347p. 10 maps. (Collins Independent Travellers' Guide).
Lisbon and its environs (Sintra, Cascais, Estoril, Carcavelos, Queluz) occupy nearly forty pages (p. 228-65) of this volume. Although a map and details are given of accommodation, entertainment, cuisine, shopping and transport in Lisbon, it is the twelve pages on the history of the city which mark out this guide from others. The use of a separate column for headings and sub-headings make entries particularly easy to locate.

174 **Portugal.**
Gabriel Calvo, Sabine Tzschaschel. Munich, Germany: Nelles Verlag, 1996. 254p. 14 maps. (Nelles Guide).
Very attractive colour photographs and exceptionally detailed maps make this recent addition to English-language tourist guides to Portugal particularly appealing. A chapter entitled 'Lisbon: the white city' (p. 39-64) covers the major sights and facilities for visitors. These are presented in separate sections which include city districts, museums, churches, gardens and suburbs. Both Belém and Queluz are covered, as well as Lisbon itself.

175 **Cook's Portugal: Lisbon and the Lisbon coast.**
Frank Cook, edited by Jorge Santos, Fernando C. Correia. Lisbon: Frank Cook, 1994. 18th ed. 93p. maps. (Cook's Guides).
A glossy pocket-size guide to the Lisbon area for English-speaking tourists which, because it appears on an annual basis and is produced in Portugal, can generally be relied upon to be up-to-date in the information it conveys. It is attractively produced and its many large-scale colour maps are a particularly useful feature. These cover both Lisbon and its environs, including towns across the Tagus. Details of tourist sights, shops, transport, food, accommodation and other practical aspects of any visit to Lisbon are all included.

176 **Walking in Portugal.**
Bethan Davies, Ben Cole. London: Footprint Guides, 1994. 208p. maps. (A Footprint Guide).
In this guide to walking in Portugal, there is a section dedicated to Lisbon (p. 63-74) as well as separate information on the city in sections of practical information such as 'Getting there'. The city is seen primarily as a base in which to purchase maps, supplies and equipment and information is given on sources for such walking aids in Lisbon. There is also brief information on accommodation and tourist sights in the city.

177 **Lisbon.**
Gudrun Decker, Alexander Decker. Singapore: APA, 1995. 96p. 5 maps. (Insight Compact Guides).
An authoritative and attractive companion to the main Insight City and Pocket Guides (see item nos. 187 and 191), which is only marred by a few misspellings of Portuguese names. The book is divided into sections on places, culture, leisure and practical information, and is enhanced by a multitude of generally small, but high quality,

colour photographs. The main section is arranged into six itineraries around the city and six suggested excursions out of Lisbon.

178 **Lisbon, mostly on foot.**
De Moura, Cláudia Conduto, Kathleen Joan Taylor.   Lisbon: Pergaminho, 1995. 144p.

Loosely based on walks through Lisbon, this is an English version of De Moura's Portuguese work, *Passeando em Lisboa*. It is distinguished by his artistic drawings of the city's sights and scenes.

179 **Portugal: the rough guide.**
Mark Ellingham, John Fisher, Graham Kenyon, updated by Matthew Hancock, Jules Brown, Jens Finke.   London: Rough Guide, 1996. 7th ed. 499p. maps. bibliog.

This work contains a lengthy section (p. 45-123) on Lisbon and its environs. Details are given of hotels, restaurants, sights and transport, with guidance as to cost, and ten maps are included. An opening chapter gives practical information on Portuguese custom and practice, whilst a closing section, 'Contexts', furnishes historical, artistic and cultural information. There is a particularly useful English-language bibliography for the reader wishing to become acquainted with Portuguese culture. Also aimed at the independent traveller is *Portugal* by Julia Wilkinson and John King (Hawthorn, Australia: Lonely Planet, 1997. 498p. maps), which has an extensive section on Lisbon (p. 129-201) accompanied by a small number of colour photographs and thirteen maps of the city and its environs. It is packed with practical information but its maps lack the names of many of the streets they depict.

180 **Cook's traveller's handbook to Spain & Portugal.**
Roy Elston.   London: Simpkin, Marshall Ltd., 1930. new ed. 656p. 36 maps.

Modelled on the old Baedeker format of sections of factual detail in smaller print than the main descriptive text, this is a comprehensive guide to Iberia. Lisbon and its hinterland are specifically covered (p. 504-37) but there are also itineraries of journeys from Lisbon to Leiria, Coimbra, Oporto and Badajoz elsewhere in the volume. As well as details of Lisbon's tourist sights, information is also provided on accommodation, transport and other practical matters. An excellent two-page colour map of Lisbon supports the text.

181 **Portugal.**
David J. J. Evans, revised by Kamin Mohammadi.   London: Cadogan Books, 1995. 3rd rev. ed. 468p. maps. bibliog. (Cadogan Guides).

Written in a somewhat literary style, this guide, illustrated by a small number of drawings, devotes more than forty pages of text to Lisbon (p. 289-330) and its environs. A brief history of Lisbon precedes eleven sections on different districts of the city and one entitled 'Across the River'. The book is particularly useful in its attention to practical details including the budget-end of the accommodation market in Lisbon.

182   **Hotels of character and charm in Portugal.**
Michelle Gastaut, Fabrice Camoin.   New York: Fodor's Travel
Publications, 1996. 125p. 6 maps.
A guide to those hotels in Portugal which the authors feel remain untouched by mass
tourism. These include eight hotels in Lisbon itself, such as the Hotel Metrópole,
Hotel Janelas Verdes and York House, a favourite haunt of British visitors. More than
twice this number are listed in the environs of Lisbon, in towns such as Sintra and
Estoril. Each hotel is represented by a colour photograph and a text which comprises
factual information as to its location and facilities, followed by a short assessment of
its major features. Detailed road maps are provided to assist in locating the hotels.

183   **Goldenbook of Lisbon.**
Lisbon: Vilela & Figueiredo/Interpropo, 1988- . annual.
A glossy, large-format, hardback book, often left for the consultation of guests in the
more up-market hotel rooms of Lisbon. It has many colour photographs and
descriptions of the main tourist sights of the city, interspersed with advertising matter.
Revised and reissued every December, its target audience is affluent tourists and
business people.

184   **Discover Portugal.**
Martin Gostelow.   Oxford: Berlitz, 1996. 351p.
Lisbon is covered in some depth (p. 91-120) in this attractive guide which has many
colour pictures and useful information about the city's sights. There is also abundant
practical advice on getting around the city, as well as sections on Portuguese history
and geography. The adjoining coastal area is covered (p. 121-45).

185   **Lisbon.**
Martin Gostelow.   Oxford: Berlitz, 1996. 144p. 4 maps. (Berlitz
Pocket Guides).
A full colour pocket-sized guide to the Portuguese capital, published for the first time
in 1996. Folding maps inside the covers make the volume easy to use. The text is
divided into sections on 'Lisbon and the Lisboêtas', 'A brief history', 'What to see',
'A selection of hotels and restaurants', 'What to do', 'Eating out' and 'Blueprint for a
perfect trip'. This last section is an alphabetical section of practical information on
themes such as 'Money matters'. An index is also provided.

186   **The complete guide to Portugal.**
Gordon M. Graham, Alec Israel.   London: George Philip, 1972. 172p.
2 maps.
Lisbon occupies a substantial portion (p. 31-78) of this down-to-earth precursor to
guides such as those in the Rough Guides Series (see item no. 179). Packed with
practical information and opinions on individual hotels and eating places, it also gives
details of prices for such transactions as dry-cleaning, laundry, haircuts and bus rides.
It now forms a record of Lisbon life in the immediate run-up to the 1974 Revolution.
A separate section (p. 79-94) covers the environs of Lisbon, including the towns
towards Cascais and Sintra. Colour and black-and-white photographs show everyday
scenes as well as the tourist sights.

187 **Lisbon.**
Edited by Alison Friesinger Hill; photographs by Tony Arruza; revised by Roger Williams; editorial director, Brian Bell. Singapore: APA Publications, 1995. new ed. 207p. 5 maps. bibliog. (Insight Guides, Portugal Series).

The most comprehensive and attractive current English-language tourist guide devoted solely to the Lisbon area, this Insight Guide follows the normal series format. Thus there are essays, by various authors, on different aspects of the city's history, people and places, along with practical travel tips and recommended further reading. In spite of a number of Portuguese spelling errors, the text is generally comprehensive and authoritative. It is aimed primarily at a North American audience. The dozens of superb colour photographs of Lisbon and its environs are, however, the most alluring feature of this publication.

188 **Portugal.**
Edited by Alison Friesinger Hill, update editor, Marion Kaplan, photographs by Tony Arruza. Singapore: APA Publications, [1996]. new ed. 365p. 8 maps. bibliog. (Insight Guides).

The Lisbon section of this quality tourist guide (p. 165-83) is by Marvine Howe, a *New York Times* reporter, and further sections are to be found on Cascais, Estoril and Sintra (p. 184-93). The book, aimed primarily at North American visitors, is liberally illustrated with high-quality colour photographs of Lisbon and a double-page map of the city. A final section lists hotels in the capital and gives practical information on such topics as shopping, museums and sport.

189 **Fielding's Portugal: the most in-depth guide to the intimate charms of Portugal.**
A. Hoyt Hobbs, Joy Azidgian. Redondo Beach, California: Fielding Worldwide, 1995. 360p. maps.

Lisbon and its environs, including Cascais and Sintra, are covered in depth (p. 85-160) in this guide for North American readers. Surprisingly for a contemporary guide, it carries no illustrations. The text prides itself on being entertaining and is particularly strong on accommodation detail, but prices are given in dollars only.

190 **Lisboa 94 always: roteiro/guide.**
Edited by Jorge M. Laureano Jacinto. Lisbon: Produce, 1994. 254p.

Despite its unclear layout and lack of an index, this large-format volume is a mine of practical information on Lisbon, with sections on museums, bars, clubs, architecture and many other aspects of the city's life. The selection of subjects and of topics within each section is somewhat idiosyncratic but useful information on how to get to each location by public transport is given. The text is given in English and Portuguese and is accompanied by monochrome photographs, albeit of indifferent quality, printed on low-grade paper.

191 **Lisbon.**
Written and presented by Marion Kaplan. Singapore: APA
Publications, 1993. 89p. maps. bibliog. (Insight Pocket Guides).
The middle size of the three formats of Lisbon guide in the Insight Guides Series (see
item nos. 177 and 187). It shares their striking use of colour photographs, but has a
completely original text. After a substantial history of Lisbon, the main section
comprises three full-day and ten half-day itineraries for visitors which explore the city
itself but also assume the use of a car to venture as far afield as Mafra, Queluz,
Cascais, Sintra and Setúbal. A section on practical information, covering such matters
as transport, accommodation and local custom, completes the book.

192 **Portugal.**
Michael Khorian, photographs by Bruno Barbier, Nik Wheeler.
Ashbourne, England: Moorland Publishing Co., 1995. 269p. 10 maps.
(The Insider's Guides).
A wealth of sharply-focused colour photographs of Lisbon and the rest of Portugal are the
cornerstone of this tourist guide. The first part of the text consists of brief reviews of
suggested 'top spots' for visitors to Portugal, written in informal style, with alliterative
titles such as 'Trundle on the trams' and 'Marvel at the Manueline'. Following a short
history of Portugal, Lisbon and its environs are covered (p. 108-45). All the major sights
are described and there are sections on accommodation, cuisine and shopping. A useful
colour map of the whole area from Belém to eastern Lisbon completes the section.

193 **Portugal.**
T. J. Kubiak. New York: Hippocrene Books, 1989. 260p. maps.
(Hippocrene Companion Guide).
Chapter thirteen of this tourist guide for North Americans covers Lisbon (p. 223-52).
Written as a narrative rather than as a compilation of short entries on individual sights,
the text is accompanied by indifferent black-and-white maps.

194 **Portugal: a traveller's guide.**
Susan Lowndes. London: Thornton Cox, 1989. 3rd ed. 184p. 5 maps.
The third edition of a work first produced in 1982, this book has the advantage over
many travel guides of being written by someone who has lived for many years in the
country in question. Lisbon and its environs are amply covered (p. 29-57) and two of
the book's five maps and several of its colour photographs are of the area. It is
unusually strong on information about Anglo-American residents' organizations in
Lisbon, such as the Royal British Club, British Institute, American Women of Lisbon
and the American Library, although its main emphasis is necessarily on the tourist
sights and museums. Brief details of accommodation in Lisbon and the surrounding
area are also provided.

195 **Lisbon, Sintra, Queluz, Cascais, Estoril.**
Giovanna Magi. Florence, Italy: Bonechi, 1995. 60p.
An attractive English-language edition of a guide to Lisbon and its environs which is
published in several languages. It is copiously illustrated by good quality colour
photographs. Unashamedly aimed at the tourist market, the text is informative but
somewhat uncritical in tone.

196 **Visitor's guide, Portugal.**
Barbara Mandell. Ashbourne, England: MPC, 1996. 2nd revised and
updated ed. 240p. 6 maps. (Moorland Travel Guide).
The main section of this attractive guide divides Portugal into six parts, of which one
comprises the Lisbon and Costa de Lisboa area (p. 108-44). The tourist sights are
illustrated by high-quality colour photographs and clear colour maps. The text is
written as a continuous narrative but consultation is aided by an innovative use of
symbols for each type of tourist sight (e.g. museums) in the margin of each page,
adjacent to the relevant piece of text. An alphabetical 'fact file' completes the volume.

197 **Birnbaum's Portugal.**
Alexandra Mayes. New York: Harper Perennial, 1995. 440p. maps.
There is a substantial section on Lisbon (p. 103-48) in this guide for North American
visitors to Portugal. The city is described in distinct sections dedicated to each of its
geographical areas. These encompass a large number of tourist sights and museums,
whilst lists of restaurants and hotels are also included.

198 **Portugal, Madeira, The Azores.**
Michelin Tyre PLC. Watford, England: Michelin Tyre Public
Limited Company, 1995. 271p. maps. bibliog. (Tourist Guide).
One of the Michelin 'green guide' series. Following detailed information on
Portuguese history, geography, culture, food and traditions, the book is arranged
alphabetically by place-name. The Lisbon section (p. 110-30) includes four colour
maps, accompanied by a brief street index. Most of the many city sights which are
described are grouped into seven timed itineraries arranged by district or theme. A
separate section at the back of the book gives details of opening times of these sights.
Numerous colour photographs accompany the text and short entries are also to be
found on Sintra (p. 169-72), Cascais (p. 71) and Estoril (p. 87).

199 **Lisbon, Cascais, Sintra touristic guide.**
Carlos Nunes, photographs by Paulo Roberto. Lisbon: Sage, 1989.
160p.
A well-illustrated tourist guide to the Lisbon area which is unusual for an English-
language guidebook in that it has been written by a native Portuguese who has a
thorough knowledge of the Lisbon area.

200 **Lisbon and Lisbon coast.**
Orange Guide. Lisbon: Convergência, 1985. 240p. maps.
A tourist guidebook which very clearly follows the model of the traditional Michelin
'green guides' both in physical format and in internal arrangement. Thus, rather than
photographs, line drawings of buildings and monuments are used and in addition to
the description of individual locations, sections on history and culture are included.
The book covers not only the Lisbon side of the Tagus estuary, including the Cascais
area, but also the southern side and such places as Almada.

201   **Lisboa: o que o turista deve ver. Lisbon: what the tourist should see. Edição bilingue.** (Bilingual edition.)
Fernando Pessoa, translated by Maria Amélia Santos Gomes.   Lisbon: Livros Horizonte, 1992. 153p. map.

Pessoa, Portugal's leading 20th-century poet, was brought up in South Africa and was therefore fluent in English. He wrote this guidebook in English and here it is presented in a parallel English and Portuguese edition, derived from a manuscript found in 1987 in the Biblioteca Nacional de Lisboa. It comprises a practical guidebook to Lisbon with two supplements: 'Lisbon newspapers' (p. 140-43); and 'A visit to Cintra via Queluz' (p. 144-53). The work was written around 1925 as part of a planned work entitled *All about Portugal*, which Pessoa never completed.

202   **Unknown Portugal: archaeological itineraries illustrated with photographs by the author.**
Georges Pillement, translated from the original French by Arnold Rosin.   London: Johnson, 1967. 248p. 10 maps.

The subtitle of this translation of the author's *Le Portugal inconnu* is a little misleading in that the book is essentially a series of nine motoring itineraries, visiting historical rather than purely archaeological sites. Five of the journeys either start or terminate in Lisbon. Although the overall emphasis is on places other than Lisbon city centre, the suburbs of Benfica, Queluz, Cascais, Estoril and Sintra are all covered.

203   **Frommer's Portugal: the best of Lisbon and the countryside.**
Dawn J. Porter, Danforth Price.   New York: Macmillan Travel, 1996. 14th ed. 403p. maps.

'What to see and do in Lisbon' is the title of section six of this book (p. 114-54) which is aimed at the North American visitor but which does also include a section on 'Lisbon for British travellers'. Unusually for a modern tourist guide, there are no colour photographs, but clear three-colour maps do support the text. Basic information on the major tourist attractions of Lisbon is furnished, with Estoril, Cascais and Sintra also being covered.

204   **Guia de Portugal, 1: Generalidades, Lisboa e arredores.** (Guide to Portugal, 1: generalities, Lisbon and surrounding area.)
Raúl Proença, introduction and notes by Sant'anna Dionísio.   Lisbon: Fundação Calouste Gulbenkian, 1991. 696p. 15 maps. bibliog.

A reproduction of the original edition of a classic guide, published by the Biblioteca Nacional de Lisboa in 1924. After a lengthy general introduction to Portugal, its history, art, ethnography and transportation, nearly 300 pages cover Lisbon (p. 163-451). Its surrounding area, including Sintra, Estoril, Cascais and Queluz, occupies another large section (p. 453-623). As well as surveying the major buildings and sights of the city, the textual detail extends to guided routes through Lisbon's major museums and even thorough listings of tram routes. Substantial bibliographies of both Portugal and Lisbon are included, as are many photographs and excellent colour maps.

205 **Portugal.**
Marc Rigole, Claude Victor Langlois.   Montreal, Canada: Ulysses
Travel Guides, 1996. 351p. 34 maps.
Lisbon and its surrounding area are covered extensively (p. 57-144) in this tourist guide which is particularly well illustrated by colour photographs and maps. There are sections both on the tourist sights and on getting about the city.

206 **Portugal.**
Ian Robertson.   London: A. & C. Black; New York: W. W. Norton,
1996. 4th ed. 335p. 21 maps. (Blue Guide).
Lisbon is covered at some length (p. 93-141) in this pocket-format guidebook. The well-researched text is largely organized as a series of tours, for which Lisbon is frequently the starting or end point. Unlike most modern tourist guides, this one contains no colour maps or illustrations.

207 **Portugal: a traveller's guide.**
Ian Robertson.   London: John Murray, 1992. 238p. 5 maps.
Seven chapters of this book are dedicated to Lisbon and its environs. After an initial chapter on Lisbon before the earthquake, the remaining coverage of the city is divided into geographical areas, such as 'The Baixa', 'Bairro Alto' and 'Eastern Lisbon'. There is also a chapter on Queluz, Sintra and Mafra. As the information on the Lisbon area is conveyed in a continuous narrative rather than in subheaded sections, the book is best read before travelling rather than as a vade-mecum. The author's knowledge of his subject is underlined by references to the writings of earlier English travellers.

208 **The road to Lisbon.**
Vivian Rowe.   London: Eyre & Spottiswoode, in association with the
B. P. Touring Service, 1962. 207p. 4 maps. (Highways to the Sun).
One of a series of guides for the motorist, this volume recounts a journey from England, via France, Spain and northern Portugal to Lisbon. Chapters fourteen and fifteen (p. 178-95) cover the approach to Lisbon via Torres Vedras, Sintra and Estoril, and the city itself, with visits to Cascais, Estoril, Carcavelos and Oeiras. In Lisbon, the sights of Belém, as well as the Estrela Basilica, the castle and the city centre are all covered.

209 **The New Michael's Lisbon.**
Michael Schichor.   Ramat Gan, Israel: Inbal Travel Information,
1995. 166p. 8 maps.
An attractive colour guide with an introductory section, 'The story of Lisbon', which covers the city's history and gives practical information on aspects such as transport. The second part of the volume provides suggestions of places to visit arranged as a series of walks, and proposes a number of day tours. The text is interspersed with colour photographs to make a visually appealing book.

210 **The charm of Lisbon: a short guide for those who do not know her.**
Secretariado Nacional de Informação.   Lisbon: S. N. I., [1950]. 36p.
map.

Thirty numbered sections on specific buildings and sights in Lisbon, with further
sections on gardens, fountains and other open spaces, comprise the text of this
somewhat fawning description of the city. There are also very brief accounts of
Queluz, Sintra, Estoril and Mafra. A number of brown-tinted photographs and a large
folding map of the whole city area are of a quality which suggests limitations imposed
by postwar austerity conditions. This is, nevertheless, an interesting example of the
Portuguese government's postwar attempts to market Lisbon as a mass tourist
destination.

211 **Living in Portugal.**
Anne de Stoop, translated by Francis Cowper, preface by Mário
Soares, photographs by Jérôme Darblay, assisted by Caroline
Champenois.   Paris; New York: Flammarion, 1995. 255p. bibliog.

Lisbon and its surrounding area occupy a substantial portion (p. 115-76) of this
sumptuously produced colour volume, which avowedly sets out to present the
customs, traditions, culture and natural riches of Portugal. The superb photographs
include many interior shots and exterior close-ups of objects such as washing lines,
rooftops, shop goods and ceramic tiles, which seek to evoke a mood rather provide the
objective pictorial record found in many more tourist-orientated books. The text
provides a wealth of practical information on life in Portugal.

212 **Essential Portugal.**
Martin Symington.   Basingstoke, England: A.A. Publications, 1995.
128p. 8 maps.

A pocket guidebook distinguished by its bright and clear maps and some attractive
colour photography. The author, a member of a port-wine shippers' family, resides in
Portugal and so provides an authoritative text. Lisbon and the Ribatejo area are
covered (p. 45-62) with brief entries on the major tourist attractions, accommodation
and services. The book also includes three maps on the Lisbon area and an
alphabetical section of 'essential information' on Portugal.

213 **Lisbon: historical and tourist guide.**
Aderito Tavares, Walter de Carvalho.   Lisbon: Margrap, 1987. 64p.

A profusely illustrated, large-format tourist guide to Lisbon which benefits from its
authors' firsthand knowledge of the city.

214 **Berlitz travellers' guide to Portugal.**
Alan Tucker, general editor.   New York; Oxford: Berlitz, 1995.
4th ed. 560p. 6 maps.

An especially full guide to Lisbon and its area is provided in this work (p. 45-159).
Unlike many other guides, its explicit aim is to provide 'exceptional information for
the experienced traveller'. This approach is reflected in the fact that, as well as the
customary description of sights and facilities within the city, there is an extensive
guide to trips out from the capital. It is produced in a handy pocket-size format, but it
lacks any illustrations.

215 **Lisbon and its surroundings.**
Pedro de Vasconcelos, photographs by Vasco Saraiva, João Abreu
Mota. Lisbon: Distri, 1985. 63p.

A large-format introduction to Lisbon and the adjacent coast and suburbs which is
richly illustrated by photographs. As an English-language book published in Portugal,
it is clearly aimed at the tourist.

216 **Lisbon: from the Castle to Belém.**
Manuela Pina Vidal. Lisbon: Câmara Municipal de Lisboa Tourist
Department, 1982. 16p.

A collection of three suggested pedestrian itineraries across Lisbon. The first is from
the Praça do Comércio to the Castelo and S. Vicente church. The second is around the
Alfama district and the third is a riverside route from Xabregas, in the east, to Belém,
in the west. Thirty-six colour photographs illustrate the locations described but these
are of a disappointing quality in terms both of faithfulness of colour and of sharpness
of focus.

217 **Portugal.**
Julia Wilkinson, photographs by Steve Vidler. Hong Kong: Odyssey,
1991. 208p. 6 maps.

The cover of this book calls it *Introduction to Portugal*, whilst the title page simply
says *Portugal*. It is generously illustrated by good quality colour photographs. The
text is arranged regionally and the section on Lisbon (p. 66-82) includes information
on getting to, from and around the city. It also embraces sections on the 'old town',
'The heart of the city, the Baixa', 'High town: the Bairro Alto' and on the city's
museums. A clear two-page colour map of Lisbon is also included.

218 **Holiday Portugal.**
Compiled and edited by Katie Wood; research co-ordinator George
McDonald. London: Fontana/Collins, 1988. 378p. 11 maps.

Wood's intended audience is distinct in that it is the reasonably affluent tourist under
forty years of age, rather than wealthy American senior citizens or young backpackers,
whom she feels are well catered for by existing guidebooks. In addition to pervasive
references, twenty pages of the book (p. 246-65) cover the history, sights, hotels and
sources of entertainment in Lisbon and the Estoril coast areas in what the author calls
an 'informal and chatty style'.

219 **The tourist's Spain and Portugal, with numerous illustrations.**
Ruth Kedzie Wood. London: Andrew Melrose, 1914. 2nd ed. 357p.

An early tourist guide, reprinted from the first New York edition of 1913, which
covers Lisbon, Monte Estoril and Sintra (p. 249-74). Factual information on Lisbon
hotels, restaurants, banks and other practical matters is included in a separate final
section of the book. In addition to details of the major tourist sights, Wood also dwells
on street scenes of fishwives, flower-sellers and other vendors in Lisbon.

What's on in Lisbon, Estoril, Sintra, Blue Coast.
See item no. 678.

Travellers' Accounts

General

220 **They went to Portugal.**
Rose Macaulay. Harmondsworth, England: Penguin Books, 1985.
443p. bibliog. (Penguin Travel Library).

First published in 1946 (London: Jonathan Cape), this is probably the best starting-point for any English-speaking reader interested in the history of Lisbon. Its fifteen sections comprise Macaulay's lively renderings of visits to Portugal by Britons from the earliest times to the 19th century, based on written accounts from the 12th century onwards. The sections are grouped under headings which include 'Writers', 'Clergymen', 'Tourists', 'Earthquake', 'Plotters' and 'Ambassadors'. Most of the visitors spent much of their time in Portugal in Lisbon itself and this book is therefore a fascinating account of the city as seen by English-speaking visitors, from many perspectives, over nine centuries.

221 **They went to Portugal too. Papers from Rose Macaulay's original manuscript for** *They went to Portugal*, **omitted when the projected two volume work was published as one volume in 1946, at a time of severe post-war paper rationing, here printed for the first time.**
Rose Macaulay, introduction by Susan Lowndes, edited by L. C. Taylor. Manchester: Carcanet Press in association with Calouste Gulbenkian Foundation, 1990. 338p. map. bibliog. (Aspects of Portugal).

With its companion volume, *They went to Portugal* (q.v.), this is an essential work for anyone interested in the British in Lisbon. Eleven unnumbered chapters, each with its own bibliography, make up this second volume of Macaulay's compilation. Some of the chapters are explicitly about Lisbon, such as 'Medieval traders: merchants in Lisbon' (p. 3-13) and 'Lisbon British, 1750-1815' (p. 140-72). Other chapters have significant Lisbon relevance, not least 'Consuls' (p. 95-139), and Macaulay's Lisbon despatches to *The Spectator* which form the chapter entitled 'A western oasis'. Fourteen photographic plates complement the text, though most of these are relatively conventional portraits, including ones of Sir Francis Drake and Sir Richard Fanshawe.

18th century

222   **A journey from London to Genoa, through England, Portugal, Spain and France.**
Joseph Baretti, introduction by Ian Robertson.   Fontwell, England: Centaur Press, 1970. 2 vols.

A large-format photographic reprint in two volumes of the four-volume English 1770 edition of Baretti's travels from Falmouth to Genoa via Lisbon, a detour enforced by the closure of the Dover to Calais route because of Anglo-French hostilities. The original Italian edition appeared in 1761. Giuseppe Baretti (1719-89), a friend of Dr Johnson and tutor to the Thrale family, reached Lisbon on 30 August 1760. He stayed in the Buenos Aires district, until 17 September, at a house owned by an Irishman. Letters XVIII to XXXII (p. 75-201 of volume one) were all written during his stay in Lisbon and provide a vivid picture of the city as it recovered from the 1755 earthquake. As well as an account of the earthquake, Baretti describes visits to a bullfight, an excursion to Sintra and observations of everyday urban types such as pickpockets and the city's Jews. After Lisbon, he journeyed via Estremoz to Spain and Italy.

223   **Italy, with sketches of Spain and Portugal, by the author of 'Vathek'.**
William Beckford.   London: Richard Bentley, 1834. 2 vols.

In the second volume of this title, written in the form of letters, the wealthy Beckford recounts his departure from Falmouth to Portugal in 1787. Letters VII to XXXIV (p. 23-255) include accounts of Lisbon, Sintra, Colares and Mafra. In Lisbon he encounters 'mobs of old hags, children and ragamuffins' and like many other contemporary visitors remarks on the howling of stray dogs. The sights he visits include the aqueduct in the Alcântara valley, the cathedral and the monastery of Belém. Beckford's original account of his visit is transcribed in *The journal of William Beckford in Portugal and Spain, 1787-1788*, edited by Boyd Alexander (London: Rupert Hart-Davies, 1954. 340p. 2 maps).

224   **Recollections of an excursion to the monasteries of Alcobaça and Batalha, by Wm Beckford with his original journal of 1794.**
William Beckford, introduction and notes by Boyd Alexander.
Fontwell, England: Centaur Press, 1972. 228p.

It was not until 1835 that Beckford published his account of a twelve-day excursion he made whilst in Portugal in 1794. As well as visiting Alcobaça, Batalha and Óbidos, Beckford completed his journey at Queluz, near Lisbon. He gives an extensive account of his visit to the Portuguese Court at the royal palace of Queluz. His version of events diverges at times from that recorded at the time they happened.

225 The British and the grand tour.
Jeremy Black.   London: Croom Helm, 1985. 273p. bibliog.

A fascinating review of the European grand tours undertaken by upper-class British travellers in the 18th century. Black draws on both unpublished and published accounts which include those of visits to Lisbon by Lords Pembroke, Pelham, Clinton, Tyrawly and Ladies Craven and Tavistock. Ironically, given Lisbon's reputation as a health resort, a surprising number of the British travellers died there, including Henry Fielding, William Montagu, MP and Lady Tavistock.

226 Sketches of society and manners in Portugal in a series of letters from Arthur William Costigan, Esq., late a Captain of the Irish Brigade in the service of Spain, to his brother in London.
William Costigan.   London: T. Vener, 1788. 2 vols.

Although the whole of the second volume and part of the first comprise letters sent from Lisbon in 1779, many describe military figures rather than the city. However, the account of the post-earthquake reconstruction and of social events such as dinner at the home of the British Consul General in Lisbon inadvertently convey the sense of superiority of the writer and his colleagues as they view the 'indolent manner of life all Portuguese lead'. The letters also cover visits to Oeiras and to Sintra. Costigan was the pseudonym of Diogo, or James, Ferrier or Ferriere. Born in Scotland in 1734, of a Huguenot family, he served in the Portuguese army from 1762 until 1780.

227 Memoirs of Richard Cumberland written by himself, containing an account of his life and writings, interspersed with anecdotes and characters of several of the most distinguished persons of his time, etc.
Richard Cumberland.   London: Lackington, Allen & Co, 1806. 533p., plus a supplement of 72p., published in 1807.

In May 1780, the dramatist, Richard Cumberland, was sent to Lisbon with his wife and daughters to pose as innocent travellers. In reality he was on a secret government mission and was to await instructions on arrival in the Portuguese capital. After an eventful voyage during which his ship, *Milford*, captured a frigate and its 155 French and American crew, Cumberland lodged at Mrs Duer's in the Buenos Aires district of Lisbon. As well as meeting the Minister at Lisbon, Mr Walpole, he took time to watch a Corpus Christi procession and visit Sintra, Queluz and the Alcântara aqueduct before receiving instructions to leave for Spain. A number of his letters from Lisbon to the Earl of Hillsborough are also reproduced here.

228 Travels through Spain and Portugal, in 1774; with a short account of the Spanish expedition against Algiers, in 1775.
William Dalrymple.   London: J. Almon, 1777. 187p. map.

Major Dalrymple set out from his Gibraltar garrison to visit Madrid but carried on to make a five-month circular journey which encompassed Lisbon. He arrived via Sintra, which he found 'romantic and agreeable' but otherwise unimpressive. His account is written in the form of letters, of which number XIV is dated Lisbon, 25 October 1774.

He gives a rather disordered account of the city, predictably paying most attention to its military aspects. Although he is critical both of Pombal for his self-aggrandisement and cruelty, and of Lisbon's dirty old quarters, he does admire some features, such as the recently-built aqueduct.

229   **An account of Portugal as it appeared in 1766 to Dumouriez, since a celebrated general in the French Army.**
Charles François Duperrier Dumouriez.   London: C. Law, 1797. 274p.

Dumouriez was sent to Lisbon by the French Minister of Foreign Affairs to assess the means by which Portugal might be attacked or defended. In this abridged translation of his report, published as *État présent du royaume de Portugal* (Lausanne, 1795), Dumouriez adds much information on politics, government, commerce and manners. The work is divided into four 'books' covering geographical description, the Portuguese colonies, the army, and national character and government. In Lisbon, Dumouriez finds 'the streets full of filth ... uneven, hilly and illpaved', and 'the inhabitants are robbers, misers, traitors, brutal, fierce and morose'.

230   **Memoirs.**
William Hickey, edited by Peter Quennell.   London: Hutchinson, 1960. 452p.

In 1782 Hickey sailed from Falmouth to Lisbon, where he hoped to obtain a passage to India. His companion was Charlotte, the so-called Mrs Hickey, who fell ill whilst in Lisbon and was forced to return to England. She recovered in time to reach Lisbon for an unexpected reunion with Hickey before he left for India. Hickey was favourably impressed by Lisbon although his account (p. 347-61) is largely concerned with his friendship with an Indian born merchant, Mr Baretto, and with his dealings with the English community, including the consul and English Factory.

231   **Letters from Barbary, France, Spain and Portugal.**
By an English Officer, [i.e. Alexander Jardine].   London: T. Cadell, 1788. 2 vols.

Volume II of these *Letters* includes a substantial number written from Portugal in 1779, in which Lisbon is described as a 'mixture of luxury and misery'. The author expresses admiration for some of Pombal's reforms but feels that his rebuilding of Lisbon would have been more succesful had he held an open competition for its replanning. He comments extensively on the flouting of Pombal's reforms and practices in the immediate aftermath of the Minister's fall from grace in 1777.

232   **Travels in Portugal, through the provinces of Entre Douro e Minho, Beira, Estremadura and Alem-Tejo, in the years 1789 and 1790, consisting of observations on the manners, customs, trade, public buildings, arts, antiquities &c. of that kingdom.**
James Murphy.   London: A. Strahan and T. Cadell and W. Davies, 1795. 308p. map.

The author, an Irish bricklayer who became an architect, not only dedicates this work to Don John, Prince of Brazil, but also draws on quotations from Portuguese writers, both facts indicating his favourable view of the country about which he writes. Lisbon is described at length (p. 131-240) with visits to numerous churches, the English cemetery, the aqueduct and Belem interspersed with observations on such diverse topics as Lisbon butchers' meat, its Jews, and the city's birth, death and marriage statistics. Amongst the thirty-four plates are a superb engraved map of Lisbon and three other city sights.

233   **William Beckford & Portugal: an impassioned journey, 1787, 1794, 1798. Exposição, exhibition, Palácio de Queluz, Maio – Novembro, 1987.**
       Maria Laura Bettencourt Pires.   Lisbon: Instituto Português do Património Cultural, 1987. 197p. bibliog.
A catalogue of an exhibition, written in parallel Portuguese and English texts, to commemorate the bicentenary of Beckford's first trip to Portugal. A section of the catalogue is entitled 'The capital of the enchanted kingdom, Lisbon: form, character and urban poetry' (p. 100-19). This includes several contemporary panoramas of the city and reproductions of prints of such sights as the Águas Livres aqueduct and the Feira da Ladra (Thieves' Market).

234   **An account of the most remarkable places and curiosities in Spain and Portugal.**
       Udal ap Rhys (Uvedale Price).   London: J. Osborn, A. Millar, J. and J. Rivington and J. Leake, 1749. 332p.
This book is important as an English-language account of Lisbon in the period immediately before the 1755 earthquake which destroyed the heart of the city. It therefore depicts the Royal palace on the waterfront, the Torre de Belém in mid-river and many of Lisbon's churches and buildings which failed to survive the cataclysm. Rhys also provides statistical and historical information on the city, and offers accounts of the suburbs of Belém, Sintra, Colares and Almada. Details are also given of various English establishments in Lisbon, such as the English College seminary and the English nunnery, as well as the Sion House convent at Belém. The book ends with an alphabetical index and numerous tables of distances for journeys, which include six itineraries ending in Lisbon. The book was republished in 1750 as *A tour through Spain and Portugal*.

235   **Journal of a lady of quality; being the narrative of a journey from Scotland to the West Indies, North Carolina and Portugal in the years 1774 to 1776.**
       Janet Schaw, edited by Evangeline Walker Andrews in collaboration with Charles McLean Andrews.   New Haven, Connecticut: Yale University Press; London: Oxford University Press, 1939. 351p. 8 maps.
This text reproduces a British Museum manuscript account of an Edinburgh woman's journey to North America from which she returned via Lisbon, where she arrived in December 1775. Having avoided a period of quarantine in the Lazareto, courtesy of a forged health certificate, Miss Schaw made the rounds of expatriate English and French society in Lisbon. She visited tourist sights such as St Rock (S. Roque) church, the aqueduct and the Baixa area. However, her accounts of less celebrated locations are particularly striking, such as her visit to the menagerie at the royal palace of Belem, with its lions, panthers and bears, and her trip to the theatre where she discovered that all female parts had to be played by males.

236   **Journals of a residence in Portugal 1800-1801 and a visit to France 1838. Supplemented by extracts from his correspondence.**
Robert Southey, edited by Adolfo Cabral.   Oxford: Clarendon Press, 1960. 285p. 2 maps.

The editor of this volume uncovered two private journals of Southey's in Bristol in 1949, which are here published for the first time. The first recounts the author's arrival in Lisbon in late April 1800 and chronicles his activities. As well as encounters with society, Southey visited remaining ruins from the 1755 earthquake and observed how the citizens of Lisbon despised the many negroes in their city. The volume also includes a number of unpublished letters written from Portugal in 1800-01, including several from Lisbon and Sintra.

237   **Letters of Robert Southey: a selection.**
Robert Southey, edited with introduction and notes by Maurice H. Fitzgerald.   London; New York; Toronto; Melbourne: Oxford University Press, 1912. 552p.

Nine letters written by Southey concerning or during his two visits to Lisbon are included in this collection. One is from his first visit in 1796 and the rest relate to 1800-01, when he returned, with his wife, to research his *History of Portugal*. Unlike many of his fellow-countrymen who visited Lisbon, Southey attempted to learn Portuguese and understand the people and their history. In Lisbon he describes the religious processions and bullfight which he witnessed and a visit to Fielding's grave, as well as commenting on the city's populace, its street life and its crime. Sintra, he declares, 'is too good a place for the Portuguese'.

238   **Letters written during a short residence in Spain and Portugal, with some account of Spanish and Portugueze [sic] poetry.**
Robert Southey.   Bristol, England: Joseph Cottle, 1797. 551p.

In 1796 Southey visited Lisbon and Sintra for the first time and, despite an initial lack of enthusiasm, he became sufficiently interested in the locality to return in 1800-01 to research a history of Portugal. On this first visit, which included a visit to the Bridgettine convent, he found Lisbon dirty and uncivilized, but was somewhat more enthusiastic about Sintra.

239   **The tour of his Royal Highness Edward, Duke of York, from England to Lisbon, Gibraltar, Minorca, Genoa, Alexandria, Asti, Turin, Milan, Parma, Florence, Leghorn, Pisa, Lucca, Pistoja, Sienna, Rome, Bologna, Mantua, Verona, Vicenza, Padua, Venice & c. with an introduction and a circumstancial [sic] and historical detail of each place through which he passed, etc.**
Dublin: P. Wilson, S. Cotter, J. Potts and J. Williams, 1764. 47p.

In October 1763, Edward Augustus, Duke of York, spent three and a half weeks in Lisbon as part of a one-year European tour. This tract describes his reception by the Portuguese Royal Family at Queluz, where a concert and comic opera were put on for him. The Duke met the chief minister, Pombal, and was waited upon by the Deputy British Consul and representatives of the British Factory of merchants. A general description and brief history of Lisbon are given, together with a discourse on bullfighting.

240   **Travels through Portugal and Spain in 1772 and 1773, with copper plates and an appendix.**
      Richard Twiss.   London: Published by the Author, 1775. 465p. map.

After an eighteen-day delay waiting for favourable winds, Twiss sailed for Lisbon from Falmouth in November 1772. His travel diaries are characterized by detailed observation which includes subscription prices for visitors to the English Factory meeting rooms, an appendix of journey times and distances, and an estimate that Lisbon's black and mulatto population is a fifth of its total. He describes Lisbon as 'pretty nearly in the same ruinous state it was the day after the earthquake in 1755'. During his eleven-week stay in the area he mixed with English society including the consul, Mr Walpole, visited the theatre and took excursions to Belém, St Julian's fort at Carcavelos, Sintra, Cabo da Roca, Odivelas, Mafra and Caluz (Queluz), before moving on to Alcobaça.

19th century

241   **Sketches in Portugal during the Civil War of 1834, with observations on the present state and future prospects of Portugal.**
      John Edward Alexander.   London: James Cochrane & Co., 1835. 328p.

Alexander, a Lieutenant-Colonel in the Portuguese Service, went to a turbulent Lisbon, beset by conflict between liberals and conservatives, to arrange for a Royal Geographical Society venture to be granted access to Mozambique. The first ninety-two pages of this book concern his journey from Falmouth and his stay in Lisbon. After passing through the Royal Navy squadron in the Tagus, Alexander landed and found lodgings at Cais do Sodré. In Lisbon he met dignitaries such as the British consul, Lord Howard de Walden, Lady St Vincent, the Duke de Terceira and even encountered the former king, Pedro, at the opera. More interesting, however, are his walks through Lisbon's streets in which he describes middle-class fashions as well as more mundane sights such as the fish-market, beggars, stray dogs and harbour activity. After an excursion to assess the state of the civil war being waged in the country, Alexander returned to Lisbon where he comments on the military and political situation, before visiting Sintra and Mafra. An appendix includes statistics of Anglo-Portuguese trade.

242   **A visit to Portugal, 1866.**
      Hans Christian Andersen, translated from the Danish, with an introduction, notes and appendices by Grace Thornton.   London: Peter Owen, 1972. 105p. bibliog.

A translation of *Et besøg i Portugal, 1866,* with accompanying black-and-white photographs, including a number of Lisbon. Several of the chapters cover Andersen's time in Lisbon in 1866, where his visits included outings to the aqueduct and, curiously, the Alto de S. João cemetery. He makes a point of stating that the city was not as dirty as he had been led to expect. Andersen suffered greatly from the heat in Lisbon before moving on by boat to Bordeaux.

243 **Rough leaves from a journal kept in Spain and Portugal during the years 1832, 1833 & 1834.**
Lovell Badcock. London: Richard Bentley, 1835. 407p.

Lt. Col. Badcock arrived in the Tagus in 1832 on HMS *Britannia*, with Lord William Russell and Colonel Hare, on a mission to rebuild Anglo-Portuguese relations after their disruption by D. Miguel's usurpation of the Portuguese crown (1828-34). Badcock observed D. Miguel himself cruising up and down the Tagus at Lisbon and he reports on the air of unease in the city as to his intentions. After a brief exploration of the city's 'horribly filthy streets' and a visit to Sintra, he journeyed into Spain to assess reports of Spanish advances into Portugal. Having returned briefly to Lisbon, he moved north to Oporto. Badcock understood the Portuguese distrust of Britain, which he attributed to his own country's lowering of duty on rival French wines, its failure to acknowledge the role of the Portuguese army in the Peninsular War and its prevarication regarding the Portuguese royal succession.

244 **The Tagus and the Tiber; or, Notes of travel in Portugal, Spain and Italy in 1850-1.**
William Edward Baxter. London: Richard Bentley, 1852. 2 vols.

In almost seventy pages on Lisbon and its environs, Baxter finds the city largely devoid of foreign visitors and, contrary to received opinion, judges it less dirty than other European cities such as Naples, Marseilles and Trieste. Indeed, he is firm but relatively balanced in his opinions, criticizing drunkenness amongst Royal Navy sailors in Lisbon as well as the alleged laziness of the lower class local citizenry, yet praising the smartness of the Portuguese army. Baxter is of a progressive outlook, advocating the canalization of parts of the Tagus and eulogizing the travel benefits of steam navigation, which brought him to Lisbon. Baxter is also highly critical of the royal usurper, D. Miguel, and considers the then Queen of Portugal, Maria II, to be 'a coarse-looking, overgrown woman'. As well as Lisbon, he also visited Sintra, Colares, Torres Vedras and, across the River Tagus, Cacilhas.

245 **Journal of a ride post through Portugal and Spain, from Lisbon to Bayonne.**
Charles Beaufoy. London: T. and W. Boone, 1846. 97p.

Beaufoy sailed to Lisbon in March 1820 and lodged at Reeve's Hotel in the Buenos Aires district. He paints a grim picture of dirty streets, packs of stray dogs, night-time stabbings and discharges of waste water from upper windows onto unsuspecting passers-by. He also finds the Lisbon opera inferior to that found in France and Italy. Beaufoy's general disregard for the city is reflected in his misspelling of a large number of street, building and place-names. In early April he moved on to Sintra and Caluz (Queluz), before leaving for Madrid after almost a month in the Lisbon area.

246 **The Bible in Spain; or, The journeys, adventures and imprisonments of an Englishman in an attempt to circulate the scriptures in the Peninsula.**
George Borrow. London: Constable; New York: Gabriel Wells, 1923. 2 vols. (The Norwich Edition).

The title of this travel classic, first published in 1843, conceals the fact that more than a hundred pages of its narrative takes place in Portugal, much of it in and around

Lisbon. Borrow relates his arrival at Belém, in late 1835, and describes the city, which he did not greatly enjoy. He observes many remaining ruins from the 1755 earthquake and writes about the Lisbon Jewish quarter. As a militant Protestant, he had an uneasy encounter with the Catholic clergy at the English College.

247 **The works of Lord Byron. A new revised and enlarged edition with illustrations. Letters and journals. Vol. I.**
Lord Byron, edited by Rowland E. Prothero. London: John Murray, 1898. 365p.

This edition of Byron's correspondence includes two letters about the poet's stay in Lisbon in July 1809. In the first, to Francis Hodgson, he describes his visit to Sintra which he rates as one of the most beautiful villages in Europe. He also refers to swimming in the Tagus and conversing with local monks in Latin. In the second letter, to his mother, he alludes to Lisbon's 'filthy streets and filthy inhabitants' in contrast to Sintra which he describes as 'delightful'.

248 **Portugal and Gallicia, with a review of the social and political state of the Basque provinces.**
The Earl of Carnarvon. London: John Murray, 1861. new ed. 376p.

The first edition of this book came out in 1836. It commences with a voyage undertaken in 1827 from Plymouth to Lisbon, in whose environs the author spent approximately four weeks. Whilst staying at Reeve's Hotel in Lisbon and in Sintra, he consorted with the Ambassador, Sir William a'Court, Sir William Clinton and other upper class notables, both native Portuguese and expatriate British. In chapter VIII the author turns from an interpolated account of an earlier visit to Spain back to Lisbon in 1827. Here he addresses the political situation including the roles of General Saldanha and the Portuguese Cortes. Following a journey around the Alentejo, the Earl records the proclamation of Dom Miguel as monarch in 1828, before setting sail back to England.

249 **A voyage to Cadiz and Gibraltar up the Mediterranean, Sicily and Malta in 1810 & 11 including a description of Sicily and the Lipari Islands and an excursion in Portugal.**
Sir George Cockburn. London: J. Harding, 1815. 2 vols. maps.

Lisbon is covered in the second volume (p. 130-216) of this handsome edition, illustrated by colour plates, one of which is of Sintra. Ominously, Cockburn finds that Lisbon 'looks well at a distance' but during his stay at Baron Quintella's palace, he concludes that it is 'the most dirty, filthy, stinking town I ever was in' whilst its male citizens 'are dirty, filthy objects'. He also makes the customary reference of overseas visitors to the city's packs of stray dogs. In diary form he records excursions to Belém, St Julien's [sic] fort, Sintra, Colares, Mafra, Torres Vedras and Vimiera [i.e Vimeiro]. Cockburn's army background is evident in his thorough observation of battle sites and military buildings.

250 **Ship and shore in Madeira, Lisbon and the Mediterranean.**
Rev. Walter Colton, revised from 'The journal of a cruise in the frigate *Constellation*' by *Rev.* Henry T. Cheever. New York: A. S. Barnes, 1851. 313p.

Chapter VII covers the sea-passage from Madeira to an anchorage near Ajuda, Lisbon and provides a detailed description of Lisbon (p. 104-26) including street scenes, visits to the Alcântara aqueduct and S. Roque church, as well as an account of the 1755 earthquake. Chapter VIII relates an excursion to Sintra, whilst chapter IX describes the voyage from Lisbon to Gibraltar.

251 **The modern traveller: a popular description geographical, historical and topographical, of the various countries of the globe. Spain and Portugal.**
Josiah Conder. London: James Duncan; Edinburgh: Oliver & Boyd; Glasgow, Scotland: M. Ogle; Dublin: R. M. Tims, 1826. 2 vols.

In vol. 2 of this first-person account of Lisbon (p. 295-310) and Sintra (p. 310-14), Conder conveys a generally positive impression of what he sees, which includes such sights as Belém, the British Factory and the aqueduct. Indeed, he portrays Sintra as 'the Richmond of Lisbon'. He draws heavily on the writings of previous visitors to Lisbon, such as Marianne Baillie, Henry Matthews and Robert Semple (see item nos. 1, 263 and 269). Among the more interesting aspects of his own account is its estimate of the negro and mulatto population at a fifth of Lisbon's total, a figure which concurs with Twiss's earlier estimate (q.v.), and the author's observation of 'Moorish' porters at work in the city.

252 **The invalid's guide to Madeira, with a description of Teneriffe, Lisbon, Cintra, Mafra etc, and a vocabulary of the Portuguese and English languages.**
William White Cooper. London: Smith, Elder & Co., 1840. 116p.

Unusually for a mid-19th-century guide, Cooper emphasizes the value of the traveller's acquiring some knowledge of spoken Portuguese. In other respects, such as his description of Queen Maria II as 'of a ponderous size, with a decidedly un-intellectual countenance', he was decidedly less well-disposed to his hosts. Cooper stayed at the English 'Madame de Belém's hotel' from which he found the streets of Lisbon generally clean but overrun by stray dogs and rats. He admired the Jerónimos, S. Roque and Estrela churches, as well as Lisbon's fountains. He also visited Sintra and in his account Byron is quoted at some length.

253 **A loafing trip to Lisbon.**
Cornhill Magazine, new series, vol. 12 (January-June 1889), p. 584-94.

An unsigned account of an upper-class Englishman's visit to Lisbon, which he describes as 'Fairyland' on his arrival there by ship. However, after exploring the city and experiencing its 'fishy and fetid' odours, its raucous street vendors and the animals in its streets, he has a less favourable impression long before his departure. The author also visited a Lisbon bullfight and made an excursion to Sintra and Mafra.

254 **Recollections of a long life. With additional extracts from his private diaries.**

John Cam Hobhouse, Lord Broughton, edited by his daughter, Lady Dorchester. London: John Murray, 1910. reprint. 2 vols.

A reprint of the 1909 edition of Lord Broughton's memoirs. In 1809, as John Cam Hobhouse, he visited Lisbon with Lord Byron. During a two-week stay in the area, based initially in the Buenos Aires Hotel, they visited the theatre and famously met the ill-educated monks of the Jerónimos monastery at Belém. In chapter II of these *Recollections*, Hobhouse provides fascinating detail of street crime and stray dogs in Lisbon, as well as of life in the city under the French occupation of Junot. Despite a more pleasing visit to Sintra, Hobhouse concludes that 'avarice and immorality appear to be the reigning passions of the Portuguese'.

255 **An overland journey to Lisbon at the close of 1846; with a picture of the actual state of Spain and Portugal.**

T. M. Hughes. London: Henry Colburn, 1847. 2 vols.

In October 1846, Hughes arrived in Lisbon, after an eventful journey through France and Spain, and devoted almost two hundred pages of the second volume (p. 279-464) to the city and its surrounding area. His account is a mixture of travelogue and factual and critical comment on the state of Lisbon, its history, politics, military aspects, culture and natural characteristics. In Lisbon, he disliked the Terreiro do Paço and equestrian statue but admired the sunset views from the Buenos Aires district. Outside the city centre he explored Belém, Alcântara and Sintra.

256 **Fair Lusitania. With twenty illustrations from photographs.**

Catherine Charlotte, Lady Jackson. London: Richard Bentley & Son, 1874. 402p.

A sumptuous volume with fine illustrations of sights such as the Bar of Lisbon, the Torre de Belém, Camões's statue, the Teatro D. Maria and the Jerónimos monastery. Of the twenty-seven chapters, the first twelve cover Lisbon and the next three, Sintra. The final chapter marks a return to the capital. Lady Jackson was a fervent admirer of Portugal, with some knowledge of the language. This book is based on diaries she kept on a visit there in 1873, following a number of years' absence from the country. With this work, she hoped to redress the generally negative perception of Portugal which she ascribed to her fellow-countrymen.

257 **Travels in Portugal, being an account of a visit to Lisbon, Cintra, Mafra and Torres Vedras.**

Charles Johnson. London: Wood & Son Printers, 1875. 40p.

Based on a letter sent to his brother in China, this short book records Johnson and his friend Coutts's visit to Lisbon in August 1874. His entertaining account is written in a light-hearted and lively style, reminiscent of that of Jerome K. Jerome, with characters such as Mr and Mrs T. Caddy as well as portions of dramatic dialogue. Nevertheless, Johnson is attentive to detail, not least in his description of a gruelling journey on the Larmanjât steam tramway from Torres Vedras to Lisbon and of Royal Navy sailors buying up Lisbon's stock of canaries in the belief that they were genuinely from the Canary Islands.

258   **Portugal; or, The young travellers, being some account of Lisbon and its environs and of a tour in the Alemtejo in which the customs and manners of the inhabitants are faithfully detailed, from a journal kept by a Lady during three years' actual residence.**
A Lady.   London: Harvey & Darton, 1830. 275p.

The authoress visited Lisbon in the period shortly before the return of King João VI from Brazil in 1821. Her account is curiously written in a literary form, with dialogue recorded between the characters. The book relays the journey of a Mr and Mrs Grey to Lisbon, where they hoped that the ailing health of their daughter Sophia would be improved by the favourable climate. In their initial stay in Lisbon (p. 14-89), they resided at Mrs Reeve's hotel in the Buenos Aires district, favourite lodgings for English visitors. Their explorations took in the Baixa, Belém and Estrela. Following a visit to Setúbal, they returned to Lisbon (p. 121 et seq.) and also travelled to neighbouring Cascais and Sintra.

259   **Travels in Portugal.**
John Latouche [pseudonym for O. J. J. Crawfurd], with illustrations by the Right Hon. T. Sotherton Estcourt.   London: Ward, Lock & Tyler, Warwick House, 1875. 354p.

Oswald Crawfurd was H. M. Consul at Oporto in the latter part of the 19th century. This is an extended version of articles which he originally published in *The New Quarterly Magazine* as 'Notes of travel in Portugal'. Latouche saw his work as complementing that of Lady Jackson's *Fair Lusitania* (see item no. 256) insofar as he followed the 'bye-paths' of Portugal whereas she concentrated on the tourist sights. Chapter eight covers Lisbon with the author commenting on the corrupt local press, bullfighting and art, as well as describing everyday city life.

260   **Iberian sketches: travels in Portugal and the North-West of Spain.**
Jane Leck, with illustrations by Robert Gray.   Glasgow, Scotland: Wilson & McCormick, 1884. 166p.

Records a seven-week tour made in 1883. The authoress has little regard for Lisbon, compared with Naples, Geneva or Rome, and she describes it as 'infested with half-starved mangy-looking cats' (p. 77). Amongst the sites described are the churches of S. Vicente, S. Roque and Estrela, as well as the Academy of Fine Arts and Belém. Leck also portrays 'the dirty little steamers' which cross the Tagus.

261   **Travels in Portugal, and through France and Spain, with a dissertation on the literature of Portugal and the Spanish and Portuguese languages.**
Henry Frederick Link, translated from the German by John Hinckley. London: T. N. Longman & O. Rees, 1801. 504p.

This work recounts the visit to Portugal, between 1797 and 1799, of the German amateur naturalist, the Count of Hoffmansegg and Henry (Heinrich) Link, a botanist and mineralogist. Their purpose was to gather material for a book on the flora and fauna of Portugal. After an account of their travels through France and Spain from their starting-point in Hamburg, they take a figure-of-eight journey around Portugal, passing through Lisbon three times and also taking in Sintra and Queluz. Although their purpose was primarily scientific, Link also recorded their observations on the public institutions and amusements of Lisbon, as well as on its climate and history. The travellers' receptiveness to Portugal is further underlined by Link's two essays on Portuguese literature and language at the end of the book.

262 **A little about Madeira, Spain (Andalusia), Lisbon, Cintra and Tangiers: diary.**
F. C. Marshall.   Grimsby, England: printed by Albert Gait, 1881. 44p.

In April 1880, at their father's expense, the well-heeled author and his brother sailed as young men to Madeira. In May, they sailed on to Lisbon with a number of acquaintances, and spent four enjoyable days in the city and in Sintra, visiting the latter's sights on hired donkeys. After a sojourn in southern Spain, they returned to Lisbon in early June and stayed for over a fortnight, amusing themselves at the Teatro Trindade and bullring, as well as visiting the local sights, although their activities were limited by the illness of their invalid companion, Warschawsky. Their stay in Lisbon coincided with the three-day street celebrations for the tercentenary of the death of Camões, which failed to impress this laconic diarist.

263 **The diary of an invalid; being the journal of a tour in pursuit of health in Portugal, Italy, Switzerland and France in the years 1817, 1818 and 1819.**
Henry Matthews.   Paris: Galignani, 1825. 419p.

Chapter one relates a voyage to Lisbon and Sintra, by sea, from Plymouth. Matthews found Lisbon a less than congenial destination whose views of the Tagus were 'overrated by travellers' and whose streets were populated by scavenging dogs. Given these jaundiced views, it is not surprising that the author moved on from Portugal to visit allegedly more congenial parts of Europe.

264 **Peninsular sketches during a recent tour.**
John Milford.   London: John Richardson & J. Hatchard, 1816. 212p.

Milford visited Lisbon in 1812 and describes his experiences in chapter VII, whilst the following chapter covers Sintra and other parts of Portugal. In a text laced with literary and classical allusions, he portrays the city in a favourable light, going so far as to describe the Praça do Comércio as 'one of the noblest in Europe'. Milford was also impressed by the 18th-century aqueduct, the shops of the Baixa area, the Lisbon opera and the local ladies. In the environs, he visited Sintra and Belém, remarking on the latter's 'Arabesque gothic' architecture.

265 **Peeps at Portugal.**
M. O'Connor Morris.   London: Harrison & Sons, 1891. 129p.

Seeking a cure for his bronchitis, Morris sailed from Shadwell to Oporto. From there he took the overnight train to Lisbon, which he found clean and enjoyable but whilst there he 'did not see much that excited curiosity'. In Sintra he visited Monserrate and the palaces before enjoying a bullfight in the Sintra Colyseu at which he admired the popularity of the Portuguese prince, Henrique. Morris's spelling of Portuguese names and words is less than perfect but he nevertheless conveys a genuine enjoyment of his visit and of the local people.

266 **A month in Portugal.**
Rev. Joseph Oldknow.   London: Longman & Co.; Birmingham,
England: R. H. Leather, 1855. 165p.

Oldknow visited Portugal for the first time with the more well-travelled cleric, J. M.
Neale, whose own resulting *Handbook for travellers in Portugal* (q.v.), with its
comprehensiveness and balance, contrasts with the more ecclesiastically skewed and
discontented tone of Oldknow, who confesses that 'I do not like the Portuguese – at
least the lower orders'. In the final chapter (p. 130-65), Oldknow, having arrived by
steamer from Vila Franca de Xira, describes Lisbon as a 'painted sepulchre' but
asserts that it '*is* now one of the most cleanly cities in Europe'. He enjoyed the relative
creature comforts of the capital compared with the rest of Portugal. His tour of the city
was dominated by visits to churches, including S. Roque, S. Vicente, the cathedral and
the Irish and English Colleges. He made the customary visitor's excursion to Sintra
but even 'the scenery of Cintra somewhat disappointed me'.

267 **Anecdotes of the Spanish and Portuguese revolutions.**
Count Giuseppe Pecchio, with an introduction and notes by
E. Blaquiere.   London: G. & W. B. Whittaker, 1823. 197p.

Originally published in 1822 as *Tre mesi in Portogallo*, Pecchio's letters to 'Jenny'
soon appeared in French, German and English. The work comprises eleven letters
written between February and June 1822. As well as conveying the poverty of many
of Lisbon's citizens, the letters also capture the political ferment of a period which
coincided with the process of independence of Brazil from Portugal. A modern
Portuguese edition, *Cartas de Lisboa, 1822* (Letters from Lisbon, 1822), appeared in
1990 (Lisbon: Livros Horizonte).

268 **Journal of a few months' residence in Portugal and glimpses of the
south of Spain.**
Dorothy Quillinan.   London: Edward Moxon, 1847. 2 vols.

Dorothy Quillinan, Wordsworth's daughter, visited Lisbon (vol. II, p. 73-81) in 1846,
arriving from Sintra. Whilst in Lisbon, she visited the opera, theatre and Torre do
Tombo archives, where she met Alexandre Herculano, the librarian and historian, who
disliked the English. Amongst the other sites she visited were the Estrela basilica, the
English cemetery, Belém and Lisbon Cathedral, where she describes the sight of
recently-dead child corpses left in the church.

269 **A second journey in Spain in the spring of 1809, from Lisbon,
through the western skirts of the Sierra Morena to Sevilla,
Cordoba, Granada, Malaga and Gibraltar; and thence to Tetuan
and Tangiers. With plates, containing 24 figures illustrative of the
costume and manners of the inhabitants of several of the Spanish
provinces.**
Robert Semple.   London: C. & R. Baldwin, 1809. 306p.

In January 1809, following the invasion of Spain by the French, Semple left Falmouth
to assess the effects on Cádiz and Sevilla (Seville). The first chapter concerns
Semple's stay in Lisbon *en route*. His vivid depiction of rumour and chaos, as the
news of Moore's reverse at Corunna reached Lisbon, includes portrayals of the Royal
Navy's ships in the Tagus, the British Army in a state of indecision, English

merchants packing to leave and the raising of a keen, but ill-armed, Portuguese force to repel the advancing French. Semple also describes his unsuccessful intervention to try to save the life of an English servant who was mistaken for a Frenchman and beaten to death by a Lisbon mob. Semple's outspoken criticism of his own country's support for an unpopular Portuguese government and his acknowledgement of the success of the Junot administration (1807) in cleaning up the Lisbon streets mark him out as a balanced and well-informed chronicler.

270 **Three pleasant springs in Portugal.**
Henry N. Shore. London: Sampson, Low, Marston & Company, 1899. 395p. map.

The section entitled 'Spring, the first' covers the author's experience of Lisbon, which he generally admires. However, his intolerance of Catholicism is implicit in his somewhat condescending attitude towards the annual festivities in Lisbon in honour of St. Anthony which he regarded as excessive for what was, to his mind, an unimportant historical event.

271 **Narrative of a spring tour in Portugal.**
Rev. Alfred Charles Smith. London: Longmans, Green & Co., 1870. 220p.

The first five chapters cover the visit of Smith, vicar of Yatesbury and a keen ornithologist, and his photographer-father to Lisbon and Sintra. Father and son spent seven weeks in Portugal for only fifty pounds a head. Smith enjoyed Lisbon, which he explored in detail, including Belém. However, after what he pointedly states was a longer visit to Sintra than those of most of his English predecessors, he judged that the town was somewhat overrated by such as Byron. Nevertheless, he spent a week happily exploring Sintra's estates and tropical gardens, where a highlight for him was his shooting of a large lizard as a specimen for his collection. The final chapter, as well as detailing dozens of bird species to be found in Portugal, also includes references to Lisbon museums.

272 **Winter travels in sunny climes. Seven lectures.**
James C. Street. Belfast: Wm. Henry Greer, 1875. 374p.

To seek a remedy for ill-health, the author sailed from Liverpool, intending to by-pass Portugal. However, a problem with the vessel forced a stop in Lisbon, which is described at length (p. 1-46). After an initial encounter with Portuguese bureaucracy whilst attempting to come ashore, Street forms an adverse impression of the country, although he grudgingly admits that he was 'favourably impressed with the people' despite their 'low morals' and 'the indecency hourly taking place in the open streets'. Apart from encountering many beggars and even prisoners, who solicited passers-by from their cell windows, he surprisingly met members of the royal family walking in the streets. As well as Lisbon, he also visited Sintra, Colares and Mafra, from whence he returned by steam tramway to Lisbon.

273   **The letters of Alfred, Lord Tennyson.**
Alfred, Lord Tennyson, edited by Cecil Y. Lang, Edgar F. Shannon.
Volume II, 1851-70.   Oxford: Clarendon Press, 1987. 585p.

A modern edition of Tennyson's four rather sombre letters to his wife Emily, written
from the Braganza Hotel in Lisbon and from Sintra, between 21 August and 2
September 1859. The poet had gone to Portugal with F. T. Palgrave and his student
friend, Grove. Tennyson tells his wife of his initial disappointment with Lisbon and of
visiting the church of S. Vicente, the Botanical Gardens, the locked British Cemetery
and a bullfight whilst there. He was also disappointed by Sintra, where he climbed up
to the Pena Palace. Back in Lisbon he was courted by Portuguese society, including
the King's chamberlain and the Duque de Saldanha.

274   **Alfred, Lord Tennyson: a memoir. Volume I.**
Hallam Tennyson.   London: Macmillan & Co., 1897. 516p.

This publication, by Lord Tennyson's son, includes *My father's letter-diary: journey
to Portugal with F. T. Palgrave and F. C. Grove* (p. 438-42). This comprises letters
from Tennyson to his wife, written from Lisbon and Sintra in August-September 1859.
Interspersed with these letters are extracts from Palgrave's record of the same visit
which reveal the extraordinary lengths taken by an ailing Tennyson to protect himself
from the city's mosquitoes and how he suffered from the strong sun to the extent that
he thought he might join Fielding in a Lisbon grave.

275   **Lord Byron's Iberian pilgrimage.**
Gordon Kent Thomas.   Provo, Utah: Brigham Young University
Press, 1983. 92p. map. bibliog.

Byron visited Lisbon in 1809, on his way, via Spain, to Gibraltar. Thomas retraces the
journey through extensive reference to *Child Harold's Pilgrimage*, which includes
scenes set in both Lisbon and Sintra. The volume includes three photographs of
Lisbon and five illustrations of the Sintra area, albeit of indifferent quality of
reproduction.

276   **Notes of a journey from Cornhill to Grand Cairo by way of Lisbon,
Athens, Constantinople and Jerusalem, performed in the steamers
of the Peninsular and Oriental Company.**
M. A. Titmarsh.   London: Chapman & Hall, 1846. 2nd ed. 221p.

Mr Titmarsh packed a great deal into a short stay in Lisbon when his vessel called
there on its way to Cádiz and, eventually, Cairo. In a very readable second chapter he
recounts his generally favourable impressions of such Lisbon sights as St Rock (S.
Roque) church, the Necessidades royal palace and the Belém district. This book,
whose first edition also appeared in 1846, evolved out of articles submitted to the
magazine *Punch*. It was only in its third edition (London: Smith, Elder & Co., 1865.
208p.) that M. A. Titmarsh was explicitly identified as a pseudonym of William
Thackeray. An attractive modern edition, *Notes of a journey from Cornhill to Grand
Cairo*, was published in 1991 (Heathfield, England: Cockbird Press, 1991. 160p.).
This edition is embellished by many 19th-century engravings and paintings, both in
colour and monochrome. Five of these illustrations are of the Lisbon area and the
volume also includes an informative introduction by Sarah Searight.

277 **A steam voyage to Constantinople by the Rhine and Danube in 1840-41 and to Portugal, Spain &c. in 1839.**
C. W. Vane, Marquess of Londonderry. London: Henry Colburn, 1842. 2 vols.

Volume two (chapters XX-XXI) of this work includes the Marquess's visit to Lisbon and its environs, including Mafra and Sintra, and is entitled *Journey of a tour in the southern part of Spain, including Tangier, Ceuta and Tetuan, performed in the Autumn of 1839.* As might be expected from such an upper-class visitor, it is the nobility of Lisbon and the expatriate British community who constituted his main contact with Lisbon life. Outside these circles he witnessed only 'poverty and decay' and the 'horror and abominations of the narrow streets' (p. 131). Equally appalled by the alleged squalor of Lisbon was the Marchioness of Londonderry, who recorded her impressions of the 1839 tour in *A journal of a three months' tour in Portugal, Spain, Africa, &c.* (London: J. Mitchell, 1843. 134p.).

278 **Narrative of a voyage to Madeira, Teneriffe and along the shores of the Mediterranean, including a visit to Algiers, Egypt, Palestine, Tyre, Rhodes, Telmessus, Cyprus and Greece with observations on the present state and prospects of Egypt and Palestine, and on the climate, natural history, antiquities, etc of the countries visited.**
W. R. Wilde. Dublin: William Curry, 1840. 2 vols.

In 1837 the author, father of Oscar Wilde, went on the above-mentioned journey as the medical attendant to an invalid. One of their first ports of call was Lisbon (p. 40-82). Wilde admired the bustle of the harbour and was a keen observer of street life, taking a particular interest in the efficient water-supply system, both of the aqueduct and of the large numbers of Galician water-carriers. As a medical man, he made a visit to the St Joseph Hospital and his informed observations on Lisbon medical services are an unusual aspect of a travel narrative. He visited much of Lisbon, including the Buenos Aires and Belém districts, as well as the cathedral, parliament and the churches of S. Roque and Carmo. Although many aspects of Lisbon impressed Wilde, its alleged backwardness and the incessant howling of packs of dogs at night led him to conclude that 'the city is worthy of a people degraded by ignorance and the grossest superstition' (p. 58). He also describes his visits to Sintra and Mafra.

20th century

279 **A winter holiday in Portugal, with a coloured frontispiece map and 40 original drawings by the author.**
Granville Baker. London: Stanley Paul & Co., 1912. 324p. map.

Captain Baker visited Lisbon, as a self-styled holiday-maker, shortly after the 1910 Revolution, yet his book reveals little of the political chaos at the time, other than a few favourable references to the overthrown Portuguese monarchy. Chapters three to six chronicle his visit to Lisbon, the Cascais coastal area and Sintra (p. 46-161) and are accompanied by pleasant monochrome drawings by the author which match the somewhat genteel tone of the text. In addition to description of street scenes and buildings, Baker provides a history of Lisbon and of Portuguese art and culture, but unfortunately his spelling of Portuguese names is poor.

280 Portuguese panorama.
Oswell Blakeston.   London: Burke, 1955. 224p. map.

The author here describes his journey with fellow-painter, Max Chapman, through Portugal. Nine of the fourteen chapters are wholly or substantially set in Lisbon or its immediate environs. These are not typical visitors, for they presented their credentials at the Palácio Foz in Lisbon and were accorded an official government guide. Moreover, they rubbed shoulders with the likes of Amália Rodrigues, Portugal's most celebrated *fado* singer of the era, and met a number of artists and writers in Lisbon. The book is illustrated by black-and-white photographs and has a helpful, if idiosyncratic, index which includes entries such as 'ices', 'lavatories and bathrooms' and 'Lisbon tummy'.

281 Afoot in Portugal.
John Gibbons, with a foreword by G. K. Chesterton.   London: George Newnes, 1931. 207p.

Gibbons arrived in Lisbon, unusually for a British visitor, on the Tagus river ferry from Cacilhas, having travelled from southern Portugal and Spain. Chapter seven describes his wanderings and chance encounters around Lisbon, its theatres and clubs. He seems to be only moderately informed about the city, pleading factual ignorance on a number of occasions where a minimum of research or inquisitiveness would have lent his superficial accounts more authority.

282 To Portugal.
Douglas Goldring.   London: Rich & Cowan Ltd., 1934. 294p. map. bibliog.

Goldring here sets out to be 'chatty, discursive, precisely informed and engagingly readable'. The book, as the writer admits, is a conscious work resulting from research rather than the spontaneous recollections of someone long familar with the country. Lisbon is covered in chapter II (p. 66-91), whilst its environs are described in the following chapter (p. 92-111). Chapter II also includes Sintra, Queluz and Cascais. The author's wide reading on the subject of his travels is reflected both in frequent references to sources within the text and in a useful bibliography.

283 My tour in Portugal.
Helen Cameron Gordon, Lady Russell.   London: Methuen & Co., 1932. 287p. map.

Chapters eighteen to twenty-five (p. 194-277) of these memoirs of a trip to Portugal include perceptive accounts of the 'Portuguese Riviera', Sintra and Lisbon. The Riviera section includes visits to Estoril, Cascais, Carcavelos and, unusually, to the Aquário Vasco da Gama at Dafundo. The sections of Lisbon are divided into historical sections, with a closing chapter entitled, 'The light side', on carnival time in Lisbon.

284   **An Easter cruise on the S.S. 'Ophir' to Lisbon and the Peninsula, April 12th to 29th, 1906.**
P. Heywood Hadfield.   Ross, England: Published by the author, [c1906]. unpaginated.

An expensively produced account and photographic album recording the visit of a group of British medics to the Fifteenth International Congress of Medicine, held in Lisbon in 1906. These delegates made up about half of the 250 passengers on the cruise from Tilbury, via Vigo and Tangier, to Lisbon. A detailed account of the party's stay in Lisbon is given. As well as enjoying the main city sights, the party attended a royal garden party at Sintra, and a bullfight at Campo Pequeno in Lisbon. The author's own high quality photographs include sixteen of Lisbon and Sintra.

285   **A journey to Gibraltar.**
Mrs Robert Henrey.   London: J. M. Dent, 1943. 169p. map.

Produced on war-grade paper, almost all of the first seven of the twenty-two chapters of this book discuss wartime Lisbon, to which the authoress flew in 1941. She remarks both on the well-stocked shops and on the juxtaposition of German and English newspapers in the kiosks. From this accessible range of international newspapers, she was able to glean information on the living conditions of occupied France. As well as visiting Lisbon bookshops, a tea-dance and nightclubs, she also observed more traditional tourist sights both in the city and in Estoril.

286   **Portuguese journey.**
Garry Hogg.   London: The Travel Book Club, [1954]. 208p. 2 maps.

The author and his wife relate a backpacking journey through Portugal of which Lisbon was the twice-visited highlight, interrupted by a journey to the Algarve. Hogg enthuses about the city at a time, in the early 1950s, before large-scale tourism had reached it. The sights visited include Belém, Sintra and the Lisbon bullring. However, as they were travelling on foot, it is their description of Lisbon street life, with its fishwives, news vendors, fruitsellers, shoeblacks and other characters which make this a lively contrast to the less adventurous journals of more wealthy contemporary travellers such as Blakeston or Merle (q.v.).

287   **In and about the Mediterranean, with chapters upon Corunna, Oporto, Lisbon, Tangier and Casablanca. Illustrated by the author's and other photographs.**
Clive Holland.   London: Herbert Jenkins, 1934. 256p. map.

The first chapter is entitled 'Corunna, Oporto, Lisbon, Cadiz'. Holland adequately describes the main tourist sights of the city centre area but he is rather uncritical and bland, an attitude epitomized by his closing comments that 'Lisbon, on the whole, leaves upon the mind a very pleasant impression, for the city is bright, sunny and engaging'.

288   **South of Lisbon: winter travels in southern Portugal.**
Frank E. Huggett.   London: Victor Gollancz, 1960. 224p.

Despite its title, a significant portion of this book does relate to Lisbon itself, starting with the author's shock at the poverty he encounters on arrival at the Santa Apolónia railway station. Huggett goes on to record his experiences on the streets of Lisbon, rather than indulging in yet another travel-writer's tour of the city's sights. As a consequence he is led into a certain amount of analysis and comment of the Salazar régime. A number of the book's photographs depict Lisbon. The book's title derives from the author's decision to leave the capital and journey to the Algarve.

289 Through Portugal.
Martin Hume.   London: E. Grant Richards, 1907. 316p.

In this handsome volume, illustrated with forty photographs, Hume relays his sympathetic view of Portugal as he sought relief from his allegedly arduous life as a writer. His object here is to portray the country 'from the point of view of the intelligent visitor in search of sunshine, health or relaxation'. His trip from Oporto southwards takes in Sintra (chapter VII) and Lisbon (chapter VIII, p. 229-63). Whilst enjoying Belém and Monte Estoril, he found Lisbon itself 'decidedly disappointing at close quarters'. A fascinating section of 'Hints to travellers' gives unusual detail of shipping routes to Lisbon and of hotels, food and drink in Portugal.

290 Backwards out of the big world: a voyage into Portugal.
Paul Hyland.   London: Harper Collins, 1996. 269p. map. bibliog.

The author arrived in Lisbon by cargo vessel and the first quarter of the book is a lively description of the city, its sights and its history. He then ascended the Tagus by various modes of transport before reaching Alcántara on the Spanish border. A meandering route, via the Alentejo, brings him back to Lisbon and Sintra for a further three chapters. His description of his journey through Lisbon and many towns off the normal visitor's track is interspersed with digressions on Portuguese literature and history.

291 Lisbon & Cintra; with some account of other cities and historical sites in Portugal.
A. C. Inchbold, illustrated by Stanley Inchbold.   London: Chatto & Windus, 1907. 248p.

Illustrated by twenty-two finely reproduced watercolours, this book provides a detailed account of both Lisbon and the surrounding areas for the well-heeled Edwardian tourist. Its first eleven chapters cover Lisbon, Belém and as far afield as Estoril, Sintra and Setúbal. The final four chapters describe the Tagus Valley, Alcobaça, Buçaco and the cities of Coimbra, Braga and Oporto. The work has no index and the chapters have no headings, but page headers provide a guide to the contents.

292 Invitation to Portugal.
Mary Jean Kempner.   New York: Atheneum, 1969. 314p. map. bibliog.

Written by a former United States war correspondent who had a second home in Sintra, this introduction to Portugal contains much information about Lisbon interspersed amongst descriptions of travels throughout the country. In Lisbon, Kempner's hobnobbing with ambassadors, dining at prestigious restaurants and extensive use of a chauffeur-driven limousine do not bear much resemblance to the typical tourist's experience of Lisbon but are revealing of the way of life available to those with social and diplomatic connections. Many black-and-white photographs, including nine of Lisbon, are scattered throughout the text.

293   **Moments in Portugal; or, Land of the laurel.**
       Lady Lowther.   London: Luzac & Co., 1939. 132p.
Chapter one of this diary of a visit to Portugal is entitled 'Moments in Portugal:
Lisbon and environs' (p. 1-58). In it Lady Lowther describes a visit in April 1936 on
her way back from Madeira. She is largely oblivious to any defects in the city and her
style is rather effusive. She also describes visits to Sintra and Alcobaça. The volume is
enhanced by black-and-white photographs, which include the Torre de Belém and
Jerónimos monastery.

294   **On the contrary: articles of belief, 1946-1961.**
       Mary McCarthy.   London: Weidenfeld & Nicolson, 1980. 312p.
Two of the essays in this volume relate to Lisbon. The first, 'Letter from Portugal'
(p. 106-31), was written in February 1955 and records the author's arrival in Lisbon.
She found Lisbon 'charming' but gives a balanced picture of the city, revealing its
poverty, censorship and bureaucracy as well as its superficial beauty. In the second
essay, 'Mister Rodriguez', dated August 1955, she describes travelling around Lisbon
with the Director of the Economic Homes Programme. She counters his pride in his
work of providing homes for the citizens of Lisbon with gentle humour directed at his
paternalistic attitude to the working classes.

295   **A wayfarer in Portugal.**
       Philip S. Marden.   London: Methuen, 1927. 210p. map.
Chapters three and four of this account of the author's travels in Portugal cover,
respectively, Lisbon itself and its environs, including Belém and Sintra. Black-and-
white photographs, a preliminary historical essay and some concluding practical
advice for the visitor to Portugal complete the volume.

296   **Portuguese pilgrimage, July 1st – September 4th, 1947.**
       C. C. Martindale.   London: Sheed & Ward, 1949. 165p.
The account of a two-month visit to Portugal by a Jesuit priest whose interest was,
naturally, biased towards places of religious significance. His base was Monte Estoril,
near Lisbon, and much of the book concerns the environs of the city. He mixed with the
Portuguese and English upper classes as well as visiting the major tourist sights. His
account of the historical cortege, in Lisbon, organized to commemorate the 800th
anniversary of the Siege of Lisbon (1147), captures the nationalistic fervour of the times.

297   **Portuguese panorama.**
       Iris Merle.   London: Ouzel Press, 1958. 224p. 2 maps.
A rather gushing account of a journey to Madeira and Portugal, liberally illustrated by
black-and-white photographs. The portrayal of 1950s Lisbon (p. 111-25) is somewhat
superficial and uncritical.

298   **Insider's guide to Lisbon.**
       Eric Newby.   London: The Observer, 1985. 16p.
A colour supplement to *The Observer* newspaper by the celebrated travel writer. It has
many colour photographs of Lisbon street scenes which mirror the text in
concentrating on observations of everyday scenes rather than formal tourist sights.
Information is also provided on using transport and finding hotels.

299 **Portugal.**
Cedric Salter. London: B. T. Batsford, 1970. 208p.

This general introduction to Portugal for the visitor is written by a resident of Portugal. One chapter (p. 55-79) is entitled 'In and around Lisbon' and another is called 'Lisbon to the Alentejo', but the emphasis falls as much on suburban areas such as Belém, Sintra, Queluz, Cascais and Estoril, as on the capital itself. Twenty-three photographs accompany the text.

300 **Lisbon.**
Rev. John Tole. [Printed at] Plymouth, England: Underhill, [1959]. 48p.

The author spent six years in the 1920s training as a priest at the English College seminary in Lisbon and his firsthand knowledge of the city makes this guidebook worthy of a much wider circulation than it received. In ten factually-packed chapters he covers the city, largely by tram, making many historical references as well as relaying his own experience of both the 1927 earthquake and the republican insurrection of that year. There are also many allusions to British connections with Lisbon and, as might be expected, Rev. Tole is particularly well-informed on ecclesiastical aspects of the city.

301 **Lisbon: a portrait and a guide.**
David Wright, Patrick Swift. London: Barrie & Jenkins, 1971. 270p. maps.

An account of the authors' stay in Lisbon and excursions along the coast to Cascais, up the Tagus and across the river to Sesimbra. The work aims to be a serious study of the Portuguese character rather than a mere travelogue. It includes a forty-two page section on the history of Lisbon. Swift was an Irish painter who had lived in Portugal, whilst Wright was a South African poet, based in England. Monochrome photographs accompany the text.

302 **Blue moon in Portugal: travels.**
William Younger, Elizabeth Younger. London: Eyre & Spottiswoode, 1956. 298p. bibliog.

A rather routine travelogue of Portugal in which chapter XII is entitled 'Lisbon, the city of the sea' (p. 248-69). The normal tourist venues in Belém and Lisbon are visited, and an excursion is made to Cacilhas, across the Tagus. Black-and-white photographs further convey the authors' experience of 1950s Portugal.

Bibliographie des voyages en Espagne et en Portugal. (Bibliography of travels in Spain and Portugal.)
See item no. 686.

Flora and Fauna

303 **Flora da Estufa Fria de Lisboa.** (Flora of the Estufa Fria of Lisbon.)
Maria Lisete Caixinhas.   Lisbon: Verbo, 1994. 143p. bibliog.

A high-quality colour review of the flora in Lisbon's unusual Estufa Fria (Cold Greenhouse) gardens in the Parque Eduardo VII. Built in the 1920s, the Estufa Fria consists of a semi-tropical microclimate created by a vast network of protective and insulating slats. Within its confines is a profusion of exotic plants and a network of paths across man-made pools, inhabited by birds, frogs and other creatures. The book illustrates, with dozens of fine colour photographs, scores of types of plant and foliage. The text provides details of their botanical names, countries of origin and identifying characteristics. The location of each species within the gardens is given as are details of each plant's growing season.

304 **Guia do Zoo de Lisboa.** (Guide to Lisbon Zoo.)
José Dias, Maria Inácia Teles.   Lisbon: Bertrand, 1991. 70p.

An illustrated guide to Lisbon's zoo in the Laranjeiras Park at Sete Rios, north of the city centre. As well as housing more than 3,000 animals, the zoo also contains pleasant gardens and an impressive manor house.

305 **Where to watch birds in Britain and Europe.**
John Gooders.   London: Hamlyn, 1994. 262p. maps. (Hamlyn
Birdwatching Guides).

The section on Portugal includes details of sites from which to observe a wide variety of birds in the lower Tagus estuary, near Lisbon. Precise details are given on how to reach the best watching places. The river's mudflats at low tide are home, in particular, to huge numbers of waders, but other species such as egrets, herons and marsh harriers can also be seen. Detailed lists are provided of the types of birds which frequent the estuary, arranged by the seasons of the year.

306 **Where to watch birds in Spain and Portugal.**
Laurence Rose.   London: Hamlyn, 1995. 215p. maps. (Hamlyn Birdwatching Guides).

This practical, illustrated guide to birdwatching covers all of Portugal and includes short sections on the types of bird to be found in the Tagus estuary and the Berlengas Islands, near Lisbon. It also advises on the best sites from which to view them.

Travels in Portugal, and through France and Spain.
See item no. 261.

Prehistory and Archaeology

307 **Roman Portugal. Volume II Gazetteer, inventário, Fascicule 2 . . . Coimbra . . . Lisboa.**
Jorge de Alarcão. Warminster, England: Aris & Phillips, 1988.
142p. 5 maps. bibliog.
Part of a work comprising two volumes in four fascicules, this book covers Roman Lisbon in a section (p. 110-42) which is divided into a brief introduction, a list of 373 Roman sites with brief details, a bibliography, an index and illustrative plates. Two of the accompanying folding maps relate to Lisbon. The text is in both Portuguese and English and is accompanied by eight line drawings and site plans in the Lisbon section. An extensive bibliography, predominantly of journal articles, and an index of locations complete the work.

308 **The Roman towns of Portugal.**
Jorge de Alarcão, Spanish Ministry of Culture. In: *The Hispano-Roman town.* Madrid: Minister [sic] of Culture/Àmbit Servicios Editoriales, 1993, p. 206-23. bibliog.
Jorge de Alarcão's essay covers the emergence of Olisipo (Lisbon) and the excavations of Mirobriga (Santiago de Cacém) to the south. Amongst the finds discussed are those of pottery from the second Iron Age in the Lisbon cathedral area, the Roman theatre excavations in the present-day Rua da Saudade in Lisbon's Alfama district and the *thermae*, or baths, under the Rua da Prata in the Baixa quarter of the city. This finely illustrated folio book was produced to accompany an exhibition for the 14th International Conference on Classical Archaeology, which was held in Tarragona, Spain. The final section of the volume is a catalogue of that exhibition.

309 **Portugal, 1001 sights: an archaeological and historical guide.**
James M. Anderson, M. Sheridan Lea. Calgary, Canada: University
of Calgary Press; London: Hale, 1995. 180p. 5 maps. bibliog.

Accompanied by eighty-seven black-and-white illustrations, this is a very readable
survey of Portuguese archaeological sites, preceded by a history of ancient
civilizations in Portugal from palaeolithic times. The section on Lisbon includes a
brief account of its successive occupations by Romans, Alans, Visigoths and Muslims.
Lisbon sites described are those of the Roman theatre in the Alfama district, the
Roman baths under the Rua da Prata and a garum manufactury found near the Casa
dos Bicos. Separate sections cover nearby towns such as Oeiras, Estoril and Cascais.

310 **The bell beaker cultures of Spain and Portugal.**
Richard J. Harrison. Cambridge, Massachusetts: Peabody Museum of
Archaeology and Ethnology, 1977. 257p. 15 maps. bibliog. (American
School of Prehistoric Research, Peabody Museum, Harvard Museum,
Bulletin no. 35).

A review of the beaker pottery culture of the late Neolithic period in Iberia. Chapter
four covers the Tagus estuary around Lisbon, including sites at São Pedro do Estoril,
Parede and the Praia das Maçãs, near Sintra. Harrison discusses the origins of the
beaker culture and suggests that whilst one source is local to Iberia, its roots are also
to be traced to central Europe. One hundred and ten figures illuminate the text.

311 **Subterranean Portugal.**
Museu Nacional de Arqueologia. Lisbon: Electa, 1994. 278p. 7 maps.
bibliog.

Published to accompany an exhibition in the Museu Nacional de Arqueologia, Lisbon
(26 February to 31 December 1994), this colourful book is divided into two undefined
parts. The first (p. 8-132) comprises a preface and twenty-three chapters by differing
authors on topics which include 'Lisbon before Man', 'Moslem Lisbon' and 'The
estuary of the River Tagus'. The second part (p. 141-274) is a catalogue of the
exhibition. Each part has a bibliography (p. 133-39 and p. 275-78) which includes a
small number of English-language publications, but no index is provided. Throughout,
the book is lavishly illustrated with high-quality colour photographs of both exhibits
and contextual material.

312 **Spain and Portugal: the prehistory of the Iberian peninsula.**
H. N. Savory. London: Thames & Hudson, 1968. 323p. 23 maps.
bibliog. (Ancient Peoples and Places, vol. 61).

Profusely illustrated with sixty-six photographs and sixty-eight line drawings of
artefacts and archaeological sites, this book covers the ancient history of the Lisbon
area in a number of its chapters. Most relevant are chapter five, 'Rock-cut tombs and
the Tagus culture' (p. 117-37), and the two succeeding chapters on beaker culture and
metalworkers. Amongst the archaeological finds discussed are those made at São
Pedro do Estoril, Sintra and Licea (Oeiras).

Unknown Portugal: archaeological itineraries.
See item no. 202.

Guide to the Archaeological Museum.
See item no. 632.

Inventário do Museu Nacional de Arqueologia: colecção de escultura romana. (Inventory of the National Museum of Archaeology: collection of Roman sculpture.)
See item no. 640.

Portugal das origens à época romana. (Portugal from its origins to the Roman period.)
See item no. 645.

History

General

313 **The Portugal story: three centuries of exploration and discovery.**
John Dos Passos. London: Robert Hale, 1969. 402p. 2 maps. bibliog.
Although largely concerned with Portuguese maritime expansion, part one, 'How
Portugal began', contains much of relevance to Lisbon's growth, in particular, a
section (p. 22-34) which helpfully paraphrases *De expugnatione Lyxbonensi*, the
contemporary Latin account of the siege of Lisbon by Afonso Henriques in 1147. In
part five (p. 259-71), there is also a protracted depiction of the Lisbon Court of King
Manuel the Fortunate (1495-1521).

314 **Dicionário da história de Lisboa.** (Dictionary of the history of Lisbon.)
Edited by Francisco Santana, Eduardo Sucena. Lisbon: Carlos
Quintas, 1994. 991p. bibliog.
Probably the best modern Portuguese introduction to the history of Lisbon, this is an
alphabetically-arranged dictionary in which each entry has its own bibliography.
Although it contains a thematic index, it is not easy to find specific references to
names or places included within entries. The volume is illustrated by a number of
monochrome photographs but these are uncaptioned.

315 **Lisboa no passado e no presente. Lisbon: past and present.**
Lisbonne: le passé et le présent. Lissabon: Gestern und Heute.
Vol. 1.
Edited by Jorge Segurado, preface by General França Borges.
Lisbon: Edições Excelsior, 1971. 360p.
A magnificent folio volume, with well over 100 black-and-white photographs and full-
page colour plates of Lisbon. The text comprises five sections covering the period up
to the late 15th century.

316　**The British Army in the records of St. George's Church, Lisbon.**
Rev. H. F. Fulford Williams. *Journal of the Society for Army Historical Research*, vol. XVII (1938), p. 179-80.
Many of the records of the English Cemetery in Lisbon for the Stuart Period were lost in a shipwreck, but the existing church registers date from 1721. The author has studied these from the point of view of identifying military victims of the Seven Years War (1756-63), the American Revolutionary War (1775-83) and the 1797 expedition to Lisbon under General Charles Stuart, as well as of 19th- and 20th-century conflicts including the Peninsular, Boer and Great Wars. In all, he has traced burial records at St George's of 754 British soldiers and sailors over this period.

British Historical Society of Portugal Annual Report and Review.
See item no. 672.

Historical Society, Lisbon Branch, Annual Report.
See item no. 674.

Subsídios para a bibliografia de história local portuguesa. (Contributions to the bibliography of Portuguese local history.)
See item no. 685.

To 1147 AD

317　**De expugnatione Lyxbonensi: the conquest of Lisbon.**
Edited from the unique manuscript in Corpus Christi College, Cambridge, with a translation into English by Charles Wendell David. New York: Octagon Books, 1976. Reprint of 1936 ed. by Columbia University Press. 201p. map. bibliog. (Records of Civilization, Sources and Studies, no. XXIV).
A fascinating account in Latin, with parallel English translation, of the siege of Lisbon in 1147 when the city was wrested from Moorish possession. This chronicle was written by an Anglo-Norman crusader in the service of the Portuguese king, Afonso Henriques. Contrary to some interpretations, David believes that the text is addressed to a Suffolk nobleman, Osbert of Bawdsey, by a knight who signed himself with the initial R. Others believe Osbert (or Osbern) is the author.

318　**The English Crusaders in Portugal.**
H. A. R. Gibbs.　In: *Chapters in Anglo-Portuguese relations.*　Edited by Edgar Prestage.　Watford, England: Voss & Michael Ltd., 1935, p. 1-23. bibliog.
The capture of Lisbon from the Moors in 1147 by Afonso Henriques, with the help of north European Crusaders is recorded in *De expugnatione Lyxbonensi* (q.v.), of which Gibbs here provides a substantial summary. He also provides details of the earlier attempt by the Crusaders, in 1140, to displace the Moors from Lisbon before chronicling their activities to the south of Lisbon after 1147. The text is based on a public lecture given at King's College, London in 1934.

319 **The 'Conquest of Lisbon' and its author.**
Harold Livermore. *Portuguese Studies*, vol. 6 (1990), p. 1-16.
A piece of scholarly detective work in which the celebrated historian of Portugal, Harold Livermore, attempts to resolve the riddle of the authorship of the *De expugnatio Lyxbonensi* (q.v.). His conclusion is that the writer was Raol, a priest, who addressed the text to Osbert of Bawdsey, in the abbreviated form Osb. Osbert has been seen by some other scholars as the writer himself.

320 **Conquista de Lisboa aos Mouros, 1147. Narrações pelos Cruzados Osberno e Arnulfo, testemunhas presenciais do cêrco. Texto latino e sua tradução para português.** (The Conquest of Lisbon from the Moors, 1147. Accounts by the Crusaders Osbern and Arnulfo, eye-witnesses of the siege. Latin text and Portuguese translation.)
Edited and translated from the Latin by José Augusto de Oliveira.
Lisbon: S. Industriais da C.M.L., 1936. 174p.
Reproduces the celebrated account by an Anglo-Norman crusader, here assigned the name Osbern, who assisted Afonso Henriques in the recapture of the Lisbon from the Moors in 1147. The second account, by another Crusader, Arnulfo, comprises a letter addressed to the Bishop of Therouanne in France which is somewhat more succinct in its relation of events.

321 **The Moors in Spain and Portugal.**
Jan Read. London: Faber & Faber, 1974. 268p. 4 maps. bibliog.
Read provides a detailed account of the recapture of Lisbon from the Moors in 1147 with a lengthy critical commentary on the *De expugnatione Lyxbonensi* (q.v.). Also, in chapter XVIII, 'A kingdom is born: the origins of an independent Portugal, 1087-1179', Read explains the factional skirmishes on both the Christian side, between the putative Portugal and León, and amongst the Moorish caliphs.

322 **Osbernus, De expugnatione lyxbonensi.** (Osbern, the siege of Lisbon.)
Edited by William Stubbs. In: *Rerum britannicarum medii aevi scriptores; or, Chronicles and memorials of Great Britain and Ireland during the Middle Ages, 38. Chronicles and memorials of Richard I, Volume I, Itinerarium peregrinorum et gesta regis Ricardi.* London: Longman, Green, Longman, Roberts & Green, 1864, cxlii-clxxxii.
This edition of the original Latin text of the *De expugnatione* occupies p. cxlii-clxxxii of the preliminary section of this volume. It is included in this volume as an illustration of the activities of English Crusaders during the reign of King Richard I of England. The editor attributes authorship to Osbernus, who is seen by modern editors to have been the text's recipient rather than its originator. A short English introduction to the Latin text is supplied by Stubbs.

The history of the siege of Lisbon: a novel.
See item no. 579.

Mediaeval and Renaissance periods, 1147-1580

323 **Lisbon in the Renaissance. A new translation of the *Urbis Olisiponis Descriptio*.**
Damião de Góis, translated by Jeffrey S. Ruth. New York: Italica Press, 1996. 76p. 11 maps. bibliog.

Damião de Góis was a humanist acquaintance of Erasmus whose Latin account of Lisbon was published in 1554 when the city was enjoying commercial and political importance as the hub of Portuguese expansion overseas. His text provides a detailed description of the city's history from classical times and of its contemporary architectural appearance. This is all the more valuable given Lisbon's destruction by the earthquake of 1755. In this edition the text is enhanced by a substantial introduction and a detailed map of Lisbon published in Cologne in 1598 which, unfortunately, is printed in eleven separate sections scattered through the book. The original Latin text, with Portuguese translation, was published by Raúl Machado in 1937, *Lisboa de Quinhentos: descrição de Lisboa* (Lisbon: Livraria Avelar Machado).

324 **Lisbon in the days of King Manuel I, 1495-1521: promenades.**
Instituto Português de Museus. Lisbon: Instituto Português de Museus, [1995]. 72p. map. bibliog.

An illustrated guide, in colour, to the reign of King Manuel during which Portugal undertook the most momentous of the Voyages of Discovery. An impression of the city of Lisbon at this time is captured through a number of suggested itineraries around Lisbon. Colour photographs, including sights at Belém as well as in Lisbon itself, accompany the description.

325 **The festivities of December 1552 in Lisbon.**
Harold V. Livermore. Coimbra, Portugal: Revista Universitária, 1984. 20p.

An offprint from the *Revista da Universidade de Coimbra*, vol. 31 (1984), p. 321-36, which studies a manuscript in the Robert Southey archive held in the British Library. From it, Livermore recounts the arrival of the Emperor Charles V's daughter, the Princess D. Joana, at Barreiro on the River Tagus opposite Lisbon. She was to marry the Portuguese prince, João, who later died of fever in Lisbon in 1554. King João III escorted the princess from Barreiro and a crowd of 100,000 inhabitants lined the streets between Xabregas and Boa Hora. The celebrations were soured by an English protestant, Robert Gardner, who snatched church plate from the royal chaplain and was consequently burned at the stake, after having his hands amputated and being led through the streets of Lisbon in an ox-cart.

326 **The English in Portugal, 1367-87. Excerpts from the Chronicles of Dom Fernando and Dom João.**
Fernão Lopes, introduction, translation and notes by Derek W. Lomax, R. J. Oakley. Warminster, England: Aris & Phillips, 1988. 368p. 4 maps. bibliog.

In this parallel text edition, in Portuguese and English, of extracts from the Chronicles of Fernão Lopes, (c.1385-c.1460) there are copious references to the role of Lisbon, whilst the editors' introduction addresses in detail the 1383 rebellion, largely orchestrated from Lisbon, which led to the accession of King João I. Amongst the historical events in the Chronicles are the Castilian fleet's sacking of Lisbon in 1382 and Nun'Alvares's retaliation on the Castilians at the battles of Alcântara and Aljubarrota.

327 **Ambassador from Venice: Pietro Pasqualigo in Lisbon, 1501.**
Donald Weinstein. Minneapolis, Minnesota: University of Minnesota Press, 1960. 112p.

Using the only copy in the United States of the 1501 edition of the *Oration* by Pietro Pasqualigo, Venetian Ambassador to Portugal, Weinstein assesses the Venetians' reaction to the Portuguese discovery of the Ocean route to India by Vasco da Gama. Pasqualigo's *Oration* included a request for King Manuel I of Portugal to assist the Venetians against the Turks. As well as a facsimile, transcript and commentary on the *Oration*, Weinstein includes an account of the Ambassador's experiences at the Royal Court in Lisbon.

Atlas de cidades medievais portuguesas, séculos XII-XV, vol. I. (Atlas of mediaeval Portuguese towns, XIIth-XVth centuries, vol. I.)
See item no. 114.

Spanish rule, 1580-1640

328 **The principal navigations, voyages, traffiques & discoveries of the English nation made by sea or overland to the remote and farthest distant quarters of the earth at any time within the compass of these 1600 years.**
Richard Hakluyt. London: Dent, 1926-36. 8 vols.

Amongst the events recounted here are the Lisbon involvement in the Spanish Armada, from whence the fleet sailed in 1588 (vol. ii) and the subsequent maritime exploits in the Lisbon area of John Evesham (vol. iv), Thomas Stevens (vol. iv), Francis Drake and Sir John Norris (vol. iv), Robert Devereux, Earl of Essex (vol. v) and Robert Tomson (vol. vi). For a fuller account of the abortive Lisbon mission of Drake, Norris and Essex, see item no. 330.

329 **Livro das grandezas de Lisboa. Contém fac-simile da edição original de 1620 e texto actualizado.** (Book of the splendours of Lisbon. Contains a facsimile of the 1620 edition and modernized text.) *Frei* Nicolau de Oliveira, edited by Maria Helena Bastos. Lisbon: Vega, 1991. 703p. (Colecção Conhecer Lisboa).

A photographic reprint of a classic survey of 17th-century Lisbon which was first published in 1620. This is followed by a modern version of the text which starts with a geographical definition of Portugal and a survey of the ancient Kings of Spain and Portugal. Approximately one half of the book, its central sections, constitutes a detailed census of Lisbon's parishes, major institutions and buildings. An explanation is also given of Lisbon's administrative apparatus, with a thorough listing of the number of occupants of each job-title within many of Lisbon's major institutions, such as the Customs House and the Casa da India, the body which regulated trade with Portugal's overseas territories.

330 **The expeditions of Sir John Norris and Sir Francis Drake to Spain and Portugal, 1589.** Edited by R. B. Wernham. Aldershot, England: Temple Smith for the Navy Records Society, 1988. 380p. 5 maps. bibliog.

Two hundred and two contemporary letters and documents make up this volume, which begins with a sixty-six page prefatory narrative of the expeditions which they cover. Following the defeat of the Spanish Armada, which had set off from Lisbon, England decided to press home its success by burning the surviving vessels in Lisbon and Seville and by seizing the Portuguese capital, prior to an assault on the Portuguese Azores. After landing his forces at Peniche, 70km west of Lisbon, Norris and the Earl of Essex expected local supporters of António, Prior de Crato, the royal pretender, to rally to their anti-Spanish cause. When this, and their planned rendezvous with Drake, who had lingered at Cascais, failed to materialize, Norris himself withdrew to that town. Approximately 2,000 soldiers died in this failed campaign.

331 **Alarms and excursions in Lisbon under Castilian domination: the case of Captain Richard Butler.** Michael E. Williams. *Portuguese Studies,* vol. 6 (1990), p. 94-114.

A fascinating study, using historical sources, of Richard Butler, an Irish Catholic who was arrested by King Philip II of Spain after landing in Portugal in 1592, when Portugal was ruled by the Spaniards. Butler's exciting life as a servant to Walter Raleigh and sometime sailor and pirate is itself of great interest, as is Williams's account of the intrigue afoot amongst expatriate Britons and Irishmen in Lisbon. This article goes on to recount his trial by the Spaniards which culminated in a death sentence, a punishment later commuted to service in the King's galleys.

Independence, 1640-1754

332 The Royalists at sea in 1650.
R. C. Anderson. *The Mariners' Mirror: the Journal of the Society for Nautical Research*, vol. XVII (1931), p. 135-68.
Virtually all of this article concerns the confrontation in the Tagus between the Royalist fleet of Prince Rupert and the Commonwealth ships under Admiral Blake. Details are also given of the ships snatched as 'prizes' by the Royalist fleet and, in particular, the furore caused by its capture of *The Roebuck*, a ship bound for Lisbon with goods for the city's merchants. Indeed, the Portuguese were forced to take steps to prevent Prince Maurice from operating as a privateer from the safety of Lisbon. Another article by the same author, 'The Royalists at sea in 1649' (*The Mariners' Mirror*, vol. XIV [1928], p. 320-37) also briefly touches upon this naval confrontation in the Tagus.

333 Lord Tyrawly in Lisbon: an Anglo-Irish Protestant at the Portuguese Court, 1728-41.
C. R. Boxer. *History Today*, vol. 20 (November 1970), p. 791-98.
Tyrawly was sent to Lisbon in 1728 to replace Brigadier General Dormer who had sensationally attempted to murder the British Consul General in a Lisbon street. Tyrawly disliked the English Factory, Roman Catholics and Lisbon. However, Boxer shows that despite his gambling habit and his irascibility, Tyrawly had personal skills which he used to cultivate the advisers of King João V. When his request for a recall from Lisbon was finally successful, in 1741, he allegedly returned with three 'wives' and fourteen children.

334 Memoirs of Lady Fanshawe, wife of Sir Richard Fanshawe Bt., ambassador from Charles II to the Courts of Portugal & Madrid, written by herself, containing extracts from the correspondence of Sir Richard Fanshawe.
Lady Fanshawe, edited, with an introduction, by Beatrice Marshall. London; New York: John Lane, The Bodley Head, 1905. 312p.
Lord Fanshawe arrived in Lisbon as English representative in September 1662 and stayed there, with his wife, until August 1663. Lady Fanshawe records not only their social and diplomatic contact with the Portuguese Court but also their experience of a popular uprising in Lisbon in May 1663 and the battle of Évora, at which the Spanish army of Don Juan de Austria was defeated by Anglo-Portuguese forces. There is also a well-observed account of Lisbon life and trade which conveys the writer's favourable impression of the city: 'Lisbon with the river is the goodliest situation that ever I saw'.

335 John Methuen and the Anglo-Portuguese treaties of 1703.
A. D. Francis. *The Historical Journal*, vol. III (1960), p. 103-24.
An account of the protracted diplomacy in Lisbon of John Methuen, who was first appointed as Minister to that city in 1691, and of his son, Paul, who succeeded as Minister in 1696. However, John himself returned to Lisbon in 1702 to conduct delicate negotiations with the Portuguese Crown aimed at extricating Portugal from a

treaty with the French and gaining privileges for the Royal Navy in Portugal. Having been elevated to the title of Ambassador to Lisbon, John Methuen ceremonially entered the city in September 1703 and three months later successfully completed the Treaty negotiations by which Portuguese wines were to be charged a lower tariff on import to England whilst English cloth would be admitted to Portugal.

336   The Methuens and Portugal, 1691-1708.
A. D. Francis.   Cambridge, England: Cambridge University Press, 1966. 397p. map. bibliog.

John Methuen rose from relative obscurity in Wiltshire to become the British minister at Lisbon in 1691, a post which he then held alternately with his son Paul Methuen, who was appointed to the rank of ambassador in 1706 after his father's death. John Methuen was instrumental in persuading Portugal to break its alliance with France. The Methuen Treaties allegedly did more damage to Portugal by allowing British woollen goods into Portugal, than they benefitted the country by facilitating the export of wine to England.

337   Portugal, 1715-1808: Joanine, Pombaline and Rococo Portugal as seen by British diplomats and traders.
David Francis.   London: Tamesis Books, 1985. 291p. map. bibliog.
(Colección Támesis, Serie Monografías, CIX).

As well as a section dedicated to the Lisbon earthquake (chapter six), the volume also covers court life, Anglo-Portuguese trade and the activities of the Marquis of Pombal in the capital. An appendix addresses 'The Strangford-Sidney Smith controversy' concerning the respective roles of these two Britons in the evacuation from Lisbon of the Portuguese Regent shortly before the advancing French forces entered the city in 1807.

338   Prince Rupert at Lisbon.
Samuel Rawson Gardiner.   London: Royal Historical Society, 1902. 21p. (The Camden Miscellany, vol. 10).

An edition of various documents contemporary to the confrontation in 1650 in the Tagus estuary between the Commonwealth fleet of Admiral Blake and the Royalist ships under Prince Rupert of the Rhine. Gardiner uses British Museum manuscripts to demonstrate that the Portuguese monarch, João IV, actively sided with the Royalist forces. The documents are printed in their original English orthography.

339   Lisbon in the age of Dom João V, 1689-1750: promenades.
Instituto Português de Museus.   Lisbon: Instituto Português de Museus, [1995]. 72p.

An illustrated history of the period of King João V (1706-50) told by means of a guided walk through the present-day city. In the early 18th century, bolstered by revenue from Brazil, Lisbon enjoyed a period of splendour in which João built a splendid opera house and initiated work on the palace at Queluz. However, the earthquake of 1755 swept away much of this grandeur in the city itself.

340   **The private correspondence of Sir Benjamin Keene, K.B.**
Sir Benjamin Keene, edited with introduction and notes by *Sir* Richard
Lodge.   Cambridge, England: Cambridge University Press, 1933.
548p.

In 1746, Keene went to Lisbon as Envoy Extraordinary to the Court of Portugal.
During his two years in the Portuguese capital he was particularly beguiled by the
charms of nearby Sintra. His experiences in Lisbon were partly recorded in the five
letters reproduced here, dating from 1748-49. However, his later letters from Madrid
also convey his reaction to the Lisbon earthquake of 1755, which he himself felt
whilst at the Escorial Palace in Spain.

341   **The Lisbon of Rupert and Blake.**
Dora Greenwell McChesney.   *Cornhill Magazine,* 3rd series, vol. XXII
(1907), p. 227-44.

A slightly pompous account of the dispute in 1650 between the Royalist fleet of Prince
Rupert, anchored near the Torre de Belém and the Commonwealth fleet under Admiral
Blake, massed slightly further from Lisbon, off Oeiras. This involved the diplomatic
efforts of King João IV who tried to steer a course between his instinctive support for
another European monarchy and his wish to avoid giving offence to the new masters
of England.

Late 18th century, 1755-1806

342   **Une ville des Lumières: la Lisbonne de Pombal.** (A city of the
Enlightenment: the Lisbon of Pombal.)
José-Augusto França.   Paris: S.E.V.P.E.N., 1965. 259p. 3 maps.
bibliog.

The original, French-language edition of a study depicting pre-earthquake Lisbon as
well as describing the cataclysm itself. França also describes the efforts, orchestrated
by Pombal, to rebuild the city. In addition, the work has a useful critical bibliography
and black-and-white illustrations.

343   **The genuine legal sentence pronounced by the High Court of
Judicature of Portugal upon the conspirators against the life of his
most faithful Majesty, with the just motives for the same. Literally
translated from the original Portuguese, as printed at the Court of
Lisbon, by order and authority of the said tribunal.**
London: E. Owen & T. Harrison, 1759. 40p.

Published in England in the same year as Coustos's gruesome account of the tortures
of the Lisbon Inquisition, this account of the sentencing of the Távora conspirators
who attempted to assassinate King José I in Lisbon in 1758 reveals the equally brutal
punishments handed out by the royal courts in the Portuguese capital. After a one-
sided and vitriolic presentation of the evidence, the main conspirators were first to be

strangled, then have their eight leg and arm bones broken, be tortured on the wheel and then burnt, with their bodies finally being thrown into the sea. The sentences were carried out at Belém, where a small monument remains today.

344 **Lisboa e o Marquês de Pombal. Exposição comemorativa do bicentenário da morte do Marquês de Pombal, 1782-1982, Museu da Cidade, Lisboa, 10 de Novembro a 31 de Dezembro de 1982.**
(Lisbon and the Marquis of Pombal. Commemorative exhibition to mark the bicentenary of the death of the Marquis of Pombal, 1782-1982, City Museum, Lisbon, 10 November to 31 December 1982.)
Irisalva Moita.   Lisbon: Museu da Cidade, 1982. 3 vols. bibliog.

Photographic plates comprise some 285 pages of this three-volume catalogue from a major exhibition on Pombal. These concentrate, in volume one, on portraits of Pombal and his contemporaries, in volume two on depictions of the 1755 earthquake and the reconstruction of Lisbon and in volume three on the ceramic output of the Pombaline era, particularly from the Fábrica do Rato in Lisbon. The text describes more than 600 exhibits which include documents, books, medallions, paintings and ceramic ware.

345 **The historical and the posthumous memoirs of Sir Nathaniel William Wraxall, 1772-1784.**
Sir Nathaniel William Wraxall, edited with notes and additional chapters by Henry B. Wheatley.   London: Bickers & Son, 1884.
5 vols.

Wraxall visited Lisbon as a young man at the start of a grand tour of Europe. In the early part of volume one he describes, rather drily, his experience of Lisbon in 1772. He provides fascinating detail of the monarch José I who, at the time of writing, was still refusing to sleep other than in tents or wooden barracks for fear of a repeat of the 1755 earthquake. Although Wraxall opines that 'no royal house in Europe was so musical as that of Portugal', he finds court life in Lisbon and nearby Salvaterra lacking in public spectacle. As well as discussing such figures as the Marchioness of Távora, Pombal and José's Spanish Queen, Mariana Victoria, Wraxall describes enjoyable visits to the collection of royal carriages, then held at Alcântara, to Fielding's grave, bullfights, the opera, Lisbon cathedral and Belém.

Dictator of Portugal: a life of the Marquis of Pombal, 1699-1782.
See item no. 378.

Pombal: paradox of the Enlightenment.
See item no. 383.

19th century, 1807-99

346 **The journal of an army surgeon during the Peninsular War.**
Charles Boutflower. Manchester, England: Refuge Printing
Department, 1912. 181p.

Boutflower made two visits to Lisbon during his Peninsular War service, both of
which are recorded here in diary form. His first was in August 1809 when, having
arrived in Lisbon, he was obliged to walk three miles to Belém and was disgusted by
the filth and squalor that he encountered on the way. After military duties took him
across the Tagus to Aldeia Galega (now Montijo) and thence to Elvas, Badajoz and
elsewhere, he returned to the Portuguese capital for several days in January 1811. He
experienced a minor earthquake but otherwise found Lisbon's citizens going about
their work largely oblivious to the military activities around them.

347 **The life and times of Henry, Lord Brougham.**
Lord Brougham. Edinburgh, London: William Blackwood, 1871.
3 vols.

In 1806 Brougham was part of the British naval mission to Portugal, led by Lord St
Vincent and Lord Rosslyn on the warship *Hibernia*. Their purpose was to mount guard
in the Tagus at a time of threatened French invasion of Portugal. Brougham describes
not only his own intrigues in Lisbon, including plans to kidnap the Prince Regent and
take him to Brazil, but also how the Royal Navy held court to Portuguese dignitaries
on their vessels in the Tagus. After the departure of the fleet, Brougham remained in
Lisbon and several of his letters from there to Lord Rosslyn and Viscount Howick are
reproduced here.

348 **A treatise on the defence of Portugal, with a military map of the
country, to which is added a sketch of the manners and customs of
the inhabitants and principal events of the campaigns under Lord
Wellington.**
William Granville Eliot. London: T. Egerton, 1811. 2nd ed., with
considerable additions. 302p. 5 maps.

Chapter X is entitled 'Lisbon and the environs: amusements of the Portuguese'
(p. 169-90), but the city is also evident in many other parts of this book. Like other
English visitors, the author finds Lisbon attractive from a distance but dirty from a
closer perspective. Eliot was a Royal Artillery captain but his keen observation goes
well beyond comments on the military aspects of the Lisbon area and indeed his
account is much more readable than its austere title suggests. He found time to admire
S. Roque and S. Vicente de Fora churches, the equestrian statue of D. José and the
Baixa amongst other Lisbon sights. He also writes authoritatively of the Lisbon opera
and theatres. In addition, he travelled to Queluz and Sintra. The latter part of the book
contains a wealth of practical information on such matters as the Portuguese language,
manners, prices, weights and measures.

349 **Britannia sickens: Sir Arthur Wellesley and the Convention of Cintra.**
Michael Glover.   London: Leo Cooper, 1970. 207p. 3 maps. bibliog.

An account of Wellington's Portuguese campaign in 1808. Glover sees his victory over General Junot, the commander of the French army, as a triumph also over the inefficiency and traditions of his superiors in the British Army. The Convention of Cintra (Sintra) in 1808 confirmed the safety of Lisbon, but its generous terms towards the occupying French army aroused much controversy. The volume is illustrated with black-and-white photographs, mostly reproductions of paintings and sketches of the personalities and incidents of the campaign.

350 **Surgeon Henry's trifles: events of a military life.**
Walter Henry, edited, with an introduction and notes by Pat Hayward.
London: Chatto & Windus, 1970. 281p.

In 1811, whilst attached to the 2nd Battalion of the 66th Foot as a surgeon during the Peninsular War, Irishman Walter Henry visited Lisbon three times. He first arrived from Portsmouth in May, observing of Lisbon that 'though all is majestic and magnificent without, all is stench and filth within'. He lodged with a minor Portuguese nobleman with whom he could only communicate in Latin. After a brief interlude in the Coimbra area, Henry was sent back to Lisbon with 200 wounded men in July, and he remained there for four months, mixing gruesome amputations with observations of street life and the consumption of Colares and Carcavelos wines. During his final visit, in December, he witnessed Christmas church celebrations and visited the Jerónimos monastery at Belém as well as Sintra.

351 **Portugal and the Anglo-Russian naval crisis, 1808.**
Donald D. Horward.   *Naval War College Review,* vol. 34, no. 3 (1981), p. 48-74.

A study of the confrontation between the ostensibly neutral Russian fleet and the Royal Navy in the Tagus at Lisbon in 1808, at a time of conflict with the French. Britain's assertion of its naval strength against the Russians reinforced the land victories of the Duke of Wellington against the French in Portugal. Horward claims that the Lisbon incident was a key moment in the reconquest of the Iberian peninsula from the French and, ultimately, in the collapse of Napoléon's empire.

352 **Adventures in the Rifle Brigade in the Peninsula, France and the Netherlands from 1809 to 1815.**
J. Kincaid.   London: T. & W. Boone, 1830. 351p.

An account of Captain Kincaid's arrival at Lisbon during the Peninsular War and of his involvement at the Lines of Torres Vedras occupies chapters two to four of these memoirs. Kincaid was one of many British visitors to declare, whilst observing Lisbon from the River Tagus, that 'there are few cities in the world that can promise so much and none, I hope, that can keep it so badly' (p. 5).

353 **Letters from Portugal and Spain, comprising an account of the operations of the armies under their excellencies Sir Arthur Wellesley and Sir John Moore, from the landing of the troops in Mondego Bay to the battle of Corunna. Illustrated with engravings from drawings made on the spot.**
Adam Neale.   London: Richard Phillips, 1809. 116p. map.

As with Eliot (see item no. 348), the militaristic title of this volume belies its inclusion of a great deal of descriptive detail of Lisbon and its surroundings. This includes accounts of the 1755 earthquake, of General Junot's occupation of Lisbon in 1807, and of visits to the Lisbon aqueduct, the Ajuda palace, Belém, Torres Vedras, Queluz and Sintra. Neale finds Lisbon to have a 'delightful character' despite 'the extreme inequality of the ground' and his visit is well illustrated by engravings from his own drawings.

354 **The Lines of Torres Vedras: the first three Lines and fortifications south of the Tagus.**
A. H. Norris, Robert W. Bremner.   Lisbon: British Historical Society of Portugal, 1986. 3rd rev. ed. 63p. 4 maps. bibliog.

In October 1809 Wellington, from Lisbon, instigated the construction of the Lines of Torres Vedras, which were successfully to repel the French advance on the Portuguese capital, led by Masséna in 1810. In this third edition of a work first published in 1972, Norris describes the construction of the first two Lines, north of Lisbon, and quotes from contemporary sources as to their effectiveness (Part I), before surveying 'The Lines today' (Part II). In Part III, Bremner describes the third Line, built between Junqueira and Oeiras to provide protection for an orderly escape, should the French have broken through the first two Lines. He also writes of the fortifications south of Tagus, between Caparica and Almada, built to forestall any French attack from the south.

355 **Letters from Portugal and Spain written during the march of the British troops under Sir John Moore, with a map of the route and appropriate engravings.**
An Officer.   Cambridge, England: Ken Trotman, 1985. 320p. map.

The reprint of a text first published in London in 1809. The first six letters (p. 1-82) cover Lisbon and its environs in considerable detail. The appearance of Lisbon citizens, their leisure activities and the sights of the city are amply covered. The author is not impressed by Lisbon, which he depicts as 'a chaos of nastiness, poverty and wretchedness'. Excursions to the suburbs include Belém and St Julian's fort, on the Tagus estuary.

356   A concise and accurate account of the proceedings of the squadron
under the command of Rear Admiral Sir Will. Sidney Smith in
effecting the escape, and escorting the Royal Family of Portugal to
the Brazils on the 29th of November, 1807 and also the sufferings
of the Royal fugitives during their voyage from Lisbon to Rio de
Janerio [sic], etc.
Thomas O'Neill.   London: Published by the Author, 1809. 79p.

An account by a British officer of the machinations in Lisbon involving Smith and the
British minister, Strangford, to secure the escape to Brazil of the Portuguese royal
family and their entourage from the capital, just before the city was taken by Junot's
advancing army in November 1807.

357   War in the Peninsular.
Jan Read.   London: Faber & Faber, 1977. 256p. maps. bibliog.

Read successfully sets out to produce 'a book for the general reader' which covers, in
some detail, the French occupation of Lisbon in 1807 and Wellesley's subsequent
success behind the Lines of Torres Vedras. Read also concisely explains the
complexities of the Convention of Sintra (1808), whereby the French were allowed to
evacuate their forces from the city. The book has a full bibliography and a most useful
chronology of the campaigns.

358   A sketch of the causes and consequences of the late emigration to
the Brazils.
Ralph Rylance.   London: Longman, Hurst, Rees & Orme, 1808. 78p.

Rylance explains the background and the preparations for the naval mission of Rear-
Admiral Smith and the Earl of St Vincent to Lisbon. Their goal of extricating the
Portuguese Regent and his entourage from Lisbon before the arrival there of the
French invasion forces was accomplished in November 1807. The Royal Navy
ensured their safe transport from the Tagus to Rio de Janeiro.

359   Narrative of the Peninsular War from 1808 to 1813.
Charles William Vane, Marquess of Londonderry.   London: Henry
Colburn, 1828. 2 maps.

Vane was a colonel in the 10th Royal Hussars during the Peninsular War. Here he
provides an account both of Junot's occupation of Lisbon in 1807 and of the entry into
the city of British troops following the signing of the Convention of Sintra (1808).
There is also a chapter on Wellesley's (Wellington's) activities in Lisbon. Two fine
colour maps illustrate the complex logistics of the War.

360   The story of Wordsworth's 'Cintra'.
John Edwin Wells.   Studies in Philology, vol. 18 (1921), p. 15-76.

An account of how, in 1809, William Wordsworth came to publish his tract against the
Convention of Sintra, which had been signed in 1808 between the British and French,
in the wake of the Battle of Vimeiro. The Convention had effectively obliged the
French to abandon Lisbon but allowed them an orderly escape with their booty and
forces intact. The tract is depicted by Wells as expressing Wordsworth's moral
indignation against what he saw as the British betrayal of the Spaniards in their

struggle against France. This study is completed by a thorough bibliographical analysis of the publication in its variant forms.

361   **The Convention of Cintra.**
William Wordsworth.   In: *Selected prose*.   Edited, with an introduction and notes by John G. Hampden.   Harmondsworth, England: Penguin Books, 1988, p. 166-249.

Wordsworth's longest prose work was this political tract criticizing the Convention of Sintra of 1808, whereby Hew Dalrymple had reached agreement with the French, following Wellington's success at the battle of Vimeiro. First published in 1809, this prolix document is here reproduced (p. 166-249) in an accessible, abridged form, with introductory comments by John Hampden. Wordsworth felt that the British government and generals had not obtained an agreement sufficiently beneficial to the Spaniards in their conflict with the French. Arguably a part of the text of this tract was actually written by Samuel Coleridge. The full text, *William Wordsworth's 'Convention of Cintra', a facsimile of the 1809 tract,* was edited by Gordon Kent Thomas (Provo, Utah: Brigham Young University Press, 1983. 216p.).

Early 20th century, 1900-38

362   **The first of February in Lisbon.**
Jean Finot.   *Contemporary Review,* vol. XCIII (January-June 1908), p. 287-99.

The author first bemoans the lack of overseas interest in Portugal which he sees as 'a veritable paradise, neglected by its inhabitants'. Then, following some criticism of the Portuguese monarchy, Finot recounts his meeting with João Franco, who was prime minister to King Carlos I (1889-1908). Franco's attempts to suppress opposition helped to precipitate the assassination of the King and his heir, Prince Luís Filipe on 1 February 1908 in Lisbon's Praça do Comércio. In the wake of the Lisbon regicide, Finot relays the general indifference of the populace to the event.

363   **A diplomatist in Europe.**
Sir Arthur Hardinge.   London: Jonathan Cape, 1927. 272p.

Sent as British Minister to Lisbon in 1911, Hardinge enjoyed two years in the Portuguese capital, which he chronicled in chapter VII of these memoirs (p. 222-49). In the wake of the 1910 overthrow of the Portuguese monarchy, Hardinge provides an account of the chaotic early days in Lisbon of the Portuguese Republic, with its frequently changing governments.

364 **Visitas reais entre as Cortes Portuguesa e Britânica, 1902-1910.**
Royal visits between the British and Portuguese Courts, 1902-1910.
Palácio Nacional da Ajuda and British Historical Society of Portugal.
Lisbon: Palácio Nacional da Ajuda/British Historical Society of
Portugal, 1985. 62p.

Preceded by a brief essay, this is an illustrated catalogue, in parallel Portuguese and
English texts, of an exhibition organized to mark the visit to Lisbon of Queen
Elizabeth II and the Duke of Edinburgh in 1985. It covers six royal visits; that of the
Portuguese Crown Prince Luís Filipe to the coronation of Edward VII in London
(1902), of King Edward VII to Lisbon (1903), of King Carlos I and Queen Amélia to
England (1904), of the separate visits of the Duke and Duchess of Connaught, and of
Queen Alexandra to Lisbon (1905) and of King Manuel II to England (1909). In all
there are 192 catalogue entries and a number of photographs taken on the visits. All of
the visits to Portugal were centred on Lisbon.

365 **Spring in Lisbon.**
V. S. Pritchett. *The Fortnightly Review*, new series, vol. CXXXI
(January-June 1932), p. 700-12.

An essay in four numbered sections which collectively attempt to capture the mood of
contemporary Lisbon. After a visit to the governor of a Lisbon gaol and reference to
the trial of Alves Reis, a celebrated bank fraudster, Pritchett addresses more perennial
themes such as bullfighting and *saudade*, the typically Portuguese notion of yearning
which permeates Lisbon's *fado* songs and music.

366 **My diplomatic education.**
Norval Richardson. New York: Dodd, Mead & Company, 1923.
337p.

A lively account of the worldwide diplomatic life of Norval Richardson, which
included an eighteen-month period in Lisbon as Secretary to the American Legation
there. The period after the 1910 Revolution, according to Richardson, witnessed 150
changes of occupant of the post of Portuguese Prime Minister, all of which made
diplomatic life difficult, but eventful, for the author. His lively account of dealing with
a country in which one Prime Minister, Sidónio Pais, was actually shot during the
author's period in Lisbon and his description of the US Legation's attempts to foster
good relations with Portugal combine to convey his enjoyment of his posting.

Second World War, 1939-45

367 **From Lisbon to Jamaica: a study of British refugee rescue during
the Second World War.**
Paul R. Bartrop. *Immigrants & Minorities*, vol. 13, no. 1 (1994),
p. 48-64.

Lisbon has normally been portrayed as a haven for persecuted minorities fleeing
before Hitler's advance during the Second World War. However, Bartrop here tells

how, in November 1941, the Portuguese government ordered the deportation of about 500 European Jews who had taken refuge in the city. Following the refugees' appeal to the British government they were transported from Lisbon to safety in the British colony of Jamaica.

368 Flight into Portugal.
Ronald Bodley. London: Jarrolds, 1947. 224p.

The author fled from France to Lisbon ahead of the German occupying forces in 1940. Approximately a quarter of this account is of his stay of several months in Lisbon and Sintra, where he lodged with the Marquesa do Cadaval. Above all, it was the plight of the multinational body of refugees in Lisbon which most affected him but interspersed with descriptions of wartime Lisbon are accounts of bullfighting and episodes of Portuguese history. After visiting Batalha, Coimbra and the Alentejo, Bodley left Lisbon on a refugee ship bound for New York.

369 By safe hand. Letters of Sybil & David Eccles, 1939-42.
David Eccles. London; Sydney; Toronto: The Bodley Head, 1983. 432p.

Eccles was sent to the British Embassy in Lisbon to head its commercial section and soon established himself as the British government's expert on Iberia even though, by his own admission, he was unable to make himself understood in Portuguese. Here, some seventy-five letters written by Eccles from Lisbon to his wife Sybil, are printed. They cover three separate residences in Lisbon: the first from 30 April to 13 August 1940; the second from 28 June to 19 November 1941; and the third from January to August 1942. They shed light on diplomatic activity in Lisbon during the Second World War and include accounts of discussions, held in French, with Prime Minister Salazar, whom Eccles greatly admired. The correspondence also describes wartime visits to Lisbon by celebrities such as Noel Coward, the Duke of Kent, Ian Fleming and the Duke and Duchess of Windsor.

370 Lisbon: gateway to warring Europe.
Harvey Klemmer. *National Geographic Magazine,* vol. LXXX, no. 2 (August, 1941), p. 259-76.

Abundantly illustrated with black-and-white photographs, mostly taken by the author, this essay comprises an American's personal impressions of Lisbon at the height of the Second World War, when it was 'the only major gateway between warring Europe and the world outside'. Klemmer surveys a city of relative plenty, peopled by friendly natives and a wide assortment of exiles, emigrants seeking passage to the United States and agents of both the Axis and Allies. The photographs concentrate on street and river scenes rather than the historic monuments and buildings of Lisbon.

371 European junction.
Hugh Muir. London: George Harrap, 1942. 168p.

A fascinating account of life in Lisbon in 1940-41 from a staunchly pro-British viewpoint, which is nevertheless critical of Britain's failure to win the propaganda battle against Germany. As well as portraying the bustle of Lisbon as it sought to cope with an influx of refugees and emigrés, Muir points out some ironic juxtapositions in the city. He notes British-style pillar boxes in the streets and marmalade in the shops, but also observes a Nazi German school in Lisbon and German diplomats' cars bearing the swastika. Likewise, at the airport at nearby Sintra, then allegedly Europe's busiest centre of civil aviation, he sees British airliners on the apron next to those of German and Italian airlines, and the British Overseas Airways office next door to that of Lufthansa. His interview with a British merchant seaman, rescued from a torpedoed vessel off Lisbon, is also indicative of the city's involvement in the war.

Postwar period, 1945-

372 **Footprints in time.**
John Colville. London: Collins, 1976. 287p.
The autobiography of diplomat John Colville who, in October 1949, was sent to Lisbon as Head of Chancery to the British Embassy. In a chapter entitled, 'A Portuguese interlude', he draws contrasts between the busy, understaffed and contracting British Embassy and its expanding US counterpart. He also provides a fascinating glimpse of the rivalries between the many exiled members of European royal families resident in Estoril, including the ex-kings of Romania and Italy, the ex-Regent of Hungary and the Counts of Barcelona and Paris. Colville admired the Portuguese President, Salazar, as a man of personal humility. A further chapter covers 'Portuguese colonial rule'.

373 **Lisboa, 25 de Abril de 1974: breve roteiro fotográfico. Edição comemorativa do vigésimo aniversário do 25 de Abril.** (Lisbon, 25th April, 1974: brief photographic record. Commemorative edition of the twentieth anniversary of the 25th April revolution.)
Adelino Gomes, introduction by Mário Soares. Lisbon: Contexto, 1994. unpaginated.
An evocative collection of forty-four black-and-white photographs of the 1974 Portuguese Revolution as witnessed on the streets of Lisbon. The pictures show troops and crowds in the street and the arrests of secret police (PIDE) agents. The text is limited to one-line captions and to two two-page prefaces by President Soares and Adelino Gomes.

374 **Portuguese Revolution, 1974-76.**
Chris Hunt, edited by Lester A. Sobel. New York: Facts on File, 1976. 151p. map.
Despite its title, this diary of the Portuguese Revolution actually contains a significant amount of material on the decade or more before the April 1974 *coup d'état*. It provides much detail of events in Lisbon which would otherwise only be found in newspapers, and comprises a factual record of events rather than a political analysis of the Revolution.

As paredes em liberdade. (The liberated walls.)
See item no. 114.

Biographies and Autobiographies

375 **England's wealthiest son: a study of William Beckford.**
Boyd Alexander.   Fontwell, England: Centaur Press, 1962. 308p.
William Beckford made three visits to Portugal, in 1787, 1793-95 and 1798-99, in the course of which he established himself in Sintra and endeavoured to gain full acceptance at the Royal court and in Lisbon society. He was frustrated in the former ambition largely by the hostility of Robert Walpole, British Minister at Lisbon, who reflected the British Establishment's animosity to Beckford following his involvement in a moral scandal in England. Beckford's Portuguese experiences were recorded in his own *Italy, with sketches of Spain and Portugal* (see item no. 223), and *Recollections of an excursion to the monasteries of Alcobaça and Batalha* (see item no. 224), and these are covered by Alexander in chapter ten of this book.

376 **The elusive Baron: the life of Andrew Vincent Patterson, 1867-194? [sic].**
Lionel Alves.   Lisbon: The British Historical Society of Portugal, 1990. 53p.
Born in Cleveland, Ohio, to Irish immigrants, Andrew Patterson joined the Standard Oil Company and became the Lisbon manager of their subsidiary, Colonial Oil, from 1904 until the firm was sold in 1908. For reasons which are still not clear, he became the first and last American citizen to receive a Portuguese baronetcy in 1907. Alves describes Patterson's activities in Lisbon, which included publication of the first ever Portuguese motoring road map. He then goes on to describe Patterson's three marriages and his corresponding decline into penury before his unrecorded death sometime in the 1940s.

377 **On the twentieth anniversary of the establishment of the Calouste Gulbenkian Foundation.**
Calouste Gulbenkian Foundation.   Lisbon: Calouste Gulbenkian Foundation, 1976. 43p.
This book describes itself as 'a synthesis of the life of a Man and his Work'. It recounts how the Armenian oil millionaire, Calouste Gulbenkian, made his money and acquired a marvellous collection of paintings and *objets d'art*. It goes on to print sections of his will and of the statutes of the Foundation established to house his collection in Lisbon.

378 **Dictator of Portugal: a life of the Marquis of Pombal, 1699-1782.**
Marcus Cheke.   London: Sidgwick & Jackson, 1938. 315p. bibliog.
Until the publication by Maxwell (see item no. 383) this was the standard biography of Pombal, the man for ever associated with the rebuilding of Lisbon after the 1755 earthquake and the power behind the throne of King José I. Although the book incorporates a bibliography, this is of limited use as all entries, except one, lack any imprint details.

379 **Where I fell to earth: a life in four places.**
Peter Conrad.   London: Chatto & Windus, 1990. 252p.
The autobiographical account of an Oxford academic's search, as a young man, for alternative homes after leaving his native Tasmania. He recounts a period of his life spent commuting between the four cities of Oxford, London, New York and Lisbon, his experiences in each place being interwoven with those elsewhere. In many respects he felt most at home in Lisbon, where he was virtually adopted by the family of a Portuguese scientist friend he had made at Oxford. However, Conrad goes beyond mere recollection to examine the way in which man orders his experiences and makes use of them as a source for art.

380 **Mr Five Per Cent: the biography of Calouste Gulbenkian.**
Ralph Hewins.   London: Hutchinson, 1957. 254p. map.
On his death in Lisbon in 1955, Gulbenkian reputedly left some 70 million dollars in cash and an income from his oil investments estimated at between 50 and 100 million dollars a year. This less than reverential volume briefly covers Gulbenkian's years of residence in Lisbon's Hotel Aviz and also depicts the unused burial plot which he reserved in the British Cemetery in Lisbon. His art collections, including Egyptology, paintings, furniture, ceramics and carpets, are today housed in Lisbon's Gulbenkian Museum.

381 **William Beckford.**
James Lees-Milne.   Tisbury, England: Compton Russell, 1976. 124p. map. bibliog.
This biography of William Beckford covers his Portuguese sojourns in chapter three. Lees-Milne believes that Beckford's journal of his visit to Portugal and Spain in 1787-88 was the writer's best work. As well as describing Beckford's close friendship in Sintra and Lisbon with the Marquis of Marialva, he also explains how the Englishman was unable to gain the audience with the Portuguese monarchy which he craved because of the moral scandal surrounding a relationship with a young man at Powderham, which had caused him to leave England.

382 **Gulbenkian: an interpretation of Calouste Sarkis Gulbenkian.**
John Lodwick, in collaboration with D. H. Young.   London;
Melbourne; Toronto: Heinemann, 1958. 289p.

Commissioned to write a biography of the millionaire Calouste Gulbenkian, who had
recently died in Lisbon, Lodwick sought out a fellow Barcelona resident David
Young. Young, by then an old man, had been Gulbenkian's private secretary from
1908 and was therefore an important source. Lodwick's resulting biography is written
largely in conjectural direct speech between Gulbenkian and his associates.

383 **Pombal: paradox of the Enlightenment.**
Kenneth Maxwell.   Cambridge, England: Cambridge University
Press, 1995. 200p. bibliog.

A well-produced biography of Sebastião de Carvalho e Melo, subsequently Conde de
Oeiras and Marquês de Pombal. He is most famous for his orchestration of the
rebuilding of Lisbon after the 1755 earthquake. Illustrated by colour and black-and-
white plates, the text covers the entire period of Pombal's virtual dictatorship during
the reign of King José I (1750-77). A helpful bibliographical essay on the published
literature relating to Pombal is appended to the volume.

384 **Calouste Gulbenkian, collector.**
José de Azeredo Perdigão, translated from the Portuguese by Ana
Lowndes Marques.   Lisbon: Calouste Gulbenkian Foundation, 1969.
237p.

Plans reached an advanced stage in the late 1930s to house the valuable art collections
of Calouste Gulbenkian (1869-1955) in a building adjacent to the National Gallery,
London. However, the insensitive British classification of Gulbenkian as a 'technical
enemy' during the Second World War resulted in his eventually bequeathing the
collections to Portugal, his final home, where they are now housed in the impressive
Calouste Gulbenkian Museum in Lisbon. As well as this story, Perdigão conveys the
Armenian's passion for travel and for collecting works of art as varied as Egyptology,
Lalique ware, Old Masters and Persian carpets. The book is lavishly illustrated with
mostly colour photographs of items from Gulbenkian's collections and a smaller
number of monochrome pictures of Gulbenkian himself.

385 **Memoirs of the Marquis of Pombal, with extracts from his writings
and from despatches in the State Paper Office never before
published.**
John Smith.   London: Longman, Brown, Green & Longmans, 1843.
2 vols.

These memoirs of the Marquis of Pombal, Portugal's major statesman of the 18th
century, by the private secretary to his great-grandson, the Marshal Marquês de
Saldanha, cover a period of over thirty years. Volume one, chapter four (p. 83-105),
covers the Lisbon earthquake whilst volume two (p. 195-213) includes the observations of Pombal on the erection of the equestrian statue of King José I in the Praça do
Comércio.

Immigrants and Expatriate Communities

386 **The 'British Assembly' in Lisbon, 1771-1819.**
Agostinho Araújo, translated by Margaret Kelting.   Lisbon: The
British Historical Society of Portugal, 1988. 40p. (Occasional Paper).
An illustrated history of the British Assembly, which occupied a building owned by
the Marquês de Marialva on the corner of the Rua das Flores and Largo do Barão de
Quintela, near the Chiado, in Lisbon. The Assembly was the scene of large expatriate
social gatherings, balls, meetings and concerts. The building also housed a tearoom,
billiards room and kitchens. In 1819, after the difficult period of the Peninsular War
and the abolition of the English Factory, the British Assembly was supplanted in the
same premises by a short-lived Assembleia Estrangeira (Foreigners' Assembly), a
multinational recreational organization which included some British members. The
activities and organizations of modern-day British residents in Lisbon are admirably
chronicled in d'Arcy Orders's *British community handbook* (Lisbon: APN Publications, 1990. new revised ed. 107p.). Details are provided of bodies as diverse as the
Royal British Club and English-run boarding kennels.

387   **The Royal British Club, Lisbon: the first seventy-five years,
1888-1963.**
L. A. Griffith, foreword by HRH The Prince Philip.   Lisbon:
Tipografia da Liga dos Combatentes da Grande Guerra, 1963. 102p.
Published to raise funds for a permanent home for the Royal British Club, an
expatriate social organization, this work is divided into thirteen chapters which are
accompanied by several photographs, including one of King Edward VII's visit to the
Club in 1903. The book ranges over events as diverse as the Club's role in the two
World Wars and repairs to its billiards table. Humorous extracts from the members'
suggestions book about topics such as the Club's provision of dry biscuits and the
failings of the nightwatchman provide a fascinating insight into the preoccupations of
some of its early members. A further twenty-five years of the Club's existence, up to
its centenary, are covered in *The Royal British Club, Lisbon, 1888-1988* by d'Arcy
Orders (Lisbon: The Royal British Club, 1988. 126p.). Illustrated by many

monochrome and colour photographs this volume reports on the recovery of the Club in the 1980s following a period of decline.

388 **The Royal Society of St George, Lisbon Branch, 1960-1985.**
d'Arcy Orders.   Lisbon: Published by the Author, [1985]. 28p.

A history of the Lisbon branch of the Royal Society of St George which enrolled with its parent body in London in 1959 and held its first meeting in 1960. It is an expatriate social organization which also raises funds for charitable causes back in Britain, such as ex-servicemen and the restoration of St George's Chapel, Windsor. In addition, the Lisbon branch sponsors prizes for British schools in the Lisbon area, and has raised money for the British Hospital in the city and for Portuguese causes such as the marking of the 500th anniversary of the death of Henry the Navigator. A history of a more formal expatriate body is to be found in the same author's *The British Community Council, Lisbon* (Lisbon: The British Historical Society of Portugal, 1996. 32p.). The Council was established during the Second World War to raise funds and provide support for Britain's war effort but still exists to raise funds for charitable causes and to coordinate expatriate involvement in official functions such as royal visits to Lisbon.

389 **A social history of black slaves and freedmen in Portugal, 1441-1555.**
A. C. de C. M. Saunders.   Cambridge, England: Cambridge University Press, 1982. 283p. 4 maps. bibliog.

This work aims to 'study the social, economic, legal and intellectual developments associated with the growth of a community of black slaves and freedmen in Portugal'. From 1512 Lisbon became officially, if not in practice, the sole Portuguese port at which slaves could be landed. By the 18th century a fifth of the city's population was estimated to be black or mulatto. Although many of the records of the Casa da Guiné (Guinea Office) and the Casa dos Escravos (Slaves' Office) were destroyed in the Lisbon earthquake of 1755, Saunders explains how taxes were levied at Lisbon on incoming slaves and how slave law was administered in spheres as diverse as employment and burial. His study is completed by a survey of race relations and of the relationship between blacks and the Catholic Church.

390 **The Lisbon Slave House and African trade.**
James L. Voigt.   *Proceedings of the American Philosophical Association*, vol. 117, pt. 1 (1973), p. 1-16.

In 1486 King João II of Portugal set up the Casa dos Escravos (Slaves' Office) in Lisbon to regulate the import of slaves, to collect import dues and to let trade privileges in Africa and the Atlantic islands of Portuguese ownership. This article explains its role and how it was supplanted after 1521 by the Casa da Índia (India House) and Casa da Mina (Mina House).

The English Crusaders in Portugal.
See item no. 318.

The Moors in Spain and Portugal.
See item no. 321.

The English in Portugal.
See item no. 326.

Women's Royal Voluntary Service, Lisbon Branch, 1939/1987.
See item no. 434.

The British Hospital in Lisbon.
See item no. 441.

The Portugal trade: a study of Anglo-Portuguese commerce, 1700-1770.
See item no. 455.

The English Factory at Lisbon: some chapters in its history.
See item no. 457.

The British Factory in Lisbon and its closing stages ensuing upon the Treaty of 1810.
See item no. 464.

The residence of the British Ambassador at Lisbon.
See item no. 509.

The Lisbon Players, 1947/1987, and including an account of the Estrela Hall.
See item no. 606.

APN, the Anglo-Portuguese News.
See item no. 655.

The British Historical Society of Portugal Annual Report and Review.
See item no. 672.

The Historical Society, Lisbon Branch, Annual Report.
See item no. 674.

Lisbon and the English.
See item no. 690.

Religion and Religious Buildings

391 Auto de fé and Jew.
Elkan Nathan Adler.   London: Henry Frowde, Oxford University
Press, 1908. 195p. bibliog.

Much of this work, which grew out of articles in *The Jewish Quarterly Review*, is a
commentary on the pioneering research on the Inquisition by the Philadelphian
merchant and scholar H. C. Lea. Chapters XXVI-XXVII cover the Jews in Portugal,
whilst chapters XLI-XLIV are a list of the *autos-da-fé* carried out mostly in Lisbon,
Coimbra and Évora by order of the Catholic Inquisition. The first Lisbon *auto-da-fé*
was in 1531, whilst the last recorded in the city was in 1794.

**392 The trial of George Buchanan before the Lisbon Inquisition
including the text of Buchanan's defences, along with a translation
and commentary.**
James M. Aitken.   Edinburgh: Oliver & Boyd, 1939. 166p. bibliog.

The Scottish Erasmian scholar, George Buchanan, was arrested in Coimbra, where he
held a post at the University. He was immediately brought to the Inquisition gaols in
Lisbon in August 1550. There, he was induced to make a recantation of his alleged
Lutheran tendencies in order to avoid the stake. This account of his ordeal includes
parallel texts in Latin and English of Buchanan's defence. The extensive preface
includes details of the source documents to be found in Lisbon's Torre do Tombo
archives and elsewhere in Portugal.

**393 The seminary priests: a dictionary of the secular clergy of England
and Wales, 1558-1850.**
Godfrey Anstruther.   Ware, England: St. Edmund's College; Durham,
England: Ushaw College; Gt Wakering, England: Mayhew-McCrimmon,
1968-77. 4 vols.

The seminary priests were those English and Welshmen who, owing to Protestant
persecution at home, were ordained outside Britain as Catholic priests. Many of them

served in Lisbon at the English College, the Bridgettine convent or the English Residence of the Jesuits and details of their activities are recorded here. The source archives include those of the English College in Lisbon. The biographical details given here in many cases reveal lives of subterfuge, imprisonment and, in some cases, execution on return to England for holding the Catholic faith.

394 **Churches of Portugal.**
Carlos de Azevedo, photographs by Chester E. V. Brummel. Lisbon: Difel & Bertrand Editora, 1985. 199p. bibliog.

Four-fifths of this book consists of monochrome, and some colour, photographs of Portuguese churches, including many examples from the Lisbon area such as S. Vicente de Fora and the Jerónimos monastery. The English text relates the evolution of Portuguese church building from the Visigothic period to the Baroque.

395 **Hugo Gurgeny, prisoner of the Lisbon Inquisition.**
Mary Brearley. London: Jonathan Cape, 1947. 176p. bibliog.

Using Inquisition records from the Torre do Tombo archives, Brearley tells the story of Hugo Gurgeny, an Oxford graduate who, whilst on a business visit to Lisbon, was arrested in 1606 on suspicion of being an undercover Lutheran preacher. He was finally released in 1609 after making a confession which saved him from an appearance at a planned *auto-da-fé* in Lisbon. The book relates Gurgeny's denunciation by an English Roman Catholic priest and the gruesome activities of the Portuguese Inquisition, which in Lisbon alone burned at least 576 people to death between its inception in 1536 and 1821.

396 **Church of St. Rock guide book.**
Maria Filomena Brito, translated by Luís Miguel Brito. Lisbon: Santa Casa da Misericórdia de Lisboa, 1992. 54p.

A guide, rather imperfectly translated, to the Church of St. Rock (S. Roque) in Lisbon's Bairro Alto. It tells the story of both the origins of the cult of St Rock as a protector against plague and the construction of the church. Although a relic of St Rock had been obtained by King Manuel I from the saint's burial-place in Venice in the early 16th century, the present church was built in the latter part of that century by the Jesuits. The exterior is relatively plain but the church interior, amply illustrated here in colour, is a baroque masterpiece of giltwork, marble and tiles.

397 **Os conventos de Lisboa.** (The convents of Lisbon.)
Baltazar Matos Caeiro. Sacavém, Portugal: Distri Editora, 1989. 184p. 2 maps. bibliog.

A large-format directory of the extant and demolished convents of Lisbon. The nineteen convents in the latter category are illustrated with line drawings whilst the sixty-nine surviving buildings are shown in a large number of good quality colour photographs with, in some cases, additional drawings. A brief outline and history of each convent is supplied in the text accompanying each entry. Although one of the maps indicates the sites of all of the convents in Lisbon, there is no key to link a convent's name to a particular point on the map.

398 **As obras de Santa Engrácia e os seus artistas.** (The works of St Engracia church and its artists.)
Ayres de Carvalho. Lisbon: Academia Nacional de Belas Artes, 1971. 141p. map.

The 'obras de Santa Engrácia' is a phrase synonymous in Portuguese for any major undertaking which takes an age to complete. The current church of Santa Engrácia was first started in the 17th century but only in 1966 was it in a sufficiently complete state to be designated Portugal's National Pantheon. It now contains memorials to such national heroes as Prince Henry the Navigator, Vasco da Gama and Luís de Camões. This volume includes 165 photographic illustrations and plates as well as several line drawings. The text recounts the history of the church's construction and provides details of the architects and artists involved.

399 **The sufferings of John Coustos for free-masonry and for his refusing to turn Roman Catholic in the Inquisition of Lisbon ... To which is annex'd the origin of the Inquisition with its establishment in various countries.**
John Coustos. London: Published by the Author, 1746. 400p.

Coustos was born in Bern in 1716 and became a gemcutter in England and a freemason. After setting up as a jeweller in Lisbon in 1738, he was gaoled in the Inquisition's headquarters in Lisbon in 1743 after having set up a masonic lodge in the city. He was tortured on the Inquisition's rack nine times, scourged and branded, before suffering an *auto-da-fé* in June of that year. Although sentenced to four years in the galleys for being both a protestant and a freemason, he was saved from this fate by the intervention of the British Embassy in Lisbon which returned him to London in December 1744. This autobiographical account of his treatment was first published in 1745.

400 **Historical account of Lisbon College, with a register.**
Canon Croft, register by Joseph Gillow. Barnet, England: St. Andrew's Press, 1902. 275p.

Lisbon College, or the English College as it was also known, took in its first seminarians in 1628, its function being to supply Roman Catholic priests for service in England. Built in the Travessa dos Inglesinhos, in the Bairro Alto area of Lisbon, it closed as a seminary in 1971. This history, based on an earlier work by John Kirk, published in *The Catholic Magazine* in 1834-35, recalls the College's often difficult existence in a text which is supported by black-and-white photographs of both the College buildings and some of the leading characters associated with it. A register records former pupils of the College.

401 **English College, Lisbon.**
English College, Lisbon, with illustrations from original pencil drawings by W. Haeburn-Little. Lisbon: English College, [1943]. 21p.

A brief history of the English College in Lisbon is accompanied here by a series of fine drawings of the College itself and of its two estates, the Quinta da Ponte, at Luz in northern Lisbon, and the Quinta da Pera in the Caparica valley, across the Tagus from the city. The estate at Luz served as a summer house whilst the latter provided holiday accommodation for the seminarists. The College was founded in 1622 by Nicholas Ashton, with help of the Portuguese nobleman, Pedro de Coutinho, to accommodate English seminarists unable to pursue their studies freely at home. The first students arrived in 1628. A list of all twenty-three presidents of the College between 1627 and 1943 is given, as are details of famous Catholic priests who attended the College. There are also accounts of three difficult periods for the College, namely after the 1755 earthquake, during the Peninsular War and after the Portuguese Republican Revolution of 1910.

402 Buchanan in Portugal.

Guilherme J. C. Henriques. In: *George Buchanan: a memorial, 1506-1906. Contributions by various writers.* Compiled and edited by D. A. Millar. St. Andrews, Scotland: W. C. Henderson & Son, University Press; London: David Nutt, [1906], p. 60-78.

G. J. C. Henriques was legal advisor to the British Embassy in Lisbon. In this essay, he reveals his discoveries in the archives of the Lisbon Inquisition which throw light on the arrest and trial in Lisbon of the Scottish humanist, George Buchanan. His text is illustrated by photographs which include the S. Bento convent, in the Lisbon suburb of Xabregas, where Buchanan was imprisoned.

403 George Buchanan in the Lisbon Inquisition. The records of his trial, with a translation thereof into English, facsimiles of some of the papers and an introduction.

Guilherme J. C. Henriques. Lisbon: Typographia da Empreza da História de Portugal, 1906. 47p.

Buchanan was employed at the University of Coimbra when he was arrested by the Inquisition in 1550. In his introduction, Henriques speculates on the reasons for Buchanan's arrest. He goes on to use recently unearthed documents to throw light on his arrest in Coimbra with two other professors, and his immediate transfer to Lisbon. There, he was questioned thoroughly about his Catholic orthodoxy, and accused of Lutheran leanings. As well as translations of the original accounts of these sessions, the work includes photographic plates which reproduce parts of the original documents of the Inquisition.

404 Carthusian abstinence. Brigittine legislation for Syon Abbey, Lisbon. Carthusian annals.

James Hogg. Salzburg, Austria: Institut für Anglistik und Amerikanistik, Universität Salzburg; Lewiston, New York: Edwin Mellen Press, [1991]. 205p. (Analecta Cartusiana, 35:14. Spirtualität Heute und Gestern, Band 14).

In 1594 the nuns of Syon Abbey, London established a convent in Lisbon, where they found freedom from the religious persecution they had endured, first in Protestant England and, then, in the Low Countries. The bulk of this volume (p. 16-198) consists of a photographic reprint of the 1657 constitutions of St. Bridget under which the Brigittine Sisters and Brothers operated in Lisbon. In the second of the three essays by Hogg the religious legislation of the Abbey is reproduced from its original manuscript.

405 'Except the Lord build the house, their labour is lost that build it', Psalm 127. A guide to and brief record of the building of St Paul's Church, Estoril, Portugal together with an account of the origin of the Diocese to which it belonged and what became of it.
John Humphreys. Estoril, Portugal: The Friends of St Paul's, 1986. 95p.

The author was chaplain of the Anglican church of St Paul's in the Lisbon suburb of Estoril from 1957 to 1980. In the early 20th century a winter chaplaincy was established in Estoril to service the British community, many of whom were invalids. Humphreys recounts how services were variously held in the Hotel Itália at Monte Estoril and the Hotel Paris before, in 1935, a mission church was erected in the latter's grounds. This small church was finally demolished and replaced on the same site by a new church, five times its size, in 1968. Following this history, the bulk of this book comprises a detailed description of the new church, accompanied by many photographs, some of which are in colour.

406 **Syon Abbey.**
F. R. Johnston. Offprint from *South Western Catholic History*, no. 5 (1987), 13p.

The Bridgettines were the only English community to maintain convent life without interruption by the Reformation. They achieved this by fleeing to Flanders during the reign of Henry VIII and, following persecution in the Low Countries during the reign of Queen Elizabeth I, they moved to Lisbon in 1594. There, they received support from Philip II, then King of Spain and Portugal. Johnston describes the nuns' stay in Lisbon until 1861, when anti-clericalism drove them back to London. In the interim they had survived a major fire in their Lisbon convent in 1651, the 1755 earthquake and the French seizure of Lisbon in 1807.

407 **Roteiro histórico dos Jesuítas em Lisboa.** (An historical guide to Jesuit Lisbon.)
António Lopes. Braga, Portugal: Livraria Apostolado da Imprensa, 1985. 175p. 2 maps. bibliog.

Divided into four chronological sections, plus a fifth on Jesuit personalities, this book describes the Jesuits' connections with forty buildings in and around Lisbon, from 1540 onwards. As recently as 1910 Jesuits were imprisoned in Lisbon, following the declaration of the Portuguese Republic, and the prisons in which Jesuits were held in this and earlier eras are amongst the sites covered. A fine, colour, folding map locates all the places mentioned in the text very clearly. Although the author is himself a Jesuit, this is a factual work rather than one of religious propaganda. Each site in Lisbon is illustrated by photographs.

408 **Potamius de Lisbonne et la controverse arienne.** (Potamius of Lisbon and the Arian controversy.)
António Montes Moreira. Louvain, Belgium: Bibliothèque de l'Université, 1969. 349p. bibliog. (Université Catholique de Louvain, Faculté de Théologie et de Droit Canon. Travaux de Doctorat en Théologie et en Droit Canon, Nouvelle Série, Tome 1).

In the mid-4th century AD Potamius was the first recorded Bishop of Lisbon. Whilst his writings are generally orthodox, contemporary evidence indicates that he was a sympathizer with the Arian schism, whose believers denied the divinity of Christ. This biography of Potamius seeks to examine his links with Arianism through the evidence not only of his own verifiable and suppositious works, but also through a study of the writings of his contemporaries.

409 **Jerónimos.** (The Jerónimos Church and Monastery.)
Rafael Moreira, translation by George F. W. Dykes. Lisbon: Verbo, 1995. 48p. (Monumentos de Portugal).

The first half of this folio volume is a text in both Portuguese and English describing the history of the Jerónimos monastery and of the century of works, commencing in 1501, to construct the original buildings. Each section of the complex is then briefly described in turn. King Manuel I, who initiated the building programme, used a five per cent tax on gold from Guinea and spices and precious stones from India to finance this massive project, which is the prime surviving example of the Manueline style of architecture. The second half of the book consists entirely of colour photographs of the exterior and interior of the church and cloisters.

410 **St. Andrew's Presbyterian Church, Lisbon, Portugal, founded 1866: a history.**
d'Arcy Orders. Lisbon: Published by the Author, [1990]. 89p. (British Community Series).

After tracing the history of Portuguese tolerance to non-Catholic religious observance, Orders describes the establishment of a Free Church of Scotland congregation in Lisbon in 1866, initially comprising seventy persons. They used the former Carmelite Mariano convent, a 17th-century building in the Rua das Janelas Verdes in western Lisbon which is now the York House Hotel. In the 1870s a mission school was established there too, with a roll of eighty-six children in 1888. A new building was erected on the nearby Rua de Arriaga in 1899 and following the 1905 split in the Scottish Church, the church came under United Free Church of Scotland jurisdiction. By the time of publication, the Church had recovered from a slump in congregation and had an active Sunday School and Women's Guild, as well as a congregation totalling 150 at its services both, weekly, at St Andrew's in Lisbon and, fortnightly, in St Paul's Anglican church in Estoril.

411 **Notices of the English colleges & convents established on the continent after the dissolution of religious houses in England.**
Edward Petre, edited by the Rev. F. C. Husenbeth. Norwich, England: Bacon & Kinnebrook, 1899. 105p.

Included in this volume are brief sections on the history of both 'The College of Lisbon', the English seminary, and the 'Bridgettin [sic] Convent of Sion House', the nunnery which spent 267 years of its existence (1594-1861) in Lisbon after its nuns and priests were driven by persecution, firstly, from Sion House in England, seat of the Duke of Northumberland, and then from the Low Countries. Their convent in the Rua de Quelhas was later occupied by the Jesuits.

412   **The anatomie of the English Nunnery at Lisbon in Portugall.**
       Dissected and laid open by one that was sometime a young brother
       of the covent [sic].
       Thomas Robinson.   London: printed for P. Stephens and C. Meredith,
       1637. 31p.

In this work, first printed in 1622, Robinson claimed to have been forcibly ordained in Lisbon by Fr. Seth Foster, the Bridgettine chaplain at the Sion nunnery in Lisbon. Despite his lack of vocation, Robinson spent two and half years at the nunnery, where his work included copying the registers. In this often humorous account of the nunnery, Robinson claimed to be outraged by the liberal behaviour of the nuns, whom he described as entertaining the clergy with 'ribaldous songs and jigs'. Indeed, this edition's title-page engraving illustrates priests and nuns engaged in unedifying activities. Less scurrilous details of the Lisbon nunnery's priests, such as Foster and *Rev.* John Vivian, who are described by Robinson, are to be found in Anstruther (see item no. 393).

413   **Bishop Russell and John Sergeant.**
       Michael Sharratt.   *Ushaw Magazine*, no. 253 (1979), p. 22-37.
       bibliog.

From sources in the Lisbon College (English College) archives now held in Durham, Sharratt tells the story of Russell and Sergeant, two of the major mid-17th-century priests at the College. They found themselves at odds, particularly over Sergeant's alleged links with the Blacklowists, followers of Thomas White, alias Blacklow. White had been tainted by his contacts with Cromwell in the 1650s and was seen in some quarters as a rationalist who was disrespectful of authority, particularly that of the Holy See. In consequence the Lisbon College was viewed by many in England as being a centre of Blacklowism. Russell became Bishop of Portalegre, in southern Portugal, in 1671.

414   **The Lisbon Collection at Ushaw.**
       Michael Sharratt.   *Northern Catholic History* (Autumn 1978),
       p. 30-36.

An account of the scope and contents of the collection of books, archives and other material transferred from the English College, Lisbon to the archives of Ushaw College, a Catholic seminary in County Durham. The material was transferred after the College closed to seminarians in 1971. About 1,900 printed books were brought from Lisbon from a larger total held there, together with some 250 books of archive material. The archives include material relating to Pedro Coutinho, the College's initial benefactor and celebrated Catholic figures such as Bishop Russell and the Revs. John Sergeant and Thomas White, alias Blacklow. Records of visitations by the Lisbon Inquisition are also included. Various artefacts such as the College orrery, sundial, lamp and some ceramic tiles also form part of the collection. This essay is also printed in *Catholic Archives* (no. 1 [1981], p. 36-39).

415   Lisbon College, catalogue of archives. Part I: correspondence.
      Michael Sharratt.   Durham, England: Ushaw College, 1986. 48p.

Ushaw College, an English Roman Catholic seminary, received the archives of the
English College, Lisbon in 1974, three years after the Portuguese institution ceased its
role as a seminary for English students. The College in Lisbon had received its first
students from Douai in 1628 and Ushaw is the direct descendant of that French
college. Much of the 17th-century documentation from the English College did not
survive the vicissitudes of time, particularly the Peninsular War. However, Michael
Sharratt has listed that which survives by name of writer, each entry being
subarranged by correspondent and date of the communication.

416   Lisbon College register, 1628-1813.
      Edited by Michael Sharratt.   [London]: Catholic Record Society,
      1991. 252p.

The Colleges of Saints Peter and Paul, also known as Lisbon College and English
College, Lisbon, were opened in 1628 and remained operative as a seminary until
1971. This transcription of the College register comprises alphabetical entries by
surname of the students and their 'superiors', with the original Latin text accompanied
in each case by an English summary. The College archives are now held at Ushaw
College in County Durham, England.

417   Histoire du Collège de Campolide et de la Résidence des Jésuites à
      Lisbonne. Texte latin écrit par les pères des deux maisons,
      acompagné [sic] de la traduction française avec une préface par le
      Prof. Emm. Borges Graïnha. (History of Campolide College and of
      the Jesuit Residence in Lisbon. Latin text written by the clergy of the
      two houses, accompanied by a French translation with a preface by
      Prof. Emm. Borges Graïnha.)
      Societas Iesu.   Lisbon: Imprimerie A Editora Limitada, 1914. 184p.

Illustrated by photographs, this is an edition of the formal reports of activities at the
Jesuit Order's College at Campolide in north-west Lisbon and at their Residence in the
city. The College reports span the years 1854 to 1900, whilst those of the Residence
date from 1864. The text is in French, with the Latin original at the foot of each page.

418   Sé de Lisboa. (Lisbon Cathedral.)
      Elísio Summavielle, Jorge Salazar Braga, photographs by Henrique
      Ruas, Delfim Ferreira.   Lisbon: Teorema for the Instituto Português
      do Património Cultural, Departamento de Museus, Palácios e
      Fundações, 1986. 27p. bibliog.

In this brief guide to Lisbon Cathedral, there are twenty-nine photographs of which
the majority are in colour. These show both the changing exterior of the building and
internal features such as tombs and ceilings. In addition, five clear floor plans show
the evolution of the cathedral from the mid-12th century to the present day and these
are supplemented by a chronology of the same period. The cover-title differs from the
title-page in calling this work *Igreja de Santa Maria Maior, Sé de Lisboa.*

419   **The treasure of São Roque: a sidelight on the Counter-Reformation.**
William Telfer.   London: Society for Promoting Christian
Knowledge, for The Church Historical Society, 1932. 222p.
(Church Historical Society Publications, New Series).

The church of S. Roque in Lisbon gained its name from the relics of St Rock procured
by King Manuel I from Venice, in 1506, in the hope that their veneration would help
to reduce the effects of plague on Lisbon. Here, the author seeks to authenticate many
other holy relics by means of a detailed academic study, based on a university thesis,
of the contents of a tin box of 16th-century deeds found at the church.

420   **A brief account of some Lent and other extraordinary processions
and ecclestiatical entertainments seen last year at Lisbon, in four
letters to an English friend.**
George Whitefield.   London: printed for W. Strahan, 1755. 29p.

Whitefield was a leading Calvinistic Methodist and chaplain to the Countess of
Huntingdon. This is an account of his visit to Lisbon where he called *en route* to
North America with a shipload of orphans. Whitefield disapprovingly recounts his
observations of Catholic religious observance and superstition in the Portuguese
capital.

421   **Inscriptions in the British Cemetery, Lisbon, connected with
Devon and Cornwall.**
H. F. Fulford Williams.   *Devon and Cornwall Notes and Queries,*
vol. 22 (1946), p. 364-68.

The British community in Lisbon were granted the right to a Lisbon burial ground in a
treaty of 1656 between Cromwell and the Portuguese. Because the Exeter wool trade
exported to Lisbon and, also, because for many years the Falmouth packet was the
chief maritime passenger route to Lisbon, many Westcountrymen came to the city.
There are therefore numerous graves of such visitors and residents including John
Jeffrey (died 1822), the British Consul, and members of the Stephens family, from
Exeter, whose family established an important glass works in Portugal in Pombal's
time. The author reproduces the inscriptions of some three dozen tombstones.

422   **'Os Inglesinhos de Lisboa'.** (The young Englishmen of Lisbon.)
Michael E. Williams.   In: *Centenário do Tratado de Windsor,
de 15 a 18 de Outubro de 1986.*   Oporto, Portugal: Faculdade de
Letras do Porto, Instituto de Estudos Ingleses, 1988, p. 241-44.
(Proceedings of the Conference Commemorating the Sixth Centenary
of the Treaty of Windsor, 15-18 October, 1986).

Despite its Portuguese title, this article is in English and relates the history of the
Catholic seminary, the English College in Lisbon's Bairro Alto. Williams relates how
the College was founded in 1622, but closed in 1973 as a consequence of changing
Roman Catholic ideas on seminary training and a shortage of teaching staff.

423   **The origins of the English College, Lisbon.**
Rev. Michael E. Williams.   *Recusant History,* vol. 29, no. 4 (1991), p. 478-92.

An account of how Fr William Newman, a banished English Recusant, planned the establishment of a seminary, the English College, in Lisbon with the patronage of Dom Pedro Coutinho. However, the Jesuits ordered Newman back to England and Joseph Hervey was selected to be first President of the College, arriving in Lisbon in 1626. The College opened on a site in the Rua da Rosa (now Rua S. Boaventura) in 1628, from which it operated for over three hundred years.

424   **Gould's history of freemasonry, embracing an investigation of the records of the origins of the fraternity, etc.**
Revised, edited and brought up to date by Dudley Wright.   London: Caxton Publishing Company Limited, 1931. 5 vols.

Chapter eight of volume four traces freemasonry in Portugal in substantial detail from its origins there, around 1735 up to 1929. The Masons suffered various periods of persecution, as evidenced by the torture by the Lisbon Inquisition of the English jeweller and freemason, John Coustos in 1743-44 and the actions of Pina Manique (1780-1805) under the regency of the future João VI. Yet by 1812 there were thirteen active masonic lodges in Lisbon and despite further oppression, fourteen existed in the capital in 1885. The leaders of the revolution which brought about the Portuguese Republic in 1910 were mostly freemasons.

425   **The Lisbon massacre of 1506 and the royal image of the *Shebet Yehudah*.**
Yosef Hayim Yerushalmi.   Cincinnati, Ohio: Hebrew Union College, 1976. 91p. (Hebrew Union College Annual Supplements, no. 1).

A scholarly study of Solomon Ibn Verga's work, *Shebet Yehudah*, and related documents. In 1497 King Manuel ordered the forcible conversion of Portugal's Jews to Christianity. Nine years later many of these New Christians were slaughtered in a popular rising against them in Lisbon, orchestrated by the Dominicans, and it is this massacre which is described here. An appendix includes a contemporary German account of the event and a number of relevant Portuguese royal edicts.

Serious thoughts occasioned by the earthquake at Lisbon.
See item no. 157.

A letter from a clergyman at London to the remaining disconsolate inhabitants of Lisbon.
See item no. 158.

Portuguese pilgrimage, July 1st-September 4th, 1947.
See item no. 296.

Guia do Museu Antoniano. (Guide to the St. Anthony Museum.)
See item no. 641.

Spanish and Portuguese Jewry: a classified bibliography.
See item no. 691.

Social Conditions

426 **Jovem Portugal: after the Revolution.**
Jason Lauré, Ettagale Lauré. New York: Farrar, Straus & Giroux,
1977. 153p. map.
An illustrated English-language account of the experiences of nine Portuguese young
people. These include an Angolan girl who returned to Lisbon following that
country's independence from Portugal, a girl who lives in a Lisbon shanty-town and
an eighteen-year-old Communist militant who is active in the city. The text and the
numerous black-and-white photographs depict an everyday experience of life which is
absent from most English-language guides to Lisbon.

427 **Lisboa: luxo e distinção, 1750-1830.** (Lisbon: luxury and distinction,
1750-1830.)
Nuno Luís Madureira. Lisbon: Fragmentos, 1990. 110p. 2 maps.
bibliog.
This highly illustrated volume seeks to portray everyday life during the late 18th and
early 19th century in Lisbon. It covers topics such as leisure, fashion, music, dancing,
games, water supply, public health and transport. Many of the numerous colour plates
are from contemporary descriptions of Lisbon, especially those by foreign visitors,
such as Batty, Kinsey and L'Évêque (see item nos. 2, 18 and 618). These include
magnificent panoramas of Lisbon and portrayals of city 'types'. Textual sources
include popular literature and posthumous inventories of individuals' possessions.

428 **Daily life in Portugal in the late Middle Ages.**
A. H. de Oliveira Marques, translated by S. S. Wyatt, drawings by
Vítor André. Madison, Wisconsin: University of Wisconsin Press,
1971. 355p. 3 maps. bibliog.
Translated from *A sociedade medieval portuguesa: aspectos da vida quotidiana*
(Lisbon: Sá da Costa, 1964), this is a fascinating survey of every aspect of late
mediaeval life in Portugal, with particular reference to Lisbon throughout. The chapters
are entitled 'The Table', 'Dress', 'The House', 'Hygiene and Health', 'Affection', 'Work',

120

'Faith', 'Culture', 'Amusements' and 'Death'. Ninety-nine illustrations, some of which are photographs, accompany the text.

429 **Lisboa em movimento – Lisbon in motion, 1850-1920. A modernização da cidade entre 1850 e 1920, da Regeneração à Grande Guerra. A transformação do urbanismo, das infraestruturas, dos transportes e serviços, dos espaços sociais e públicos. Exposição no pavilhão, pátio e jardins do Museu da Cidade, Campo Grande, Lisboa, junho/outubro 1994.** (Lisbon in motion, 1850-1920. The modernization of the city between 1850 and 1920, from the Regeneration to the Great War. The transformation of the city, its infrastructure, transport and services, its social and public spaces. Exhibition held in the pavilion, patio and gardens of the City Museum, Campo Grande, Lisbon, July to October, 1994.)
Sociedade Lisboa 94, Departamento de Intervenção Urbana.   Lisbon: Livros Horizonte/ Sociedade Lisboa 94, 1994. 404p. bibliog.

Although it also constitutes the catalogue of an exhibition, this book is essentially a richly illustrated review of the modernization of Lisbon between 1850 and 1920 and 'movement' is seen as the unifying feature of this process. However, it is much more than a coffee-table book, for in its five sections, the text explains changes in urban planning, infrastructure, public transport, civic services such as the fire brigade, and 'urban spaces' such as shops and cafés. Each section has an English text as its conclusion, giving the volume as a whole over forty pages in English. There is a wealth of colour and monochrome photographs and illustrations depicting buildings, vehicles, street scenes, city plans and technical drawings.

430 **Southern Europe transformed: political and economic change in Greece, Italy, Portugal and Spain.**
Edited by Allan Williams.   London: Harper & Row, 1984. 295p. bibliog.

Chapters four and eight of this work are concerned with Portugal. In the former, M. Porto surveys twenty years of political change in Portugal, including Lisbon. In the latter, Jorge Gaspar addresses 'Urbanization: growth, problems and policies' with specific reference to Lisbon (p. 208-35). Here he discusses social and political movements, the housing situation including the growth of squatting and shanty towns in Lisbon, and the strains on aspects of the urban infrastructure such as water supply and sewerage services.

Housing

431 **Portugal.**
J. R. Lewis, A. M. Williams.   In: *Housing in Europe.*   Edited by
Martin Wynn.   London, Canberra: Croom Helm; New York:
St Martin's Press, 1984, p. 281-325. 4 maps. bibliog.
Chapter ten of this work, written by academic geographers J. R. Lewis and A. M.
Williams and illustrated by black-and-white photographs, describes the housing
situation in Portugal since the 1974 Revolution, particularly in Lisbon and Oporto. It
discusses the growth of Lisbon's shanty towns and clandestine building, civic housing
programmes and the need for reform of the building industry and of government
policies toward cities.

432 **Lisbon housing and city development: a contribution to their
study. Report.**
Luís Guimarães Lobato.   Lisbon: Câmara Municipal, 1952. 20p.
A report presented to the XXI Congress of the International Federation for Housing
and Town Planning on the progress made in Lisbon in providing accommodation for
the city's growing postwar population.

433 **Bairros degradados da cidade de Lisboa.** (Rundown quarters of
Lisbon.)
Luís Soczka, Paulo Machado, Mário João Freitas.   Lisbon:
Laboratório Nacional de Engenharia Civil, 1990. 36p. map. bibliog.
(Laboratório Nacional de Engenharia Civil, Memória no. 751).
A study of the Musgueira Sul shanty town, near the airport in northern Lisbon. It is a
reworking of a study first published in *Povos e Culturas*, no. 3 (1988). A very short
summary is given in broken English.

Women

434 Women's Royal Voluntary Service, Lisbon Branch, 1939/1987.
d'Arcy Orders.   Lisbon: Published by the Author, [1987]. 35p.

This illustrated pamphlet tells how, in 1939, forty British women in Lisbon formed the
Women's War Work Organisation, following the example of the Women's Voluntary
Service, founded in Britain the previous year. The Lisbon body soon changed its name
to the Women's Relief Work Organisation and had 250 members by 1945. During the
Second World War they supplied garments and bandages to Britain, to local refugees
and to others in need, such as rescued seamen. In 1945 they became the Lisbon branch
of the W.V.S. and since then they have carried out much fundraising and work for
charitable causes both in the Lisbon area and in Britain.

Health and Medicine

435 The thermal springs and the climate of Estoril in chronic rheumatism and gout during winter.
D. G. Dalgado.   Paris: Henri Jouve, 1910. 56p.

One of a number of publications by Dr Dalgado aimed at stimulating visits to the Estoril area by the infirm. He gives details of the water sources and climate of Estoril, before concluding with a section entitled 'Social arrangements at the three Estorils', which furnishes information on local hotels and tourist sights. Dalgado calls for the building of a modern hydropathic establishment at Estoril to ensure that it 'makes its mark as a winter thermal resort', following the lead of nearby Monte Estoril which he classifies as a 'winter climatic resort'.

436 Change of climate considered as a remedy in dyspeptic, pulmonary and other chronic affections, with an account of the most eligible places of residence for invalids in Spain, Portugal, Algeria, etc. at different seasons of the year, etc.
D. J. T. Francis.   London: John Churchill, 1853. 339p.

Dr Francis here draws on five years' overseas residence, including a period in Lisbon, during which he discussed the city's health with Dr Mackenzie of the British Hospital. Chapter VII (p. 115-30) remarks on the city's decline as a resort for British invalids before citing temperature, wind, rain and sunshine data for Lisbon and commenting on the often high diurnal temperature ranges in the city. These variations and the winds detracted from the city's appeal to many invalids. Francis's fascinating account of prevalent illnesses in Lisbon includes the locals' alleged 'predisposition to cerebral affections', as well as to consumption, apoplexy, palsy, rheumatism and even leprosy. An account of the healthy attractions of Sintra is also given, although its winter climate is dismissed as damp and cheerless.

437   **James Boswell and Dr Kennedy's Lisbon diet drink.**
Colby H. Kullman. *Mississippi Folklore Register*, vol. 15, no. 2
(Fall 1981), p. 57-62.

Kullman recounts how James Boswell sought, in London, a cure from gonorrhoea
through infusions of the fashionable Lisbon diet drink purveyed by the aged Dr
Kennedy, who held university qualifications from Rhiems and Oxford. The drink was
a decoction containing sarsparella, guaiacum wood, antimony, syrup, water and
various other substances which was believed to be helpful to sufferers from venereal
and other diseases. Lisbon sarsparella is believed to have originated in Pará in Brazil,
from whence it entered Europe via Lisbon. Despite consuming a bottle of the diet
drink every day, Boswell was not cured until he submitted himself to the surgical
knife of a Dr Forbes.

438   **A dissertation on the properties and efficacy of the Lisbon
diet-drink, a medicine for many years successfully used in
Portugal in the cure of the venereal disease and scurvy, in which
its comparative excellence with mercury and guaiacum is
considered, etc.**
J. Leake.   London: J. Clarke, 1757. 67p.

The author, a surgeon, wrote this book to describe the fashionable Lisbon drink
remedy at a time when he thought that the 1755 earthquake might deprive Englishmen
of the chance to visit the city to benefit from its curative effects for diseases as varied
as rheumatism, gout, dropsy and gonorrhoea. Leake himself had studied the effects of
the drink at first hand in Lisbon, where it had originally been known as the German
diet drink because of its introduction by a German physician to the Portuguese royal
court. The book is in three sections, covering respectively the drink's efficacy, the
improper use of mercury as a cure and, finally, an account of particular cases in which
the Lisbon drink proved beneficial.

439   **On change of climate: a guide for travellers in pursuit of health,
illustrative of the advantages of the various localities resorted to by
invalids for the cure or alleviation of chronic diseases, especially
consumption, with observations on climate and its influence on
health and disease. The result of extensive personal experience of
many southern climes: Spain, Portugal, Algeria, Morocco, France,
Italy, the Mediterranean Islands, Egypt, &c.**
Thomas More Madden.   London: T. Cautley Newby, 1864. 387p.

Dr Madden's four-year residence in Lisbon informs his thorough account of the city
which constitutes Chapter VII of this book. He describes the topography, population,
chief buildings and amusements of Lisbon before detailing its climate through the
seasons. His appreciation of the city is epitomized by his recommendation of
Portuguese hotels over their more expensive, foreign-owned counterparts. Madden
judges the city's climate as being of benefit to sufferers from certain types of
consumption, dyspepsia, mental exhaustion, and as affording relief from sedentary
pursuits, melancholia and hypochondria. Brief reference is also made to the attractions
to Lisbon residents of Sintra's cool summers.

Health and Medicine

440 **An account of the Lisbon diet drink in venereal cases.**
Donald Monro. *Essays and observations physical and literary, read before the Philosophical Society in Edinburgh and published by them*, vol. III (1771), p. 402-06.

Dr Monro was physician to St George's Hospital in London. Here he draws on information gleaned from several physicians in Lisbon to present a prescription for a decoction known as the Lisbon diet drink. This contained sarsparella, antimony and other substances and was credited, when taken after mercury treatment, with curing venereal diseases. Monro goes on to outline his successful use of the drink on a patient who was required to drink a quart of it per day. The Lisbon diet drink became a fashionable medicine in late 18th-century London.

441 **The British Hospital in Lisbon.**
A. H. Norris. Lisbon: The British Historical Society of Portugal, 1973. 132p.

Although treatment centres for Britons in Lisbon existed in earlier times, the hospital set up in the Rua da Estrela by the English Factory in 1793 is the one initially described in detail in this book. Gerald de Visme, an Englishman of Huguenot extraction, and a Lisbon resident for over forty years, largely financed the project whose chief aim was to assist the visiting merchant seamen from Britain, upon whom the Factory depended for transporting their goods. Following the winding-up of the Factory in the early 19th century, the hospital ceased to operate. Norris goes on to describe how, in 1910, the present British Hospital opened in the former British Protestant School in Lisbon's Rua Saraiva de Carvalho. A statistical appendix shows that in 1972 the Hospital admitted 351 patients and performed 152 operations.

442 **Medical climatology; or, A topographical and meteorological description of the localities resorted to in winter and summer by invalids of various classes, both at home and abroad.**
R. E. Scoresby-Jackson. London: John Churchill, 1862. 509p.

Dr Scoresby-Jackson here includes Lisbon in his review of health resorts. After describing its geographical setting, he outlines the major local ailments, including inflammation of the lungs, pleurisy, bronchitis, laryngitis and leprosy. Consequently, he cannot recommend Lisbon for English pulmonary consumptives. Considerable detail of climate readings is supplied and the author makes much of the effect of temperature variations in Lisbon on causing catarrh and related complaints. The elevated suburbs of Campolide, Sete Rios, Benfica, Calhariz, Campo Grande and Lumiar are recommended for the summer months, as is Sintra which is otherwise 'foggy, raw and dull'.

The invalid's guide to Madeira, with a description of Teneriffe, Lisbon, Cintra, Mafra, etc.
See item no. 252.

The diary of an invalid; being the journal of a tour in pursuit of health in Portugal, Italy, Switzerland and France in the years 1817, 1818 and 1819.
See item no. 263.

126

The journal of an army surgeon during the Peninsular War.
See item no. 346.

Surgeon Henry's trifles: events of a military life.
See item no. 350.

Constitution and Law

443 **Assembleia da República: breves notas sobre o Parlamento Português e o Palácio de São Bento.** (The Portuguese Assembly: brief notes on the Portuguese Parliament and the Palace of São Bento.) Assembleia da República. Lisbon: Assembleia da República, [1991]. 2nd ed. 34p.

A large-format guide to the Portuguese Parliament building in Lisbon, the Palace of S. Bento, and to the parliamentary process. Many colour photographs reveal the splendour of the architecture of the late 16th-century building, a former Benedictine monastery, and its interior artwork. The text and photographs also cover the library, cloister and gardens of the palace.

444 **The Portuguese bank note case: legal, economic and financial approaches to the measure of damages in contract.** John Tillotson. Manchester, England: Centre for Law and Business, Faculty of Law, University of Manchester, 1992. 33p. (Working Paper, no. 13).

A study from the legalistic point of view of the famous fraud perpetrated in Lisbon against the Banco de Portugal by Artur Virgílio dos Alves Reis in 1924-25. The first part of the study is an enthralling account of Reis's fraud by which he deceived the prestigious British firm of Waterlow into printing unauthorized 500 escudo notes. Approximately one million pounds' worth of notes were produced before the fraud was discovered. The second part of the work assesses the legal arguments surrounding the amount of restitution which Waterlow was ordered to pay to the Banco de Portugal in 1932.

The genuine legal sentence pronounced by the High Court of Judicature of Portugal upon the conspirators against the life of his most faithful Majesty.
See item no. 343.

Administration and Local Government

445   **The Lisbon *juiz do povo* and the independence of Brazil,**
       1750-1822: an essay in Luso-Brazilian populism.
       Harry Bernstein.   In: *Conflict and continuity in Brazilian society.*
       Seminar on Latin American History, 1967.   Edited by Henry H. Keith,
       S. F. Edwards.   Columbia, South Carolina: University of South
       Carolina Press, 1969, p. 191-226. bibliog.

The post of Lisbon's *juiz do povo* (people's judge) existed from 1375 to 1835. He was
the elected head of the Lisbon guildhall or *Casa dos Vinte e Quatro* (House of the
Twenty-Four), so-called because it comprised the twenty-four guilds of Lisbon. The
juiz enjoyed the same status as that of a royal minister in terms of gaining access to
the monarch. This academic study of the office's populist role links its demise to the
same historical process which resulted in Portugal's loss of control of Brazil in the
early 19th century.

446   **The Lord Mayor of Lisbon: the Portuguese tribune of the people**
       and his 24 guilds.
       Harry Bernstein.   Lanham, Maryland; New York; London: ARP/
       University Press of America, 1989. 193p. bibliog. (Atlantic Studies on
       Society in Change, no. 57).

A study of the *Casa dos Vinte e Quatro* (House of the Twenty-four), a body comprising representatives of the craft guilds of Lisbon. The *juiz do povo* (people's judge)
was elected annually to preside over the Casa and thus was effectively the Lord Mayor
of Lisbon. Through him the city enjoyed privileged access to the monarch from the
late 14th century until the early 19th century and, Bernstein argues, it was one of the
most liberal administrative bodies in the world.

447   **Lisboa, II Congresso das Capitais do Mundo.** (Lisbon, II
Congress of the World's Capital Cities.)
Lage Simões Coelho, Marques da Costa.   Lisbon: Congresso das
Capitais do Mundo, 1950. unpaginated.

This large book, which marks a seven-day conference attended by mayors and other
representatives of capital cities held at the Palácio Galveias, is divided into three
sections. The first comprises eight chapters on Portugal, including four on Lisbon
itself, whilst the second is an account of the conference proceedings. Both sections
have text in Portuguese with either a full translation or résumé in French. The chapters
on Lisbon, illustrated by many black-and-white photographs and drawings, cover the
historic and modern aspects of the city, as well as its local customs and touristic
aspects. The final section of the book comprises 114 numbered pages of commercial
advertisements interspersed with text, again in French as well as Portuguese, on
different aspects of Portuguese exports and products.

448   **Lisbon: two steps forward on the road to democracy.**
José Tudella.   Lisbon: Imprensa Municipal, [c1975]. 36p. 3 maps.

This paper was given by Tudella, as President of Lisbon City Council, to the
Conference of Mayors of the World's Major Cities held in Milan, Italy, in 1975.
Coming exactly a year after the Portuguese Revolution, it is not surprising that
Tudella concentrated on the problems of grappling with new legislation and the
avoidance of political and planning anarchy. His concerns with housing shortages,
shanty towns and reorganization of Lisbon's municipal districts are uppermost here.
The text is accompanied by eight drawings by J. P. Barata which show different types
of Lisbon dwelling, taken from the Lisbon *Master Plan* of 1967.

Economy

449 Limits to competition.
The Group of Lisbon.   Cambridge, Massachusetts: The MIT Press,
1995. 167p.

The Group of Lisbon comprised nineteen assorted businessmen, academics, politicians
and bureaucrats drawn from Europe, Japan and North America who met regularly
under the aegis of the Calouste Gulbenkian Foundation during the early 1990s as a
continuation of the Portugal 2000 project. The name of Lisbon was chosen not only
because the Group met there but because the city's role as the hub of the Portuguese
Discoveries symbolized the contrast between Europe's history of expansion by
imposition and the Group's converse aim of promoting a cooperative pact between
North America, Europe and Japan in preference to competition.

Finance and Banking

450   The man who stole in Portugal.
   Murray Teigh Bloom.   New York: Charles Scribner's Sons, 1966.
   306p.

A thorough study of the fraud perpetrated against the Banco de Portugal in Lisbon and
the London banknote printing firm of Waterlow, by Alves Reis, from late 1924. Reis
was tried in 1930 and sentenced to a period of gaol and hard labour. Bloom
thoroughly researched thousands of pages of trial transcripts from both Portugal and
England, as well as following up the case's Dutch connections. His attention to the
personalities of those involved makes interesting reading of the potentially dry,
technical details of fraud.

**451   The Portuguese bank note case: the story and the solution of a
   financial perplexity.**
   Sir Cecil H. Kisch.   London: Macmillan & Co., 1932. 284p.

Divided into three sections, 'The Story', 'The Legal Solutions' and 'The Financial
Solution', this authoritative book by a banking expert tells of the massive fraud
perpetrated in Lisbon against the Banco de Portugal and their bank note printers,
Waterlow of London, by Alves Reis during 1924/25. In that period he put into
circulation 200,000 notes to the value of over one million pounds and had a further
380,000 notes printed. The latter part of this book concentrates on the legal question
of whether Waterlow should have had to pay merely the printing costs of the fraud or
the market value of the circulated notes.

The Portuguese bank note case.
See item no. 444.

The man from Lisbon.
See item no. 547.

Trade and Commerce

452 **O Porto de Lisboa: estudo de história económica, seguido de um catálogo bibliográfico e iconográfico. Quinto centenário do Infante D. Henrique.** (The Port of Lisbon: an economic history, followed by a bibliographical and iconographic catalogue. Fifth anniversary of Prince Henry the Navigator.)
José Bacellar Bebiano.   Lisbon: Administração Geral do Porto de Lisboa, 1960. 405p. 2 maps. bibliog.
A magnificent folio volume illustrated by a number of colour photographs, reproductions of engravings, tables and maps. It recounts the evolution of the port of Lisbon from before the Voyages of Discovery to the time of publication. An English summary is provided (p. 367-72) and an extensive bibliography directs the reader to further, related sources.

453 **A Feira da Ladra.** (The Thieves' market.)
Marina Tavares Dias.   Lisbon: Ibis Editores, 1990. 97p. bibliog.
(Guias de Lisboa pelos Olisipógrafos, no. 2).
The Feira da Ladra takes place today in the Campo de Santa Clara, near the church of S. Vicente de Fora in Lisbon's Alfama area. Formerly it was sited in the Campo de Santana. Its stalls nowadays sell clothes, shoes and all manner of second-hand bric-à-brac. As early as 1272 a market was held near the castle but the name Feira da Ladra was first documented in 1610. This well-illustrated volume includes 19th- and 20th-century photographs as well as engravings of earlier periods. The text comprises extracts by Fialho de Almeida, Xavier da Cunha, Júlio César Machado and Eduardo Coelho, all celebrated 19th-century writers on Lisbon.

454   **Lisbon, its English merchant community and the Mediterranean in the eighteenth century.**
H. E. S. Fisher.   In: *Shipping, trade and commerce: essays in memory of Ralph Davis.*   Edited by P. L. Cottrell, D. H. Aldcroft.   Leicester, England: Leicester University Press, 1981, p. 23-44. bibliog.

Fisher's paper explains how the English commercial community (The English Factory), based in Lisbon, dominated Portugal's trade with the Mediterranean in the 18th century, as well as trading directly with England and Brazil. The native Portuguese merchants concentrated their efforts on trade with the Portuguese settlements in Africa and Asia, largely leaving the Mediterranean to other nationalities. Much of the English trade through Lisbon with the Mediterranean was to Italy, but the traders also acted as agents for English-based firms buying commodities such as sugar in Lisbon and transporting them to Turkey. Because English shipping documents were some help in warding off Barbary pirates, other nations took to forging them and masquerading as English traders between Lisbon and the Mediterranean ports.

455   **The Portugal trade: a study of Anglo-Portuguese commerce, 1700-1770.**
H. E. S. Fisher.   London: Methuen & Co. Ltd., 1971. 171p. 2 maps. bibliog.

This detailed study of 18th-century Anglo-Portuguese commerce covers Lisbon's trade with England, particularly in textiles, grain, wine, bullion, diamonds and Brazilian goods. Also covered are the activities of the English Factory in Lisbon and the Lisbon Custom House, as well as the effects of the 1755 earthquake on trade. Statistical tables give details of shipping movements in the port of Lisbon. The work is a development of the author's doctoral thesis and has an extensive bibliography. It is illustrated with photographs which include a view of Lisbon in 1752 and a Falmouth to Lisbon packet-boat, the chief means of passenger communication between Britain and Lisbon in the 18th century.

456   **Lisbon as a port town in the eighteenth century.**
Stephen Fisher.   In: *Lisbon as a port town, the British seaman, and other maritime themes.*   Edited by Stephen Fisher.   Exeter, England: University of Exeter, 1988, p. 9-36. (Exeter Maritime Studies, no. 2).

A paper from the 19th Datini Conference held at Prato in 1987. Using extracts from contemporary printed sources, mostly accounts by visitors or foreign residents in Portugal, Fisher shows how Lisbon grew by the mid-18th century to be a major world port, yet, by the end of that century was lagging behind competitors such as London. This decline is attributed to the sluggish local economy and, subsequently, to the Napoleonic Wars which cost Portugal a substantial share of its direct trade with Brazil. Four of the illustrations, plus that on the cover, are of Lisbon or its environs.

457   **The English Factory at Lisbon: some chapters in its history.**
Sir Richard Lodge.   *Transactions of the Royal Historical Society,* series 4, vol. 16 (1933), p. 211-47.

The text of a paper given to the Royal Historical Society in 1932 which initially describes the major treaties of the 17th and 18th centuries between England and

Portugal, including the Methuen Treaties of 1703. The English Factory was a mercantile depot, which levied a duty on imports from England and whose presiding officer was the Consul-General in Lisbon. Although the exact date of foundation is unknown, it was certainly flourishing in the 18th century. Lodge recounts the various grievances between the Factory and Portugal which necessitated London's involvement and its survival of Pombal's attacks on it in the 18th century. The Factory was defunct by the mid-19th century.

458 **Mercado 24 de Julho.** (24th July Market.)
José Alberto Maio, Manuel Pedro Serra, José Melo Carvalheira,
photographs by Carlos Gil. Lisbon: Câmara Municipal de Lisboa,
Direcção Municipal de Abastecimento e Consumo, 1991. unpaginated.
bibliog.
About a half of this volume comprises twenty-eight, mostly colour, photographs and drawings of the Mercado 24 Julho, the animated Lisbon market situated on the busy Avenida 24 de Julho, at Cais do Sodré, near the riverside. The text explains how the market was established in 1882 and rebuilt after a fire in 1893. Further building work took place in 1940 and 1980. Today the market covers 10,000 square metres and predominantly sells flowers and vegetables with, until recently, an overflow of stalls across the road selling fish and fruit.

459 **Lojas antigas de Lisboa.** (Old shops of Lisbon.)
Carlos Laranjo Medeiros. Lisbon: Programa das Artes e Ofícios
Tradicionais, 1994. 2 vols.
A full colour survey of the many ornate shop exteriors and interiors which survive in Lisbon. Volume one covers the Baixa, the commercial heart of Lisbon, whilst volume two covers fifty-two shops in the upper city quarters of the Chiado, Carmo and Trindade, which are mostly small and privately owned. The text provides historical and descriptive detail as well as addresses and opening hours. The emphasis is on the social history and the personalities embodied in the shops rather than on their architectural features. Useful indexes are provided both by trading name and by type of merchandise sold. A few restaurants are included as well as shops.

460 **Lisboa: lojas de um tempo ao outro.** (Lisbon: shops from one era to
another.)
Jorge Ribeiro, Júlio Conrado. Lisbon: Editorial Notícias, 1994. 178p.
A large-format survey of Lisbon shops with many colour and black-and-white illustrations. Most of the premises covered are in the city centre and include many of the surviving specialist shops such as the Casa dos Carimbos (The rubber-stamp shop).

461 **Trade, Inquisition and the English nation in Portugal, 1650-1690.**
L. M. E. Shaw. Manchester, England: Carcanet in association with
the Calouste Gulbenkian Foundation, 1989. 230p. bibliog.
Part I of this book, based on a doctoral thesis, covers the Portuguese Inquisition and the era of treaties with England, whilst part II addresses the English nation in Portugal, 1650-90. This latter section includes chapters on 'The English College and Anglo-Portuguese relations' and 'The life of a consul'. The latter describes the

activities of the consul in Lisbon, Thomas Maynard. Shaw shows how the series of Anglo-Portuguese treaties turned Portugal into a virtual colony of Britain and how the Inquisition and War of Spanish Succession sapped the economy further.

462 **Stratégie des affaires à Lisbonne entre 1595 et 1607: lettres marchandes d'Évora et Veiga.** (Business strategy in Lisbon between 1595 and 1607: commercial correspondence of Évora and Veiga.) J. Gentil da Silva. Paris: Librairie Armand Colin, 1956. (printed 1957). 442p. 43 maps. (École Pratique des Hautes Études VIᵉ Section, Centre de Recherches Historiques: Affaires et Gens d'Affaires, IX).

After a calendar of contemporary events and a chapter on contemporary Lisbon's commercial connections with Medina del Campo in Spain, the bulk of this volume comprises business letters sent by Rodrigo Lopes d'Évora, Manuel da Veiga, Lopo Rodrigues d'Évora and their relatives to the Roiz Embito family of merchants at Medina del Campo. The letters are in Castilian Spanish and give detailed information of commercial activity in Lisbon, which is illuminated by a commentary in French by the editor.

463 **Mercado de Santa Clara.** (Santa Clara market.) Emília Maria Velasco. Lisbon: Câmara Municipal de Lisboa, 1991. 24p. bibliog.

Santa Clara market was opened in 1877 as the Mercado Oriental do Campo de Santa Clara, behind the church of S. Vicente in the Alfama area of Lisbon. Colour photographs depict the market hall, local gardens, and the nearby churches of S. Vicente and of Sta Engrácia, the latter being Portugal's national pantheon. Adjacent to the market is the Feira da Ladra (Thieves' market), well-known to tourists in Lisbon for its wide range of bric-à-brac, cheap footwear and clothing stalls. The Feira da Ladra has a history going back to the reign of Afonso II (1211-23), but it only moved definitively to its present site in 1882.

464 **The British Factory in Lisbon & its closing stages ensuing upon the Treaty of 1810. Compiled from original documents.** A. R. Walford. Lisbon: Instituto Britânico em Portugal, 1940. 200p. bibliog.

A history of the British (or English) Factory, an assembly of expatriate merchants and factors, the origins of which date back to the 17th century. Because of the close relationship between trade and political relations, this work is an account of the work of the British consuls in Lisbon as well as of the trading activities of the Factory. Its fourteen chapters are in broadly chronological sequence with some thematic digressions on topics such as the Factory's Protestant burial ground. The work's index is almost exclusively by name rather than subject.

Antigos lugares de vender, Anciens lieux de vente, Old selling places. *See* item no. 54.

The elusive Baron. *See* item no. 376.

On the twentieth anniversary of the establishment of the Calouste Gulbenkian Foundation.
See item no. 377.

Mr Five Per Cent: the biography of Calouste Gulbenkian.
See item no. 380.

Gulbenkian: an interpretation of Calouste Sarkis Gulbenkian.
See item no. 382.

Centros de comércio e serviços na cidade de Lisboa. (Commercial centres and services in the city of Lisbon.)
See item no. 525.

Transport

Aerial

465 **Imagem: jornal do Aeroporto de Lisboa. Lisbon Airport Journal.**
Aeroportos e Navegação Aérea.   Lisbon: ANA, Aeroportos e
Navegação Aérea, 1994- . bi-monthly.

A bilingual Portuguese and English tabloid newspaper produced by the Lisbon Airport authority and which enjoys a circulation of 100,000 copies. It is a mixture of practical airport information and news and statistics of the airport's developments, all presented attractively with colour photographs, charts and diagrams.

466 **The Lisbon story.**
N. C. Baldwin.   Sutton Coldfield, England: The Aero Field, [1965].
10p. (A Popular Pamphlet).

This reprint from *The Aero Field* is a fascinating account of aviation in Lisbon, starting with the pioneering 1922 seaplane flight of Cabral and Coutinho from the Tagus to Rio and concluding with the cessation of flying-boat services from Lisbon to Madeira in 1958. The much-celebrated 1922 flight is revealed actually to have taken over two months to complete and involved the use of three different aircraft, as the first two crashed *en route*. The story of Portuguese airmail is also told and a number of illustrations of airmail cancellations are included. The pamphlet ends with a chronological table of significant events in Lisbon aviation history between 1922 and 1958.

467 **Report on the air crossing from Lisbon to Rio de Janeiro.**
Sacadura Cabral, Gago Coutinho, translated by Bryan de Avelar.
Lisbon: Academia Internacional da Cultura, 1972. 141p. map.

Consists of a general account of the first air crossing between Brazil and Portugal in 1922, written by Sacadura Cabral, the pilot and commander, followed by a technical report by the navigator, Gago Coutinho. The former includes substantial detail on the preparations for their seaplane flight from the River Tagus at Belém, on the western outskirts of Lisbon, whilst the latter goes into much technical detail, including navigational and mathematical calculations undertaken on the flight. The book is illustrated by thirty-four photographs. The surviving aircraft is today preserved in Lisbon's Naval Museum.

468 **Aircraft museums and collections of the world, Volume 4: Austria, France, Portugal, Spain and Switzerland.**
Bob Ogden. New York: Published by the Author, 1993. 128p.
Included in this specialist guide to aeronautical collections is a description of the Museu do Ar da Força Aérea Portuguesa (Portuguese Air Force Aviation Museum) housed at Alverca, about 25km north of Lisbon. The museum houses aircraft, engines and models on a site near the River Tagus. Although half a million people have visited the museum since its foundation in 1971, it has inadequate room. The author believes that if its planned relocation materializes, it will become one of Europe's major aviation museums. Its envisaged new site is the Granja do Marquês airbase, near Sintra, which served as Lisbon's international airport before and during the Second World War.

469 **European airports.**
Alan J. Wright. London: Ian Allan, 1992. 2nd ed. 96p. (ABC Series).
In this survey of major European airports, aimed at civil aviation enthusiasts, there is a brief entry for Lisbon's international airport at Portela de Sacavém, 7km north of the city, which opened towards the end of the Second World War. Details are given of runway lengths and orientation, as well as air traffic control radio frequencies and viewing facilities.

Maritime

470 **The discovery of the Atlantic.**
Costa Brochado. Lisbon: Comissão Executiva das Comemorações do Quinto Centenário da Morte do Infante D. Henrique, 1960. 126p. 5 maps.
Translated from *Descobrimento do Atlântico*, this is a nationalistic eulogy of Portuguese navigational exploits by sea and by air, orginating from Lisbon. As well as addressing the maritime voyages of Bartolomeu Dias, Vasco da Gama and Pedro Álvares Cabral, who set off from the Tagus in the latter years of the 15th century and reached India and Brazil respectively, the book also includes a chapter on the 1922 seaplane crossing from the Tagus at Belém to Rio de Janeiro by Gago Coutinho and Sacadura Cabral. By implication this modern flight is put on a par with these earlier maritime exploits.

471 **Veleiros de Portugal. Sailing vessels in Portugal.**
Francisco Correia Figueira, translated by Wendy Graça.   Lisbon:
Edições Inapa, 1994. 125p. bibliog.
A parallel text in Portuguese and English provides the captions to a series of superb
19th- and early 20th-century photographs of Portuguese sailing vessels. Many of these
are traditional Lisbon vessels, depicted at home in the Tagus in locations such as
Belém, Alcântara, Cascais, Montijo or in the docks of Lisbon itself.

472 **Boats of the Lisbon river: the fragata and related types.**
Cangueiro, bote and bote de meia-quilha, bote fragata, falua, bote
de tartaranha; barcos de quatro cintas.
Manuel Leitão.   London: Trustees of the National Maritime Museum,
1980. 2nd revised ed. 154p. bibliog.
Published in duplicated typescript in A4 format and accompanied by black-and-white
photographs and line drawings, this is a comprehensive guide to traditional Lisbon
river craft. The book is aimed at the specialist with much technical detail provided;
every named part of the boats is given in both Portuguese and English.   There are six
unnumbered chapters, each on a different type of vessel, but no index is provided.

473 **Referências históricas do Porto de Lisboa.** (Historical references of
the Port of Lisbon.)
Ministério das Obras Públicas, Transportes e Comunicações.   Lisbon:
Administração do Porto de Lisboa, 1991. 223p. map. bibliog.
A profusely illustrated history of the port of Lisbon from mediaeval times to the
mid-20th century. Subjects covered include boat construction, maritime transport,
immigration, quarantine procedures, entrepôt arrangements, seaplane operations and
aspects of navigation of the Tagus river. The book includes many sepia-tinted
photographs of the port of Lisbon and a number of colour illustrations.

Terrestrial

474 **Tram tours of Lisbon.**
Joseph Abdo.   Lisbon: Represse, 1991. 98p. 10 maps.
Although only a small-format publication, this work is illustrated with high-quality
colour and black-and-white photographs of tram scenes. It has a section on each extant
tram route, accompanied by a map showing every tram-stop. The accompanying text
identifies points of interest on the route and is angled to the tourist rather than the
tramway specialist. Also included is a brief history of public transport in Lisbon and a
useful list of places to visit along the tram routes which is organized by type of sight,
such as museums and churches. Unfortunately some of the routes have since been
converted to bus operation but the itinerary information remains largely valid.

475 **Lisbon public transport.**
N. R. Bartlett, with additional material by Geoffrey Morant.
Chelmsford, England: Westbury Marketing, 1985. 60p. 2 maps.
bibliog.

This pocket-sized volume has eleven sections, an eight-item bibliography and is illustrated by thirty-two black-and-white photographs. The sections each relate to a different form of transport, such as tram, bus, coach, ferry-boat, funicular, train or elevator. Brief histories of the various urban transport undertakings are given, along with fleet lists. The work also gives practical hints on ticketing and on using the various forms of transport. The forthcoming (1997) *Bus fleets of Lisbon and Oporto,* by Ron Phillips (PSV Circle. 2nd ed.) should effectively update much of this work. Photographs of Lisbon area buses can be found in *The buses of Portugal: a pictorial review* by Bruce Tilley (Elizabeth, South Australia: Railmac Publications, 1988, p. 4, 13-18).

476 **Engineering as civic art: the Santa Justa elevator in Lisbon.**
Gonçalo Byrne. *Lotus International,* vol. 45 (1985), p. 118-32.

An account, accompanied by colour and monochrome photographs as well as many architectural drawings, of the two stylish vertical street-lifts known collectively as the Elevador de Santa Justa (Santa Justa elevator). This connects Lisbon's Rua Áurea, near Rossio, with the Largo do Carmo in the elevated Chiado district. It was designed by the Oporto-born engineer, Raoul Mesnier du Ponsard and was opened in 1901. It continues to operate daily as a busy part of the Lisbon transport system operated by Carris. The text is in both English and Italian.

477 **Lisboa: a cidade dos elevadores.** (Lisbon: the city of the elevators.)
Edite Estrela. Lisbon: Carris, 1986. 49p.

An account of the evolution and present state of Lisbon's three street funiculars and the Santa Justa elevator, with a summary in English. Published by the Lisbon transport undertaking, Carris, which operates these services to the hilly parts of the city, this book is illustrated by many colour and monochrome photographs and drawings. Short sections are included on Lisbon funiculars and street-lifts which no longer exist and on literary references to these modes of Lisbon transport.

478 **The tramways of Portugal: a visitor's guide.**
B. R. King, J. H. Price. London: Light Rail Transit Association,
1995. 4th ed. 92p. 11 maps. bibliog.

Approximately half of this book is given over to an account of Lisbon's railed transport systems. This includes a thorough history of the Lisbon tram system and funiculars as well as short sections on the Metro underground network and the coastal railway line from Lisbon to Cascais. Although written primarily for light-rail enthusiasts, its text is straightforward for the general reader and is a most helpful guide to getting around Lisbon by public transport. The text is accompanied by many black-and-white photographs and the maps show the evolution and recent contraction of the Lisbon tram system. There is also a section on the Sintra tramway, which runs to the Atlantic coast. The text is updated by news reports in the same publisher's monthly journal, *Light Rail and Modern Tramway.*

479   **O livro da Carris. The book of Carris.**
       José Lagrange, António Alçada Baptista.   Lisbon: Companhia Carris
       de Ferro de Lisboa, 1993. 98p.

Carris is the main Lisbon public transport undertaking founded in 1872, curiously as a company based in Rio de Janeiro. This attractive large-format volume depicts in words and photographs ten past and present examples of the company's trams and trailers, nine classes of bus, three street funiculars and one street elevator. This diverse fleet is illustrated by fine colour photographs which, almost exclusively, concentrate on details such as seats, wheels and handles, rather than the vehicles in their entirety. The text, which is in both Portuguese and English, outlines the history of the Carris company and its vehicles and provides basic technical data on each vehicle.

480   **Lisbon docks and Cintra railway.**
       J. D. Powles.   London, [1859]. 38p. map.

John Diston Powles, the retired Secretary to the London Docks, was hired to report on the feasibility of an English company taking over, from the failed French Count Lucotte, the concession for the building of docks, a dyke and a railway to Sintra on the banks of the Tagus to the west of Lisbon. His report, accepted by the Portuguese government, concluded that the value of newly reclaimed flat land along the industrialized sector between the Praça S. Paulo and Belém would ensure the viability of the dock project but that the railway should be built as a separate project due to the uncertainty of its financial success, particularly of the final stretch to Sintra. It was not until 1895 that the section between Pedrouços (Torre de Belém) and Cais do Sodré was completed, whereas the link to Sintra was never built.

481   **Spain and Portugal by rail.**
       Norman Renouf.   Chalfont St Peter, England: Bradt, 1994. 326p.
       maps.

This book for the international rail-traveller includes a section which, in fact, provides more detail on places of interest in Lisbon than practical transport information on the city. Descriptions, addresses, telephone numbers, transport route details and timetables are given to assist visitors to reach the sights described. A plan is included of the layout of the Santa Apolónia international station in Lisbon but no information is forthcoming on the Rossio Station in the city centre.

482   **Railway holiday in Portugal.**
       D. W. Winkworth.   Newton Abbot, England: David & Charles, 1968.
       158p. 4 maps. bibliog.

Chapter nine of this nationwide account of Portuguese railway travel covers Lisbon and Sintra. Black-and-white photographs of Lisbon's underground, funiculars and railways illustrate the text. The emphasis is on Lisbon's local rail services, including the underground network and suburban lines to Cascais and Sintra rather than the main-line connections to other cities. Lisbon's tram and funicular system are also covered.

An historical journey along the Marginal.
See item no. 95.

Planta da rede dos transportes públicos da Carris. (Map of the public transport network of Carris.)
See item no. 106.

Encenar a cidade: intervenções artísticas nos tapumes das obras do Metropolitano de Lisboa. (Decorating the city stage: artistic works on the construction hoardings of the Lisbon Metropolitan railway.)
See item no. 584.

Azulejos no Metropolitano de Lisboa. (Tiles on the Lisbon Underground.)
See item no. 594.

The Lisbon coaches in history.
See item no. 633.

Museu Nacional dos Coches, National Coach Museum, Musée National des Carrosses.
See item no. 637.

Great maritime museums of the world.
See item no. 646.

Museu de Marinha visitor's guide.
See item no. 650.

Environment

483 **Science, technology and European cultural heritage. Proceedings of the European Symposium, Bologna, Italy, 13-16 June, 1989.**
Edited by N. S. Baer, C. Sabbioni, A. I. Sors. Oxford: Butterworth-Heinemann, 1991. 980p. bibliog.

This record of a European symposium includes two reports on the effects of pollution on Lisbon's architectural heritage at Belém. 'Chemical characterisation of the weathering crust of the Jerónimos monastery' by E. Roekens and others (p. 863-67) identifies sulphates as the most important product of weathering. In the paper by L. Aires-Barros and others, 'Stone decay: effects of weathering and air pollution. The case of the Jerónimos monastery, Lisbon, Portugal' (p. 876-80), the authors describe their use of a monitoring system to assess the micro- and nano-climate of the site. Amongst their proposals are screening the structure against wind, rain and pigeons and the implementation of traffic and industrial limitations in the vicinity.

484 **A study of rainwater acidity in Greater Manchester and Greater Lisbon.**
S. E. Hare, J. W. S. Longhurst, A. Marques da Costa. *The Environmentalist,* vol. 11, pt. 4 (1991), p. 267-80.

A comparative evaluation over a three-month period of rainwater acidity using data collected by ten schools in Manchester and a further ten in the Lisbon area.

485 **Survey of metal contamination along the Lisbon – Estádio national highway, Portugal.**
A. Gama Xavier, M. Kersten. In: *Proceedings of the International Conference on Environmental Pollution, ICEP-1, Lisbon, 1991.* Geneva, Switzerland: Interscience Enterprises, 1991, p. 388-93.

A scientific study of the pollution, caused predominantly by exhaust emissions, along the busy trunk road running west out of Lisbon past the national sports stadium at Cruz Quebrada.

Architecture

General

The *Distrito de Lisboa* includes fifteen *concelhos* of which the Lisbon city area is one.
The three tomes of volume five of this survey are devoted to the city of Lisbon and
these were published in 1973, 1975 and 1988 to form part of a multi-volume set which
covers the entire administrative area of the *Distrito de Lisboa*. The three tomes share a
common format of between 147 and 196 pages of text each, interspersed with a
number of full-page colour photographs and followed by between 127 and 154
monochrome photographs of the monuments and buildings described. Although the set
comprises a most extensive visual portrayal and description of Lisbon's buildings and
monuments, its ease of use is not enhanced by the lack of an overall alphabetical
index.

Conceived and, for the most part, written by one of Lisbon's most esteemed
historians, this work comprises twelve large-format fascicules, generally of around
sixty pages in length and each of which covers a particular group or groups of
building, public space or monument to be found in Lisbon. Overall, the work
constitutes a census of buildings and sites of architectural or historical merit in
Lisbon, which is well illustrated by black-and-white photographs and by drawings.

488   **Guia urbanístico e arquitectónico de Lisboa.** (Urban and architectural
       guide to Lisbon.)
       Associação Arquitectos Portugueses.   Lisbon: Associação Arquitectos
       Portugueses, 1987. 311p. 24 maps. bibliog.

Lisbon is divided into five areas in this comprehensive guide to the architecture of the
city, which contains over 600 black-and-white photographs of buildings and structures. As well as the common tourist sights, there are fewer common edifices included,
such as apartment blocks, fountains and bandstands. Overall, this is an excellent visual
introduction to the city for the visitor as well as for the student of architecture. Date of
construction and the architect's name are given for each entry and a detailed set of
street maps shows the precise location of every building mentioned. Floor plans and
elevation drawings are also provided for some of the more notable buildings. Indexes
by type of building and by architects' names maximize the usefulness of the volume.
Summaries are provided in both French and English, the latter being entitled 'An
approach on city development' (p. 296-303).

489   **Solares portugueses: introdução ao estudo da casa nobre.**
       (Portuguese country houses: introduction to the study of the stately
       home.)
       Carlos de Azevedo.   Lisbon: Livros Horizonte, 1988. 207p. bibliog.

This extensive guide to Portuguese houses of the nobility includes an English
summary of each chapter (p. 187-92) and in addition to the pagination noted above,
the book has an appendix of 160 pages of black-and-white photographs of such
houses. In the Lisbon area, these include various buildings in Sintra, the Palácio
Pombal in Oeiras and the Palácio Fronteira in Benfica. The text covers the period from
mediaeval times to the end of the 18th century.

490   **Guia de arquitectura Lisboa 94.** (Architectural guide, Lisbon 94.)
       Edited by Francisco Gentil Berger, Luís Bissau, Michel Toussaint.
       Lisbon: Associação dos Arquitectos Portugueses; Sociedade Lisboa
       1994; Faculdade de Arquitectura da Univ. [sic] Técnica de Lisboa,
       1994. 394p. map.

A useful parallel-text guide, in Portuguese and rather stilted English, to the
architectural landmarks of Lisbon, accompanied by black-and-white photographs of
each of the 147 sites covered. The work is arranged in ten main chapters which cover
Lisbon's architectural history chronologically. For each site the appropriate Lisbon
bus or tram route-number is given, as well as architectural and historical details.

491   **Country manors of Portugal: a passage through seven centuries.**
       Marcus Binney, introduction by Nicolas Sapieha, photographs by
       Nicolas Sapieha, Francesco Venturi.   Woodbridge, England: Antique
       Collectors' Club, 1987. 231p. map. bibliog.

Abundantly illustrated with fine colour photographs, this volume looks at fifty-nine
country manors, grouped by region. Belying the title, houses in Madeira, the Azores
and even Brazil are included. 'Greater Lisbon' and 'Sintra and surroundings'
constitute two of the chapters (p. 16-69), whilst a further section, entitled 'The Tagus
river', covers the south side of the river. Amongst the buildings represented in the
Lisbon area are the Palácio dos Marqueses de Fronteira at Benfica, the Quinta Real de

Caxias, the Palácio do Marquês de Pombal at Oeiras and Sintra's palaces of Seteais and Monserrate.

492   **Arcos e arcadas de Lisboa.** (Archways and arcades of Lisbon.)
      Baltazar de Matos Caeiro.   Sacavém, Portugal: Distri Editora, 1991.
      142p. 5 maps. bibliog.

A large-format anthology of mostly colour photographs of some 120 of Lisbon's public archways and arcades. They are arranged in broadly chronological order, with about a third being of structures which no longer exist. Some of this category are illustrated by drawings or old engravings. A brief textual description accompanies each illustration. The subject matter varies enormously and includes the Águas Livres aqueduct, the Rossio station tunnel and the Rua Augusta arch, but the majority of examples are utilitarian structures supporting roads or buildings, many of which are centuries old.

493   **Aquedutos em Portugal. Aqueducts in Portugal.**
      Joaquim Caetano.   Lisbon: Liber, 1991. 111p.

This profusely illustrated survey of Portuguese aqueducts is written in parallel English and Portuguese texts. As well as describing and portraying, in colour, the Águas Livres aqueduct of Lisbon which was linked to the city in 1748, others in the area, such as the Águas Livres tributary to Queluz and the system at the Quinta do Marquês de Pombal at Oeiras, are also covered. The text is not excessively technical and is therefore of interest to the general reader.

494   **Cemitérios de Lisboa: entre o real e o imaginário.** (Cemeteries of
      Lisbon: between the real and the imaginary.)
      Francisco Moita Flores.   Lisbon: Câmara Municipal de Lisboa, 1993.
      167p. bibliog.

High-quality colour photographs adorn this portrayal of Lisbon's cemeteries, produced in A4 format. In addition to depictions of cemeteries at Alto de S. João, Prazeres and elsewhere in Lisbon, there is comparative reference to, and illustration of, cemeteries in France and Italy. The book has nineteen sections which are not coherently drawn into a whole, and these address topics as diverse as epitaphs, gypsies, freemasonry and anti-Fascist symbolism.

495   **Palácios portugueses. 1º volume.** (Portuguese palaces, 1st volume.)
      Raúl Lino.   Lisbon: Secretaria de Estado da Informação e Turismo,
      1972. unpaginated.

A folio-size portrayal, using many colour and black-and-white photographs, of eight Portuguese palaces, including four in the Lisbon area. These are the Paço Real and Castelo da Pena in Sintra, the Palácio de Queluz and, in Lisbon itself, the Palácio da Ajuda. With a text for each building in English and French, as well as Portuguese, this volume is an impressive introduction to the major royal palaces of the Lisbon area.

496 **Roteiro cultural dos pátios e vilas da Sétima Colina.** (Cultural survey of the courtyards and townships of the Seventh Hill.) Rui Matos, Paula Teixeira. Lisbon: Contexto, 1994. 94p. bibliog.

This work, published under the auspices of the Lisboa 94 European Cultural Capital initiative, has a brief summary in English. Lisbon is said to be built on seven hills and this work is arranged as two itineraries through the Sétima Colina, or Seventh Hill, the area between Cais do Sodré on the Tagus riverside, to the west of the city centre, and the Largo do Rato, a square in the north-west of Lisbon. Illustrated by black-and-white photographs and line drawings of buildings, the volume aims not only to convey architectural and historical information but also to awaken an interest in the need for restoration and renewal of this area of the capital.

497 **O livro de Lisboa.** (The book of Lisbon.) Edited by Irisalva Moita. Lisbon: Livros Horizonte, 1994. 527p. bibliog.

Published as a project of the Departamento de Intervenção Urbana da Sociedade Lisboa 94, this high quality publication seeks to present the history of Lisbon through its buildings. Its eleven chapters, each by a different author and ornamented by fine colour illustrations, cover a period of Lisbon's evolution from prehistoric times to the present. Detailed bibliographies augment each chapter and a general bibliography of 200 items completes the work. Unfortunately, no overall index is provided for this otherwise excellent volume, which is an essential starting point for the study of the city.

498 **Quintas e palácios nos arredores de Lisboa.** (Estates and palaces in the outskirts of Lisbon.) Anne de Stoop, photographs by Maurício Abreu. Oporto, Portugal: Livraria Civilização, 1986. 420p. 9 maps. bibliog.

A magnificent folio volume packed with hundreds of colour photographs of fine houses, palaces and their gardens in the Lisbon area. As well as profusely illustrating the Palácio Fronteira and Quinta dos Azulejos in Lisbon itself (p. 79-99), the neighbouring towns of Loures, Amadora, Oeiras, Cascais, Sintra, Sesimbra and Setúbal are also represented. Excellent colour maps show the locations of the buildings featured. The volume is completed by an inventory of other notable houses which do not merit a full, individual entry.

499 **Portuguese architecture.** Walter Crum Watson. London: Archibald Constable & Company, 1908. 280p. map. bibliog.

The nineteen chapters of this finely produced volume are arranged chronologically, with extensive reference to Lisbon buildings throughout. The emphasis is predictably on the major ecclesiastical and royal buildings, including the cathedral, the churches of Carmo, Estrela, S. Vicente, Conceição Velha and the Ajuda palace. A separate chapter is devoted to the Manueline treasures of Belém. Over 100 black-and-white photographs illustrate the book which, although now dated, has yet to be superseded in range by any more modern work in English.

To 1599

500   **Torre de Belém: English guide.** (Tower of Belém: English guide.)
Isabel Cruz de Almeida, translated by Nicolau Anderson Leitão, Ana
Mântua.   Lisbon: IPPAR, Instituto Português do Património
Arquitectónico e Arqueológico, [1995]. unpaginated.

The official guide to the Tower of Belém which was built well out into the River
Tagus as part of the defences of Lisbon but which, since the 1755 earthquake altered
the river's course, has stood at its southern edge. It was built for King Manuel I by
Francisco de Arruda, between 1514 and 1520. Arruda's experience in military
building in North Africa was allied to the prevailing late Gothic architectural style,
now known as Manueline. In addition to historical and architectural information, the
guide includes colour photographs, a cross-section and a floor plan of the Tower.

501   **Apontamentos sobre o manuelino no Distrito de Lisboa.** (Notes on
Manueline architecture in the Lisbon District.)
Fernando Pereira Bastos.   Lisbon: Imprensa Nacional-Casa da Moeda,
1990. 198p. map.

Manueline architecture is the late Gothic style which developed in the reign of King
Manuel I (1495-1521) and coincided with many of the celebrated Voyages of
Discovery. This folio volume is a monochrome catalogue of hundreds of architectural
drawings of Manueline features to be found in the Lisbon District, which encompasses
fifteen councils, including Oeiras, Cascais and Sintra, as well as Lisbon itself. The
Lisbon section naturally includes many examples from the Belém area but less well-
known buildings in the city are also featured. The provenance of the subject of each
drawing is given but, otherwise, there is minimal textual accompaniment.

502   **Mosteiro dos Jerónimos: English guide.** (Jerónimos Monastery:
English guide.)
Luís Chimeno, translation by the British Council.   Lisbon: IPPAR,
Instituto Português do Património Arquetectónico e Arqueológico,
[1995]. unpaginated.

A large-format, brief, colour guide to the magnificent Jerónimos monastery at Belém,
on which work began in early 1501 and which has been a Unesco World Heritage site
since 1984. This official guide, which includes floor plans of the church and cloisters
and eleven colour photographs, also provides a brief history of its building phases and
of its 19th-century alterations.

503   **Portuguese plain architecture: between spice and diamonds,
1521-1706.**
George Kubler.   Middletown, Connecticut: Wesleyan University
Press, 1972. 315p. bibliog.

A fine large-format study of the *estilo chão*, or 'plain architecture' which succeeded
the more flamboyant and wealthy Manueline period in Portugal. About a quarter of the
126 photographic plates are of Lisbon buildings and numerous architects' drawings
further enhance the text which covers many of the capital's major tourist sights. The

149

Lisbon buildings include the churches of S. Roque, Sta. Engrácia, S. Vicente de Fora and the Cathedral. Chapter seven is entitled 'The joyeuse entrée at Lisbon in 1619' and concerns the public ceremony whereby an oath was sworn by the Portuguese sovereign to guarantee traditional municipal rights. An extensive bibliography completes the work.

504 **Belém Palace: its guests, its secrets and its daily life.**
José António Saraiva, translated by Amélia Salavisa Brooker.
Lisbon: Editorial Inquérito, 1991. 2nd ed. 146p. 2 maps. bibliog.

Illustrated by many colour and black-and-white photographs, this work recounts the history of what is now the Portuguese President's residence at Belém, in the western outskirts of Lisbon. The origins of the palace go back to the 16th century but there have been many alterations and additions since then. The palace was purchased by João V in 1726 and he was there when the 1755 earthquake struck and destroyed the royal palace in Lisbon itself. Nowadays its use for ceremonial functions has been somewhat usurped by the palaces of Ajuda and Queluz.

17th and 18th centuries

505 **The Palace and gardens of Fronteira: seventeenth- and eighteenth-century Portuguese style.**
José C. Neves.   New York: Scala Books; Woodbridge, England: Antique Collectors' Club, 1995. 148p.

A well illustrated presentation of the magnificent palace of the Marqueses de Fronteira which is situated at Benfica, in the north-western outskirts of Lisbon. The palace is particularly renowned for its extensive ceramic tilework and gardens which are both fully depicted here.

506 **João Frederico Ludovice, an eighteenth-century architect in Portugal.**
Robert C. Smith.   *The Art Bulletin*, vol. XVIII (1936), p. 273-370.

Ludovice, whose original German name was Johann Friedrich Ludwig, was a goldsmith who brought his German and Italian experience to Portugal in 1701. As well as his architectural works on the royal palace at Mafra and at Évora, he also worked in Lisbon on the Paços da Ribeira, the royal palace on the waterfront which was destroyed by the 1755 earthquake, and S. Domingos church, which still stands despite a disastrous fire in 1959. Smith shows how, although Ludovice was a derivative architect insofar as he borrowed much from the Roman architects of the Seicento and from Germany, he nevertheless transformed Portuguese building. This article is illustrated with many black-and-white photographs.

507   **Carlos Mardel and his Lisbon architecture.**
Hellmut Wohl.   *Apollo: the Magazine of the Arts*, vol. 97 (April 1973),
p. 350-59.

Mardel was a Hungarian military engineer who was instrumental in bringing Rococo architecture to Portugal. The author records how Mardel was involved in the construction of the massive Lisbon aqueduct, completed in 1748, and related water-supply projects in Lisbon. With Eugénio dos Santos he was also a leading figure in the reconstruction of post-earthquake Lisbon and the author contrasts the outlooks of the two men; Santos being pragmatic whilst Mardel sought more sophisticated solutions to planning problems. Illustrations included in this article show several of Mardel's works in Lisbon.

19th and 20th centuries

508   **Tomás Taveira.**
Andrea Bettella, art editor.   London: Academy Editions, 1994. 144p.
(Architecture Monographs, no. 37).

Following two brief introductory essays, this book contains fifteen sections on different projects of the architect Tomás Taveira, with a brief concluding section of biography. Thirteen of the projects detailed are buildings in Lisbon or its immediate environs. These include the enormous, multicoloured Amoreiras shopping centre, the Chelas housing project, the monumental and controversial Cultural Centre at Belém, the D. Carlos I Building in Lisbon and, on a smaller scale, a record shop in Cascais.

509   **The residence of the British Ambassador at Lisbon.**
T. A. Bull.   Lisbon: The British Historical Society of Portugal, 1995.
82p. bibliog.

A history of the house in the Lapa district of western Lisbon which accommodates the British Ambassador. The author briefly mentions the various residences of the British envoys and ambassadors to Lisbon before concentrating on the residence in the Rua S. Francisco de Borja, which although occupied by the British envoy in the 1830s was not purchased by the British government until 1875. An account is given of its celebrated visitors over the years and of the Embassy's activities to the present day. The book is well illustrated by colour and black-and-white photographs as well as by reproductions of watercolours by John Coates. An appendix includes a complete list of British diplomatic representatives appointed to Lisbon from 1555 to 1993.

510   **Centre for Modern Art and Acarte, Lisbon: the background, the new buildings 1983-4 and the first five years.**
Calouste Gulbenkian Foundation.   Lisbon: Calouste Gulbenkian Foundation, 1991. 67p. bibliog.

A profusely illustrated book which brings together for the general reader articles previously published in specialist architectural journals. Included are contributions from Luís de Guimarães Lobato, Leslie Martin, Patrick Hodgkinson and José Sommer Ribeiro. The text is arranged into six sections covering the history and development of the Gulbenkian Centre site and the creation of Acarte (The Department of Cultural Promotion, Artistic Creation and Education through Art). The Centre for Modern Art shares its site with the Gulbenkian Museum.

511 **Chiado, Lisbon: Álvaro Siza and the strategy of memory.**
Bernard Colenbrander, translated from the Dutch by Michael O'Loughlin. Rotterdam, the Netherlands: Nederlands Architectuur Instituut, 1991. 45p.

On 25 August 1988 an area approximately 100 metres by 200 metres of the Chiado area of central Lisbon was destroyed by a fire started by an electrical fault in the Grandella department store. The architect Álvaro Siza's plans to rebuild the affected area were approved by Lisbon City Council in 1990. The full text of these plans is reproduced in this illustrated volume.

512 **Arquitectura do princípio do século em Lisboa, 1900-1925: levantamento e classificação da arquitectura do 1º quartel do séc. XX na cidade de Lisboa.** (Early 20th-century architecture in Lisbon, 1900-25: survey and classification of the architecture of the first quarter of the 20th century in the city of Lisbon.)
José Manuel Fernandes, Maria de Lurdes Janeiro, Ana Cristina Tostões, Fernanda Dália Moniz da Câmara. Lisbon: Câmara Municipal de Lisboa, 1991. 199p. 71 maps. bibliog.

This companion volume to the following item is the outcome of a project in the late 1980s to identify and classify Lisbon's outstanding architectural heritage. Each surveyed building is accorded between one and four stars according to merit. In this volume, which is finely illustrated with colour reproductions of fine watercolours as well as with many black-and-white photographs, all of the buildings which have been accorded a rating of two or more stars are described. They are arranged in six geographical groupings but are otherwise quite difficult to locate as the work lacks an index of buildings.

513 **Arquitectura modernista em Lisboa 1925-1940: levantamento e classificação de arquitectura modernista na cidade de Lisboa, 1925-1940.** (Modernist architecture in Lisbon, 1925-40: survey and classification of Modernist architecture in the city of Lisbon, 1925-40.)
José Manuel Fernandes, Maria de Lurdes Janeiro. Lisbon: Câmara Municipal de Lisboa, 1991. 114p. 40 maps. bibliog.

A companion volume to the preceding entry but lacking any of the fine coloured drawings which enhanced that volume. Nevertheless, numerous black-and-white photographs, accompanied only by brief textual description, create an impressive panorama of Lisbon's Modernist architecture. As in the companion volume, the buildings are given star ratings, up to a maximum of four, and are arranged in six geographical areas. Only buildings with two or more stars are depicted or described. Detailed maps show precise locations of each site, but the lack of an index is a considerable drawback to rapid reference to specific buildings.

514 **Álvaro Siza.**
Brigitte Fleck.   London: E & F. N. Spon, 1995. 143p. bibliog.
(Architecture Collection).
Heavily illustrated with colour and black-and-white photographs and architectural
plan drawings, this is a survey of the work of the Portuguese architect Álvaro Siza.
Siza has carried out many projects in Lisbon and as well as a general review of this
work, a section of this book is dedicated to his plans for the rebuilding of the Chiado
district of the city, following the major fire in 1988 which destroyed buildings in four
blocks of this historic area.

515 **Centro Cultural de Belém: o sítio, a obra.** (Belém Cultural Centre:
the place, the works.)
António Luíz Gomes.   Lisbon: Centro Cultural de Belém/Sociedade
de Gestão e Investimento Imobilário, 1993. 225p.
With a short summary in English and French, this large volume tells the story both of
the Centro Cultural de Belém and of the surrounding district. The imposing Centre
was opened to coincide with Portugal's Presidency of the European Community in
1992. Dozens of colour photographs show both the interior and exterior of this
architecturally controversial building, located in a sensitive historical suburb of the
city. Several other neighbouring institutions in Belém are also described, including the
Jockey Club, the Ermida (hermitage) and the Convento de Bom Sucesso.

516 **Calouste Gulbenkian's garden: Cultural Centre, Lisbon.**
Patrick Hodgkinson.   *Architectural Review*, no. 178, pt. 9 (1985),
p. 22-31.
In this appraisal of the work of architects Leslie Martin and Ivor Richards, the author
evaluates for a professional readership the Gulbenkian Centre for Modern Art in the
light of the completion of its final component, the Children's Pavilion. Both the
pavilion and the art centre occupy, with other museum buildings and an open-air
theatre, a magnificently landscaped park at Palhavã in north-central Lisbon. The
article is accompanied by colour and black-and-white photographs.

517 **História do Prémio Valmor.** (History of the Valmor Prize.)
José Manuel Pedreirinho.   Lisbon: Publicações Dom Quixote, 1988.
237p. map.
The Prémio Valmor is a prize awarded jointly to the architect and the owner of what is
judged to be the finest new or restored building in Lisbon in any particular year. Its
total of forty-six awards between the first, in 1903, and 1984, are covered here. A map
reproduced on the front and back end-papers curiously only marks the location of
forty-two of these sites. The book includes more than 200 illustrations, comprising
photographs and plans of prizewinning buildings. A list of prizewinners completes the
work.

518 **Portugal, architecture, 1965-1990.**
Nuno Portas, Manuel Mendes. Paris: Éditions du Moniteur, 1992.
178p. bibliog. (Tendances de l'Architecture Contemporaine).
A French-language publication which includes more than sixty case-studies of modern Portuguese buildings by Portuguese architects. These are all illustrated with photographs, some in colour, as well as architectural drawings. Amongst the works in Lisbon which are depicted and described are projects at Chelas, Restelo, Olivais Norte, the Gulbenkian Foundation and Lloyd's Bank.

519 **Recent works of Tomás Taveira.**
Architecture and Urbanism: A+U, vol. 87:01, no. 196 (January 1987), p. 29-138.
This 'special feature' of the Tokyo publication *A+U* is dedicated to the work of the Portuguese architect, Tomás Taveira, whose works grace Portugal, Macao, Angola, Cape Verde and the United Arab Emirates. Following an introductory essay by Michel Toussaint Alves Pereira (p. 31-36), there are fourteen case-studies of Taveira's work. These are predominantly projects realized in Lisbon, such as the Amoreiras shopping centre tower, the Chelas housing complex and Lisbon East bus station. Each study includes colour photographs, and reproductions of Taveira's architectural plans and drawings.

Pena: palácio nacional. (Pena: national palace.)
See item no. 89.

O Palácio Nacional de Sintra: residência querida de D. João I e D. Filipa de Lencastre. The Royal Palace of Sintra, favourite residence of John I and Philippa of Lancaster.
See item no. 91.

Sintra: Palácio Nacional. (Sintra: National Palace.)
See item no. 99.

Churches of Portugal.
See item no. 394.

Church of St. Rock guide book.
See item no. 396.

Os conventos de Lisboa. (The convents of Lisbon.)
See item no. 397.

Jerónimos. (The Jerónimos Church and Monastery.)
See item no. 409.

Planning

520 **Lisbon: a vulnerable city. Álvaro Siza's Chiado.**
Gonçalo Byrne. *Lotus International,* vol. 64 (1989), p. 32-53.
On 25 August 1988 eighteen buildings in Lisbon's central Chiado area were destroyed by a fire which started in a department store in the former Palácio Barcelinhos. Byrne explains how his fellow architect Álvaro Siza Vieira planned to 'reclaim' rather than 'change' the essential character of the affected area yet also sought to open up some new public spaces. He suggests that the fire in some respects was useful for it focused planning attention on a declining area and also revealed many unlicensed building alterations within the damaged area. The text is accompanied by numerous architectural drawings, photographs and quotations from Siza.

521 **Rebuilding the city: Pombal's Lisbon.**
Gonçalo Byrne. *Lotus International,* vol. 51 (1986), p. 6-24.
This account of the rebuilding of Lisbon after the 1755 earthquake, by the modern architect Gonçalo Byrne, is presented in parallel English and Italian texts. It explains the evolution of the rebuilding plans which were initially hindered by the order to retain all of the many former ecclesiastical sites and lay out the new streets around them. Eight pages of excellent colour reproductions of the contemporary plans show how the planners of the Casa do Risco das Obras Públicas (Public Works Design Office), under Manuel da Maia, gradually arrived at the present-day grid-iron layout of the city centre. The text is also illuminated by reproductions of contemporary engravings of Lisbon.

522 **Crescimento e diferenciação das áreas suburbanas de Lisboa e do Porto. With an English summary.** (Growth and differentiation of the suburban areas of Lisbon and Oporto.)
Maria Lucinda Fonseca, Deolinda Reis. Lisbon: Centro de Estudos Geográficos, Universidade de Lisboa, 1980. 93p. bibliog. (Estudos para o Planeamento Regional e Urbano, no. 13).
Attempts to define the suburban areas of both Lisbon and Oporto and to account for the factors determining their growth. Socioeconomic differentiation of the inhabitants is noted as progressively decreasing in the districts to the west of Lisbon. Copious charts and diagrams support the text, indicating such factors as population age, television ownership and electricity consumption in different parts of Lisbon.

523 **Lisbon of 1750-1850: the significance of its structural evolution.**
José-Augusto França. In: *Portugal and Brazil in transition.* Edited by Raymond S. Sayers. Minneapolis, Minnesota: University of Minnesota Press, 1968, p. 265-73. bibliog.
França's article in this collection of essays is followed by a short critical commentary by Carlos de Azevedo. França concentrates on the 1755 earthquake and the subsequent plans for the rebuilding of Lisbon, which included serious consideration of relocating to Belém. He also describes the erection of the nearby royal palace at Queluz, which commenced in 1748.

524 **Pombaline Lisbon and art in the days of the Marquis of Pombal.**
José-Augusto França, translated by Angus Malcolm. *Apollo: the Magazine of the Arts*, vol. 97 (April 1973), p. 340-49.

An illustrated review of the rebuilding of Lisbon after the 1755 earthquake which was carried out under the aegis of the Marquis of Pombal, chief minister to the ineffective King José (1750-77). The text also covers the construction of the nearby royal palace at Queluz, commenced in 1748, and briefly touches on Oporto. A number of large black-and-white illustrations of Lisbon buildings enhance the text.

525 **Centros de comércio e serviços na cidade de Lisboa.** (Commercial centres and services in the city of Lisbon.)
Jorge Gaspar, Fernando Correia, Maria Júlia Ferreira, João Ferrão, Graça Branco. *Finisterra: Revista Portuguesa de Geografia*, vol. X, no. 20 (1975), p. 230-72. maps.

An academic study, which includes both an English and French summary, of the patterns of distribution of individual trades and services in nine Lisbon districts. Survey data on these commercial activities and on local inhabitants' purchasing behaviour are assessed in the context of various urban planning theories and of studies of other European and American cities. The text is accompanied by sixty-eight figures and three tables.

526 **A dinâmica funcional do centro de Lisboa.** (The functional dynamics of the centre of Lisbon.)
Jorge Gaspar. *Finisterra: Revista Portuguesa de Geografia*, vol. XI, no. 21 (1976), p. 37-150. maps. bibliog.

A study of the human geography of Lisbon, with an English and French summary, which accounts for the growth of Lisbon city centre and the locations of various trades and commercial activities in particular streets and areas. Many maps and charts show the changing pattern of commercial activity in particular locations from the early 20th century onwards. From this time the main east-west commercial axis of the Baixa, Chiado and Cais do Sodré gave way to a north-south one from the Baixa, via Rossio to the Avenida da Liberdade. A second edition, without the English summary, has appeared in book-form (Lisbon: Livros Horizonte, 1985).

527 **A distribuição das actividades terciárias na cidade de Lisboa, segundo as estatísticas fiscais.** (The distribution of tertiary activities in the city of Lisbon, based on fiscal statistics.)
João Gaspar, Fernando Correia. *Finisterra: Revista Portuguesa de Geografia*, vol. X, no. 20 (1975), p. 193-229.

A study, with English and French summaries, of the distribution patterns of various retail activities in the city of Lisbon, and of the relationship between these activities and the population of the areas in which they are sited. The authors recommend a unification of the differing spatial divisions of Lisbon which exist for purposes such as taxation, administration and postal services. A detailed assessment is made of four types of retail activity, denominated as daily, occasional, special and food services. The work is completed by a statistical annex.

528 **Urban development in southern Europe: Spain and Portugal.**
E. A. Gutkind. New York: The Free Press; London: Collier
Macmillan Limited, 1967. 534p. maps. bibliog. (International History
of City Development, vol. III).

A large-format textbook in which Lisbon is covered in some detail (p. 62-77). The text
provides the history of the site of Lisbon from pre-Roman times, accompanied by
three maps of the Lisbon area and a number of black-and-white photographs of the
city and its environs. Geological and demographic details of Lisbon are also supplied
and there is a substantial account of the Pombaline plans for the rebuilding of the city
after the 1755 earthquake. The modern demographic and social development of
Lisbon is covered in *Urban dominance and labour market differentiation of a
European capital city: Lisbon 1890-1990*, edited by Pedro Telhado Pereira and Maria
Eugénia Mata (Boston, Massachusetts; London; Dordrecht, the Netherlands: Kluwer,
1996. 186p.). Its seven chapters derive from an EC-funded universities' project,
EUROCIT.

529 **The reconstruction of Lisbon following the earthquake of 1755:
a study in despotic planning.**
John K. Mullin. *Planning Perspectives*, vol. 7 (1992), p. 157-79.
bibliog.

Mullin argues how, following the 1755 earthquake in Lisbon, the Marquês de Pombal
seized the opportunity to demonstrate through his rebuilding programme that it was
the merchant, bureaucrat and common man who were the new forces in the land, as
opposed to the formerly dominant Crown, nobility and Church. His role and that of
General Maia, the Royal Engineer in Chief, are examined here. Mullin also outlines
the four options of rebuilding the city as it was, rebuilding with minor improvements,
rebuilding with major improvements or adopting a fresh location and starting to
rebuild a city from scratch. Plan drawings of the various schemes are provided.

530 **Bairros clandestinos na periferia de Lisboa.** (Clandestine districts on
the periphery of Lisbon.)
Teresa Batista Salgueiro. *Finisterra: Revista Portuguesa de
Geografia*, vol. XII, no. 23 (1977), p. 28-55. 4 maps. bibliog.

This study of the factors behind the location and growth of illicit housing on the
periphery of Lisbon includes an English-language summary. Salgueiro shows how
clandestine building in Lisbon was tolerated by the local authorities in the late 1970s
as it acted as a kind of safety valve, taking pressure off the legally built housing
market.

Une ville des Lumières: la Lisbonne de Pombal. (A city of the
Enlightenment: the Lisbon of Pombal.)
See item no. 342.

Science and Technology

531 The Academy of Sciences of Lisbon, founded in 1779.
Academia das Ciências de Lisboa. Lisbon: Academia das Ciências de
Lisboa, 1994. 31p.
Founded as the Academia das Ciências de Lisboa in 1779, but later known as the Real
Academia das Ciências de Lisboa, this body's 200-year history is concisely conveyed
here, with the help of illustrations.

**532 História e desenvolvimento da ciência em Portugal, I Colóquio. Até
ao século XX. Lisboa 15 a 19 de Abril de 1985.** (History and
development of science in Portugal, first colloquium. The period up to
the twentieth century, Lisbon, 15-19 April, 1985.)
Academia das Ciências de Lisboa. Lisbon: Academia das Ciências de
Lisboa, 1986. 2 vols. (Publicações do II Centenário da Academia das
Ciências de Lisboa).
Over 1,400 pages of text comprise these proceedings of the wide-ranging conference
on Portuguese scientific history held in Lisbon in 1985. Each of the forty-eight papers
is preceded by an English-language summary and the vast majority refer to
developments in Lisbon in the particular branch of science in question. Thus in
Barahona Fernandes's paper 'O nascimento da psiquiatria em Portugal' (The birth of
psychiatry in Portugal), vol. I, p. 577-93, he describes the work of the Rilhafoles and
Todos-os-Santos hospitals in Lisbon; in J. Tiago de Oliveira's 'As matemáticas em
Portugal: da Restauração ao Liberalismo' (Mathematics in Portugal: from the
Restoration to the Liberal period), vol. I, p. 81-110, the activities of the Jesuits' Santo
Antão college in Lisbon are recounted; whilst in Alberto Iria's 'A fundação da
Academia das Ciências de Lisboa' (The founding of the Lisbon Academy of
Sciences), vol. II, p. 1,283-99, an account of the late 18th-century origins of the
prestigious Lisbon Academy is to be found.

533   **Scientific expeditions to the Portuguese overseas territories, 1783-1808 and the role of Lisbon in the intellectual-scientific community of the late eighteenth century.**
William Joel Simon.   Lisbon: Instituto de Investigação Científica Tropical, 1983. 193p. 4 maps. bibliog. (Estudos de Cartografia Antiga, no. 22).

Based on the American author's doctoral thesis, this is a study of the pioneer Portuguese naturalists who explored the territories of Angola, Mozambique, Cape Verde and Brazil, and of the scientific environment in Lisbon from which they set out and to which they and their specimens, for the most part, returned. It covers the foundation of the Royal Academy of Sciences of Lisbon, the Ajuda Botanical Garden and the proposed Natural History Museum in Lisbon.

Literature

English works and non-Portuguese translations

534 I like it here. Sixth impression.
Kingsley Amis.   London: Gollancz, 1966. 208p.
This early novel by Kingsley Amis, originally published in 1958, is perhaps the best known 20th-century English literary work to be set in Lisbon. In it, hack-writer Garnet Bowen is commissioned to go to Lisbon to investigate the whereabouts and activities of the elusive novelist Wulfstan Strether and he sets out with his wife and children by ship from Southampton. Whilst carrying out this mission, the flavour of Salazar's Portugal is conveyed through encounters with locals and expatriate Britons.

535 The lady from Lisbon.
Vanessa Blake.   London: Robert Hale, 1971. 189p.
A romantic novel in which Rosanna Pentaillon, who had been living in Lisbon with her father Charles, moves back to the family home in Cornwall on his death. After his burial in the British Cemetery in Lisbon, and an escape from the clutches of a scheming upper-class Portuguese called Dom Luíz, the remainder of the narrative concerns events in England and an eventual reconciliation of Rosanna with her neighbour Hugo.

536 Facts and fictions.
Ann Bridge [pseudonym for Mary Dolling, Lady O'Malley].   London: Chatto & Windus, 1968. 215p.
Lady O'Malley uses her pen-name to recount, in a mixture of fact and fiction, her experiences as a diplomat's wife in Lisbon in 1945 (chapter 14, p. 188-204). She concentrates on her dealings with the upper echelons of Portuguese and British expatriate society, as well as her encounters with the assorted exiled European

monarchy to be found in Estoril. She recounts at length the condescension of both Portuguese and British 'society' in Lisbon towards the lowly-born wife of the Portuguese President, Carmona. Her meeting with the Duke and Duchess of Palmela at their Lisbon residence resurfaces in fictional form in the author's novel *The Portuguese escape* (see item no. 537).

537 **The Portuguese escape.**
Ann Bridge [pseudonym for Mary Dolling, Lady O'Malley]. New York: Berkley Publishing Corporation, 1958. 272p. (A Berkley Medallion Book, X895) (A Julia Probyn Story).
One of a series of novels involving the fictional journalist Julia Probyn. Here she involves herself in the escape of a Hungarian refugee and attempts to foil the kidnappers of a young Hungarian heiress, Hetta Páloczy, in Lisbon in the late 1940s. The narrative ranges across a backdrop of Lisbon, including the Lapa and Chiado districts, as well as nearby Cascais, Cabo da Roca and Sintra. All of these locations were well known to the authoress, the wife of a British diplomat who was based for a time in the Portuguese capital. She further draws on her real life experience of diplomatic life in her portrayal of the fictional British First Secretary in Lisbon who becomes engaged to Hetta at the book's conclusion.

538 **Childe Harold's pilgrimage: a romaunt.**
Lord Byron. In: *Byron's poetical works.* Edited by Frederick Page, new edition corrected by John Jump. London: Oxford University Press, 1970, p. 179-252.
Cantos XIV to XXX of Byron's celebrated *Childe Harold's pilgrimage* are set in Portugal, and specifically Lisbon, Sintra and Mafra. Though impressed by the natural surroundings of Sintra in particular, the narrator depicts 'dingy denizens [. . .] rear'd in dirt' and muses dismissively 'Why, Nature, waste thy wonders on such men?' Many British travellers, inspired by this poem, subsequently sought out Sintra during the 19th century.

539 **Lovers in Lisbon.**
Barbara Cartland. London; Sydney: Pan Books, 1987. 144p. (Pan Original).
A typical Barbara Cartland romance, which involves Felicita and the Marques Alvaro de Oliveira Vasconles. The Lisbon setting, at the end of the 19th century, is lacking in detail and the idiosyncratic choice of spuriously Portuguese names and titles both confirms the authoress's lack of deep acquaintance with the city and the famed speed with which she produces her work. Nevertheless, the novel is an example of how Lisbon is used as a touchstone of romantic exoticism. Another example of the genre of historical love story is *Lisbon: a novel* by Valerie Sherwood (New York: New American Library, 1989. 535p.).

540 **The cockney of Lisbon.**
Douglas Castle, illustrated by Imre Hofbauer. London: Blackie & Son, [1953]. 253p.
In this novel, Lieutenant Peter Watson of the Naval Intelligence Service arrives by passenger boat in Lisbon. He becomes embroiled there in the shady activities of a

fellow-traveller, the cockney scrap-metal dealer, Robbins. After a series of nautical adventures, Watson and colleagues succeed in thwarting Robbins's criminal plans.

541 **A tale of Lisbon.**
Marcus Cheke. Oxford: Shakespeare Head Press, 1937. 37p.

A curious historical poem in two cantos, comprising seventy-five nine-line stanzas, which tells of the arrival in Lisbon of a sailor, José, from Viana do Castelo in northern Portugal. Canto II concerns the temporal Bishop of Lisbon, Dom Vasco Bourbon Hapsburg de Braganza, who takes a fancy to a young girl, Perlita, only being resigned to leaving her to José when his ambition to become a cardinal is realized.

542 **Lord Byron's 'Childe Harold's Pilgrimage to Portugal' critically examined.**
D. G. Dalgado. Lisbon: Imprensa Nacional, 1919. 97p.

The author, otherwise a medical climatologist, attempts to explain why Byron was so antipathetic to the Portuguese in his *Childe Harold*. That work is partly set in Sintra and Lisbon, which Byron had visited in 1809. Dalgado concludes that the same egotism which led to Byron's literary brilliance accounted for his refusal to judge the Portuguese objectively.

543 **Rendezvous in Lisbon.**
Iris Danbury. London: Mills & Boon, 1967. 189p.

A romantic novel about Janice Bowen, the new secretary of the feared Mr Everard Whitney. Unexpectedly, Janice is asked to travel with her boss to Lisbon where he is to transact business over a period of several weeks. The novel ends predictably with the two having fallen in love. In the interim, the narrative ranges over much of central Lisbon, with visits to a concert at the Estufa Fria tropical garden and to the Avenida Palace hotel, Carmo, the Chiado and Black Horse Square (Praça do Comércio) amongst the highlights. Trips are also made to suburban locations such as Queluz and Sintra.

544 **Eighteenth-century vignettes. First series. Second series.**
Austin Dobson. London; New York; Toronto: Oxford University Press, 1951. 308p. + 306p. (The World's Classics).

In the first series of these vignettes, is an essay written in 1897 on 'Fielding's voyage to Lisbon'. Dobson recounts how the ailing Fielding left his home in north London in 1754 and, after a nightmare journey, arrived in Lisbon seven weeks later. Although somewhat fawning in his attitude towards Fielding, Dobson does nevertheless point out that the published version of the author's *Journal* is a sanitized version of a somewhat more acerbic original.

545 **Five passengers from Lisbon.**
M. G. Eberhart. Bath, England: Chivers Press, 1993. 260p. (Scarlet Dagger Crime).

A Second World War 'whodunnit' story involving five passengers from Lisbon who were rescued from a small cargo ship which sank three days out of the Portuguese capital, near the Azores. One of the crew is found murdered when the life raft is located by a hospital ship. The novel is an example of how Lisbon is used as a literary device, being one of the few places where passengers of such diverse origins, both Nazi and Allied, could come together in a credible narrative of intrigue. The novel was first published in 1946.

546 **The journal of a voyage to Lisbon.**
Henry Fielding, edited with an introduction and notes by Tom Keymer. Harmondsworth, England: Penguin Books, 1996. 142p. (Penguin Classics).

The dramatist and novelist, Henry Fielding, sailed to Portugal for his health's sake in the summer of 1754. The journal of his voyage there was completed in Lisbon, shortly before his death on 8 October of that year. He was buried in the English cemetery in Lisbon where his grave has become a much-visited tourist landmark, even though Fielding himself described the city as dirty and expensive. This new edition has useful explanatory notes and an introduction which draws parallels between Fielding's work and the novel of Kingsley Amis, *I like it here* (see item no. 534), which is set in Lisbon and incorporates a scene at Fielding's tomb.

547 **The man from Lisbon.**
Thomas Gifford.   London: Futura Publications, 1978. 418p.

Gifford, a newspaper editor from the USA, has produced here a riveting, fictionalized account of the story of Alves dos Reis who, in 1924-25, defrauded the Banco de Portugal of over a million pounds. Much of the story is set in Lisbon and Gifford draws on sources, such as Lisbon newspapers, for the factual basis of the narrative.

548 **One day to Sintra & back.**
Walter Hamady.   Mt. Horeb, Wisconsin: Perishable Press, 1970. unpaginated.

Four poetic works occasioned by a visit to Lisbon and Sintra make up this book. They are entitled respectively 'Lisbon, 22 August 1969', 'Perpétua', 'For Professor Dos Santos' and 'At the Palace'. The verse in this slim volume, produced on 'variegated shadwell paper', is accompanied by a drawing by Bartolomeu dos Santos who accompanied Hamady to Sintra.

549 **Mist in the Tagus.**
Tom Hopkinson.   London: The Hogarth Press, 1946. 184p.

A romantic novel about a two-week holiday spent near the Tagus at Marinha and Vallado, near Lisbon. Before returning home from Lisbon, the heroine, Caroline Page, a one-time shop assistant, is engaged in a romantic tryst with Robert Krantz, a German doctor, for whose affections she competes with his male friend, Leo.

550 **The Judas code.**
Derek Lambert.   London: Hamish Hamilton, 1983. 340p.

Although the central purpose of this novel is to seek an explanation for Stalin's failure to take seriously the reality of Hitler's invasion of Russia, despite advance warnings from Churchill, much of its action takes place in wartime Lisbon whose neutrality facilitated the juxtaposition of Allied and Axis agents. Against the backdrop of Estoril, the Alfama and other recognizable Lisbon landmarks, a cast of exiles, refugees, spies and covert Gestapo officers create a labyrinth of intrigue.

551   **Almada Hill: an epistle from Lisbon.**
William Julius Mickle.   In: *The works of the English poets from Chaucer to Cowper including the series edited, with prefaces biographical and critical, by Dr Samuel Johnson and the most approved translations. The additional lives by Alexander Chalmers. vol. XVII.* London: J. Johnson, 1810, p. 534-40.
Mickle is best known as an early translator of Camões into English but he also enjoyed a reputation as a poet in his own right. His lengthy poem, *Almada Hill,* was mostly written in Portugal after his visit, in December 1799, to the ruins of Almada castle on the south bank of the Tagus, overlooking Lisbon. It takes up the Portuguese historical vein of *The Lusiads* using Almada Castle as its impetus, since that was the site given to those English crusaders who remained in the Lisbon area after their successful involvement in the freeing of the city from the Moors in 1147. His sonnet, *On passing the bridge of Alcantara, near Lisbon,* is also included in this volume (p. 540) as is a biography of Mickle. An account of Mickle's stay in Lisbon is to be found in S. George West's *The visit to Portugal in 1779-1780 of William Julius Mickle, translator of 'Os Lusíadas'* (Lisbon: Junta de Investigações do Ultramar, 1972. 13p.).

552   **Byron Portugal 1977.**
F. de Mello Moser, J. Paço d'Arcos, J. Almeida Flor, E. Santos Mattos, C. Estorninho.   Lisbon: Byron Society, 1977. 159p. bibliog.
Described as a 'symposium volume' of the Portuguese Committee of the Byron Society, this book consists of four essays each reproduced in English and Portuguese, followed by a bibliography of Portuguese Byroniana. The essays are entitled 'Three approaches to Byron', 'Rosa Corder; or, An autograph of Lord Byron's', 'A Portuguese review of *Childe Harold's Pilgrimage*' and 'A poet finds the new Eden'. The third paper largely comprises a commentary written in 1812 which complains about Byron's scorn for the Portuguese, whilst admitting to the filth of Lisbon's streets. The final essay concerns the poet's visit to Sintra and is illustrated by photographs of the Lawrence Hotel, where he stayed.

553   **The stone cutter of Lisbon.**
William Henry Peck.   New York: Robert Bonner's Sons, 1870. 436p.
Written by a Professor of History at the University of the State of Louisiana, this novel is set in 1755, the year of the Lisbon earthquake. It relates the 'romantic adventures' of the unconvincingly named Stonio the stone cutter and other equally misnamed pseudo-Portuguese characters, against a background of the ruins of Lisbon. The book is also available in libraries as part of the *Wright American Fiction* microfilm series, volume III, reel P-11, item number 4154.

554   **The conspirators: a novel.**
Frederic Prokosch.   London: Chatto & Windus, [1943]. 169p.
This is a suspenseful novel by an American author set in wartime Lisbon. The plot involves a Dutchman, Vincent van der Lyn, who is commissioned to assassinate the Axis sympathizer, Hugo van Mohr in Estoril. The planning of the murder and the amatory involvement of the Russian, Irina Pedrova, with both assassin and victim take place in the Alfama and other districts of Lisbon before the action moves, via the

coastal railway, to Estoril, Cascais and Guincho. An explosion in Lisbon is the pivotal episode of another more recent thriller, *Back toward Lisbon: a novel of suspense* by Allison Cole (New York: Dodd, Mead, [1985]. 212p.).

555 Lady Good for Nothing.

Sir Arthur Quiller-Couch. London; Toronto: J. M. Dent & Sons Ltd; New York: E. P. Dutton & Co., 1928. 291p. (The Tales & Romances of Sir Arthur Quiller-Couch. The Duchy Edition).

First published in 1910, this is an historical novel based on the lives of Sir Harry Frankland and Agnes Surridge. Set in the mid-18th century it tells of Sir Oliver Vyell and his wife Ruth. The couple are caught in the Lisbon earthquake of 1755, in which Sir Oliver is injured. 'Lisbon and after' (p. 247-83) is the title of the last of the five 'books' which comprise this novel. Quiller-Couch reproduces eyewitness accounts of the earthquake taken from such sources as *The Gentleman's Magazine* to support his own portrayal of Lisbon and Belém. His narrative incorporates historical characters such as Abraham Castres, the British envoy and Mr Hay, the British consul at Lisbon.

556 The night in Lisbon.

Erich Maria Remarque, translated by Ralph Manheim. London: Hutchinson, 1964. 287p.

A novel by the author of *All quiet on the Western Front* set in Lisbon in 1942. It tells how the narrator, a refugee from Fascism, meets Schwarz, another refugee, who offers him his tickets for a voyage to safety in the United States in return for the narrator's spending the night listening to his account, in a Lisbon bar, of his travels through Europe to Portugal. The novel conveys the atmosphere of Lisbon as a haven for emigrés *en route* to the United States during the Second World War.

557 Declares Pereira: a true account.

Antonio Tabucchi, translated from the Italian by Patrick Creagh. London: The Harvill Press, 1995. 136p.

Tabucchi is an Italian who has lived in Portugal for many years. This novel, translated from the original Italian, *Sostiene Pereira,* is set in Lisbon in 1938 and tells the story of Pereira, who is responsible for the newly-created cultural section of a fictional evening newspaper called *Lisboa.* His struggle with his own sense of inadequacy is heightened by his young colleague's challenge to him to oppose the limitations imposed by Salazar's political régime. This narrative is related against a detailed Lisbon topography.

558 Candide & Zadig.

François Marie Arouet de Voltaire, translated by Tobias George Smollett, edited with an introduction by Lester G. Crocker. New York: Washington Square Press, 1962. 217p.

This edition of *Candide; or, The optimist,* first published in 1759, tells of the eponymous youth who is expelled from a baronial court in Westphalia for kissing Cunegund, the Baron's daughter. His subsequent travels take him via Bulgaria to Portugal where his former master, Dr Pangloss, is hanged in an *auto-da-fé.* The events related whilst in Lisbon include a tempest, shipwreck and earthquake, the last being modelled on the 1755 earth movement which destroyed so much of the city. The work, as a whole, is seen as a critique of the prevailing philosophy of optimism.

559   **Together in Lisbon.**
       Fran Wilson.   London: Silhouette Books, 1984. 189p. map.
       (Silhouette Romance, no. 277).

A romantic tale in which Pratt Fenton, the owner of Fenton Canneries, is obliged to
take his wife Bria on a business trip to Lisbon. There, after a trip on the Tagus and to
Sintra, the couple's troubled relationship is restored to harmony.

English translations from Portuguese

560   **José Rodrigues Miguéis: Lisbon in Manhattan.**
       Edited, with an introduction by Onésimo T. Almeida.   Providence,
       Rhode Island: Gávea-Brown, 1994. 216p.

A collection of essays on the Portuguese-born writer, Rodrigues Miguéis who
continued to publish in his native language despite living in the USA from 1936 until
his death in 1978. His vivid portrayals of Lisbon, as in *Happy Easter* (q.v.), recall how
many of the evocations of the city by Eça de Queiroz were likewise written while
resident abroad. A number of the essays collected here relate to his writings on
Lisbon, especially 'Miguéis, witness and wanderer' by Gerald M. Moser, where it is
claimed that in order to write *Páscoa feliz* (Happy Easter), *Saudades para a Dona
Genciana* (Yearning for Dona Genciana) and *Regresso à cúpola da Pena* (Return to
the cupola of the Pena Palace), the author had 'to know Lisbon as intimately as Balzac
had known the Paris of his time'.

561   **The Lusiads.**
       Luís Vaz de Camões, translated by William C. Atkinson.
       Harmondsworth, England: Penguin Books, 1973. 249p. (Penguin
       Classics).

A re-issue of the 1957 translation of *Os Lusíadas*, the most celebrated work in
Portuguese literature. In this national epic poem, modelled on *The Aeneid*, the
departure of Vasco da Gama from Belém in 1497 is described, as is his triumphant
return. The poem reviews various earlier heroic episodes of Portuguese history
including Afonso Henriques's seizure of Lisbon from the Moors in 1147, João I's
Lisbon rising against Dona Leonor in 1383 and the triumph of Nun'Álvares against
the Spaniards at the battle of Aljubarrota (1385). The supposed founding of Lisbon by
Ulysses is also recounted.

562   **A Lisboa de Fernando Pessoa.** (The Lisbon of Fernando Pessoa.)
       Marina Tavares Dias.   Lisbon: Ibis Editora, 1991. 101p. map. bibliog.
       (Guias de Lisboa, Extra-Colecção).

Fernando Pessoa (1888-1935) was Lisbon and Portugal's major 20th-century poet and
this volume consists mostly of monochrome photographs of sites in Lisbon which
figured either in the poet's life or his work.   A map identifies these sites with a
coloured dot but, curiously, it does not link these to specific photographs in any way.
Pessoa spent his adult life in Lisbon, where he was employed as a commercial translator.

563 **Cousin Bazilio.**
José Maria Eça de Queiroz, translated by Roy Campbell. Manchester, England: Carcanet, in association with The Calouste Gulbenkian Foundation, 1992. 295p. (Aspects of Portugal).

A translation of *O Primo Basílio* (1878), which has often been compared with Flaubert's *Madame Bovary*. In it, Eça (1845-1900) recounts the affair of the married Luísa with her suave cousin Basílio, which leads to their blackmail by her servant, Juliana. The moral turpitude and pomposity of upper middle-class Lisbon society are captured by Eça with characteristic irony.

564 **The Maias.**
José Maria Eça de Queiroz, translated by Patricia McGowan Pinheiro, Ann Stevens. Manchester, England: Carcanet, in association with The Calouste Gulbenkian Foundation, 1993. 633p. (Aspects of Portugal).

A translation of *Os Maias* (1888), Eça's lengthy chronicle of the Lisbon family, the Maias. Carlos da Maia, heir to Afonso da Maia, has pretensions to be a doctor, artist and politician yet achieves nothing more than a life of dilettantism in a Lisbon society riven by pomposity, self-absorption and hypocrisy. As usual with Eça, humour and bathos are never far from the forefront of the narrative.

565 **The mandarin and other stories.**
José Maria Eça de Queiroz, translated by Richard Franko Goldman. London: The Bodley Head, 1966. 185p.

A translation of four stories by Eça, the longest of which is the comic masterpiece, *The Mandarin* (*O mandarim, 1880*), a novella in which the protagonist is Teodoro, a Lisbon clerk in the civil service. Reading second-hand books, Teodoro is beguiled by a story in which he is offered the prospect of untold wealth if he will ring a bell, the side-effect being that a man will die in far-off Mongolia. Eça's depiction of this moral dilemma takes place against a humorously naturalistic backdrop of lower middle-class pretensions, particularly amongst his acquaintances in his boarding house in Lisbon's Travessa da Conceição. The other stories here are *Peculiarities of a fair-haired girl, A lyric poet* and *José Matias*.

566 **The relic.**
José Maria Eça de Queiroz, translated by Margaret Jull Costa. Sawtrey, England: Dedalus, 1994. 320p. (European Classics).

A translation of *A relíquia* (1887) in which an orphan, Teodorico, lives with his aunt, Titi, a religious fanatic in Lisbon's Campo de Sant'Ana area. After an affair he gains his freedom when his aunt sends him off to the Holy Land.

567 **To the capital.**
José Maria Eça de Queiroz, translated into English by John Vetch. Manchester, England: Carcanet, in association with The Calouste Gulbenkian Foundation, 1995. 368p.

A translation of the novel, *A capital*, which was left by Eça in an unfinished state and completed by the author's son, twenty-five years after the novelist's death in 1900. It tells of Artur Corvelo who inherits a legacy and decides to move to Lisbon. There he seeks to win acclaim in literary and intellectual circles but his efforts come to nought and he returns to the provinces. As ever, Eça captures the affectations of Lisbon society with humour and irony.

568 **The yellow sofa and Three portraits.**
José Maria Eça de Queiroz. 'The yellow sofa' translated by John Vetch, 'Three portraits': 'A lyric poet' translated by Richard Franko Goldman, 'José Mathias', 'A man of talent' translated by Luís Marques. Manchester, England: Carcanet, in association with The Calouste Gulbenkian Foundation, 1993. 181p. (Aspects of Portugal).

The yellow sofa, a translation of the novella *Alves e Cª* (Alves and Co.), was found among Eça's papers after his death in 1900. It tells of the inoffensive Lisbon clerk, Godofredo Alves, who is deceived by his business colleague, the elegant Machado. In the humorously drawn context of Lisbon petit-bourgeois life, Machado steals Alves's wife from him, before a belated reconciliation is effected between the three of them. *José Mathias* (1897) is a short story, also set in Lisbon. The narrator recalls the life and decline of the once wealthy Mathias as he proceeds to the city's Prazeres cemetery to his funeral.

569 **'Cintra's glorious Eden': time and space in 'Desencontro' by Maria Judite de Carvalho and 'Regresso à Cúpula da Pena' by José Rodrigues Miguéis.**
David Frier. In: *Portuguese, Brazilian and African studies: studies presented to Clive Willis on his retirement.* Edited by T. F. Earle, N. H. Griffin. Warminster, England: Aris & Phillips Ltd., 1995, p. 255-64.

An analysis of two short stories by Maria Judite de Carvalho and José Rodrigues Miguéis which both involve actual or proposed escape from the city of Lisbon to the rural tranquility of nearby Sintra. Frier draws a parallel between this process and the similar dichotomy in Byron's *Childe Harold's pilgrimage*, in which Sintra is likewise cast as a bucolic haven in contrast to the dirt and misery of Lisbon.

570 **Travels in my homeland.**
J. B. da Silva Leitão de Almeida Garrett, translated by John Parker. London: Peter Owen, 1987. 256p.

A translation of *Viagens na minha terra* (1843), a work which has been described as a mixture of Laurence Sterne and Walter Scott. It tells, in literary form, the story of Garrett's journey from Lisbon to Santarém, along the Tagus valley, in the context of the civil strife between King Pedro IV and his brother, the usurper, D. Miguel.

571 **Lisboa na ficção contemporânea, séculos XIX e XX.** (Lisbon in contemporary fiction, nineteenth and twentieth centuries.) Instituto da Biblioteca Nacional e do Livro. Lisbon: Instituto da Biblioteca Nacional e do Livro, 1995. 74p. bibliog.

A catalogue of 383 novels and short stories which have Lisbon as a setting. It is based on an exhibition held at the National Library in Lisbon in 1995. All of the items are Portuguese editions but a number, by authors such as José Saramago and Eça de Queiroz, have been translated into English. The catalogue is interspersed with reproductions of title pages, book jackets, illustrations and photographs of Lisbon from some of the listed volumes.

572 **Happy Easter.** José Rodrigues Miguéis, translated from the Portuguese by John Byrne. Manchester, England: Carcanet, in association with The Calouste Gulbenkian Foundation, Instituto da Biblioteca Nacional e do Livro, Instituto Camões, 1995. 115p. (From the Portuguese, no. 2).

First published in 1927, as *Feliz Páscoa,* this is a first-person narrative, set in Lisbon, of a paranoid schizophrenic who recounts his fantasies leading up to his incarceration.

573 **The book of disquiet.** Fernando Pessoa, edited by Maria José de Lancastre, translated by Margaret Jull Costa. London: Serpent's Tail, 1991. 262p. map.

A translation of a posthumous prose work, entitled *O livro do desassossego,* by Lisbon and Portugal's pre-eminent 20th-century poet. The work, written as a diary, is set in Lisbon and ostensibly written by Bernardo Soares, one of Pessoa's many literary persona. It recounts Soares's loneliness and life of routine in the city. Two other English translations of this title also appeared in 1991, published by Carcanet Press and Quartet Books.

574 **A centenary Pessoa.** Fernando Pessoa, edited by Eugénio Lisboa with L. C. Taylor. Translations: poetry by Keith Bosley, prose by Bernard McGuirk, Maria Manuel Lisboa, Richard Zenith. Manchester, England: Carcanet, in asssociation with The Calouste Gulbenkian Foundation, The Instituto Camões, The Instituto da Biblioteca Nacional e do Livro, 1995. 335p. bibliog. (Aspects of Portugal).

An essential volume for all English readers of Portugal's major 20th-century poet, Fernando Pessoa. Pessoa spent most of his life in Lisbon where he was employed as a commercial translator and frequented its bars. Lisbon is also the context of a number of his works, not least the 'Lisbon revisited' poems and the prose work *O livro do desassossego* (The book of disquiet), both of which are included here in whole or in part. As well as English translations of many of Pessoa's works, this edition also incorporates critical comments and an excellent bibliography, which includes English editions of Pessoa's work. Photographs depict the poet at various stages of his life and there are a number of colour reproductions of Pessoa as a subject of artists and painters.

575 **Selected poems.**
Fernando Pessoa, translated by Jonathan Griffin. Harmondsworth, England: Penguin Books, 1974. Reissued, 1996. 128p. (Penguin Modern European Poets).

A compilation of eighty poems by Pessoa (1888-1935) which constitute the most readily available selection of his work in English. Many of the works are inspired by Pessoa's mundane existence in Lisbon, where he was employed as a commercial translator and which he rarely left during the last thirty years of his life. A brief introduction surveys the poet's life and works.

576 **The Lisbon of Jorge Ferreira de Vasconcellos.**
Anson C. Piper. *Luso-Brazilian Review*, vol. 4, no. 1 (1967), p. 17-25.

A study of the portrayal of 16th-century Lisbon in Ferreira de Vasconcellos's three dramatic novels, *Comédia Eufrosina* (1555), *Comédia Ulisipo* (earliest known edition 1618) and *Comédia Aulegrafia* (earliest known edition 1619). From his experience as a courtier Vasconcellos was able to incorporate much detail of Lisbon palace life into his works. Contemporary attitudes to fashion, negroes and the relations of country and city are amongst the evidence to emerge from these 'plays', as are depictions of both Lisbon and its surroundings, including such places as Cacilhas and Almada.

577 **Lisboa. Vol. I, poesia.** (Lisbon. Vol. I, poetry.)
Edited by Tomaz Ribas, with assistance from António Valdemar. Lisbon: Livraria Bertrand, [1969]. (Antologia da Terra Portuguesa, no. 18).

An anthology of Portuguese poems relating to Lisbon, the earliest being from the 13th century. Of the ninety-eight poets represented, thirty-three are contemporary to the date of publication.

578 **Lisboa. Vol. II, prosa.** (Lisbon. Vol. II, prose.)
Edited by Tomaz Ribas, with assistance from António Valdemar. Lisbon: Livraria Bertrand, [1969]. 250p. (Antologia da Terra Portuguesa, no. 19).

An illustrated anthology of prose writings in Portuguese on Lisbon in which Fernão Lopes and João de Barros alone represent the pre-19th-century period. In all, sixty-four writers are represented, thirty-nine of whom are contemporary to the date of publication.

579 **The history of the siege of Lisbon: a novel.**
José Saramago, translated by Giovanni Pontiero. London: The Harvill Press, 1996. 312p.

An excellent translation of the 1989 novel, *História do cerco de Lisboa*, by Portugal's leading contemporary novelist. It tells the story of Raimundo Silva, a Lisbon proof-reader, who inserts an alteration into the text of 'The history of the siege of Lisbon', which has the effect of claiming that the Crusaders did not, in fact, assist in the recapture of Lisbon from the Moors in 1147. The narrative interweaves the 20th-century life of Raimundo in Lisbon, including his affair with his proofreading supervisor, with the alternative version of the 12th-century conquest of Lisbon which he writes at her suggestion.

580 **The year of the death of Ricardo Reis.**
José Saramago, translated from the Portuguese by Giovanni Pontiero.
London: Harvill, 1992. 358p.

A translation of *O ano da morte de Ricardo Reis*. The narrative concerns the Ricardo Reis, a heteronym of the 20th-century Portuguese poet Fernando Pessoa. Here, Reis outlives his real-life creator, Pessoa, by nine months and returns to 1930s' Lisbon where he sets up as a locum in the Rua de Santa Catarina. He wanders the streets of Lisbon, sometimes even accompanied by the deceased Pessoa, and has strained romantic involvements with both a chambermaid and a woman with a paralysed hand.

581 **Requiem: a hallucination.**
Antonio Tabucchi, translated by Margaret Jull Costa.   London:
Harvill, 1994. 110p.

A novel, originally published in Lisbon in 1991, by the Italian professor, Antonio Tabucchi which mixes fact with fantasy as the narrator waits for an encounter with the long-dead poet, Fernando Pessoa. The narrative is set in contemporary Lisbon and has been described as a 'picaresque ramble' through the city.

582 **On being a Westerner: a translation of 'O sentimento dum ocidental'.**
Cesário Verde, translated by Keith Bosley. *Portuguese Studies*, vol. 2 (1986), p. 120-24.

A rhymed translation of Cesário Verde's poetic masterpiece, published in 1880 to commemorate the tercentenary of the death of Luís de Camões. It is arguably the best known Portuguese poem written about Lisbon and conveys the experience of a lone narrator in the increasingly threatening streets of the city as night falls. Copious references and allusions to Lisbon topography and street scenes allow the work to be read as a prosaic, descriptive account of the city as well as a poetic work which prefigures many of the themes and techniques of the subsequent European existentialist and surrealist movements. Verde (1855-86) ran his family's ironmonger's shop in the capital's Rua dos Fanqueiros and has been posthumously recognized as Portugal's leading poet of the 19th century.

Sintra na literatura romântica inglesa. (Sintra in English Romantic literature.)
See item no. 90.

Poem upon the Lisbon disaster.
See item no. 156.

The works of Lord Byron.
See item no. 247.

England's wealthiest son: a study of William Beckford.
See item no. 375.

William Beckford.
See item no. 381.

Arts

Visual

583 **The 'torreão' of the Lisbon Palace and the Escorial Library: an artistic and iconographic interpretation.**
Barbara von Barghahn, Annemarie Jordan. *Arquivos do Centro Cultural Português*, vol. XXII (1986), p. 25-114.

After Philip II of Spain assumed the throne of Portugal in 1580 he modified the Royal Palace in Lisbon by adding a large tower on the waterfront side of the building. Its four floors included an arsenal, nobles' apartments, a library and galleries, an Ambassadors' Hall and Royal Throne Room. In this illustrated study, the authors argue that the design and artistic decoration of the library of the Escorial Palace, built by Philip in Spain, was based on that in the Lisbon Palace, which was destroyed in the 1755 earthquake.

584 **Encenar a cidade: intervenções artísticas nos tapumes das obras do Metropolitano de Lisboa.** (Decorating the city stage: artistic works on the construction hoardings of the Lisbon Metropolitan railway.)
Photographs by Homem Cardoso, text by Isabel Carlos, Margarida Mira. Lisbon: Metropolitano de Lisboa, 1994. 164p. map.

Illustrates, through colour photographs, the murals painted on the hoardings erected at the various sites in Lisbon where the underground Metropolitano railway was being extended in the early 1990s. However, the photographs of these locations, mainly in the northern part of the city, are perversely outnumbered by colour pictures of other parts of Lisbon, unaffected by the railway works, such as the Praça do Comércio.

585 **Gravuras de aguarelas de Belém.** (Watercolour prints of Belém.)
John Coates. Lisbon: British Historical Society of Portugal, 1990.
unpaginated.

A companion publication to the earlier *Watercolour prints of Lisbon* (see item no.
586). It comprises eleven large, colour reproductions of watercolours by John Coates,
a resident in Portugal since 1972. They show the following sites: the Jardim Botânico
da Ajuda (Ajuda botanic garden); Chafariz do Largo da Princesa (fountain in the
Largo da Princesa); Cemitério da Ajuda (Ajuda cemetery); Torre da Capela Real da
Ajuda (Ajuda Royal Chapel tower); Teatro Luís de Camões (Camões theatre); Igreja
da Memória (Memória church); Casa do Galvão (Galvão house); Palácio Calheta
(Calheta palace); Convento das Salésias (Salesians' convent); and two aspects of the
Palácio da Ajuda (Ajuda palace). The accompanying descriptive text is taken from
Monumentos e edifícios notáveis do Distrito de Lisboa (see item no. 486).

586 **Watercolour prints of Lisbon. Gravuras de aguarelas de Lisboa.**
John Coates. Lisbon: British Historical Society of Portugal, 1985.
unpaginated.

A collection of eight large (47cm x 32cm) colour reproductions of watercolours by
Canadian-born artist John Coates, produced to commemorate the visit to Lisbon of
Queen Elizabeth II in 1985. They show eight buildings in the city which have British
or Irish connections. These are the church of Corpo Santo, the British Ambassador's
residence, the English College, the Parsonage of St George's Church, the British
Hospital, Bemposta Palace, Henry Fielding's tomb in the English Cemetery and the
Bom Sucesso convent. An accompanying text in both English and Portuguese gives a
brief history of each building.

587 **Lisboa na moderna pintura portuguesa.** (Lisbon in modern
Portuguese painting.)
José Gomes Ferreira. Lisbon: Realizações Artis, 1971. 15p.

The brief textual introduction in this volume is outweighed by forty-two plates, some
in colour, of portraits of Lisbon by twenty-six artists born between 1881 and 1931.
Amongst those represented are Carlos Botelho, Bernardo Marques and Abel Manta.

588 **Lisboa velha, Ancient Lisbon, Lisbonne la vieille.**
Alfredo Roque Gameiro. Lisbon: Vega, 1992. 36p.

Rather than the brief textual element of this book, it is the additional 100 repro-
ductions of portraits of Lisbon's buildings and streets by the painter, Alfredo Roque
Gameiro (1864-1935), which are its major attraction. The introductory essay is in
Portuguese, English and French.

589 **As paredes em liberdade.** (The liberated walls.)
Photographs by José Marques. Lisbon: Editorial Teorema, 1974.
unpaginated.

A collection of uncaptioned monochrome photographs, taken in May and June 1974,
of the ubiquitous wall-slogans to be found in Lisbon's streets immediately after the
Revolution of 25 April. Whilst, predictably, these are mostly the work of the extreme
Left political parties, such as the Maoists (MRPP) and Communists (PCP), other
parties, such as the Monarchists (PPM), Socialists (PS) and Popular Democrats (PPD)

are also represented. None of the more artistic graffiti of the 1974 Portuguese Revolution is depicted here.

590   **The art of Portugal, 1500-1800.**
      Robert C. Smith.   London: Weidenfeld & Nicolson, 1968. 320p. map.
      bibliog.

A comprehensive study of three centuries of Portuguese art which according to the author is the first such work in English wholly dedicated to this subject. It is lavishly illustrated with 264 black-and-white plates and 16 in colour. These include many Lisbon landmarks, whilst the text is an authoritative source of information on every aspect of art in the Portuguese capital, from the Águas Livres aqueduct to the Gil Vicente monstrance in the Museu de Arte Antiga. The chapters cover architecture, gilt-wood church interiors, sculpture, painting, ceramics, silverware, furniture and textiles. Access to the text is facilitated by a detailed index.

Decorative

591   **Design Lisboa 94.** (Design Lisbon 94.)
      Lamartine de Campos Ladeira.   Lisbon: Electa Grupo Dimensão,
      1994. 211p.

A finely produced catalogue of examples of the work of contemporary Lisbon artistic designers. The volume abounds in colour photographs of a wide array of furnishings, furniture, ornaments and other modern artefacts.

592   **The art of azulejo in Portugal: Portuguese glazed tiles.**
      José Meco.   Lisbon: Bertrand, 1994. 2nd ed. 95p. bibliog. (Collection
      Portuguese Patrimony).

A concise but thorough introduction in English to the Portuguese ceramic tile tradition, presented in chronological sequence. Many colour illustrations of Lisbon and Sintra tilework are included which are noteworthy for incorporating everyday examples from bars and roadsides as well as from historic monuments and palaces. The work first appeared as *Azulejaria portuguesa*.

593   **Five centuries of jewellery, National Museum of Ancient Art,
      Lisbon.**
      Leonor d'Orey.   Lisbon, London: Instituto Português de
      Museus/Zwemmer, 1995. 128p. bibliog.

Illustrated throughout with high-quality colour plates, this book records the new permanent exhibition of jewellery installed in Lisbon's Museum of Ancient Art in 1994. Most of the exhibits come from convents closed by the Liberals in the early 19th century and from the Barreto family collection.

594   **Azulejos no Metropolitano de Lisboa.** (Tiles on the Lisbon
       Underground.)
       João Castel-Branco Pereira.   Lisbon: Metropolitano de Lisboa, 1990.
       114p.

A finely produced colour panorama, with a brief textual history, of the modern tile
designs to be found on the stations of Lisbon's underground railway system, the
Metropolitano. Opened in late 1959, the Metropolitano was initially devoid of artistic
adornment. However, the system is continuing to expand and this growth, combined
with the need to adapt many of the older stops, has provided the opportunity to make
the stations a subterranean gallery of modern ceramic art. This book commemorates
the thirtieth anniversary of the Metro system and concentrates on details of the designs
rather than their overall effect. It includes a short summary in English, as well as a
brief essay which places the stations' tiles in the context of the last 400 years of tile
decoration in Portugal. Photographs of a number of Portuguese tiles from earlier eras
are interspersed with those of the Metropolitano system.

595   **Portuguese tiles from the National Museum of Azulejo, Lisbon.**
       João Castel-Branco Pereira.   Lisbon, London: Instituto Português de
       Museus/Zwemmer, 1995. 128p. bibliog.

Fully illustrated with colour photographs, this volume provides a useful introduction
for the English reader to the history and design of the world-famous Portuguese
ceramic tilework, known as *azulejo*. The book includes a history of the Manueline
Madre de Deus church in the eastern coastal area of Lisbon, in which the recently
established National Museum of Tiles is located, and an account of the collections
themselves. Modern tilework is being added to the collections, including a number of
replicas of the artistry to be seen on Lisbon's underground railway stations.

596   **A fronteira. Tradução de Pedro Tamen. Azulejos do Palácio
       Fronteira. Bestiário fotografado por Nicolas Sapieha e Paulo
       Cintra. Nota sobre os jardins por José Meco.** (The frontier.
       Translated by Pedro Tamen. Tiles of the Fronteira Palace. Bestiary
       photographed by Nicolas Sapieha and Paulo Cintra. Note about the
       gardens by José Meco.)
       Pascal Quignard.   Lisbon: Quetzal Editora, 1992. 2nd ed. 146p.
       bibliog.

Although a literary essay on Portuguese history occupies half of this volume, this is
interspersed with colour plates of tiles from the Fronteira Palace. For the non-
Portuguese reader, however, it is the remainder of the book which is the more
interesting. This section comprises a substantial array of colourful photographs of
ceramic tiles, all depicting animals, which are to be found in the Palace and its
grounds, at Benfica in the north-west quarter of Lisbon. The volume is completed by
an essay on the tiles and Palace gardens by José Meco, which is also finely illustrated
by high-quality colour photographs.

597 **Azulejos de Lisboa do século XX.** (Lisbon tiles of the twentieth century.)
Teresa Saporiti.   Oporto, Portugal: Afrontamento, 1992. 242p. bibliog.

With text in both English (translated by Susan Pérez Castillo), and Portuguese, Teresa Saporiti surveys the magnificent range of Portuguese ceramic tiles produced in the 20th century. A wealth of colour plates illustrates the volume, which is completed by brief biographies of the artists and factories responsible for the tiles depicted.

598 **Azulejos em Lisboa à luz duma cidade.** (Ceramic tiles in Lisbon by the light of a city.)
Marylène Terol.   Lisbon: Dinalivro, 1995. unpaginated.

Decorative ceramic tilework is a Lisbon tradition which has undergone a renaissance in the 1980s and 1990s. This large-format album, with abundant colour illustrations, reflects the decorative range of this craft. The bilingual text is in Portuguese and French.

Plastic

599 **Estatuária de Lisboa.** (Statuary of Lisbon.)
Rafael Laborde Ferreira, Víctor Manuel Lopes Vieira.   Lisbon: printed by Amigos do Livro, 1994. 447p. 4 maps.

In this work nearly 400 Lisbon statues are described and illustrated with monochrome photographs. Biographical information on the sculptors is provided and there are indexes of subjects, locations and sculptures in chronological order.

600 **Lisboa: de pedra e bronze, in stone and bronze. A estatuaria no caminho da cidade. The statuary in public places of the city.**
Photographs by Luís Leiria de Lima, text by Isabel Salema, translation by Patricia Thorburn.   Lisbon: Difel, 1990. 173p.

Lisbon is a city of many fine public monuments and sculptures and this is a sumptuous survey of these, comprising colour photographs of 105 different works. Twelve of the examples are from the gardens of The Gulbenkian Foundation and the rest from the streets of the capital. They are split into various categories according to subject matter. Those classed as monuments enjoy up to nine pages of photographic detail per statue. The parallel Portuguese and English text provides historical or biographical detail of the subject of each work as well as background information on its creator and on the context, location and date of its erection in Lisbon.

O povo de Lisboa: tipos, ambiente, modos de vida, mercados e feiras, divertimentos, mentalidade. Exposição iconográfica. Junho/ Julho, 1978-1979. (The working class of Lisbon: social types, environment, ways of life, markets and fairs, entertainments, mentality. Iconographic exhibition, June/ July, 1978-79.)
See item no. 22.

Calouste Gulbenkian, collector.
See item no. 384.

As obras de Santa Engrácia e os seus artistas. (The works of Santa Engracia church and its artists.)
See item no. 398.

The Palace and gardens of Fronteira: seventeenth- and eighteenth-century Portuguese style.
See item no. 505.

Centre for Modern Art and Acarte, Lisbon: the background, the new buildings 1983-4 and the first five years.
See item no. 510.

Inventário do Museu Nacional de Arqueologia: colecção de escultura romana. (Inventory of the National Museum of Archaeology: collection of Roman sculpture.)
See item no. 640.

Guia do Museu Rafael Bordalo Pinheiro. (Guide to the Rafael Bordalo Pinheiro Museum.)
See item no. 643.

Museu do Chiado: arte portuguesa, 1850-1950. (Chiado Museum: Portuguese art, 1850-1950.)
See item no. 644.

The Berardo Collection.
See item no. 649.

Music

601 **Opera in Portugal in the eighteenth century.**
Manuel Carlos de Brito. Cambridge, England: Cambridge University Press, 1989. 254p. bibliog.
The four sections of this book, based on a 1985 doctoral thesis, cover 'Opera during the reign of João V (1708-50)', 'Court opera during the reign of José I, (1750-77)', 'Court opera and music during the reign of Maria I, (1777-92)' and 'Commercial

opera, 1760-93'. It is therefore very much a history of opera in Lisbon, at a time when the Portuguese court was a leading European patron of this art form. The text is illustrated by eight contemporary drawings of theatres and palaces in Lisbon. A substantial portion of the text comprises a chronology of operas performed in Portugal during the 18th century, the vast majority being staged in Lisbon and its environs.

602   **O Teatro Nacional de S. Carlos.** (The S. Carlos National Theatre.)
      Manuel Ivo Cruz.   Oporto, Portugal: Lello & Irmão Editores, 1992.
      80p.

A large-format, well illustrated guide to Lisbon's São Carlos theatre and opera house, which was inaugurated in 1773. There are abundant colour photographs and black-and-white illustrations of the interior and exterior of the building, as well as of productions and personalities associated with the theatre. The building was so run-down that it closed in 1935, only to be refurbished and reopened to coincide with the 300th anniversary of the 1640 assertion of independence from Spain. Today it is Lisbon's leading opera house.

603   **Lisbon, for wind quintet.**
      Percy Aldridge Grainger.   London: Schott & Co., Ltd., 1971.
      unpaginated. (British Folk Music Settings, no. 40).

A setting for a traditional English folk-song about Lisbon. The original tune was collected by Grainger from an elderly workhouse inmate in Lincolnshire, around 1906. As well as the score, there are part-scores for flute, oboe, clarinet in B-flat, horn in F and bassoon.

604   **The Lisbon story: a play with music.**
      Book and lyrics by Harold Purcell, music by Harry Parr Davies. Vocal
      score.   London: Chappell & Co., 1948. 138p.

A two-act score, performed to acclaim in London in 1943, which includes the classic song, *Pedro the fisherman*, in which Nina forsakes the absent Pedro to marry Miguel. The narrative takes place in Summer 1942 in Lisbon, Cascais and Paris. It was adapted in 1946 into a British-made film depicting the intrigue surrounding a French atomic scientist's rescue from the clutches of the Axis.

605   **Southern Baroque revisited.**
      Sacheverell Sitwell.   London: Weidenfeld & Nicolson, 1967. 306p.

As well as a number of passing references to Lisbon, this erudite work contains a substantial account of the work of the Italian composer Domenico Scarlatti and of the architect, Guarino Guarini. Scarlatti served King João V's Court, establishing Lisbon's reputation as a leading European musical centre. Guarini built the magnificent city church of Santa Maria da Divina Providência (Our Lady of Divine Providence) which was destroyed in the earthquake of 1755.

Film and theatre

606 **The Lisbon Players, 1947/1987, and including an account of the Estrela Hall.**
    d'Arcy Orders. Printed at Monte Estoril: APN, [1987]. 92p.

This volume opens with an account (p. 7-12) by Dr Grace Thornton of the Estrela Hall, home to the Lisbon Players, an English-language theatrical group. d'Arcy Orders then briefly relates the history of over a century of British expatriate theatrical productions in Lisbon, before concentrating on the activities of The Lisbon Players, formed in 1946. Details of all its productions, accompanied by black-and-white photographs and reproductions of theatre programmes, underline the range of plays and revues mounted for the expatriate community.

607 **Lisboa a 24 imagens.** (Lisbon in 24 images.)
    Manuel Costa e Silva. Lisbon: Caminho, 1994. 121p.

A fascinating review of Lisbon as a film location. Included are those films which aimed to portray Lisbon as a film setting and those which were filmed in the city but where the location purported to be somewhere else, such as Rome. In addition to a series of short essays by film-makers and writers on the themes of Lisbon and film, there is a list and summary of over sixty Portuguese films and more than fifty foreign-language films (English, French and German) which have used Lisbon as an identified or anonymous setting. The volume is illustrated with many 'stills' and a number of colour reproductions of film posters.

Customs and Costume

608 **Portugal: a book of folk-ways.**
Rodney Gallop. Cambridge, England: Cambridge University Press, 1936. 291p. bibliog.

Roughly sixty pages of this volume refer to the folklore or customs of Lisbon and its environs. These include more than twenty pages on the *fado* music of the capital (p. 245-65). Amongst the sixteen pages of photographs and sixty drawings in this volume are depictions of Lisbon street vendors, carnival participants and the traditional 'dança da luta' of Lisbon, a kind of human pyramid.

609 **Costume of Portugal.**
Henry L'Évêque. London, 1814.

A collection of fifty coloured plates depicting Portuguese 'types' of whom a large proportion are explicitly depicted from the streets of Lisbon. These include portrayals of women going to church, with the Carmo convent behind them, a waterseller, streetporter, blind man, washerwoman and a depiction of the celebrated Lisbon custom of throwing out slops from an upper window onto the street below, a tradition noted by many a travel writer of the 19th century. The text is in both English and French and describes not only each plate but also the social or historical background to the depicted scene.

O povo de Lisboa. (The working class of Lisbon.)
See item no. 22.

Food and Drink

610 **The wines of Spain and Portugal.**
Charles Metcalfe, Kathryn McWhirter.   London: Salamander, 1988.
160p. maps. bibliog.
A very attractive colour guide to Iberian wines which covers those of the Lisbon area
and the Ribatejo to the north of the capital, as well as the produce of Torres Vedras (p.
134-35), Cartaxo (p. 136-37), Colares (p. 138-39), Bucelas (p. 140-41) and Carcavelos
(p. 141-42). As well as colour photographs of the areas and descriptive text, colour
reproductions of wine labels are also included. An important forerunner as a guide to
the wines of Lisbon was *Facts about port and madeira, with notices of the wines
vintaged around Lisbon and the wines of Tenerife*, by Henry Vizetelly (London: Ward,
Lock & Co., 1880. 211p.).

611 **The wines of Portugal.**
Jan Read.   London; Boston, Massachusetts: Faber & Faber, 1982.
Revised, 1987. 190p. 3 maps. bibliog.
The fourth chapter of this authoritative guide to Portuguese wine covers the
'Demarcated wines of the Centre'. It includes details of the wines produced in the
Carcavelos and Colares areas, to the west of Lisbon, as well as in Bucelas, some 40km
to the north of the capital. Carcavelos white wine became popular with the English
through its hearty consumption by Wellington's officers in the Peninsular War, whilst
red Colares, produced in very limited quantities between Sintra and the Atlantic coast,
is arguably Portugal's best red wine. Both Carcavelos and Colares wines are produced
in small vineyards threatened by modern winemaking methods and urban
encroachment on the vineyards.

Sport

612 **Cavaliers of Portugal, with a glossary of bullfighting terms.**
Huldine Beamish. London: Geoffrey Bles, 1966. 146p. bibliog.
Written by a lady who farmed in the Alentejo area of Portugal, this volume covers the role of the bulls, horses and men in bullfighting, as well as explaining the main techniques of the sport. She includes accounts of major incidents and events in the Lisbon bull rings of Campo de Santana and Campo Pequeno, as well as at the nearby Algés and Cascais venues. In a closing chapter on the bullrings of Portugal, she gives details of the above arenas as well as of historical sites of bullfighting in Lisbon which included the Terreiro do Paço and Salitre areas. The text is illustrated with many photographs and drawings.

613 **Benfica: Semanário do Sport Lisboa e Benfica.** (Benfica: Weekly Newspaper of the Sport Lisboa e Benfica Club.)
Lisbon: Sport Lisboa e Benfica, 1943- . weekly.
In Lisbon, sports newspapers are sold alongside the general press and individual clubs also have their own titles. *Benfica* is a long-established weekly tabloid, published on Wednesdays, for supporters of this most famous of Portuguese sporting clubs. It has plenty of photographic content, some in colour and in its normal editions of thirty-two pages it covers the full range of the club's activities, which include athletics, roller hockey, volleyball, handball and, of course, football. As with the comparable publication, *Sporting* (q.v.), there is also much coverage of supporters' club activities and reporting of club finances and administrative meetings.

614 **Sport Lisboa e Benfica: fotobiografia.** (Sport Lisboa e Benfica: photobiography.)
Rui Guedes. Lisbon: Publicações Dom Quixote, 1987. 223p.
A large and well-illustrated history of the Benfica club, best known in Britain for its football team, but actually a club with leading teams in a number of sporting disciplines. Benfica's magnificent headquarters, the Estádio da Luz, is situated in the northern suburbs of Lisbon.

615   **The Guinness guide to international motor racing.**
Peter Higham.   Enfield, England: Guinness, 1995. 544p.
In the section on racetracks in this volume there is information on Portuguese circuits. These include the current Estoril grand prix track and the former Lisbon Monsanto circuit, which used to host the Portuguese Grand Prix on a track which included a stretch of the Marginal, the public coast road between Lisbon and Cascais. As well as plans of these circuits, details are given of the past winners of the Portuguese grand prix and of other sports car races at these and other venues in Portugal.

616   **The football grounds of Europe.**
Simon Inglis.   London: Collins Willow, 1990. 288p. bibliog.
A brief section on Lisbon outlines the rivalry of the Sport Lisboa e Benfica and Sporting Club de Portugal football clubs and the background to the location of their current stadia. Colour photographs depict Sporting's Alvalade stadium and the Restelo stadium of the Lisbon suburban team, Belenenses.

617   **One afternoon in Lisbon.**
Kevin McCarra, Pat Woods, photographs by Oscar Marzaroli.
Edinburgh: Mainstream Publishing, 1988. 240p.
An illustrated account of the Glasgow Celtic football team's successful quest for the European Champions' Cup which culminated in victory over Inter-Milan at the National Stadium in Lisbon in 1967. After recounting the team's odyssey around Europe to reach the Final, the closing chapter, which shares the book's title 'One afternoon in Lisbon' (p. 193-228), tells the story of the build-up for the match and of the game itself. The experiences of the team's supporters in Lisbon are relayed, as are those of the British consulate which had to organize return journeys for many impecunious fans. Photographs of the stadium at Cruz Quebrada and of the match itself are included. Andy Dougan's *The Lisbon lions* (London: Virgin, 1997. 243p.) also covers the Glasgow club's successful European campaign in 1966-67.

618   **A Praça de Toiros de Lisboa, Campo Pequeno.** (The Lisbon
bull-ring, Campo Pequeno.)
António Manuel Morais.   Lisbon: Published by the Author, 1992.
1,079p. bibliog.
Written in 1991, the centenary year of Lisbon's Campo Pequeno bullring, this extensive volume is effectively an encyclopaedia of bullfighting in Lisbon. With well over 1,000 photographs, some in colour, it covers every aspect of bullfighting, even giving details of many of the bands which have provided music at bullfighting spectacles. The illustrations depict bullfighting personalities, including breeders, horsemen and matadores, and there are also a number of colour reproductions of posters advertising bullfights.

619   **Cricket in Portugal.**
d'Arcy Orders.   Lisbon: Published by the Author, [1990]. 74p.
Orders notes that as early as the 1730s disputes provoked by cricket arose between British sailors and residents of Lisbon and Belém. However, the heart of this book is the story of Lisbon Cricket Club, formed in 1865, and of Carcavelos Cricket Club, formed nine years later by British employees of the Eastern Telegraph Company

which administered the submarine communications cable connecting England to India. The Campo Pequeno bullring now occupies the site on which the Lisbon club first played. Full details, including a substantial statistical appendix, are given for the Lisbon versus Oporto cricket matches which have taken place virtually every year since 1861. More recent developments have included six-a-side cricket in Lisbon and tours to England by an *Iberians* side. Orders also touches on football in Lisbon.

620   **Sporting.**
Lisbon: Sporting Clube de Portugal, [1922]- . weekly.

Issued every Tuesday, this newspaper is aimed at the supporters of the club known to British football fans as Sporting Lisbon. Although obviously partisan, it refrains from sensationalism and, indeed, devotes pages to lengthy reports of club supporters' meetings. It is typically a thirty-two page, illustrated tabloid, with several pages of colour, and a supplement. The paper's circulation is 25,000 issues. The Sporting Clube de Portugal runs teams in many sporting disciplines, such as athletics, cycling and swimming, all of whose activities are covered in the newspaper.

621   **Barclays world of cricket: the game from A to Z. A new and revised edition.**
General editor, E. W. Swanton.   London: Willow Books, 1986. 724p.

The section on Portugal, by Gordon White, recounts the origins of cricket in Lisbon when sailors from Royal Navy ships were recorded as playing there. By 1810 cricket matches were taking place in Lisbon amongst the Peninsular War forces, and scorecards survive from games played between British residents in Lisbon and visiting sailors. The Lisbon club was founded in the 1860s and for over a century, with few exceptions, an annual cricket match has taken place with the Oporto cricket club, with the games in Lisbon normally taking place on matting wickets rather than grass. White provides details of a number of sides to have visited Lisbon and of tours of England by Lisbon cricketers.

622   **Torbay to Lisbon International Sail-Training Ships Race, July 1956. Over thirty photographs of the entries with a list of the finishing times, the presentation of the trophies & the sinking of the *Moyana*.**
The Times.   London: The Times Publishing Company Ltd., 1956. 31p.

An account of the inaugural 'tall-ships' race, won by the British ketch *Moyana* which unfortunately sank in a storm on the return journey from Lisbon. The book depicts the vessels and the Lisbon prize-giving ceremonies, overseen by President Craveiro Lopes of Portugal.

Recreation

623 **Gardens of Portugal.**
Text by Patrick Bowe, photographs by Nicolas Sapieha. Lisbon: Quetzal, 1989. 223p. map. bibliog.
A folio volume packed with colour photographs of Portuguese gardens, accompanied by a history and description of each location. A section of the book is entitled 'Lisbon area' (p. 19-107) and this is divided into thirteen sections. The gardens covered include those of the Palácio de Queluz, the Gulbenkian Centre, the Estufa Fria, the Palácio Fronteira and various gardens in Sintra, Belém and other suburbs of Lisbon.

624 **Portuguese gardens.**
Hélder Carita, Homem Cardoso. Woodbridge, England: Antique Collectors' Club, 1991. 320p. bibliog.
With 362 illustrations this is a colourful review of Portuguese gardens including many in the Greater Lisbon area. It is translated from the Portuguese original, *Jardins em Portugal*, and includes a preface by the anglophile journalist and politician Miguel Esteves Cardoso.

625 **Tratado da grandeza dos jardins em Portugal; ou, Da originalidade e desaires desta arte.** (Treatise on the grandeur of Portuguese gardens; or, On the originality and inelegance of this art form.)
Hélder Carita, photographs by Homem Cardoso. Lisbon: Published by the Authors, 1987. 319p. bibliog.
A fully-illustrated colour volume which highlights the magnificence of Portuguese gardens. The text goes back to the Graeco-Roman garden tradition before tracing the development of Portuguese gardens in chronologically arranged chapters. Amongst the gardens in the Lisbon area which are illustrated and described are those of the Quinta do Tojal, Palácio Fronteira, Ajuda, Paço do Lumiar, Quinta dos Azulejos, Real Jardim Botánico, Belém, Queluz, Sintra and the Quinta de S. Mateus at Dafundo. The

bibliography includes a section on non-Portuguese writers who have described Portuguese gardens and the English-language authors cited include Costigan, Dalrymple, Murphy and Southey.

626 **Jardins de Lisboa.** (Gardens of Lisbon.)
Alfredo Cunha, Luís Vasconcelos.   Lisbon: Perspectivas & Realidades, 1988. 94p. (Retrato de Lisboa).

More than three quarters of this small volume consists of matt colour photographs of scenes, structures, animals and people in a large number of Lisbon's gardens. Many of these are close-ups of such features as railings, fountains, bandstands and playgrounds which try to convey the spirit of the locations rather than portray them in their entirety. The book concludes with a list of the addresses of forty-six gardens in the city.

Palace of Queluz: the gardens.
See item no. 87.

Flora da Estufa Fria de Lisboa. (Flora of the Estufa Fria of Lisbon.)
See item no. 303.

The palace and gardens of Fronteira: seventeenth- and eighteenth-century Portuguese style.
See item no. 505.

A fronteira. (The frontier.)
See item no. 596.

Libraries and Archives

627 **A Torre do Tombo e os seus tesouros.** (The Torre do Tombo archive and its treasures.)
Martim de Albuquerque.   Lisbon: Edições Inapa, 1990. 347p. bibliog.
Founded in mediaeval times, the Torre do Tombo is the Portuguese national archive. This luxurious volume portrays, in large-format, colour photographs, many of its treasures which include manuscripts, incunabula and items such as mediaeval document seals. One of its English-language holdings, illustrated in this work, is a letter written by Abraham Lincoln to King Pedro V of Portugal. In the late 1980s the archive moved to purpose-built premises near Lisbon University.

628   **Libraries and library services in Portugal.**
Nell Buller.   Halifax, Canada: Dalhousie University, School of Library and Information Studies, 1988. 121p. 2 maps. bibliog.
(Occasional Papers Series, no. 46).
Despite its country-wide title, this detailed study of Portuguese library systems does not actually cover many libraries outside Lisbon. As well as an account of the growth and activities of the National Library, there are sections on eight university libraries in Lisbon and fifteen public, special and foreign libraries in the city and environs. There is also an account of the holdings of the Torre do Tombo (national archives). This helpful, practical guide for those intending to make use of Lisbon libraries is preceded by a brief essay on the history and educational system of Portugal. There are illustrations of several of the libraries and copies of some of their printed guide material but these, as well as the two maps, have not reproduced well in the book.

629 **Guide to the National Library.**
Editorial director, Fátima Libório, translated by Nitah Camotim.
Lisbon: Ministry of Culture, National Library and Book Institute,
1996. 83p. bibliog.

A profusely illustrated guide to the National Library of Lisbon, produced to commemorate the 200th anniversary of the founding of the Royal Public Library, the forerunner of the National Library, in 1796. After an essay on 'The National Library: a chronicle of 200 years', there are sections on the various existing library departments, all interspersed with colour photographs of many of the Library's treasures and of its present-day facilities. The Library's regulations and floor plans are also included, making this both a practical, as well as historical, guide.

630 **Major libraries of the world: a selective guide.**
Colin Steele.   London; New York: Bowker, 1976. 479p.

Lisbon is here represented by entries for both the National Library and the library of the Ajuda royal palace. As well as a photograph of both institutions, details are given of each library's history, special collections, opening hours, admission procedures and accessibility.

Catalogue of the Library of the Instituto Britânico em Portugal (and supplement).
See item no. 688.

Museums

631   Guia do Aquário Vasco da Gama. (Guide to the Vasco da Gama
Aquarium.)
Aquário Vasco da Gama.   Oeiras, Portugal: Câmara Municipal, 1990.
102p.
An illustrated guide to the Vasco da Gama Aquarium which is situated, adjacent to the
Cascais to Lisbon railway line, at Dafundo, some 10km west of Lisbon. The aquarium
exhibits examples not only of the neighbouring Atlantic Ocean's marine life, but also
tropical and freshwater fish. Amongst its historical treasures are the collections of
King Carlos I (1889-1908), who was a keen ichthyologist.

632   Guide of the Archaeological Museum.
Associação dos Arqueólogos Portugueses.   Lisbon: Associação dos
Arqueólogos Portugueses, 1994. 39p.
A guide to the eclectic archaeological museum located in the ruins of the 14th-15th
century Carmo monastery in Lisbon. In 1864 the ruins were given over to the
forerunner of the Associação dos Arqueólogos Portugueses. This illustrated book is
both a guide to the ruined church premises and to the artefacts in the collection.

633   The Lisbon coaches in history.
Carlos de Azevedo.   *The Connoisseur Yearbook*, (1955), p. 32-41.
A survey of the horse-drawn and other historic coaches in the Museu dos Coches, at
Belém, which constitute the major collection of their kind in the world. This large-
format essay is accompanied by excellent colour and black-and-white illustrations of
the exhibits.

634 **Calouste Gulbenkian Foundation.**
Calouste Gulbenkian Foundation. Lisbon: Calouste Gulbenkian
Foundation, 1995. 53p.

The posthumous creation of the Gulbenkian Foundation in Lisbon, based on the fabulous personal collections of art of the oil entrepreneur, Calouste Sarkis Gulbenkian (1869-1955), gave the city a major international cultural resource. This book is an account of the history and work of the Foundation since its creation in 1956, together with brief biographical information on Calouste Gulbenkian himself. Although the book is almost entirely focused on the Lisbon headquarters of the Foundation, it does also refer to its activities in London and Paris. Many colour photographs illustrate the Lisbon buildings of the Foundation which include two art museums, a theatre and library. Floor plans are also provided, although the volume is not primarily intended as a guidebook to the Foundation's public buildings.

635 **Ricardo do Espírito Santo Silva Foundation.**
Fundação Ricardo do Espírito Santo Silva, text by Maria João Espírito
Santo Bustorff Silva, photographs by A. Homem Cardoso. Lisbon:
Fundação Ricardo do Espírito Santo Silva, 1995. 293p. bibliog.

A large-format introduction to a hidden gem of Lisbon, the collection of mostly 17th- and 18th-century furniture, silver tapestries and other decorative arts for the most part bequeathed to Lisbon by Ricardo do Espírito Santo Silva. Also known as the Museu de Artes Decorativas (Museum of Decorative Arts), the collection is housed in the 17th-century Palácio Azurara in the Alfama district. Cardoso's photographs, some of which are in colour, illustrate the treasures of this recently renovated museum.

636 **Museums discovered: The Calouste Gulbenkian Museum.**
Rona Goffen, and fifteen essays contributed by Priscilla Soucek.
New York: Woodbine Books, 1982. 298p. bibliog.

A large-format, illustrated study of Lisbon's world-famous Gulbenkian Museum, opened in 1969 to display the priceless collections of the Armenian oil magnate, Calouste Gulbenkian, who spent his final years in the city. The Museum's strong holdings in areas such as Egyptology and European art are well represented in this volume which provides a comprehensive introduction to the collections. The book's publication predated the erection on the same site of the Centro de Arte Moderna (Centre of Modern Art) and, hence, that building's collections are not included here.

637 **Museu Nacional dos Coches, National Coach Museum, Musée National des Carrosses.**
Natália Correia Guedes, photographs by A. Homem Cardoso. Lisbon:
A. P. Edições, 1991. 83p. bibliog.

A finely produced, large-format guide to the magnificent collection of horse-drawn and other coaches held in the former riding school and stables of the royal palace at Belém. The text, in parallel Portuguese, English and French versions, tells the story of the museum's foundation in 1905 at the instigation of Queen Amélia. Today it is Lisbon's most visited museum. Superb colour photographs illustrate the collection, the oldest item in which is a 16th-century Spanish carriage allegedly brought to Portugal by King Philip II of Spain. Equally well-illustrated and similar in format is *O Museu Nacional dos Coches* (The National Coach Museum), written by its director, Silvana Bessane (Lisbon: Instituto Português de Museus, 1993. 126p.).

638   **The National Museum of Costume, Lisbon.**
Natália Correia Guedes.   *Museum: Quarterly Review Published by Unesco*, vol. XXXIII (1981), p. 94-98.

In spite of Portugal's historical tradition of textile production, the Museum of Costume (Museu do Traje) was only established in Lisbon after the 1974 Revolution, although a number of temporary exhibitions had previously laid the ground for its creation. In this illustrated article, the authoress describes the creation of the museum in the Ageja Palace and reveals how much of the collection has come from donations by the public. The museum has a restoration unit and was one of the first in Portugal to run its own educational service.

639   **The Portuguese discoveries and Renaissance Europe.**
Yudhishthir R. Isar.   *Museum: Quarterly Review*, no. 142 (1984), p. 92-98.

An illustrated panorama of the coordinated Lisbon exhibitions to commemorate the Portuguese overseas discoveries, held in five of the city's buildings; the Madre de Deus church, the Casa dos Bicos, the Museu de Arte Antiga, the Torre de Belém and the Jerónimos monastery. Photographs, some in colour, show all five sites, where a wide range of artefacts and works of art related to the Discoveries were exhibited to a total of over a million visitors in 1983.

640   **Inventário do Museu Nacional de Arqueologia: colecção de escultura romana.** (Inventory of the National Museum of Archaeology: collection of Roman sculpture.)
José Luís de Matos.   Lisbon: Instituto Português de Museus, 1995. 208p. bibliog.

A full-colour catalogue of the exhibits of Roman sculpture in Lisbon's National Museum of Archaeology. A total of 202 items, all stone sculptures, are depicted and briefly described. These are derived from many sites across Portugal, including Lisbon and Sintra.

641   **Guia do Museu Antoniano.** (Guide to the St. Anthony Museum.)
Irisalva Moita.   Lisbon: Câmara Municipal de Lisboa, 1991. 24p.

A museum dedicated to St Anthony of Padua, who was born as Fernando de Bulhões in Lisbon in 1195, is situated in an annexe to the church of St Anthony, adjacent to Lisbon cathedral. There has been a cult of St Anthony in Lisbon since the end of the 12th century but the 1755 earthquake wiped out the original church built in his honour and the current building was erected between 1757 and 1767. Most of this guidebook comprises black-and-white photographs of the sculpted, ceramic and artistic items held in the museum, which was opened in 1962. 12 June, the eve of his feast day, is still celebrated by parties in Lisbon's streets.

642   **Guia do Museu da Cidade.** (Guide to the City Museum.)
Irisalva Moita.   Lisbon: Museu da Cidade, 1991. 70p.

A full-colour guide to Lisbon's City Museum, sited in the mid-18th-century Palácio Pimenta, at Campo Grande. The eighty-five illustrations depict the palace, as well as its artefacts. These date back to pre-Roman Lisbon and also include paintings and documents. Although the City Museum has its origins in the Museu Olisiponense (Museum of Lisbon), which was set up in the Carmo Museum in 1922, it only opened on its present site and scale in 1984, although sections of the museum had been open to the public in the Palácio Pimenta since 1979.

643 **Guia do Museu Rafael Bordalo Pinheiro.** (Guide to the Rafael Bordalo Pinheiro Museum.)
Irisalva Moita. Lisbon: Câmara Municipal de Lisboa, 1991. 67p.

Apart from six pages of text, this work comprises a colour catalogue, with captions, of sixty items from the Lisbon museum dedicated to Rafael Bordalo Pinheiro (1846-1905). He achieved fame as a caricaturist in both the graphic arts and ceramics, but he also produced accomplished, serious works in these media. The text relates the history of the museum and provides biographical details of the artist. It has been housed at Campo Grande, Lisbon, in the former home for seventy years of Artur Ernesto de Santa Cruz Magalhães whose collection formed the basis of the museum.

644 **Museu do Chiado: arte portuguesa, 1850-1950.** (Chiado Museum: Portuguese art, 1850-1950.)
Museu do Chiado. Lisbon: Instituto Português de Museus/Museu do Chiado, 1994. 380p. bibliog.

One beneficial side-effect of the disastrous Chiado fire in Lisbon in 1988 was that the hurried evacuation of the paintings from the nearby Museu de Arte Contemporânea (Museum of Contemporary Art), which was threatened by the flames, brought to a head the pre-existing problems of this moribund museum. With generous help from the French state and commerce, the original museum, opened in 1911, was revamped and opened as the Museu do Chiado in 1994. The collections were widened to include 20th- as well as 19th-century Portuguese art. This finely produced colour guide illustrates over 250 paintings and other art works from the museum, arranged thematically under headings such as Romanticism, Naturalism and Modernism. An appendix covers the museum's collection of French sculpture.

645 **Portugal das origens à época romana.** (Portugal from its origins to the Roman period.)
Museu Nacional de Arqueologia e Etnografia. Lisbon: Museu Nacional de Arqueologia e Etnografia; Instituto Português do Património Cultural, 1989. 102p. bibliog.

The Museum of Ethnology in Lisbon was established in 1903 in the former dormitory wing of the Jerónimos monastery at Belém. This publication contains numerous colour photographs and descriptions of exhibits shown to mark the reopening of the refurbished museum. Amongst the items illustrated are ceramic ware, tools and statuary.

646 **Great maritime museums of the world.**
Edited by Peter Neill, Barbara Ehrenwald Krohn. London: Abrams, 1991. 304p.

A lavishly illustrated guide to maritime museums which includes a section on the holdings of the impressive Museu de Marinha at Belém, Lisbon by R. Freire Montez and J. Martins e Silva. The extensive museum occupies part of the Jerónimos monastery but has a connected modern extension housing its larger artefacts, which include royal barges and aircraft.

647   **Grandes museus de Portugal.** (Great museums of Portugal.)
      O Público.   Lisbon: O Público, [1995]. 383p. bibliog.

A compendium of large-format fascicules produced by the Lisbon newspaper *O Público*, each of which is dedicated to a particular Portuguese museum. Those in the Lisbon area include the Museus de Etnologia, Arte Antiga, Coches, Azulejo, Teatro and Traje (Museums of Ethnology, Ancient Art, Coaches, Tiles, Theatre and Costume). Each museum is lavishly illustrated with colour photographs and the text provides details of the collections, their origins and, usefully, information on published catalogues and descriptions.

648   **Guia dos museus de Portugal. Guide to museums in Portugal.**
      Edição bilingue. Bilingual edition.
      José Ramos, translation by Wally Rylat.   Paço de Arcos, Portugal:
      Margens, 1995. 83p.

Arranged alphabetically by place-name, this guide provides entries for each museum in both Portuguese and in an idiosyncratic English translation. Forty-four museums in Lisbon are included. Addresses, opening hours, admission charge information and an outline of holdings are provided for each museum.

649   **The Berardo Collection.**
      Sintra Museum of Modern Art.   Sintra, Portugal: Sintra Museum of
      Modern Art, 1996. 420p.

The newly-formed Sintra Museum of Modern Art is seeking to establish itself on the international stage and, consequently, this large volume enjoyed a publication launch at the Serpentine Gallery in London in 1996. The book illustrates and describes a cosmopolitan collection of modern art built up by the Madeiran businessman, José Berardo, and which has been compared in importance to the initiatives of the Gulbenkian Foundation in bringing a major art collection to the Lisbon area. This volume reproduces nearly 200 of the works of art housed in this new museum in Sintra, to the north-west of Lisbon. The artists represented in the collection include many non-Portuguese, such as Bridget Riley and British pop artists.

650   **Museu de Marinha visitor's guide.** (Maritime Museum visitor's
      guide.)
      José Picas do Vale.   Lisbon: Museu de Marinha, 1995. 40p.

A well-written and informative guide to the magnificent collections of the Maritime Museum at Belém which include models, artefacts and historic examples of royal gondolas and other small vessels. The museum also houses the Fairey 17 aircraft in which Coutinho and Cabral completed their epic air crossing from Lisbon to Brazil in 1922. The guidebook, which incorporates colour illustrations, also provides helpful floor plans and gives two alternative tour routes, depending on the time available.

Subterranean Portugal.
See item no. 311.

Museums

On the twentieth anniversary of the establishment of the Calouste Gulbenkian Foundation.
See item no. 377.

Five centuries of Portuguese jewellery, National Museum of Ancient Art, Lisbon.
See item no. 593.

Portuguese tiles from the National Museum of Azulejo, Lisbon.
See item no. 595.

Printing

651 **Pedro Craesbeeck & Sons: 17th century publishers to Portugal and Brazil.**
H. Bernstein. Amsterdam: Hakkert, 1987. 229p. bibliog.

A history of the Craesbeeck family of printers and publishers who came to Lisbon, via Spain, from the Low Countries in the shape of Pedro Craesbeeck, in about 1597. He and his descendants remained active as major printers in Lisbon for almost a century, until 1690. The latter portion of this book (p. 171-229) comprises a catalogue of the family's printing output.

652 **A descriptive catalogue of printing in Spain and Portugal, 1501-1520.**
F. J. Norton. Cambridge, England; London; New York; Melbourne, Australia: Cambridge University Press, 1978. 581p. bibliog.

Lisbon was the second oldest known site of printing in Portugal, its earliest products being Hebrew titles, of which the first was dated 1489. This catalogue itemizes the titles known to have been printed in Lisbon between 1501 and 1520. Full catalogue details are given for each item, as well as locations of extant copies and references to articles or books about each title.

Children's Publications

653 **Let's go to Portugal.**
Keith Lye.   London; New York; Sydney; Toronto: Franklin Watts, 1986. 32p. 2 maps.

A large-print children's introduction to Portugal, which includes a section on Lisbon. The book has surprisingly good quality colour photographs of Lisbon and elsewhere in Portugal for a book aimed at a young audience.

654 **We live in Portugal.**
Ana de Skalon, Christa Stadtler.   Hove, England: Wayland, 1986. 60p. (Living Here).

Comprises twenty-six brief essays on individual representatives of different professions from around Portugal. These include a Lisbon tram driver and a local politician. Each section is illustrated with colour photographs of the individual in question and his or her local environment.

Newspapers

655   **APN, the Anglo-Portuguese News: the paper of the international community in Portugal.**
Estoril, Portugal: APN Publicações Lda, 1937- . weekly.
The placing of this newspaper's initials before its full title and its subtitle's reference to the international community reflect the Anglo-Portuguese News's attempts to appeal to a readership beyond its initial constituency of the expatriate English community. Consequently, the paper is not parochial, but, rather, it relays a wide range of developments in Portugal for an English-reading audience. However, local news is still carried of such institutions as St. Julian's English School at Carcavelos, the British Council (Instituto Britânico) and the Lisbon Casuals cricket team. The schedules of BBC's world radio and television services are also printed. Its current circulation is 8,500 (1996) for a tabloid, typically of sixteen pages, with colour on its front page.

656   **A Capital.** (The Capital.)
Lisbon: Medipress, 1968- . daily.
A Capital, a tabloid, is now Lisbon's only surviving daily evening newspaper, having been established in its present form in 1968. Local editions are produced, for example for the Cascais area, in addition to the main city version. The paper typically comprises a main section of forty-eight pages plus varied supplements. Colour is used on the front and back covers as well as in the centre spread. Although there is necessarily much coverage of local crime, accidents and sport, the paper is not sensationalist and, indeed, carries serious articles on music, literature and entertainment.

657   **Correio da Manhã.** (Morning Post.)
Lisbon: Presselivre, 1979- . daily.
One of the higher circulation (c.100,000) Lisbon tabloid morning papers, founded in 1979. Its cover is often dominated by colour photographs and large headlines, with no actual text. Typical weekday issues consist of eighty pages, made up more or less

equally of a main news section and extra supplements on topics such as sport, health and small advertisements. Its more expensively priced Sunday issue typically comprises 144 pages, including a colour magazine. The target readership includes young and middle-aged upper-working class people and its content is largely of Portuguese relevance with little international news outside that emanating from the former Portuguese colonies.

658   **O Dia.** (The Day.)
Lisbon: Fólio, 1975- . daily.

A rather sober daily tabloid morning newspaper with heavy coverage of Portuguese politics. Indeed, much of its photographic content consists of politicians' faces. It does, however, include less weighty matters such as sport, albeit on a smaller scale than most of its competitors.

659   **O Diabo: semánario.** (The Devil: Weekly.)
Lisbon: Edições V. L., 1976- . weekly.

Published every Tuesday, this Lisbon tabloid is more expensive than its weekly and daily rivals yet achieves a respectable circulation of 38,900 (1996). Its forty-eight pages lack colour and contain an often irreverent look at domestic politics, with minimal reference to international news.

660   **Diário de Notícias.** (Daily News.)
Lisbon: Diário de Notícias, 1864- . daily.

Founded by Eduardo Coelho in 1864, this is Lisbon's oldest and most well-known morning national newspaper. Now a tabloid, with a circulation of 62,758 (1996), it is available in Britain and in electronic form. A forty-eight page main section is augmented by a differently themed supplement each day of the week. It is strong on sports coverage as well as more serious national and international news. Colour is used on its front and back pages and for its weather page, as well as for its Sunday supplement.

661   **Diário de Notícias: primeira página, 1864-1994.** (Daily News: front page, 1864-1994.)
António Rego Chaves, Mário Bettencourt Resendes.   Lisbon: Editorial Notícias, 1994. 288p.

A large-format reproduction of over 200 front pages from editions of Lisbon's leading morning newspaper, the *Diário de Notícias*. It adds examples of front pages from the period 1985-94, some of which are in colour, to those previously published in the same format in *Diário de Notícias: primeira página, 1864-1984*, edited by António Valdemar and Mário Mesquita (Lisbon: Editorial Notícias, 1984).

662   **Expresso.** (Express.)
Lisbon: Grupo Controljornal, 1973- . weekly.

Founded shortly before the Portuguese Revolution of 1974, *Expresso* has grown to be one of Portugal's most respected newspapers. It appears every Saturday, with an array of supplements to its broadsheet main section which can total nine or more. The paper can often comprise well over 300 pages of tabloid and broadsheet content. As well as its depth of reporting in current domestic and international affairs, the paper is strong in its arts and literary coverage. Its circulation of nearly 166,020 (1996) is the largest for a weekly newspaper in Lisbon and its readership is predominantly educated or business orientated. A superb, full-colour guide to the Lisbon area, the *Guia Expresso das cidades e vilas históricas de Portugal, 15, Lisboa, Sintra e Cascais* (Expresso guide to the historic cities and towns of Portugal, 15, Lisbon, Sintra and Cascais) (126p. maps) was published as a supplement to the newspaper in August 1996.

663 **O Independente: semánario de informação geral.** (The Independent: general information weekly.)
    Lisbon: O Independente, 1977- . weekly.
An independent weekly (Friday) newspaper which now enjoys a circulation of 115,000 (1996) and is particularly strong in its political, economic and financial coverage. Tabloid in format, with colour photography on its cover and a separate colour supplement entitled *Vida* (Life), it can provide well over 150 pages of reading to its predominantly middle-class readership.

664 **A palavra 'Lisboa' na história do jornalismo.** (The word 'Lisbon' in the history of newspapers.)
    Albino Lapa.   Lisbon: Câmara Municipal de Lisboa, 1967. 233p. bibliog.
A catalogue of newspapers published in and about Lisbon from the 17th century to 1952. It excludes Lisbon's national titles such as the *Diário de Notícias*. Although most of the titles are naturally Portuguese, the list does include a number of English and French newspapers published in Lisbon from the 19th century onwards. Dates of first issue and details of publisher, frequency and publishing history are given for each title.

665 **The *Gazetas de Lisboa*: an archive of Portugal.**
    Jane Manaster.   *Portuguese Studies*, vol. 9 (1993), p. 149-59.
In 1921 the University of Texas Library, at Austin, acquired a nearly complete run of the weekly newspaper, the *Gazeta de Lisboa*, which ran from 1715 to 1833. Manaster surveys the collection's content, with its mix of routine news of the Portuguese Court and shipping movements, alongside more striking reports of *autos-da-fé*, the Napoleonic Wars and exotic overseas developments. There is also extensive coverage of the 1755 Lisbon earthquake. Manaster's article includes various illustrations from the *Gazeta*.

666 **The *Gazetas de Lisboa*: introduction to an eighteenth-century newspaper archive.**
    Jane Manaster.   *Iberian Studies,* vol. 16, no. 1-2 (1987), p. 103-14.
An account of the almost complete holdings of the *Gazetas de Lisboa* held in the archives of the University of Texas. Manaster argues that these are a particularly rich resource for historians because of the destruction of so much other documentary and printed material by the Lisbon earthquake of 1755.

Newspapers

667   **O Público.** (The Public.)
Lisbon: O Público, 1990- . weekly.
A serious national newspaper which appears every day including Sundays, founded in Lisbon in 1990. Its average daily circulation of 75,303 (1996) is now ahead of the long-time leader, the *Diário de Notícias* (see item no. 660). Its audience is predominantly from the educated and professional classes and the paper has extensive domestic political and economic coverage. A colour magazine (c.80 pages) is produced in the Sunday edition but, otherwise, colour is used sparingly. *O Público* was one of the first Portuguese papers to appear in an electronic version.

668   **O Semanário.** (The Weekly.)
Lisbon: Semanário Sociedade Editora, 1985- . weekly.
A three-part weekly paper, which appears on Saturdays. It comprises a main news section, a features supplement which principally contains serious articles but also includes television listings and 'soap' plot summaries, and a glossy colour tabloid magazine. The magazine, entitled *Olá Semanário,* tends to concentrate on news of media celebrities, albeit on a smaller scale than its Spanish model, *Holá.* The main and features sections use colour on their front pages where the only text is headlines. The three sections typically comprise a total of 180 pages. The paper has a circulation of 75,000 (1996), chiefly in the middle to upper socioeconomic strata of the population.

669   **What next in Lisbon?**
Diana Smith.   *Index on Censorship*, vol. 4, no. 3 (Autumn 1975), p. 26-32.
The first of three articles by Smith surveying the Lisbon newspaper publishing scene in the wake of the Portuguese Revolution of April 1974. It comprises an interview with Francisco Pinto Balsemão, editor of *Expresso* (*see* item no. 662), which emphasizes the problems encountered with the State censorship system before 1974. The second article, 'Turmoil in Portugal' (*Index on Censorship*, vol. 4, no. 4 [Winter 1975], p. 15-22), is an analysis of Lisbon newspaper press ownership and an outline of the celebrated case of the Lisbon left-wing newspaper, *República*, whose production staff seized editorial control in the post-Revolutionary period of socialist idealism in 1975. The third, 'Letter from Portugal' (*Index on Censorship*, vol. 5, no. 2 [Summer 1976], p. 35-40), discusses Lisbon newspaper publishing in 1976, followed by an exchange of letters between Smith and Peter Sedgwick on Lisbon newspapers and the dispute over Rádio Renascença.

670   **Tal & Qual.** (This and That.)
Lisbon: Repórteres Associados, [1980]- . weekly.
A popular weekly tabloid, appearing every Friday and enjoying a circulation of 82,000 (1996), despite its modest number of pages (typically twenty plus a sixteen page supplement). However, these are mostly filled with text rather than advertisements. It is a popular newspaper with an interest in social campaigns rather than heavyweight political analysis. Although it has considerable coverage of television programmes, it is far less obsessed with that medium than its British tabloid equivalents. Colour is used on its cover pages.

Lisboa: imagens d'*A Capital*. (Lisbon: images from *A Capital*.)
See item no. 38.

Imagem: jornal do Aeroporto de Lisboa. Lisbon Airport Journal.
See item no. 465.

Benfica: Semanário do Sport Lisboa e Benfica. (Benfica: Weekly Newspaper of the Sport Lisboa e Benfica Club.)
See item no. 613.

Sporting.
See item no. 620.

Periodicals

671 **Agenda Cultural.** (Cultural Diary.)
   Lisbon: Pelouro da Cultura, Câmara Municipal de Lisboa, [1989]- .
   monthly.

The official publication of the Lisbon City Council (CML), which is also available via the Internet. In its customary eighty to a hundred pages, it provides illustrated details of current and forthcoming cultural events in Lisbon such as exhibitions, ballets, concerts, sports and meetings. There are also regular sections on books, records and cassettes, as well as extensive listings of libraries, museums and gardens. There are regular features on individual city parishes, libraries and museums. Although the text is in Portuguese, the transport directions to all of the many exhibition, concert and museum venues are given in English too.

672 **The British Historical Society of Portugal Annual Report and Review.**
   Lisbon: The British Historical Society of Portugal, 1974- . annual.

The British Historical Society of Portugal has grown since its foundation in 1974 to a body of nearly 300 members, mostly from the expatriate English community in Portugal. Despite its somewhat formal title, its journal has developed into an important historical periodical, attracting contributions from internationally-known scholars as well as local experts. Well over half of its articles are on aspects of Lisbon's history. Each volume comprises 150 pages, although initial issues were somewhat thinner. An index to the first twenty-one numbers is to be found in the 22nd *Report*, published in 1996.

673 **Cultura.** (Culture.)
   London: Portugal 600, 1986- . irregular.

An English-language arts magazine published by the cultural organization, Portugal 600. It is the best source in Britain for news and articles on artistic and cultural events in Lisbon, in particular, and Portugal, in general. The Spring 1994 issue, for example, has much on Lisbon's role as European Capital of Culture.

674 **The Historical Society, Lisbon Branch, Annual Report.**
Lisbon, London: Historical Society, Lisbon Branch, 1937-54. annual.
This body, an offshoot of the London-based Historical Society, was formed by the British community in Lisbon and was the forerunner of the British Historical Society of Portugal (BHSP). Its *Annual Report* includes English-language articles on Anglo-Portuguese history, with particular emphasis on buildings, events or persons connected with Lisbon. An index to the *Report* for the period 1937-54 is to be found in the BHSP's *Nineteenth annual report and review, 1992*, published in 1993 (see item no. 672).

675 **Lisboa: Revista Municipal.** (Lisbon: Municipal Review.)
Lisbon: Câmara Municipal de Lisboa, 1939-73; 1979-88.
This publication of the Lisbon city council underwent a number of changes of format and title in its long history. It was formerly known as *Revista Municipal*, which subsequently became its subtitle. It is an outstandingly rich source of information on the history of Lisbon, and its pictorial content increased in its latter years. In fact, the more recent volumes included a number of good quality photographs, many in colour, as well as drawings, to accompany the essays on past and present aspects of Lisbon which appeared in each issue.

676 **Analíticos da *Revista Municipal*, 1939-1973.** (Index to the *Revista Municipal*, 1939-73.)
Edited by Maria da Assunção Judice Moreira, with Eunice Relvas.
Lisbon: Gabinete de Estudos Olisiponenses/Câmara Municipal de Lisboa, 1991. 189p. (Estudos Olisiponenses, no. 1).
A thorough index, albeit arranged in a non-chronological order, of articles published in the *Revista Municipal* from 1939 to 1973. The *Revista Municipal* was dedicated to material relating to the history and life of Lisbon, and it was later renamed *Lisboa: Revista Municipal* (see item no. 675).

677 **Olisipo: Boletim do Grupo Amigos de Lisboa.** (Lisbon: Journal of the Group Friends of Lisbon.)
Lisbon: Grupo Amigos de Lisboa, 1938-85.
The organ of Lisbon's most celebrated local historical and cultural association, the Amigos de Lisboa (Friends of Lisbon). Its contributors included many of the major names of Lisbon's historiography.

678 **What's on in Lisbon, Estoril, Sintra, Blue Coast.**
Lisbon: Publiotel, 1985?- . monthly.
A useful monthly magazine produced for English-speaking visitors to Lisbon, its hinterland and the Blue Coast area around Setúbal, across the River Tagus. It includes maps of Lisbon in each issue and texts on the tourist sights and museums of Lisbon. Sections on leisure, gastronomy, shopping and accommodation are also included. Illustrations are in black and white but are not always very clear. However, the up-to-date text and lists of events make this an invaluable publication for the visitor.

Encyclopaedias

679 **The Encyclopaedia Britannica: a dictionary of arts, sciences and general literature. Volume XIV.**
Edinburgh: Adam & Charles Black, 1882. 9th ed. p. 690-93. 2 maps.

One of the most reliable sources of information on Lisbon over the last century has been the *Encyclopaedia Britannica* and arguably the editions of 1882 and 1911 were the most impressive in this respect. In the 1882 edition, a general overview of Lisbon is provided (p. 690-93) which includes its geological situation and a review of its history. Although a 'great improvement' is noted in the city's cleanliness, the tone is somewhat dismissive in respect of its commercial facilities and the city is portrayed as 'destitute of high works of art'. In the *Supplement*, which is also designated the tenth edition (vol. XXX, 1903), new roads, buildings and organizations are described and updated statistics are provided. A more positive and informed approach is to be found in the eleventh edition (vol. XVI, 1911, p. 771-73. bibliog.). *The New Encyclopaedia Britannica* (1987) has a brief entry in the *Micropaedia* (vol. 7, p. 392) and a further entry in the *Macropaedia* (vol. 23, p. 81-85, bibliog.) which is divided into sections on 'Physical and Human Geography', and on 'History'.

680 **Grande enciclopédia portuguesa e brasileira.** (Great Portuguese and Brazilian encyclopaedia.)
Lisbon: Editorial Enciclopédia, c.1945-60. 40 vols.

The standard Portuguese encyclopaedia. The main entry on Lisbon is extensive (vol. XV, p. 190-295) and has a lengthy and wide-ranging bibliography, as well as several colour maps. The text contains separate sections on history, religion and other aspects of the city as well as a number of monochrome illustrations. The *Apéndice* (Appendix) (vols. XXXIX and XL, p. 946-54 and p. 71-3, c.1960), contains updated information and statistics on the city, a map of the underground railway system and photographs of new buildings in areas such as Areeiro and the University of Lisbon.

681   **Notice inédite sur Lisbonne en 1781.** (Unpublished information on
      Lisbon in 1781.)
      Catherine Petit.   *Bulletin des Études Portugaises et Brésiliennes*,
      vol. 35-36 (1974-75), p. 92-120.

In the latter part of the 18th century, when a reworking of Diderot and d'Alembert's
famous *Encyclopédie* was being planned under the title *Encyclopédie méthodique*, one
of its organizers, Robert de Vaugondy, wrote to the newly-formed Academia das
Ciências de Lisboa with a series of questions about Lisbon. Answering these queries
was partly assigned to a priest, José Corrêa da Serra. Petit here reproduces Serra's
extensive reply which takes the form of a description of Lisbon in the decades after
the earthquake. This covers the rebuilding programme in Lisbon, the spread of
population from the city to the suburbs, the Lisbon aqueduct, the activities of the
Academia das Ciências and reference to Sintra. Unfortunately, these details were not
included in the work when published, owing to a change in editorial personnel.

Bibliographies and Catalogues

682 **Bibliografia geográfica de Portugal. Segundo volume, 1947-1974.**
(Geographical bibliography of Portugal, volume two, 1947-74.)
Ilídio do Amaral, Suzanne Daveau.   Lisbon: Centro de Estudos
Geográficos, 1982. 427p.

A sequel to the *Bibliografia geográfica de Portugal* (Lisbon: Instituto para a Alta
Cultura, 1948. 256p.) by Hermann Lautensach and Mariano Feio. This comprehensive
bibliography includes references to almost 200 periodical articles and books on Lisbon,
most of which are accompanied by a brief description of their content. Since 1975 the
bibliography has been updated in the Lisbon geographical periodical, *Finisterra*.

683 **Exposição olisiponense: catálogo.** (Lisbon exhibition: catalogue.)
Biblioteca Nacional de Lisboa.   Lisbon: Biblioteca Nacional de
Lisboa, 1948. 207p. bibliog.

Although primarily intended to accompany an exhibition in Lisbon's National Library,
this catalogue of 811 items also effectively constitutes one of the most comprehensive
published bibliographies of Lisbon to date. The items are listed in chronological
sections from the origins of Lisbon to the Salazar era. Name, title and subject indexes
are provided.

684 **Bibliografia do rio Tejo: margens e núcleos urbanos ribeirinhos.**
(Bibliography of the river Tagus: river banks and riverside towns.)
Judite Dória.   Lisbon: Urbe, Ministério das Obras Públicas,
Transportes e Comunicações, [1990]. 561p.

An extensive bibliography of 2,679 items relating to the River Tagus which flows past
Lisbon into the nearby Atlantic Ocean, near Lisbon. The entries are not annotated and
the only subject arrangement is the assignment of each entry to one of fifteen headings
in a subject index. This results in some impractically long lists of numbers under
particular subject headings, with, for example, some 1,200 such entries under
'História e Arqueologia' (History and Archaeology). An author index and a list of
item numbers in chronological order complete the volume.

206

685 **Subsídios para a bibliografia da história local portuguesa.**
(Contributions to the bibliography of Portuguese local history.)
António Mesquita de Figueiredo.   Lisbon: Biblioteca Nacional, 1933.
425p.

This volume lists, by regions, items for the most part held in the Biblioteca Nacional de Lisboa, including a small number of manuscript items as well as printed materials. There are nearly 400 entries for Lisbon (p. 176-219) and a further five in an appendix (p. 389-90) but there also many separate sections for nearby areas such as Belas, Benfica, Carnide, Cascais, Odivelas, Sintra and the Tejo (Tagus) river. Therefore, this constitutes one of the largest published bibliographies of Lisbon. The compiler was head of the history and geography sections of the Biblioteca Nacional.

686 **Bibliographie des voyages en Espagne et en Portugal.** (Bibliography of travels in Spain and Portugal.)
Raymond Foulché-Delbosc.   Paris: A. Picard, 1896. 349p. (Revue Hispanique, vol. 3).

An invaluable chronological bibliography of 858 items which includes more than sixty travellers' accounts of Lisbon in English, as well as numerous accounts in French, German and other languages. As the beginning of each title's entry comprises a clear list of the towns and cities described within the publication, it is relatively easy to locate those relating to Lisbon. However, an overall index of such places would have further facilitated usage. Full authorship and bibliographical details are provided. A reprint was published in 1969 (Amsterdam: Meridian).

687 **Bibliografia sobre Lisboa.** (Bibliography of Lisbon.)
Vanda de Freitas.   Lisbon: Pelouro Cultura, Divisão de Biblioteca e Documentação, Câmara Municipal de Lisboa, 1992. 54p.

Compiled by the chief librarian of Lisbon's municipal libraries, this unannotated bibliography of eighty-six Portuguese items is intended primarily for teachers and their pupils, but also serves as a most useful introduction to the key works on Lisbon for anyone with an interest in the city. It has seven illustrations which are chiefly historical photographs of Lisbon's street and river life. An appendix usefully lists the addresses of thirty libraries in Lisbon.

688 **Catalogue of the Library of the Instituto Britânico em Portugal (and supplement).**
Instituto Britânico em Portugal, compiled by Carlos G. Estorninho.
Lisbon: Instituto Britânico em Portugal, 1944. 288p.

The Library was founded in November 1938 and the main catalogue here lists some 6,000 volumes, arranged by classified order. The supplement includes a further 1,600 items added to the Library up to July 1945. These catalogues are of importance, above all, for their indication of the range of material available in Lisbon for those Portuguese citizens interested in British culture. However, the inclusion of catalogues of Anglo-Portuguese material and of publications of the Portuguese Propaganda Department also reflects the comparable need of English visitors and residents in Lisbon for material on Portugal.

689   **Instituto Britânico em Portugal, XX aniversário. Exposição de vinte anos de actividade editorial luso-britânica, 1938-1958: catálogo.** (British Institute in Portugal, 20th anniversary. Exhibition of twenty years of Luso-British publishing activity, 1938-58: catalogue.) Instituto Britânico em Portugal.   Lisbon: British Council, 1958. 48p.

A bibliography of 1,037 publications grouped into categories which include Portuguese translations of English works and English translations of Portuguese works and over 130 English works on Portugal, including many titles about Lisbon. Despite its age, this remains one of the best single bibliographical sources for English-language works on the city.

690   **Lisbon and the English. Catalogue of an exhibition of books, pictures and historical documents organized by the Lisbon Branch of the English Historical Association at the Instituto Britânico em Portugal, Rua de Fernandes, 3, Lisbon, May 10th – May 23rd.** Instituto Britânico em Portugal.   Lisbon: Instituto Britânico, [1947]. 23p.

An invaluable source for the English student of Lisbon which lists 176 books, mostly in English, exhibited in the 800th anniversary year of the English crusaders' involvement in the reconquest of Lisbon from the Moors. The entries are arranged by author within sections which are ordered chronologically according to the historical period of their subject matter. A further twenty-nine exhibits from the archives of the Lisbon Branch of the English Historical Association are also noted.

691   **Spanish and Portuguese Jewry: a classified bibliography.** Robert Singerman.   Westport, Connecticut; London: Greenwood Press, 1993. 720p. (Bibliographies and Indexes in World History, no. 30).

A bibliography which includes approximately fifty references to Jews in Lisbon. It supplements the same compiler's *The Jews in Spain and Portugal: a bibliography* (New York; London: Garland, 1975. 365p.), which has another forty, earlier, entries relating to Lisbon's Jewish population.

692   **Portugal.** P. T. H. Unwin.   Oxford; Santa Barbara, California; Denver, Colorado: Clio Press, 1987. 269p. map. bibliog. (World Bibliographical Series, vol. 71).

A companion volume to the present bibliography, which embraces the whole of Portugal. It contains 787 entries and approximately 100 of these are included in the index under 'Lisbon'. It is preceded by a substantial introductory essay on the country and its history. A combined author, title and subject index completes the volume.

Appendix: Portuguese Works on Lisbon

Readers of Portuguese may wish to go beyond this bibliography to consult some of the major works on Lisbon written in that language which are not included within the scope of the foregoing bibliography. The following is a selective list of major authors and titles:

Palácios reais de Lisboa: os dois paços de Xabregas, o de S. Bartolomeu e o da Alcáçova. (Royal palaces of Lisbon: the two palaces of Xabregas, that of S. Bartolomeu and the Moorish castle.) Manuel Vaz Ferreira de Andrade.   Lisbon: Editorial Império, 1949. 144p. maps. bibliog.; Lisbon: Vega, 1990. new ed. 159p. maps. bibliog.

Legendas de Lisboa. (Legends of Lisbon.) Norberto de Araújo.   Lisbon: SPN, 1943. 215p.; Lisbon: Vega, 1994. 2nd ed. 218p.

Peregrinações em Lisboa. (Pilgrimages in Lisbon.) Norberto de Araújo.   Lisbon: Parceria A. M. Pereira, 1938. 15 vols.; Lisbon: Vega, 1992. new ed. 15 vols.

Lisboa do passado, Lisboa de nossos dias. (Bygone Lisbon, today's Lisbon.) José Joaquim Gomes de Brito.   Lisbon: Livraria Ferin, 1911. 182p.

Arquivo alfacinha. (Lisbon archive.) Francisco Câncio.   Lisbon: Imprensa Barreiro, 1953-54. 2 vols.

Lisboa no tempo do Passeio Público. (Lisbon at the time of the Passeio Público.)
Francisco Câncio.   Lisbon, 1962-63. 2 vols.

Lisboa d'outros tempos. (Lisbon in bygone times.)
J. Pinto de Carvalho (*Tinop*).   Lisbon: Parceria António Maria Pereira, 1898-99. 2 vols.; Lisbon: Fenda, 1991. new ed. 2 vols.

Lisboa antiga: primeira parte, o Bairro Alto. (Old Lisbon: first part, the Bairro Alto.)
Júlio de Castilho.   Lisbon: Typographia Academia Real das Sciências, 1879. 360p.; Lisbon: Câmara Municipal de Lisboa, 1954-66. 3rd ed. 5 vols. bibliog.

Lisboa antiga: segunda parte, bairros orientais. (Old Lisbon: second part, eastern districts.)
Júlio de Castilho.   Coimbra, Portugal: Imprensa da Universidade, 1884. 7 vols. bibliog.; Lisbon: Câmara Municipal de Lisboa, 1935-39. 2nd ed. 12 vols. bibliog.

A ribeira de Lisboa: descripção histórica da margem do Tejo desde a Madre-de-Deus até Santos-o-Velho. (The Lisbon riverside: historical description of the Tagus riverside from Madre de Deus to Santos-o-Velho.)
Júlio de Castilho.   Lisbon: Imprensa Nacional, 1893. 750p.; Lisbon: Câmara Municipal, 1940. 2nd ed. 5 vols. bibliog.

Lisboa dos nossos avós. (Lisbon of our forefathers.)
Júlio Dantas.   Lisbon: Câmara Municipal de Lisboa, 1966. 280p.

Lisboa do meu tempo e do passado. (Lisbon in my lifetime and in the past.)
João Paulo Freire (*Mário*).   Lisbon: Parceria António Maria Pereira, 1930. 2 vols.

Páginas olisiponenses. (Lisbon pages.)
David Lopes.   Lisbon: Câmara Municipal, 1968. 279p. maps. bibliog.

Lisboa de lés a lés: subsídios para a história das vias públicas da cidade. (Lisbon from one end to the other: contributions to the history of the public thoroughfares of the city.)
Luís Pastor de Macedo.   Lisbon: Câmara Municipal de Lisboa, 1940-42. 5 vols.; Lisbon: Câmara Municipal de Lisboa, 1981. 3rd ed. 5 vols.

A nossa Lisboa: novidades antigas. (Our Lisbon: old news.)
Luís Pastor de Macedo, Gustavo de Matos Sequeira.   Lisbon:
Portugália, 1945. 412p.

Arquivo municipal de Lisboa. (Municipal archive of Lisbon.)
Eduardo Freire de Oliveira.   Lisbon: Typographia Universal, 1882-1911.
17 vols.

O Carmo e a Trindade: subsídios para a história de Lisboa. (Carmo
and Trindade districts: contributions to the history of Lisbon.)
Gustavo de Matos Sequeira.   Lisbon: Câmara Municipal de Lisboa,
1939-41. 3 vols. maps. bibliog.

**Depois do terremoto: subsídios para a história dos bairros ocidentais
de Lisboa.** (After the earthquake: contributions towards the history of the
western districts of Lisbon.)
Gustavo de Matos Sequeira.   Lisbon: Academia das Ciências, 1916-22.
3 vols.; Lisbon: Academia das Ciências, 1967. new ed. 4 vols.

A cerca fernandina de Lisboa. (King Fernando's walls around Lisbon.)
Augusto Vieira da Silva.   Lisbon: Câmara Municipal de Lisboa,
1948-49. 2 vols. maps. bibliog.; Lisbon: Câmara Municipal de Lisboa,
1987. new ed. 2 vols. maps. bibliog.

A cerca moura de Lisboa: estudo histórico descritivo. (The Moorish
walls around Lisbon: historical and descriptive study.)
Augusto Vieira da Silva.   Lisbon: Typographia do Commercio, 1899.
92p. maps. bibliog.; Lisbon: Câmara Municipal de Lisboa, 1987. 3rd ed.
195p. maps. bibliog.

As muralhas da ribeira de Lisboa. (The riverside walls of Lisbon.)
Augusto Vieira da Silva.   Lisbon: Typographia do Commercio, 1900.
302p. maps. bibliog.; Lisbon: Câmara Municipal de Lisboa, 1987.
new ed. 2 vols. maps. bibliog.

Indexes

In the following pages indexes are provided by author, title and subject. As is normal practice, Portuguese compound surnames are filed under their last element, whilst the few Spanish compound surnames included are filed under their first element. Original spelling (e.g. the place-name 'Cintra') is used in the transcription of titles but modern orthography (e.g. 'Sintra') is used for surnames and headings in the subject index.

Index of Authors

214

Group of Lisbon 449
Grupo Iris 43
Guàrdia, Manuel 114
Guedes, Natália Correia 637-38
Guedes, Rui 614
Guia, A 15
Guia Turístico do Norte 111
Gulbenkian Foundation *see* Calouste Gulbenkian Foundation
Gutkind, E. A. 528

H

Hadfield, P. Heywood 284
Haeburn-Little, W. 401
Hakluyt, Richard 328
Hamady, Walter 548
Hamm, Manfred 44
Hampden, John G. 361
Hancock, Matthew 179
Hardinge, *Sir* Arthur 363
Hare, S. E. 484
Harrison, Richard J. 310
Harvard Museum 310
Hayward, Pat 350
Hebrew Union College 425
Hecht, Anthony 156
Henrey, *Mrs* Robert 285
Henriques, Guilherme J. C. 402-03
Henry, Walter 350
Hewins, Ralph 380
Hickey, William 230
Higham, Peter 615
Hill, Alison Friesinger 187-88
Hinckley, John 261
Hipergráfica 112
Historical Society (Lisbon Branch) 674
Hobbs, A. Hoyt 189
Hobhouse, John Cam 254
Hodgkinson, Patrick 516
Hofbauer, Imre 540
Hogg, Garry 286
Hogg, James 404
Holland, Clive 287

Holz, Joachim 55
Hopkinson, Tom 549
Horward, Donald 351
Howe, Marvin 188
Huber, Claude 45
Huggett, Frank E. 288
Hughes, T. M. 255
Hume, Martin 289
Humphreys, John 405
Hunt, Chris 374
Husenbeth, *Rev*. F. C. 411
Hyland, Paul 290

I

Image Bank 30
Imagem 465
Imprensa Nacional-Casa da Moeda 2, 501
Inchbold, A. C. 291
Inchbold, Stanley 291
O Independente 663
Infante, Sérgio 64-65
Inglis, Simon 616
Institut für Anglistik und Amerikanistik, Universität Salzburg 404
Instituto Britânico em Portugal 464, 688-90
Instituto Camões 574
Instituto da Biblioteca Nacional e do Livro 2, 571, 574, 629, 683, 685
Instituto de Cultura Portuguesa 6
Instituto de Investigação Científica e Tropical 533
Instituto Português de Museus 324, 339, 593, 595, 637, 640, 644
Instituto Português do Património Arquitectónico e Arqueológico 99
Instituto Português do Património Cultural 89, 233, 418
International Conference on Environmental Pollution 485

International Congress of Medicine (1906) 284
Iria, Alberto 532
Isar, Yudhishtar R. 639
Israel, Alec 186

J

Jacinto, Jorge M. Laureano 190
Jackson, Catherine Charlotte, *Lady* 256
Jacob, Neto 57
James, Henry C. 16
Janeiro, Helena Pinto 83-84
Janeiro, Maria de Lurdes 512-13
Jardine, Alexander 231
Jesuits *see* Societas Iesu
Johnson, Charles 257
Johnson, Samuel 551
Johnston, F. R. 406
Jordan, Annemarie 583
Jorge, Filipe 46, 134
Jump, John 538
Junta Distrital de Lisboa 486
Junta de Freguesia de São Domingos de Benfica 80
Junta de Investigações do Ultramar 551

K

Kaplan, Marion 17, 188, 191
Keene, *Sir* Benjamin 340
Keith, Henry H. 445
Kelting, Margaret 386
Kempner, Mary Jean 292
Kendrick, T. D. 146
Kennedy, *Dr* 437
Kenyon, Graham 179
Kersten, M. 485
Keymer, Tom 546
Khorian, Michael 192
Kincaid, J. 352
King, B. R. 478

Michell, *Rev.* John 149
Mickle, William Julius 551
Miguéis, José Rodrigues 572
Milford, John 264
Millar, D. A. 402
Minister of Culture (Spain) 308
Ministério das Obras Públicas 473, 684
Mira, Margarida 584
Missler, Eva 169
Mohammadi, Kamin 181
Moita, Irisalva 344, 497, 641-43
Monclús, Francisco Javier 114
Monro, Donald 440
Montez, R. Freire 646
Morais, António Manuel 618
Morant, Geoffrey 475
Moreira, António Montes 408
Moreira, Maria da Assunção Júdice 676
Moreira, Rafael 409
Morris, M. O'Connor 265
Moser, F. de Mello 552
Moser, Gerald M. 560
Mota, João Abreu 215
Moura, F. 429
Muir, Hugh 371
Mullin, John K. 529
Murphy, James 21, 232
Museu da Cidade 344
Museu de Artes Plásticas dos Coruchéus 22
Museu de Marinha 649
Museu do Chiado 644
Museu Nacional de Arqueologia 311
Museu Nacional de Arqueologia e Etnologia 645
Myhill, Henry 23

N

National Maritime Museum, London 472

Naval Intelligence Division 62
Navy Records Society 330
Neale, Adam 353
Neale, John 164
Nederlands Architectuur Instituut 511
Neill, Peter 646
Neves, José C. 505
Neves, Paula 30
Newby, Eric 298
Norris, A. H. 354, 441
Norton, F. J. 652
Nozes, Judite 150
Nunes, Carlos 199

O

Oakley, R. J. 326
Observatório do Infante D. Luís 127
Observer 298
Ogden, Bob 468
Oldknow, *Rev.* Joseph 266
Oldroyd, D. R. 153
Olisipo 677
Oliveira, Cristina 30
Oliveira, J. Tiago de 532
Oliveira, José Augusto 320
Oliveira, Luís Filipe Cândido de 171
Oliveira, *Frei* Nicolau de 329
O'Loughlin, Michael 511
O'Neill, Alexandre 60
O'Neill, Thomas 356
Orange Guide 200
Orders, d'Arcy 386-88, 410, 434, 606, 619
Orey, Leonel d' 593
Oyón, José Luis 114

P

Page, Frederick 538
Paiva, Niza 96
Palácio Nacional da Ajuda 364
Palácio Nacional de Sintra 91

Pardoe, Julia 24
Parker, John 570
Passos, José Manuel de Silva 51
Pavão, Luís 52
Peabody Museum of Archaeology and Ethnology 310
Pearce, E. A. 131
Pecchio, Giuseppe 267
Peck, William Henry 553
Pedreirinho, José Manuel 517
Pelouro da Cultura da Câmara Municipal de Lisboa *see* Câmara Municipal de Lisboa
Pena, António 97
Perdigão, José de Azeredo 384
Pereira, Arturo D. 101
Pereira, Camacho 53
Pereira, E. J. 151
Pereira, João Castel-Branco 594-95
Pereira, Michel Toussaint Alves 519
Pereira, Pedro Telhado 528
Pereira, Rui Viana 171
Pérez Castillo, Susan 597
Pesquiet, Renée Foulomeau 35
Pessoa, Fernando Nogueira 201, 573-75
Petit, Catherine 681
Petre, Edward 411
Philip, *Prince, Duke of Edinburgh* 387
Phillips, Ron 475
Piçarra, Mariano 54
Pillement, Georges 202
Pimenta, Alberto 43
Pinheiro, Patricia McGowan 564
Pinto, Maria do Rosário 97
Pinto, Natália 166
Piper, Anson C. 576
Pires, Maria Laura Bettencourt 233
Pires, Mário 134

219

Smollett, Tobias George 558
Soares, Mário 211
Sobel, Lester A. 374
Sociedade de Gestão e Investimento Imobilário 515
Sociedade Lisboa '94 81, 429, 490
Societas Iesu 417
Soczka, Luís 433
Sors, A. I. 483
Soucek, Priscilla 636
Sousa, Maria Leonor Machado de 150
Sousa, Vicente de 57
Southey, Robert 236-38
Spanish Ministry of Culture 308
Sporting Clube de Portugal 620
Sport Lisboa e Benfica 613
Stadtler, Christa 654
Steele, Colin 630
Stetler, Susan L. 29
Stevens, Ann 564
Stewart, Frances Anne, *Marchioness of Londonderry* 277
Stoop, Anne de 211, 498
Stoqueler, *Mr* 154
Stradling, R. A. 121
Stranger's guide in Lisbon 165
Street, James C. 272
Stubbs, William 322
Sucena, Eduardo 314
Summavielle, Elísio 418
Swanton, E. W. 621
Swift, Patrick 301
Symington, Martin 212

T

Tabucchi, Antonio 557, 581
Tal & Qual 670
Tamen, Pedro 596
Tavares, Aderito 213
Taylor, Kathleen Joan 178

Taylor, L. C. 221, 574
Teixeira, Nuno Severiano 103
Teixeira, Paula 496
Teles, Maria Inácia 304
Telfer, William 419
Tennyson, Alfred *Lord* 273
Tennyson, Hallam 274
Terol, Marylène 598
Thackeray, William 276
Thomas, Gordon Kent 275, 361
Thorburn, Patricia 600
Thornton, Grace 242, 606
Tilley, Bruce 475
Tillotson, John R. 444
Times 98, 622
Titmarsh, M. A. 276
Tole, *Rev.* John 300
Tostões, Ana Cristina 512
Toussaint, Michel 490
Trigueiros, Luís Forjaz 30, 58
Tucker, Alan 214
Tudella, José 448
Tuohy, Frank 41
Twiss, Richard 240
Tzschaschel, Sabine 174

U

Unwin, P. T. H. 692
Urban, Sylvanus 144
Ushaw College, Durham 393, 413, 415

V

Valdemar, António 577-78
Vale, José Picas do 650
Vane, Charles William, *Marquess of Londonderry* 277, 359
Vargas, José Manuel 74-76
Vasconcelos, Luís 626
Vasconcelos, Pedro de 215

Velasco, Emília Maria 463
Venturi, Francesco 491
Verde, Cesário 582
Verga, Solomon ibn 425
Vetch, John 567-68
Vidal, Manuela Pina 216
Vidler, Steve 217
Vieira, Alice 59
Vieira, Víctor Manuel Lopes 599
Vincent, Mary 121
Vizetelly, Henry 610
Voigt, James 390
Voltaire, François Marie Arouet de 156, 558

W

Walford, A. R. 464
Ward, Lynd 156
Watson, Walter Crum 499
Weightman, Jonathan 47
Weinstein, Donald 327
Wells, John Edwin 360
Wernham, R. B. 330
Wesley, John 157
West, S. George 551
Wheatley, Henry B. 345
Wheeler, Nik 192
White, Gordon Barclay 621
Whitefield, George 158, 413, 420
Wilde, W. R. 278
Wilkinson, Julia 217
Williams, Allan M. 430-31
Williams, *Rev.* H. F. Fulford 316, 421
Williams, *Rev.* Michael E. 331, 422-23
Williams, Roger 187
Willis, R. C. 569
Wilson, Fran 559
Winkworth, D. W. 482
Wohl, Alice 60
Wohl, Hellmut 60, 507
Wolfall, Richard 159
Wood, Kate 218
Wood, Ruth Kedzie 219
Woods, Pat 617

221

Index of Titles

S

Index of Subjects

Belém *contd.*
18th century 4, 223,
231-32, 234-35, 240,
343, 345, 523, 555,
619
19th century 161, 246,
249, 251-52, 255,
258, 260, 264, 268,
271, 276, 278, 346,
350, 353, 355, 480
20th century 3, 23, 26,
82, 174, 192, 208,
216, 286, 289, 291,
295, 299, 302, 467,
499, 510, 525
art 585
Centro Cultural 82, 508,
515
climate 128
gardens 623, 625
museums 633, 637,
650
Palácio de 82, 235, 504,
637
photographs 41, 48-49,
58
pollution 483
ships 471
Torre de 2, 21, 82, 234,
256, 293, 341, 480,
500, 639
see also Jerónimos,
Mosteiro dos
Belém, Madame de 252
Belenenses 82, 616
Belmonte, Palácio 85
Belvederes 67, 72
Bemposta, Palácio 586
Benavente 136
Benedictines 443
Benfica 74, 80, 165, 202,
442, 489, 492, 505,
685
climate 125
Benfica (football club) *see*
Sport Lisboa e
Benfica
Berardo, José 649
Berlengas Islands 306
Bern 399
Biarritz 124
Bible 246
Bibliographies 25, 682-91

Biblioteca Municipal de
Lisboa 687
Biblioteca Nacional de
Lisboa *see* Instituto
da Biblioteca
Nacional e do Livro
Bica 77
Biographies 375-84
Birds 257, 305-06, 483
see also Flora and fauna
Bishops 408
Blacklowism 413-14
Blake, *Admiral* 332, 338,
341
Blakeston, Oswell 286
Blankett, John 7
Blue Coast (Setúbal) 678
Boa Hora 325
Boer War 316
Bologna 327
Bom Sucesso, Convento
do 515, 586
Books 285, 344, 571, 652,
671
Bordeaux 242
Boswell, James 437
Botanic Gardens *see*
Jardim Botânico
Botany 261, 271, 303, 533
Botelho, Carlos 587
Bower, Archibald 158
Braga 291
Braganza Hotel 273
Brazil
18th century 339, 454,
456
19th century 258, 267,
356, 358, 445, 533
architecture 491-92
aviation 466-67, 650
Bridge *see* Ponte 25 de
Abril
Bridgettines 234, 238,
393, 404, 406, 411-12
Brigittines *see*
Bridgettines
Bristol 236
Britannia, HMS 243
British Assembly 386
British Broadcasting
Corporation 655
British Club *see* Royal
British Club

British College *see*
English College
British Community
Council 388
British Embassy 64, 369,
372, 399, 402, 537
see also Ambassadors,
consuls and envoys
British Factory *see*
English Factory
British Historical Society
of Portugal 36, 672,
674
British Hospital 388, 436,
441, 586
British Institute *see*
Instituto Britânico
British Library 150, 325
British Museum 235, 338
British Overseas Airways
371
British Protestant School
441
Brito, J. J. Gomes de 6
Britons in Lisbon 220-21,
300, 326, 690
12th century 317-20,
322
16th century 221, 328,
330-31
18th century 223-28,
230-40
19th century 241-60,
262-66, 268-78
20th century 279-91,
293, 295-302, 655
societies 386-88, 672,
674
theatre 606
see also English
Cemetery; English
College; English
Factory
Buçaco 291
Bucelas 610-11
Buchanan, George 392,
402-03
Buenos Aires (district)
18th century 222,
227-28
19th century 245,
254-55, 258, 278
Bulgaria 558

Earthquakes *contd.*
  1755 earthquake *contd.*
    19th-century accounts
      246, 250, 353
    artistic impact 583,
      593
    geological studies
      143, 146, 148,
      151-52
    literary and
      philosophical
      impact 141, 145,
      153, 156, 551, 553,
      555, 558
    rebuilding of city
      342, 344, 378, 383,
      385, 504, 506, 521,
      523-24, 528-29
    religious impact
      157-58, 401, 406,
      420
  19th-century
    earthquakes 1, 346
  1909 earthquake 136
  1927 earthquake 300
Eastern Telegraph
  Company 619
Eccles, Sybil 369
Economics 449, 452, 461,
  663, 667
Edinburgh, *Duke of see*
  Philip, *Prince, Duke
  of Edinburgh*
Edward Augustus (former
  Duke of York) 239
Education 9, 114, 628, 638
Edward VII (former King
  of England) 73, 364,
  387
Egypt 278, 439
Egyptology 380, 384, 636
Electricity 522
Elevador de Santa Justa
  475-77, 479
Eliot, William Granville
  353
Elizabeth I (Queen of
  England, 1558-1603)
  406
Elizabeth II (Queen of
  England) 384, 586
Elvas 126, 346
Emergency Services 115

Encarnação (Bairro Alto)
  67
Encarnação (N.E. Lisbon)
  78
Encyclopaedias 679-81
Engineering 476
English Cemetery 232,
  268, 273, 316, 421,
  464, 535, 546, 585-86
English College
  18th-century accounts
    234
  19th-century accounts
    246, 251, 266, 411
  20th-century accounts
    70, 300, 393, 400-01,
    413-16, 422-23, 461,
    586
English Factory
  18th-century accounts
    144, 147, 230, 239-40
  19th-century accounts
    251, 269, 355
  20th-century accounts
    333, 386, 427-28,
    439, 441, 454-55,
    457, 461, 464
English Historical
  Association 690
English Nunnery *see*
  Bridgettines
Engravings 5, 18, 20-21,
  53, 63, 150, 232, 240,
  269, 590
Entertainment 10, 22, 29,
  104, 163, 173, 218,
  261, 678
Entre Douro-e-Minho 231
Environment 483-85
Envoys *see* Ambassadors,
  consuls and envoys
Epitaphs and inscriptions
  421, 494
Ermida, Belém 515
Escorial, El 340, 583
Espionage *see* Secret agents
Essex, *Earl of* 328, 330
Estádio da Luz 614
Estádio Nacional 485, 617
Estoril
  in prehistory 309
  19th-century accounts
    160

20th-century accounts
  16, 23, 35, 48, 92,
  173, 188, 195,
  198-99, 208, 210,
  218, 285, 291, 299,
  372
  churches 405
  climate 124-25, 130
  geology 135
  health 435
  hotels 182
  in literature 550, 554
  maps 101-05, 107-08,
    112, 119-20
  walking 88
Estrela, Rua da 441
Estrela Basilica 23, 64,
  252, 258, 260, 268,
  499
Estrela Hall 606
Estremadura 88, 128, 162,
  165, 231
Estremoz 222
Estufa Fria 303, 543, 623
Ethnography 14, 645
European Capital of
  Culture (1994) 32-33,
  496, 673
European Champions' Cup
  617
European Community 82,
  449, 515, 528
Evesham, John 328
Évora 25, 167, 334, 391,
  506
Évora, Lopo Rodrigues d'
  462
Évora, Rodrigo Lopes d'
  462
Executions 155, 325, 343
Exeter 421
Exhibitions
  archaeology 308, 311
  arts 22, 593
  books 571, 683, 689-90
  history 344, 429, 639,
    645
  photographs 32, 36
  postcards 57
  writers 233
Existentialism 582
Expo 98 30, 75, 78
Expresso 669

241

Geology 135, 143, 146, 148, 151-52, 528
George II (King of England, 1727-60) 155
German diet drink 438
Germans 285, 506, 545, 550
  Second World War 367-71, 545, 550
Gestapo 550
Gibraltar 228, 239, 249-50, 269, 275, 285
Glasgow Celtic 617
Goethe, Johann Wolfgang von 141
Gold 135, 409
Gould, R. F. 424
Government 229, 443
Graça 68
Graffiti 589
Granada 269
Grandella 511
Grand Tour 225, 345
Granja do Marquês airfield 371, 468
Greece 278, 430
Grove, F. C. 273-74
Guarini, G. 605
Guilds 445-46
Guincho 554
Guinea 409
Gulbenkian, Calouste 377, 518, 634, 636, 649
  biography 380, 382, 384
  Centro de Arte Moderna 510
  see also Calouste Gulbenkian Foundation; Gardens
Gurgeny, Hugo 395
Gypsies 8, 494

H

Haircuts 186
Hamburg 154, 261
Hampton Court, HMS 155
Handball 613
Hare, *Colonel* 243
Hay, Edward 139, 555

Health
  18th-century accounts 225, 230, 438, 440
  19th-century accounts 13, 18, 161, 245, 249, 252, 262-63, 265, 272, 274, 278, 436, 439, 442
  20th-century accounts 29, 77, 124-25, 280, 396, 427-28, 435, 437, 441, 657
Henley, *Family of* 150
Henrique, *Infante Dom* 388, 398, 452
Henrique, *Prince* 265
Henry VIII (King of England, 1509-47) 406
Henry the Navigator *see* Henrique, *Infante Dom*
Herculano, Alexandre 268
Hermitages 65, 515
Hibernia, HMS 347
Hickey, *Mrs* Charlotte 230
Hillsborough, *Earl of* 227
Hiroshima 139
Historical Society, Lisbon Branch 674
History 7-8, 21, 25, 41, 50, 56, 60, 62, 162, 179, 181, 187, 191, 198, 209, 218, 255, 261, 283, 290, 295, 300-01, 313-16, 497, 679
  Moorish period 317-22
  Mediaeval period 323-31
  17th/18th centuries 332-45
  19th century 346-61
  20th century 362-74
  bibliography 685
  districts 64-86
  maps 113
  periodicals 672, 674-75, 677
  suburbs 87-103
Hitler, Adolf 367
Hockey 613
Hodgkinson, Patrick 510

Hodgson, Francis 247
Hoffmansegg, *Count of* 261
Holá 668
Holy Land 566
Horses 164, 612, 618, 637
Hospital de Todos-os-Santos 532
Hospitals 106, 109, 118, 278, 441, 532
Hotel Avis 73, 380
Hotel Aviz *see* Hotel Avis
Hotel Braganza 273
Hotel Itália 405
Hotel Metrópole 182
Hotel Janelas Verdes 182
Hotel Paris 405
Hotels *see* Accommodation; individual hotels by name
House of Commons 155
Housing 294, 426-28, 430-33, 448
  architecture 508, 512-13
  districts 64-86
  illegal 530
  suburbs 61
Howick, Viscount 347
Huguenots 226
Hungary 372, 507
Huntingdon, *Countess of* 413

I

Iberians Cricket Team 619
Ice cream 280
Immigrants 386-90, 473
Imperial War Museum, London 36
India 230, 327
Industry 50, 61
Inglesinhos, Travessa dos 400
Inquisition 158, 343, 395, 399, 402, 414, 461
  Jews 391-92
Inscriptions *see* Epitaphs and inscriptions
Instituto Britânico 194, 655, 688-90

Lloyd's Bank 518
Lobato, Luís de
    Guimarães 510
London 34, 36, 222, 379,
    544, 649
  docks 480
  earthquake 146
  medicine 440
  Pombal 139
Londres, Praça de 49
Looting 155, 165
Lopes, Craveiro (former
    President of Portugal)
    622
Lopes, Fernão 364, 578
Loreto 67
Loures 14, 78, 498
Low Countries 404, 411,
    651
Lucotte, *Count* 480
Ludovice, J. F. 506
Lufthansa 371
Luís, Praça Dom 51
Luís Filipe (Crown Prince
    of Portugal, 1887-
    1908) 362, 364
Lumiar 74, 442, 625
  climate 125
Lutheranism 392, 395,
    403
Luz 66, 614
Luz, Quinta da 401

M

Macao 519
Macedo, Pastor de 6
Macerata 158
Machado, Júlio César 453
Machado, Raúl 323
Mackenzie, *Dr* 436
Madeira
  19th-century accounts
    250, 252, 262, 278
  20th-century accounts
    26, 198, 293, 297,
    466
  architecture 491-92
  climate 123
Madre de Deus 595, 639
Madrid 155, 228, 245,
    262, 334

Mafra
  18th-century accounts
    223
  19th-century accounts
    163, 240-41, 249,
    253, 257, 272,
    277-78, 538
  20th-century accounts
    14, 60, 191, 210, 506
Magalhães, Artur Ernesto
    de Santa Cruz 643
Maia, Manuel da 521, 529
Málaga 269
Mamede, São 76, 85
Manchester 484
  earthquake 146
Manique, Pina 424
Manta 587
Mantua 239
Manuel I (King of
    Portugal, 1495-1521)
    99, 313, 324, 396,
    409, 419, 425
  architecture 500-01
  diplomacy 327
Manuel II (King of
    Portugal, 1908-10)
    364
Maps 11, 63, 104-21, 176,
    376
Mardel, Carlos 507
Marginal 95, 615
Maria I (Queen of
    Portugal, 1777-1818)
    87, 601
Maria II (Queen of
    Portugal, 1843-53)
    89, 244, 252
Maria dos Olivais, Santa
    see Olivais
Marialva, *Marquês de* 381,
    386
Mariana Victoria (Queen
    of Portugal, 1750-77)
    345
Marinha 549
Markets 22, 54, 77, 233,
    241, 453, 458, 463
  see also individual
    markets by name
Marques, Bernardo 587
Marseilles 244
Martin, Leslie 510, 516

Mártires 69
Marvila 75
Masséna, André 354
Mateus, Quinta de São 625
Mathematics 467, 532
Matthews, Henry 251
Maurice, *Prince* 332
Maynard, Thomas 461
Mayor of Lisbon 445-48
Meat 132, 232
Medicine 435-42
  International Congress
    of Medicine (1906)
    284
  Lisbon Medical Board
    162
  Peninsular War 346,
    350
Medina del Campo 462
Mediterranean 250, 287,
    439, 454
Melo, Fontes Pereira de 73
Memória 585
Menagerie *see* Zoos
Menorca 239
Mercado de Santa Clara
    463
Mercado da Ribeira 54, 77
Mercado 24 [vinte e
    quatro] de Julho 77,
    458
Merchants, English *see*
    English Factory
Merle, Iris 286
Mesquita, Mário 661
Methuen, John 335-36,
    457
Methuen, Paul 335-36
Metropolitano de Lisboa
    (underground railway)
    66, 478, 482, 680
  art 584
  ceramics 594-95
  map 105, 113
Michelin PLC 200
Miguéis, José Rodrigues
    560, 569
Miguel, *Dom* (King of
    Portugal, 1828-34)
    24, 243, 248, 570
Miguel, Rua de São 2
Milan 239
Milford, HMS 227

Pombal, Palácio *see*
Palácio Pombal
Ponsard, Raoul Mesnier
du 476
Ponte, Quinta da 401
Ponte Salazar *see* Ponte 25
[vinte e cinco] de
Abril
Ponte 25 [vinte e cinco] de
Abril 61
Population 114, 231, 329,
439, 522, 527, 681
Port of Lisbon
18th-century accounts
4, 21
19th-century accounts
241
20th-century accounts
48, 132, 134, 389,
452, 456, 473
Portalegre 413
Portugal 2000 Project 449
Postal services 109, 466,
527
Postcards 14, 33, 39-40,
51, 57, 63
Postcodes 106-07, 117-18
Potamius (Bishop of
Lisbon, *fl*. 360 AD)
408
Powderham 381
PPD (Partido Popular
Democrático) 589
PPM (Partido Popular
Monárquico) 589
Praia das Maçãs 310
Prata, Rua da 308
Prazeres 494, 568
Prémio Valmor 73, 517
Presbyterians 410
Prices 160, 179, 189, 348
Priests 12, 393, 395,
400-01
Printing 651-52
Prisons 72, 84-85, 163
Processions 14, 296, 325,
413, 641
18th century 227, 420
19th century 237
Propaganda 371, 688
Protestantism 246, 325,
393, 404, 464
PS (Partido Socialista) 589

Psychiatry 532
Public Record Office,
London 150
Publishing 651

Q

Quarantine 235
Queiroz, José Maria Eça
de 571
Quelhas, Rua de 411
Queluz
18th-century accounts
224, 227, 233,
239-40
19th-century accounts
165, 245, 261, 348,
353
20th-century accounts
25-26, 35-36, 41, 48,
87, 173-74, 191, 195,
201-02, 204, 207,
210, 282, 299, 339,
495, 504, 523-24
aqueduct 493
climate 128
gardens 87, 623, 625
in literature 543
Quillinan, Dora 90
Quintas 498
see also individual
Quintas by name
Quintela, Largo do Barão
de 386
Quintella, *Barão de* 249

R

Rádio Renascença 669
Railways 65, 78, 132, 478,
480-82, 554
railway tunnels 492
Raleigh, *Sir* Walter 331
Raol 319
Rato 51, 81, 344
see also Fábrica do
Rato
Rats 252
Reclamation 480
Reeve's Hotel 245, 248,
258

Refugees 367-68, 370,
434, 550, 556
Reis, Artur Virgílio dos
Alves 365, 444,
450-51, 547
Relics 419
Religion 14, 246, 391-425,
428, 679
República 669
Restelo 82, 518
stadium 616
Revista Municipal 676
Revolution (1910) 73,
279, 363, 366, 401,
407, 424
Revolution (1974) 121,
186, 373-74, 431,
589, 638, 662
Rhiems 437
Rhodes 278
Ribatejo 48, 212, 610
climate 128
transport 133
Ribeira, Mercado da *see*
Mercado da Ribeira
Ribeira, Paço Real da *see*
Paço Real da Ribeira
Ribeiro, José Sommer 510
Ricardo do Espírito Santo
Silva Foundation *see*
Fundãçao Ricardo do
Espírito Santo Silva
Richard I (King of England,
1189-99) 322
Richards, Ivor 516
Richmond, Surrey 251
Riley, Bridget 649
Rilhafoles 532
Rio de Janeiro 356, 358
aviation 466-67, 470
trams 479
Roads 48, 95, 132
Rocha Conde de Óbidos
65
Rock of Lisbon *see* Cabo
da Roca
Rodrigues, Amália 280
Rodriguez, *Mr* 294
Roebuck 332
Romania 372
Romans 84, 121, 307-09,
640, 642, 645
theatre 85

Rome 239, 260, 506
Rosa, Rua da 423
Rossio 53, 79, 476, 526
Rossio Station 481, 492
Rosslyn, *Lord* 347
Rotary Club 29
Rotunda 44, 73
Rousseau, Jean-Jacques
    145
Royal British Club 194,
    386-87
Royal Geographical
    Society, London
    241
Royal Navy
    18th century 155, 335,
        358
    19th century 241, 244,
        257, 269, 347, 351,
        356, 621
Royal Public Library 629
Royal Society of St
    George, Lisbon
    Branch 388
Royalists 332, 338, 341
Royalty
    exiled royalty in Lisbon
        area 372
    Portuguese royalty 329
    16th century 325, 327
    17th century 334, 503
    18th century 10, 87,
        224, 239, 343, 438,
        529
    19th century 162, 243,
        272-73, 356
    20th century 279, 284,
        313, 362, 364
    Spanish royalty 329
    visits to Lisbon by
        overseas royalty 364,
        386-87
    see also individual
        monarchs by name
Rubber stamps 460
Rupert, *Prince, of the
    Rhine* 332, 338, 341
Russell, *Bishop of
    Portalegre* 413-14
Russell, *Lord* William
    243
Russians 550
    fleet 351

S

Sacavém 24
St Andrew's Prebyterian
    Church 410
St George's Castle *see*
    Castelo de São Jorge
St George's Chapel,
    Windsor 388
St George's Church 316,
    586
St George's Hospital,
    London 440
St Julian's Fort 240, 249,
    355
St Julian's School,
    Carcavelos 655
St Paul's Anglican Church
    (Estoril) 410
St Peter's Anglican
    Church (Estoril) 405
St Vincent, *Lady* 241
St Vincent, *Lord* 347, 358
Salazar, António de
    Oliveira (Prime
    Minister of Portugal,
    1932-68) 288, 372,
    557, 683
Saldanha, *Duque de* 248,
    273, 385
Salesians 585
Salitre 612
Saloios 14
Salvaterra 345
Santa Apolónia Railway
    Station 288, 481
Santa Catarina 70
Santa Catarina, Rua de 580
Santa Clara, Campo de 53,
    453
Santa Clara, Mercado de
    463
Santa Engrácia 398, 463,
    503
Santa Justa elevator 476
Santa Luzia 72
Santa Maria da Divina
    Providência 605
Santa Maria dos Olivais
    see Olivais
Santana, Campo de 455,
    566, 612
Santarém 129, 570

Santiago 85
Santiago de Cacém 308
Santo Estêvão 71
Santos-o-Velho 65
Santos, Eugénio dos 507
São Bento, Palácio de 64,
    443
São Bento, Xabregas 402
São Boaventura, Rua de
    423
São Carlos, Teatro *see*
    Teatro São Carlos
São Domingos de Benfica
    see Benfica
São João 75
São Mamede, Rua de 85
São Miguel 72
São Miguel, Rua 2
São Paulo 77, 125
São Paulo, Praça de 480
São Pedro do Estoril 310,
    312
São Roque 396
    18th-century accounts
        235
    19th-century accounts
        250, 252, 260, 266,
        276, 278, 348
    20th-century accounts
        67, 396, 503
    relics 419
São Sebastião 73
São Vicente de Fora
    19th-century accounts
        260, 266, 273, 348
    20th-century accounts
        216, 394, 463, 499,
        503
Saraiva de Carvalho, Rua
    441
Saramago, José 571
Saudade 365
Saudade, Rua da 308
Sawmilling 132
Saxe-Coburg Gotha,
    Fernando de, *Prince* 89
Scarlatti, Domenico 605
Schools 29, 484
    British 388
    Scottish 410
Science 483, 531-33
Scotland 226, 235, 392,
    402, 410

Scott, *Sir* Walter 570
Sculptures 81, 599-600,
  640, 644
Sé 49, 213, 308, 503
  18th-century accounts
    223, 345
  19th-century accounts
    266, 268
  20th-century accounts
    84, 418, 641
Século, Rua do 70
Seaplanes 466-67, 473
Second World War 16, 36,
  285, 292, 367-71,
  384, 387-88
  aviation 468-69
  literature 545, 550, 554,
    556
  music 604
  women 434
Secret agents 370, 550
Semple, Robert 13, 251
Sergeant, John 413-14
Serpentine Gallery,
  London 649
Serra, José Corrêa da 681
Servants 161, 269
Sesimbra 120, 498
Seteais 491
Sete Rios 80, 304
Setúbal 120, 291, 498, 678
Seventh Hill 81, 496
Seven Years' War 316
Seville 269, 330
Shadwell 265
Sherer, J. 90
Ships and shipping
  16th century 328, 330
  17th century 332
  18th century 4, 139,
    147, 159, 454-55, 665
  19th century 244,
    248-50, 266, 272,
    277-78, 351
  20th century 132-34,
    281, 284, 289-90,
    371, 452, 473
  museums 646, 650
  sailing ships 471-72,
    622
  sailors 421, 441, 434,
    621-22
  see also Ferries

Shops 11, 173, 175, 211,
  371, 429
  architecture 459-60,
    508, 519
  geography 525, 527
  maps 104
Siege of Lisbon (1147) 48,
  65, 69, 83, 296, 313,
  317-21, 579
Sienna 239
Sierra Morena 269
Silverware 89, 590
Sintra
  Mediaeval period 94,
    114
  18th-century accounts
    4, 222-23, 226-28,
    234, 236-38, 240, 681
  19th-century accounts
    1, 5, 18, 24, 98, 160,
    162-63, 165, 241,
    243-45, 247-55,
    257-58, 260-68,
    271-75, 277-78, 348,
    350, 353, 538
  20th-century accounts
    3, 23, 26-27, 35, 88,
    93, 97, 100-01, 167,
    173, 182, 186, 189,
    195, 198-99, 201-04,
    208, 210, 219, 279,
    282-84, 289-91, 299,
    312, 340, 368, 387,
    489, 491-92, 498,
    592, 685
  airport 371, 468
  archaeology 640
  architecture 501
  art 649
  climate 124-25, 439
  coliseu 265
  customs 14
  gardens 623, 625
  geography 61
  health 436, 439, 442
  literature 90, 537-38,
    542-43, 548, 552,
    559, 569
  maps 104, 106-07
  palaces 89, 91, 99, 495
  photographs 37, 41,
    48-49, 60
  transport 478, 480, 482

  walks 88
  see also Convention of
    Sintra
Sintra, Serra de 88
Sion Abbey *see* Syon
  Abbey
Siza, Álvaro 511, 514, 520
Slave House *see* Casa dos
  Escravos
Slaves 389-90
Smith, William Sidney
  337, 356, 358
Soares, Mário 373
Sociedade Lisboa '94 32,
  497
South Africa 201, 301
Southey, Robert 6, 90, 625
Spain
  prehistory 312
  Moorish period 321
  18th-century accounts
    4, 222, 227-28, 231
  19th-century accounts
    243-44, 248, 251,
    255, 260-62, 268-69,
    275, 353, 355, 360
  20th-century accounts
    330-31, 381, 406,
    430, 461, 602
  canals 132
  commerce 462
  health 436
  maps 105
  planning 528
Spectator 221
Spices 409
Spies *see* Secret agents
Sport 15, 29, 106, 613,
  656-57, 660
  see also individual
    sports by name
Sporting Clube de
  Portugal 48, 613, 616,
  620
Sport Lisboa e Benfica 80,
  613-14, 616
Stalin, Joseph 550
Standard Oil 376
Statistics 4, 74, 234, 329,
  441, 465, 619, 680
  18th century 232, 455
  19th century 241
  20th century 527

U

Ulysses 23, 561
Underground railway *see*
    Metropolitano de
    Lisboa
Unesco 502
United Arab Emirates
    519
United States of America
    citizens in Lisbon
    18th century 235
    20th century 29, 366,
        370, 376
    Embassy 29
    in literature 556, 560
University of Lisbon 23,
    627, 680
Ushaw College, Durham
    414-16

V

Vagrants 52
Valada 133
Valdemar, António 661
Vallado 549
Vasconcelos, José Ferreira
    de 576
Vaugondy, Robert de 681
Venice 327, 396, 419
Verga, Solomon ibn 425
Verona 239
Vicente, Gil 590
Vicenza 239
Vigo 284
Vila Franca de Xira 48,
    266

Vimeiro 249, 360-61
24 [Vinte e quatro] de
    Julho, Mercado *see*
    Mercado 24 de Julho
Visigoths 84, 121, 309,
    394
Visme, Gerald de 93, 441
Vivian, *Rev* John 412
Volleyball 613
Voltaire, François Marie
    Arouet de 137, 145
Voyages *see* Discoveries
    and voyages

W

Walden, *Lord* Howard de
    241
Walking 88, 176, 178
Walpole, Robert 227, 240,
    375
Warschawsky, I. 262
Water supply 124, 278,
    427, 430, 435, 507,
    609
    see also Aqueducts;
    Fountains
Watercolours 18-19, 291,
    512, 585-86, 588
Waterlow & Co 444,
    450-51
Weights and measures
    105, 163, 348
Wellesely, Arthur *see*
    Wellington, *Duke of*
Wellington, *Duke of* 349,
    351, 353-54, 357, 359
West Indies 235

White, Thomas (i.e.
    Blacklow) 413-14
Wilde, Oscar 278
Wiltshire 336
Windsor, *Duke and*
    Duchess 369
Wines *see* Food and drink
Women 13, 264, 434
Women's Relief Work
    Organization 434
Women's Royal Voluntary
    Service 434
Wool 421
    see also Textiles
Wordsworth, William
    360
Working class 22
World War I *see* First
    World War
Wold War II *see* Second
    World War

X

Xabregas 53, 216, 325,
    402

Y

Yatesbury 271
York House 182, 410
Youth 258, 426, 653-54

Z

Zoos 80, 200, 235, 304

Map of Lisbon City Area

This map shows important features and places of interest

1	Aeroporto (Airport)	5	Aqueduto (Aqueduct)
2	Ajuda Palace	6	Assembleia Nacional
3	Alameda	7	Bairro Alto district
4	Alfama district	8	Baixa district

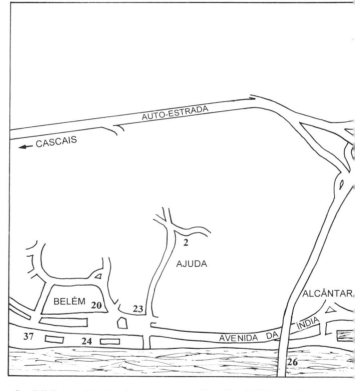

9	Biblioteca Nacional	17	Estufa Fria gardens
10	Campo Grande	18	Graça district
11	Campo Pequeno bullring	19	Jardim Botânico
12	Cais do Sodré	20	Jerónimos monastery
13	Carmo monastery	21	Madre de Deus church
14	Castelo (Castle)	22	Museu de Arte Antiga
15	Chiado district	23	Museu dos Coches
16	Estrela basilica	24	Padrão dos Descobrimento

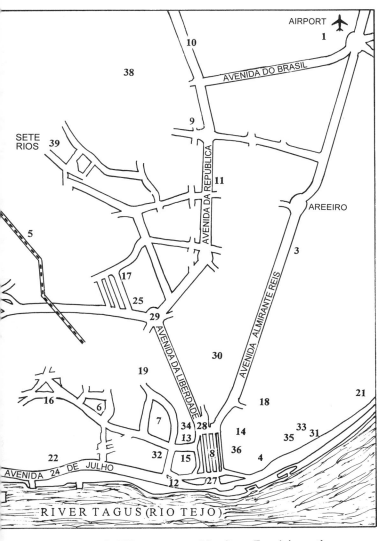

AIRPORT

1

10

38

9

SETE RIOS 39

11

AVENIDA DO BRASIL

AVENIDA DA REPUBLICA

AREEIRO

5

3

17

25

29

AVENIDA DA LIBERDADE

AVENIDA ALMIRANTE REIS

30

19

16

6

18

21

7

34 28

33

35 31

13

14

22

32

15

8

36

4

AVENIDA 24 DE JULHO

12

27

RIVER TAGUS (RIO TEJO)

ALSO FROM CLIO PRESS

INTERNATIONAL ORGANIZATIONS SERIES

Each volume in the International Organizations Series is either devoted to one specific organization, or to a number of different organizations operating in a particular region, or engaged in a specific field of activity. The scope of the series is wide-ranging and includes intergovernmental organizations, international non-governmental organizations, and national bodies dealing with international issues. The series is aimed mainly at the English-speaker and each volume provides a selective, annotated, critical bibliography of the organization, or organizations, concerned. The bibliographies cover books, articles, pamphlets, directories, databases and theses and, wherever possible, attention is focused on material about the organizations rather than on the organizations' own publications. Notwithstanding this, the most important official publications, and guides to those publications, will be included. The views expressed in individual volumes, however, are not necessarily those of the publishers.

VOLUMES IN THE SERIES